THE ACTS OF
THE APOSTLES

Bruce Milne

THE ACTS OF
THE APOSTLES

Witnesses to Him…to the
Ends of the Earth

Bruce Milne

Copyright © Bruce Milne

ISBN 978-1-84550-507-3

10 9 8 7 6 5 4 3 2 1

Published in 2010
in the
Focus on the Bible Commentary Series
by
Christian Focus Publications Ltd,
Geanies House, Fearn, Ross-shire,
IV20 1TW, Great Britain

www.christianfocus.com

Cover design by
Daniel Van Straaten

Printed and bound by
Bell & Bain, Glasgow

Mixed Sources
Product group from well-managed
forests and other controlled sources
www.fsc.org   Cert no. TT-COC-002769
© 1996 Forest Stewardship Council

Contents

Preface

'When the day of Pentecost had fully come…suddenly a sound came from heaven …' So read the opening words of Acts chapter two, and there can be few Christians anywhere whose hearts do not quicken when they hear them. The Book of Acts is of course about a great deal more than the Pentecostal happening in Jerusalem, but the associations of that unforgettable day are ineffaceable. For Acts is the story of nothing less than God's invasion of human history in the birth and subsequent spread of the Christian church; the story of what God did through a group of highly unlikely and, for the main part, quite ordinary people, in the first century of our era. It is also, as we dare to believe, the story of what our unchanging God can do again, in this twenty-first century, and in the twenty-second, and the twenty-third, or however long until the Lord Jesus Christ returns in glory.

Like each of the biblical writings, Acts has gathered about it a series of interpretative issues, such as questions of authorship and historical accuracy, which over the centuries have challenged and occupied scholarly minds within the church, and beyond it. Commentaries on specific biblical books typically devote extended introductions to addressing these issues. Having spent major periods of my life in both theological teaching and pastoral ministry I can readily appreciate how diverse an audience the Christian community is, in terms of its keen appetite for, or alternatively its frank disinterest in, these largely academic discussions. My mode in this volume is a mainly pastoral one, and hence I have decided to make a few assumptions as we set out, concerning issues such as the authorship and dating of Acts, and its general historical reliability. Proceeding in this way will allow us to enter immediately upon the text and begin our dialogue with it, and hence a dialogue also with the living God who continues to speak through its pages. The relevant academic issues will certainly not be ignored as we move along, but they will be given the more responsible discussion which they of course merit, in a series of appendices at the end of the volume. In view of this *modus operandi*, I will confine myself in this introduction to three brief considerations.

First, an issue which has been regularly debated is *the purpose of the Acts. Why did Luke write it?* We will revisit this question as we grapple with the text, not least its opening section. However it will be appropriate to offer a brief response before setting out on that journey. Obviously Luke has an historical-narrative function in mind: Acts tells the story of the rise and spread of the church. Here we uncover answers to questions such as: how did the church get started? What was the secret of its astonishing impact? What problems did it encounter in the early period, and how did it handle them? What happened to the apostles after Easter? What did Peter do? Where did Paul come from, and how did he become one of its primary leaders and propagators? Clearly Luke is writing history.

But were there other purposes which also influenced him? Bearing in mind the amount of text Luke gives to legal challenges to the Christian movement, especially from the Roman authorities, some interpreters have seen Luke's purpose as an extended apology for Christianity's political harmlessness as far as Rome is concerned, and hence for the church's right to the state protection already afforded to Judaism in the early part of the first century. Some even see the book as a defence brief for Paul's impending trial before the emperor, with Theophilus even cast as a person of possible influence with the Emperor. Others have raised the thought of an additional apologetic purpose, with respect to Judaism, in that the ministry of Jesus is consistently presented in Acts as a fulfilment of Old

Testament promises, and Paul is clearly willing at certain points to accord with Jewish traditions and scruples. Yet another school sees the book as expressing a theological purpose on the part of the author, to present Christianity as essentially a divine movement, created and directed by God the Holy Spirit. None of these positions have proved generally persuasive, though each may have some degree of pertinence.

But is there not something beyond all these? Did the Holy Spirit, in giving us the Book of Acts, not have a further purpose? The centre of the book is the story of the church as it is born, its first months and years (it covers the thirty-year period from Pentecost A.D. 30 or 33 through to A.D. 60–62, and Paul's initial 'prison ministry' in Rome), as well as Christianity's expanding geographical reach. This is surely a clue to the correct answer to Luke's primary purpose in writing. It is not just a historical record, a *description* of the earliest Christian witness. It is also *prescriptive* – telling us what the church is, why God called it into being, what are its resources, and how its ministry role fits in with the ministry role of Jesus and His mighty acts of redemption. In particular Acts is first and foremost *a book of mission*, and essentially focuses the missional role which the church is called to major on through the course of its life until the return of its Lord. Acts is not just about what the church did, but about what it exists to do, today and every day. From this perspective Luke's introduction in 1:1-11 is critical. We will see this clarified as we proceed.

A second introductory issue is *the time-line of Acts*. Many of us are used to reading the book as though one incident followed another in immediate succession, which can generate a misleading triumphalistic perspective, especially when compared with the relatively modest attainments of our churches today. Acts can then become remote from our immediate Christian lives and witness. In fact Acts covers no less a period than thirty years, from the resurrection of Jesus to the Roman imprisonment of Paul; Luke is extremely selective in the material he includes. In other words, the story

of the birth of the church and its progressively expanding witness, from Jerusalem to Judea, Samaria, and 'to
the ends of the earth', was not a matter of all-conquering,
instantly successful, Christian ministry. True, there were
high moments of outpoured blessing, as we will see, and
the eventual extent of the spread of the faith in these first
decades is an astonishing one by any account. But the
story as a whole is in essence not altogether different
from that which we commonly experience in our own
time – of faithful, persevering service for Christ in the
face of great odds and numerous setbacks. To enable that
reality to go with us into our exposition I have appended
a provisional date-line of Acts (on p. 16), as well as a possible Chronology of Paul's Life (in ch. 5).

The third introductory consideration is to underline
*how relevant the Book of Acts is for the church of the twenty-
first century.* If we are conscious today of bearing witness
to Jesus Christ in an environment where the mass of the
surrounding population, in all age groups, are largely
ignorant of, and insulated from, our convictions; where
a huge diversity of religious opinions, or their vehement
denial, meet us on every hand; where the population is
increasingly diverse by every standard of reference; where
life is largely lived in, and shaped by, dominating urban
centres; where the people of God are frequently internally divided and sometimes barely recognizable as the
people of God at all; where absolute values are an ancient
memory; and where faithfulness to Christ can prove
extremely costly, even life-threatening – then we will find
ourselves very much at home in the pages of this ancient
book. Christendom is no more, and the Western Church is
slowly and painfully learning to live without its protective
shelter. The good news of the Book of Acts is that God is
more than a match for such conditions, and that authentic
Christianity can survive and even flourish in precisely this
context.

With these provisos behind us, let us move forward,
prayerfully dependent on the same Holy Spirit who
inspired Luke in the first century, to unlock this great
text and be allowed to uncover, through its paragraphs

and chapters, the living Word of God to our hearts, our churches, and our generation.

On a personal level I greatly appreciate the invitation of Christian Focus to provide this further commentary for their widely appreciated *Focus on the Bible* series. Although I had expounded through large parts of Acts during my pastorates, the request to provide this 'full meal deal overview' proved in the event both regularly inspiring and deeply challenging. I am thankful to Regent College, Vancouver, for the opportunity to teach the entire book of Acts during their Spring School in 2008, and to the directors of the Slavic Gospel Association for the invitation to teach major sections of Acts during their annual conference at Torquay in August of the same year. I continue to be deeply indebted to my wife Valerie who put in many hours correcting early drafts of the text. My heart-prayer is that God may be pleased to use these pages to further His mission, through His people, to our desperately needy world; a world which remains 'ripe for harvest'.

Vancouver
St Andrew's Day, 2009.

Outline of the Book of Acts

The commentators offer a number of possible ways of dividing the twenty-eight chapters. We will take our cue from what appears to be Luke's own table of contents at 1:8. 'You will be my witnesses in Jerusalem, and in all Judea and Samaria, and to the ends of the earth'.

'Anointed Witnesses'

A. 'Antecedents and Anticipations': 1:1-26
   1. The Risen Lord: 1:1-3
   2. Commission and Ascension: 1:4-11
   3. Further preparations for the Mission: 1:12-26

B. 'Pentecost': 2:1-47
   1. 'A Sound from Heaven': The Spirit Comes: 2:1-13
   2. 'This is that…this is Jesus': Peter's Sermon: 2:14-36
   3. Response to the Message: 2:37-41
   4. The New Community: 2:42-47

'Witnesses in Jerusalem'

A. 'The Jerusalem Church': 3:1–5:42
   1. A Healing Miracle: 3:1-10
   2. Its Sequels
      a. A Sermon: 3:11-26
      b. A Trial: 4:1-22
      c. A Prayer Meeting: 4:23-31
   3. Community Life
      a. Positive: 4:32-37
      b. Negative: 5:1-11

    c. Signs and Ministry: 5:12-16
    d. Persecution Again: 5:17-42

B. 'The Ministry of Stephen': 6:1–8:1a
    1. A Conflict Resolved: 6:1-6
    2. Continuing Growth: 6:7
    3. Stephen's Impact and Arrest: 6:8-15
    4. His Defence before the Sanhedrin: 7:1-53
    5. The Death of Stephen: 7:54–8:1a

'Witnesses in Judea and Samaria'

A. 'Samaria and Saul': 8:1b–9:31
    1. A Scattered Church: 8:1b-4
    2. With Philip into Samaria: 8:5-25
    3. An Ethiopian Believes: 8:26-40
    4. Paul's Encounter with the Risen Lord: 9:1-19
    5. Paul's Post-Conversion Ministry: 9:20-30
    6. A Time of Peace and Progress: 9:31

B. 'Peter and Antioch': 9:32–12:25
    1. Aeneas and Dorcas: 9:32-43
    2. The Conversion of Cornelius: 10:1–11:18
    3. The Antioch Outreach: 11:19-30
    4. Peter's Miraculous Escape: 12:1-19a
    5. The Death of Herod: 12:19b-25

'Witnesses to the Ends of the Earth' (I)

A. 'Paul's First Mission Journey': 13:1–14:28
    1. The Commissioning of Barnabus and Saul: 13:1-3
    2. The Work Begins: Ministry in Cyprus: 13:4-12
    3. Pisidian Antioch: 13:13-52
    4. Iconium: 14:1-7
    5. Lystra: 14:8-20
    6. Derbe, and Return to Antioch: 14:21-28

B. 'The Consultation at Jerusalem': 15:1-35
    1. The Issue at Stake: 15:1-4
    2. Discussion and Resolution: 15:5-21
    3. The Letter to the Churches: 15:22-35

C. 'Paul's Second Mission Journey': 15:36–18:22
    1. Silas Replaces Barnabus: 15:36-41

The Time-Line of Acts [1]

A.D. 30   The founding of the church in Jerusalem
           (Acts 1–2)
32–35   Paul's conversion (Acts 9)
34–37   Paul's first visit to Jerusalem (Acts 9:26ff)
45 or 46   Famine relief sent to Jerusalem from Antioch
           (Acts 11:27ff)
           Death of James (Acts 12:2)
46 or 47   First missionary journey (Acts 13–14)
48   Apostolic Council at Jerusalem (Acts 15)
48–51   Second missionary journey (Acts 15:36–18:22)
50   Paul reaches Corinth (Acts 18)
53   Third missionary journey begins (Acts 18:23)
54–57   Paul's stay at Ephesus (Acts 19)
57–58   Paul in Greece (Acts 20)
58 (June) Paul reaches Jerusalem (Acts 21)
58–60   Imprisonment in Caesarea (Acts 24–26)
60–61   Appeal to Caesar and voyage to Rome (Acts 27)
61–63   Imprisonment in Rome (Acts 28:30).

Abbreviations

AV   Authorized Version
ESV   English Standard Version
IBD   Illustrated Bible Dictionary
JB   Jerusalem Bible
KJV   King James Version
LXX   Septuagint
NCB   New Century Bible
NDT   New Dictionary of Theology
NIV   New International Version
NIVI   New International Version Inclusive Language
        Edition
NLT   New Living Translation
REB   Revised English Bible
TDNT   Theological Dictionary of the New Testament

---

1 As offered in the *Lion Handbook to the Bible*. (Lion Publishing, 1973), and claimed to be 'accurate within a year or two either way'.

WARNING: Studying the Book of Acts can be very bad for your health.

Specifically, it may cost you a lot of money. It could involve you in conversations leading to being dismissed, even mocked. It will very possibly undermine some of your most treasured ambitions, and even require you to abandon some of your long-cherished dreams. It may involve you in profound relationships with people very different from yourself, who speak the oddest of languages and live in the poorest, most densely populated, loneliest, or trendiest of places on planet earth. It may lead to your adopting new disciplines in prayer, affect your sleeping patterns, and perhaps even shorten your life. So, be warned!

If you are ready for some or all of the above, by all means read on, because studying Acts will also very probably result in your being happier, more fulfilled and purposeful than you have ever been before. It is also likely to bring you a deeper understanding of God, a closer walk with Jesus, and a richer experience of the Holy Spirit, than you have known for a long time, maybe than you have ever known at all.

One thing is for sure, this book will not leave you where it found you. Why am I so certain about this? Because that is the kind of impact the Book of Acts has had on Christian people and churches for the last two thousand years. So, if you are perfectly content with your life, entirely happy with who you are and what you are doing to fill your days, then you had best put this commentary down immediately, quickly close your Bible, find a nice quiet corner somewhere, and have a very long sleep.

But if you are ready to read on, then please join me as we step out together into the white light of God's revealed Word, opening ourselves to Him, listening for His voice, discovering what He has done and what He can do, and… well, the rest of this sentence will have to wait for our engagement with the text; but, in general…you will need to be ready for anything!

I

Anointed Witnesses
(Acts 1:1-26)

1. Antecedents and Anticipations (Acts 1-26)

1. The Risen Lord (1:1-3)

In my former book, Theophilus, I wrote about all that Jesus began to do and teach until the day he was taken up to heaven, after giving instructions through the Holy Spirit to the apostles he had chosen. After his suffering he showed himself to these men and gave many convincing proofs that he was alive. He appeared to them over a period of forty days and spoke about the kingdom of God (1:1-3).

Most medicines issued from chemist stores come with clearly printed labels carrying important warnings and instructions 'to be read before opening'. Luke's 'Book of Acts' is no different. The first two paragraphs (1:1-11) are his label.

1:1. He begins by referring us to his **former book** (Luke's Gospel), in which he **wrote about all that Jesus began to do and teach until the day he was taken up to heaven.** In the ancient world it was common for a writer to 'organize a work into several shorter sections and to furnish each with its own brief introduction'.[1] In this opening phrase, however, Luke is very likely establishing a profounder linkage between his two works (Luke and Acts) than simply their order of publication.

---

1. I.H. Marshall, *The Acts of the Apostles* (Tyndale, 1980), 55.

The Greek word he uses (translated in the NIV as 'book') is *logos*, which is usually translatable as 'narrative' or 'account'. He does *not* use *biblos*, the usual word for 'book'.[2] This strongly suggests that Luke 'composed Acts as a single storyline extending from his Gospel'.[3] The connectedness is made explicit by his choice of verb (*erxato*) in verse one: 'all that Jesus *began* to do and teach...' The overlap of the two parts is further signalled by the repetition of the ascension account in Luke 24:50-51 and Acts 1:10-11. Luke's literary contribution to the New Testament is arguably therefore *a single book in two parts*, which we can fairly entitle 'Luke-Acts', accounting for approximately a quarter of the New Testament.

This simple fact concerning Luke's authorial intention carries significant implications for interpreting Acts. For example, it means that viewing the Gospel as 'about Jesus', and the Acts as 'about the church' is a major misunderstanding. *Both* parts are about the ministry of Jesus; His ministry on earth, personally and publicly exercised (the Gospel), and his subsequent ministry from heaven, exercised on earth through the Holy Spirit (Acts). Once we are alerted to this perspective, we discover that Acts contains a whole series of references to Jesus as the active agent, or the inspiring influence, in the 'doing and teaching' of the apostles.[4] It is Christ who sends the Holy Spirit (2:33), who energizes the witnesses, and who directs them in their mission; it is Christ who provides the supernatural power to perform miracles which by their nature express a continuity with those performed in His own ministry. Christ is the content and focus of the message which the apostles proclaim, and the one in whose name, and into union with whom, baptism is performed.[5]

---

2. cf. 1:20, the 'book of Psalms' = *biblos*.

3. D.L. Bock, *Acts* (Baker, 2007), 52.

4. See 2:3; 3:6; 4:10, 13; 4:30; 9:34; 10:48; 11:20; ; 13:38; 14:3; 14:23; 15:11; 16:7; 16:14; 16:18; 16:31f; 17:3, 7; 18:8; 19:5; 19:13f; 19:20; 20:24; 21:13f; 22:18, 21; 24:24; 28:31.

5. There are numerous other confirmatory parallels in the two narratives; e.g. the initial conferment of the Spirit, on Jesus in Luke 3:21-22; 4:1; 4:18f, and on the apostolic community in Acts. 1:5, 2:1-4; the parallel noted by David Bosch, *Transforming Mission*

Stott aptly draws attention to the uniqueness of this ministry perspective as far as teachers, prophets, and religious leaders in general are concerned. All of these luminaries and their ministries, from whatever age, in whatever place, and for whatever duration, have at some point been brought to a conclusion by the subject's death. Of Jesus alone may it be joyfully affirmed that His ministry actively continues beyond His death, and will do so 'until the end of the age' (Matt. 28:20), 'thus setting Christianity apart from all other religions. These regard their founder as having completed his ministry during his lifetime; Luke says Jesus only began his.'[6]

I vividly recall, during a visit to Pyongyang in North Korea a few years ago, being taken to the mausoleum to Kim Il Sung, 'the Great Leader' of the North Korean Marxist struggle, who died in 1994, setting in motion a three-year outpouring of national mourning. Despite all the trumpeting of his greatness, and the elaborate charade surrounding his resplendent, medal-bestrewn, mummified corpse, with its weeping bystanders, the whole effect was a pathetic demonstration of human weakness and transience; here indeed was death's sting, and here its most evident victory. By contrast no ageing effigies commemorate the life and ministry of Jesus. No visit to His tomb with its crumbling remains is incumbent upon those who would honour His earthly conquests. No sobbing ranks of mourners commemorate His final passing. Jesus lives! His ministry continues, all around the globe, fresh and vibrant in each new day; and will do so until the day of His glorious appearing, when every knee will bow and every tongue confess Him Lord of all.

(Orbis, 1991), 88, of the three-stage geographical progression in the ministry of Jesus: his ministry in Galilee (Luke 4:14–9:50), his journey from Galilee to Jerusalem (9:51–19:40), and finally the events in Jerusalem (19:41 to the end of the Gospel). In Acts the church's ministry evolves in three stages as indicated at 1:8, Jerusalem (chs. 2–7), Judea and Samaria (8–11), and 'the ends of the earth' ending in Rome(13–28). In the Gospel Jesus' preaching and healing ministry has many points of parallel in Acts (e.g. Luke 4:31-41 with Acts 5:12-16).

6. J.R.W. Stott, *The Message of Acts* (InterVarsity, 1990), 34.

Luke's sustained focus on Christ also impinges on the question of the title of the book. 'Acts' is the original title, leaving unanswered the question of whose 'acts' are in view. The early editors saw them as the acts performed by the apostles, hence the traditional title. Some other interpreters have proposed 'the acts of the Holy Spirit'.[7] Stott proposes a comprehensive, and as he admits, somewhat cumbersome, alternative: 'the Continuing Words and Deeds of Jesus by his Spirit through the Apostles.'[8] If one wished to be even more comprehensive we might expand it to '...the continuing Words and Deeds of the Risen and Exalted Jesus by his Spirit through the Apostles...'

We should note additionally the uniqueness of this connection between the Gospel and Acts. It stands apart in the New Testament. In this sense Luke's Gospel is different from those of Matthew, Mark and John. In Luke's perspective, the life of the incarnate Lord stands behind, and is inseparable from, His works of salvation and power which flow from its Easter climax. What the church has to offer the world is in the end nothing other than the life of Jesus, the ongoing of that unique ministry which is spelled out unforgettably in the records of the four Gospels. The gospel finds its heart in Jesus' death and resurrection, those unrepeatable events in which the 'tyrants' of sin, death, the devil and hell, were finally and eternally subjected; but the 'good news' is also the fact that His Easter triumph continues today in and through the life of His community in the power of His Spirit.

Hence Luke is also reminding us at the outset of Acts, that evangelism is always more than the communication of a message. It is never less than that of course, and Luke will make a major contribution in the succeeding chapters to the contents of the preached gospel (or *kerygma* as it is technically known). But evangelism is also the ever-repeated release of that unique Life through the lives, corporately and personally, of those who know Him. 'We would see Jesus' is the cry that echoes from the heart of the world in this twenty-first century as urgently, poignantly

---

7. e.g. A.T. Pierson, *The Acts of the Holy Spirit* (Marshall, Morgan and Scott, 1895).
8. Stott, 34.

and persistently as in the first. The wonder and glory of Christianity is precisely that, by grace, it can!

Luke's perspective has two other profound implications which can be noted. Firstly, this continuity between the Gospel and the Acts means that our understanding of Jesus cannot be confined to the thirty-plus years of His earthly life and ministry; it needs also to encompass this continuing ministry of the Risen Lord across the ages of history, and not least in our own day, when as never before in human history He is seen, known and passionately followed in every corner of the earth. It also needs to embrace, by implication, the entire mission of the church until the parousia. Putting the same point more technically, Christology needs to include ecclesiology.

Secondly, this means that the church cannot be understood in purely sociological terms. The church is the community of the disciples of Jesus, the people of God who seek to represent Him in the world. But it is also the body of Christ, and no matter how far it may wander from its biblical roots, in both faith and life, it remains by His grace the place where He is to be encountered. Accordingly we must never in despair give up on the church, nor pursue a Christian vocation in entire isolation from it. 'Inasmuch as you did it to one of the least of these my brothers and sisters, you did it to me.'

Theophilus is Luke's esteemed literary sponsor, met earlier in the introduction to Luke's Gospel. Dedications of this sort were common in the first century.[9] We know nothing of Theophilus apart from these references. Bruce comments, 'It is quite probable that Theophilus was a representative of the intelligent middle-class public at Rome whom Luke wished to win over to a more favourable opinion of Christianity than that which was current among them.'[10] The name clearly implies a Gentile audi-

---

9. Another example is Josephus, the first-century Jewish historian, who wrote three volumes on Jewish life and times. He begins the first by addressing his sponsor 'Epaphroditus, most excellent of men', and introduces the second volume with the words 'By means of my former volume, my most honoured Epaphroditus, I have demonstrated our antiquity....'. This is remarkably parallel to Luke here.

10. F.F. Bruce, *Commentary on the Book of Acts* (Marshall, Morgan and Scott, 1954), 31.

ence, and an audience moreover drawn from among the educated and culturally sensitive class. Luke has the world of Theophilus in his sights, the Gentile, Graeco-Roman world beyond the geographical boundaries of Palestine, and beyond the mental frontiers of Judaism and Christianity. His will be a 'Gentile-relevant' story, relating the words and deeds of Jesus to an urbane, global readership. In other words, 'by writing in this fashion Luke was claiming a place for Christianity on the stage of world history.' [11]

1.2. until the day he was taken up. Verses 1b–2 are a summary of Luke 24:46-49, which Bosch views as 'in a nutshell, Luke's entire understanding of the Christian mission',[12] and this phrase in verse 2 as a summary of Luke 24:50-52, his first account of the ascension which concludes Jesus' earthly ministry. The Greek text actually does not have the words 'to heaven'. We will offer fuller comments on the ascension at 1:10–11; however we anticipate them somewhat by reminding ourselves of Paul's observation that in so ascending Christ 'filled all things.' [13]

A further issue of interpretation in verse 2 is to which clause the phrase 'through the Holy Spirit' is to be related. The NIV links it to Jesus' 'giving instructions to the apostles' (so also ESV, REB, NLT). The positioning of the phrase in the text however allows for a possibility Marshall argues for, a link to 'whom he had chosen' (cf. Luke 6:12-16), and

---

11. Marshall, 40. Recognizing the Gentile/Imperial perspective of Luke's work, both mentally and geographically, does not mean that he is unimpressed by the Jewish-Palestinian womb of the Christian faith. Luke wrote 'his two-volume work as much for Jews as for Gentiles' (Bosch: 92), and shows 'an exceptionally positive attitude to the Jewish people, their religion and culture.' This instinct is reflected from the beginning of the Gospel in the infancy narratives (chs. 1–2) with their stress on Jesus' fulfilling of the promises to Israel, a note that continues in the 'Nazareth manifesto' (ch. 4) and the centring of so much of his account in Jerusalem (chs. 9–24). In Acts this 'Jewishness' is expressed by the re-iteration of the theme of fulfilment in the apostolic preaching, and the 'to the Jew first' pattern in Paul's ministry. 'The Gentile mission is not secondary to the Jewish mission. Neither is the one merely a consequence of the other. Rather the Gentile mission is coordinated to the Jewish mission' (Bosch: 95). Thus while many Jews reject, Luke also reports on the many who accept (2:41, 4:4, 5:14, 21:20, etc.). Israel does not so much reject the gospel as become divided by the gospel. Thus 'Jesus weeps for Jerusalem: so does Luke' (Bosch: 97); as does Paul: Rom. 9:1ff; 10:1ff.

12. Bosch, 91

13. So Calvin, I: 22.

hence an affirmation of the unique and significant status
of the apostles, a meaning which would certainly accord
well with the following contents.[14]

1:3. Note '**after his suffering**'; there is a continual
danger of so theologizing the cross that we eliminate its
human cost. 'He suffered under Pontius Pilate....' This
and similar phrases were of great importance in the
church's struggle with Gnosticism and docetism, early
heterodox views which denied the full humanity of
Christ.[15]

But these sub-Christian notions are not dead. Only too
often Christian piety and pastoral ministry is robbed of
a major ingredient through Christ's full humanity failing
to be confessed. For many believers, Christ is in many
respects a kind of 'superman' who hovers somewhere
between earth and heaven and in the process never really
identifies with our human struggles, temptations and sufferings. But 'we do not have a high priest who is unable
to sympathize with our weaknesses, but one who was
tempted in every way just as we are' (Heb. 4:15).

> 'In every pang that rends the heart,
> The Man of Sorrows had a part;
> He sympathizes with our grief,
> And to the sufferer sends relief.' [16]

As a result we can miss out on some of the deeper and
richer dimensions of our life 'in Christ'. Rutherford

---

14. Marshall, 57

15. See, *New Dictionary of Theology* (IVP, 1988), eds. Sinclair B. Ferguson and David
F. Wright, arts 'Docetism', 'Gnosticism', pp. 201f, 273f. In order to understand these
early deviations we need to appreciate the fundamental dualism of the current, universally adopted world-view. In principle God and matter were seen as simply irreconcilable. By this universally held viewpoint an incarnate, suffering God was about as possible
as a square circle. This faced these early theologians, their opponents, and ourselves
also, with the radical character of the Christian truth-claim. 'The Word became flesh' is
the fundamental datum of Christian epistemology. It is not a conclusion argued for but
the fundamental premise from which the case is argued. This is where we begin. Thus
faith-knowledge is always what we deal with. But faith gives a perspective for all else: it
is 'Faith seeking understanding' (Anselm); as Augustine argued, we believe in order to
understand (*crede ut intelligas*).

16. Scottish Paraphrases (1781)

expressed it well: 'There is no fellowship with Christ like bringing our pains and griefs to him.'[17]

...he showed himself to these men and gave many convincing proofs that he was alive. He appeared to them over a period of forty days. These phrases introduce us to the apologetic instinct in Luke's writing which is struck in both dedications to Theophilus. In his Gospel, Luke sets out his historical method involving 'careful investigation', relating to 'eyewitnesses', and an 'orderly' accounting, so that Theoplilus might 'know the certainty' (1:4) of what he had previously been taught, concerning the beginnings of the Christian story (1:1–3). In Acts, having spoken of Jesus' post-resurrection encounters with the apostles, he refers, not dissimilarly, to Jesus having therein afforded them 'many convincing proofs (1:3) that he was alive.'[18]

This claim still stands. The fact that Jesus 'appeared' to His disciples after his undoubted death on the cross, is extraordinarily difficult to dismiss. We can cite one recent apologist, N.T. Wright. After an exhaustive investigation of all the possible alternative routes by which the first disciples might have arrived at their conviction about Jesus' resurrection, and in particular his post-Calvary meetings with them which formed the core of that conviction, he comments: 'I conclude that the historian, of whatever persuasion, has no option but to affirm both the empty tomb and the "meetings" with Jesus as "historical events"... they took place as real events; they were significant events; they are, in the normal sense required by historians, provable events; historians can and should write about them. We cannot account for early Christianity without them.'[19] Hence we can detect a consistent concern on Luke's part to present his material in both Gospel and Acts as a

---

17. See Lee Strobel, *The Case for the Real Jesus* (Zondervan, 2007), 61f, interview with Craig A. Evans.

18. The Greek word is *tekmneriois*, which the Bauer, Arndt, Gingrich and Danker, *Greek-English Lexicon* renders, 'that which causes something to be known in a decisive and convincing manner, proof.' 3rd ed. (Chicago, 2000), 994.

19. N.T. Wright, *The Resurrection of the Son of God* (Fortress, 2003), 709. cf. also N.T. Wright, 'The Self-Revelation of God in History', in *There is a God* (Harper One, 2007), Anthony Flew with Roy Abraham Varghese, Appendix B.

responsible, trustworthy account of events which actually happened, and hence one which will undergird the Christian commitment and convictions of his sponsor, and other readers.

While this apologetic concern is not the entire purpose of Acts it may reasonably be seen as a not insignificant subordinate purpose, and one, moreover, which is highly relevant in a generation when the most fundamental claims of historic Christianity are regularly subjected to uncritical dismissal on the grounds that they are inherently incredible, or that the post-modern critique has established that objective truth no longer exists, and that reliable historical reconstruction is in principle not available to us. Luke's sturdy adherence to objective historical facticity is a salutary corrective.[20]

...and spoke about the kingdom of God. During this unique period Jesus appeared and reappeared among the disciples. There were *at least three purposes* to this unprecedented series of encounters; the only finally significant 'Jesus Seminar'.[21]

Firstly, our Lord brings the disciples to *absolute conviction concerning his resurrection*. That such conviction resulted is patent from the subsequent months and years of their witness-bearing. There is never the merest hint at any point, or on the part of any individual, of any diminution in their commonly held, absolute persuasion of Jesus' conquest of death. This is a fact which no historian can deny. The entire Christian movement, an indubitable reality at the heart of modern history, is predicated on the astonishing claim that Jesus Christ was raised from the dead 'on the third day', and on the disciples' undeviating commitment

---

20. For a careful assessment of the post-modern critique, see D.A. Carson, *The Gagging of God* (Zondervan. 1996), chapter 3 and passim. Also William L. Craig, *Reasonable Faith*, 3rd edn (Crossway, 2008) chapter 5; and his article 'God is not Dead Yet', *Christianity Today*, July 2008, pp. 22-7.

21. This borrows the title from a series of somewhat notorious meetings, 'The Jesus Seminar', in which radical New Testament scholars meet annually to decide, in the light of their personal, critical presuppositions, which among the reported sayings of Jesus in the New Testament, and other apocryphal sayings beyond the New Testament, are to be viewed as authentic. **See also this text, pp. 76-7.**

to it, even in face of violent state-sponsored persecution, and the consequent, agonizing suffering to the death in the case of virtually every one of the men so persuaded. The 'Easter faith' is a fact. It is explicable only as being the fruit of a repeated exposure to the Risen Christ.

Secondly, Jesus *completed his instruction* of them. He **spoke about the kingdom of God.** He had tried to help them grasp the meaning of the kingdom of God during the previous three years of his itinerant ministry in Palestine; however such was the novelty and unexpectedness of the events at its climax, events critical to its meaning, that it was only 'after the fact' that a true comprehension was possible.

What did he teach them? What do we mean by 'the kingdom of God'? (cf. Acts 8:12; 20:24f; 28:23). The key lies in grasping three realities of Old Testament revelation. *First,* God is King. 'The Lord (*Yahweh*) reigns' (Ps. 99:1) has rightly been referred to as 'the creed of Israel'. Nothing is more basic to its faith than the existence of the sovereign, creator Lord of all things, who had chosen Israel as His special possession and the initial vehicle of His historic purpose of global salvation. *Second,* God's rule is opposed. Astonishingly, tragically, His creatures rise up in rebellion against His rule – and even Israel, the covenant partner of God, falls into disobedience and idolatry. *Third,* as a growing crescendo in the great Old Testament prophetic writings, this condition of rejection of God and His rule will not be indefinitely prolonged. There is a coming, future day in which God will reign, evidently and universally over the entire created order, including humanity; a reign exercised through the instrumentality of the 'anointed One', the Messiah. That day of the Messiah's undisputed, universal reign is 'the Kingdom of God' which Jesus claimed became a present, historical reality in His ministry (Luke 4:32, 43; 6:20; 7:21-23; 8:9; 9:2; 9:20; 10:23; 11:20; 12:32; 12:50f; 13:28f; 16:16; 17:24; 18:16; 18:24f; 19:28-40; 20:17, 44; 22:16-20; 24:23f, 46-49). [22]

---

22. cf. Marshall: 57, who defines the Kingdom as 'the saving, sovereign action of God through Jesus'. cf. Stott: 41-5; Bruce: 34-6; also G.R. Beasley-Murray, *Jesus and the Kingdom of God* (Eerdmans, 1986). In Acts it is virtually a synonym for salvation. See: 8:12; 19:8; 20:25; 28:23, 31.

Thirdly, *Jesus commissioned the apostles.*

2. Commission and Ascension (1:4-11)

On one occasion, while he was eating with them, he gave them this command: 'Do not leave Jerusalem, but wait for the gift my Father promised, which you have heard me speak about. For John baptized with water, but in a few days you will be baptized with the Holy Spirit.' So when they met together they asked him, 'Lord are you at this time going to restore the kingdom to Israel?' He said to them: 'It is not for you to know the times or dates which the Father has set by his own authority. But you will receive power when the Holy Spirit comes on you; and you will be my witnesses in Jerusalem, and in all Judea and Samaria, and to the ends of the earth.' After he said this, he was taken up before their very eyes, and a cloud hid him from their sight. They were looking intently into the sky as he was going, when suddenly two men dressed in white stood beside them. 'Men of Galilee,' they said, 'why do you stand here looking into the sky? This same Jesus, who has been taken from you into heaven, will come back in the same way you have seen him go into heaven' (1:4-11).

1:4. The verb translated 'eating with' (*sunalizomai*) is commonly translated 'staying with', but sharing meals is implied. Marshall notes, 'the instruction probably took place during the meals held by Jesus with the disciples after the resurrection.' [23]

Do not leave Jerusalem, but wait for the gift my Father promised... Why this location? One suggestion is that 'the place where Jesus was rejected was to be the place where fresh witness to Him would begin.'[24] Another commentator notes the fulfilment which a Jerusalem location offered of the prophecy in Isaiah 2:3: 'for out of Zion shall go forth the law, and the word of the Lord from Jerusalem.'[25]

---

23. Marshal, 58; also Bruce, 30, fn. 5.
24. Marshall, 58.
25. W. Neill, *The Acts of the Apostles*, NCB (Marshall, Morgan and Scott, 1973), 26.

While there may well be truth in these suggestions, the location was surely primarily in anticipation of the Pentecost feast with its cross-cultural, multi-linguistic spread of the nations. They are to remain in the place where the world can be given a foretaste of the glory of the multi-national, multi-cultural, multi-linguistic, multi-generational community of the reign of God (cf. Luke 13:29; Dan. 7:14; Rev. 7:14).

We note also the need to await the Holy Spirit's enabling for the forthcoming mission. The command is clear and specific – 'wait for the Spirit.' Four things are to be deduced from Jesus' words.

First, we are confronted here by our real and continual dependence upon the ministry of God the Holy Spirit. This is the force of the command **wait!** The initiative and direction and, by implication, the enablement of the mission, does not lie with us. All ministry and all witness is dependent on His enabling. Calvin sees this utter dependence on the Spirit's ministry as a salutary reminder of the danger in Christian service of 'robbing Christ' by giving undue place to men. We only carry through the outward, the Lord imparts the inward: to Him alone be the glory![26]

Second, the Holy Spirit's enabling agency is a gift, not a reward. Thus while we may correctly note preconditions, such as waiting in prayer and personal repentance and cleanness of heart (2 Chron. 7:14f; Ps. 2:8; Acts 1:14; 4:24f; Eph. 6:18), the Spirit's ministry is never earned by us. He is always a gift of the Father and the Son.

Third, He is promised, as in Old Testament passages (such as Joel 2:28f; Isa. 32:15; Ezek. 36:27f; Jer. 31:31ff); and also promised by Jesus Himself: **which you have heard me speak about** (Luke 11:13; John 14:15-18; 14:26-27; 15:26; 16:5-15; 20:22); and probably also by implication, promised by John Baptist (Luke 3:16-17). This gives a welcome encouragement to our faith as we pray for His coming upon our lives in God's service, and upon the church, local and global. The Holy Spirit's ministry is integral to the whole redemptive plan of God; what He does in and through His

---

26. Calvin: I, 27-8.

people in the course of their mission is the fulfilment of the eternal counsel and purpose of the Living God.[27]

1:5. *Fourth,* He is a highly significant and effusive gift. Jesus uses the image of baptism, **you will be baptized with the Holy Spirit. Baptized** with its direct link to John the Baptist's rite which needed 'plenty of water' (John 3:23), and the obvious connection to the current proselyte baptism rite which called for initiates to be immersed in water, cannot but have conveyed to the disciples an image of an overwhelming experience of the Spirit's enablement. John the Baptist had by this time paid the price of his faithfulness to God's Word and been executed. His voice had been silenced, so it seemed, by the folly and cruelty of a worldly tyrant (Matt. 14:1-12). But John's words, because they were God's Word through him, did not pass away. They were to be fulfilled beyond his death. In the terms of John's enviable epitaph: 'Though he never performed a miraculous sign, all that John said about Jesus was true' (John 10:41).

A searching challenge and awesome possibility lies here for every proclaimer of the gospel, that our words, like those of John, may go on finding fulfilments and confirmations after our earthly course is concluded; and even, by His grace, become a word or sentence, in that Word 'which will never pass away' (Luke 21:33).

> *God's Word, for all their craft and force,*
> *One moment will not linger,*
> *But, spite of hell, will have its course;*
> *'Tis written by His finger.*[28]

1:6–8. This is a critically important sub-paragraph for the whole book of Acts. Indeed the entire book may be said to be an exposition of these verses. We note that the foil is the disciples' misunderstanding. **So when they met together, they asked him, 'Lord, are you at this time going to restore the kingdom to Israel?'** While such obtuseness

---

27. Stott, 36f; Marshall, 52; Bruce, 36-7.

28. Martin Luther (1483–1546); tr. Thomas Carlyle (1795–1881).

is not out of keeping with the disciples' limited levels of awareness during Jesus' ministry (cf. 9.41; Mark 8:14-21; John 14:9), there is some surprise that such misunderstanding should apparently linger on in their minds after all these days of divine instruction, and not least when one of its principal themes was 'the kingdom of God' (3). However it is likely that we should not read these verses, from verse 3 to verse 8, as though Luke's account here is in strict time sequence. 'On one occasion' (4), and 'when they were met together' (6), and 'after he said this' (9) are all, in fact, quite vague and general in their reference. Luke was not present himself during these days, and so it is very likely that what he gives us in these verses are the main themes of the conversation over the entire forty-day period as they were conveyed to him subsequently by his apostolic source, or sources. When we recognize this, our surprise at the disciples' misunderstanding is lessened. Their dim-wittedness about the meaning of the kingdom, as reflected here, may simply have been where they were when this Easter seminar commenced. And dim-wittedness there certainly was – the verb, noun, and adverb all betray doctrinal confusion about God's purpose and kingdom. 'The verb, "restore", shows they were expecting a political and territorial kingdom; the noun "Israel" that they were expecting a national kingdom, and the adverbial clause "at this time" that they were expecting its immediate establishment.' [29] Calvin notes that 'There are as many errors in this question as words.'[30]

Jesus' rejoinder, **It is not for you to know the times or dates the Father has set by his own authority**, if taken in isolation, can be read as not eliminating entirely a restoration of the Israelite kingdom at some undefined future point; however to take this saying in isolation is precisely what we must not do. The link to the immediately preceding reference in verse 3 to the kingdom of God is critical in this regard. This earlier reference is necessarily inclusive of all that Jesus taught about the kingdom as recorded in

29. Stott, 41.
30. Calvin, 29.

the Gospels, an understanding of the kingdom which, as the immense literature on this subject in the recent period clearly concludes, certainly does not culminate in a narrowly Israelite political and territorial fulfilment. Further, Jesus' response in verse 7 clearly directs their minds away from such notions to the cardinal task of global witness to the good news, and the universal implications of His death and rising.

However, while sympathizing in general with Calvin and Stott's strictures, we can at least note that the disciples are deserving of some degree of defence here, despite their misunderstandings. They *did* grasp that God's purposes have reached a climactic stage; that Jesus has power to revolutionize events; that God's kingdom is about to enter a glorious new phrase; that Jesus as the Risen One is Lord of all; and that in bringing the kingdom God will also fulfil his promise to Israel; not certainly in the nationalistic and political terms of the disciples' question, but in the deeper, profounder sense of a future universal reign of the one true Israelite, Jesus Messiah (John 15:1), a kingdom in which a believing remnant of Israel would find an honoured place (Rom. 11:1-12; Rev. 21:12) within a worshipping community which would embrace all the world's nations (Isa. 56:7; Mark 11:17). God's old covenant promise will inevitably be fulfilled in His new covenant reign. The disciples' primary error lies in their ethno-centrism, perhaps not entirely surprising in view of the ideas they had been reared with, and the depth of loyalty which is commanded by ethnic nationalism, then as now. Further, theirs was in some degree a 'fruitful' error, in that it provoked the hugely important clarification of verses 7-8, which teach at least two critical truths:

(1) *The inevitable element of mystery in God's purposes*: **It is not for you to know the times or dates the Father has set by his own authority**. The 'mystery' is particularly so with respect to the final fulfilment of his plans (cf. Mark 10:35ff; 13:32; Luke 22:24ff.). Would that this text had been clearly heard and heeded over the Christian centuries. True the expectation of the glorious return of Christ (11) is ever to be a bright and shining light of hope across the pathway

of Christian pilgrimage; the King is coming and we are travelling to meet him; there is truth to be proclaimed from the housetops! However the speculative, even obsessive, concentration on earthly theocracies, and on detailed blueprints of the 'last times', is not given any encouragement here. Such addictive 'futurology' always carries the danger that Christian resources and energies are thereby distracted from the solemn call of Christ to the far harder, more demanding task of being the light of the world and the salt of the earth, pouring our lives into seeing God's will being done on earth as it is done in heaven.[31] A divine rebuke of this mistaken focus is possibly also indicated in the angels' question (11), **Why do you stand here looking into the sky? This same Jesus…will come back**, and therefore you can trust the plans and purposes of God to him. Your task is to get on with what He has supremely asked you to do – **Be my witnesses…to the ends of the earth.**

Jesus' words were apparently heeded, as Bruce notes: 'The question in v. 6 appears to have been the last flicker of the apostles' former burning expectation of an immanent political theocracy with themselves as its chief executives. From this time forth they devoted themselves to the proclamation and service of God's spiritual kingdom, which people enter by repentance and faith and in which the chief honour belongs to those who most faithfully follow the King himself in the path of obedience and suffering.'[32]

(2) *The calling of God to His people:* **but you will receive power when the Holy Spirit comes on you; and you will be my witnesses in Jerusalem, and in all Judea and Samaria, and to the ends of the earth** (8). Here we meet the Great Commission. Each of the Gospels, including Luke's, has a version of it (Matt. 28:18-20; Mark 16:15, see note below; Luke 24:46-49; John 20:21-22). The diversity

---

31. cf. Marshall: 60. 'Since this is God's secret there is no place for human speculation.'

32. Bruce: 38.

of wording no doubt reflects the variety of occasions on which Jesus expressed His command.[33]

Mission to the ends of the earth is accordingly fundamental to the church's existence and function. It is of profound regret accordingly that this evidently primary biblical function was largely omitted during the following centuries in discussions of the essential components of the church. Referred to as 'the Marks of the Church', they were endlessly debated in the controversies of the sixteenth century and subsequent periods as the Reformers attempted to redefine the church in the light of its perceived de-formation during the medieval Catholic centuries. Thus the four traditional Catholic marks of unity, holiness, catholicity, and apostolicity were opposed by the Reformed advocacy of the faithful proclamation of the Word of God, the proper administration of the sacraments, and, on occasion, additionally, the proper exercise of church discipline.[34]

While during the ages of the Reformation mission was arguably, in an attenuated sense, included under the category of the preaching of the Word of God, mission as the expression of a universal obligation to take initiatives to bring the gospel message to the non-Christian nations of the earth, and indeed as the obligation to have the gospel shared meaningfully across local cultures and communities, was simply not on the radar in that period. It was not until the end of the eighteenth century under the influence of visionary leaders like William Carey, that Christian mis-

---

33. The final section of Mark, 16:9-20, was almost certainly not part of the original text of Mark. cf. the NIV note 'The earliest manuscripts and some other ancient witnesses do not have Mark 16:9-20'. While it therefore cannot carry final authority for faith and practice, it nevertheless offers a supportive witness to the earlier Gospels which were clearly part of the original apostolic testimony. Used in this secondary role, verse 15 is a very early witness to the fact that the church was personally mandated by the risen Jesus to set about global witness to the gospel. On this issue see for example: B.F. Westcott and F.J.A. Hort, *The New Testament in the Original Greek*, 2 vols (Cambridge, London, 1881), vol. 2: 'Appendix', 28-51.

34. On this issue, see the perceptive paper of David Wright, 'The Great Commission and the Ministry of the Word: Reflections Historical and Contemporary on Relations and Priorities'. *Scottish Bulletin of Evangelical Theology*, August 2007. Vol. 25, No. 2. The paper also traces the use of the title 'Great Commission' from its origin in the late nineteenth and early twentieth centuries up to the present.

sion, both in terms of its primary importance as well as its form and content, can be said to have begun to recover its proper biblical proportions.[35] In this sense it has taken the church nearly two millennia to get back to the book of Acts! For there can be little doubt that 1:8 is intended by Luke as a table of contents for Acts. It tells the story of the progressively expanding witness to Jesus Christ following the three-stage order of this text: 'in Jerusalem' (chs. 2–7), 'in Judea and Samaria' (chs. 8–12), and 'to the ends of the earth' (chs. 13–28). We can note also the repeated surfacing of the theme of witness-bearing through these chapters: 2:32; 3:15; 5:32; 10:39; 13:31; 22:15; etc. Acts has a number of secondary themes no doubt. History is never as simple as a single idea, and Luke is a faithful and sensitive historian. But whatever else Acts may contain, or teach, if we fail to identify its missional heart and expose ourselves to its missional challenge – to the church generally, to each local church specifically, and to our lives personally – then we have not really met God in its pages or truly heard His Word. The only history of the church that the Holy Spirit has been pleased to give us in the Holy Scriptures is a history of the Christian mission, its solemn obligations, its diverse forms, and its often desperate costliness. Hence, woe betide us if we neglect or marginalize it. Our enemy in this regard was well focused by J.H. Bavinck in his landmark study of the theology of mission of over a half century ago. 'The church loves to be occupied with itself and its own problems....People wish to remain quiet, in the peaceful little church under the high Gothic arches; they would brood about God and be preoccupied about the needs of their own souls. They do not want to be shocked by the bewildering idea that there are still many hundreds of millions of people who have never heard the gospel.'[36]

We should note, in respect of this commission:

---

35. cf. David J. Hesselgrave, art. 'Great Commission', in *Evangelical Dictionary of World Missions*, ed. A. Scott Moreau (Baker, 2000), 412-14.

36. J.H. Bavinck, *An Introduction to the Science of Missions* (Presbyterian and Reformed, 1961), 276, 277.

(1) *The activity at its heart.* The call is to be **witnesses to me**. We registered above the prevalence of 'witness-bearing' in Acts. Of its thirty-five appearances in the New Testament fifteen occur here. The idea has Old Testament roots in the role of witnesses in judicial proceedings (Num. 35:30; Deut. 17:6-7). Of particular importance for the Acts usage is Isaiah 43:10-12; and 44:8-9. Here Yahweh calls on His people to vindicate Him before the nations and their gods. Israel can bear a witness, arising from its relationship with Yahweh, that He is the true and living God, the faithful God who foretells the future, who acts in history, who saves and delivers His own. Thus witness (Gk. *martus*) has an original legal connotation, as also reflected in Jesus' use of the notion in Matthew 18:16 referring to issues of contention in a church, 'every matter may be established by the testimony of two or three witnesses.' (cf. 2 Cor. 13:1; 1 Tim. 5:19). 'A witness in this sense is someone who helps establish facts objectively through verifiable observation.'[37] This is reflected also in the concern in 1:22 that Judas' successor be a witness of the resurrection (cf. also 2:32; 3:15; 4:18, 33; 5:32; 10:41; 13:31). However there is a broader sense attached to other New Testament references where a witness is simply someone who saw or experienced something (cf. 1 Tim. 6:12; 2 Tim 2:2; Heb. 12:1; Rev. 11:3; Luke 11:48; 21:13). There is also in Revelation a developed meaning of 'witnesses' as those who seal their testimony in death, hence the root of the English 'martyr' (cf. Rev. 2:13; 17:6).

The foundational witness-bearing is incumbent on the apostles (1:8; 2:23; 3:15; 4:33; 10:39), but as the apostles begin to die (12:2), and as the witness increasingly passes beyond the geographical boundaries of Israel, 'witness-bearing' comes to be understood, both historically and theologically, as the responsibility of the entire community. Thus non-apostolic persons (in the narrower sense) like Stephen in Jerusalem, Philip in his ministry to Samaria and Ethiopia (8:4 and 35), and Stephen's disciples in Antioch (11:20), all appear as 'witnesses' in the fully

---

37. Bock, 64.

authentic sense of their being heralds of the salvation-imparting message of Jesus. 'There is already in the Lukan writings an extension of the concept of witness to people other than the apostles.'[38] Thus the foundational witness-bearing of the apostles passes to the entire church and its succeeding generations.

The fact that the legal sense of 'giving evidence' attached to the earliest meaning, indicates that the apostolic witness, which today finds permanent form in the New Testament writings, remains fundamental to the church's witness. It is a reminder that the heart of the witness we are called to bear before all nations is not so much pointing to ourselves and our experience, as pointing to Christ who can only be accounted for in terms of God's presence in Him, and who alone can account for our experience of God through Him. We note the intimate link to the Spirit's coming (cf. v. 8 and below), which underlines that witnessing is always understood as a divine-human activity: 'We are witnesses of these things, and so is the Holy Spirit' (5:32; cf. Mark 13:11).

(2) *The power for its pursuance.* **you will receive power when the Holy Spirit comes on you and you shall be witnesses to me...**As we noted for witness-bearing, so for the entire pursuance of the mission, God is at the centre. Mission operates at the matrix of the divine with the human. It is a ministry and movement in and through which God acts. This will be normatively demonstrated in the launching of the mission by the powerful 'coming on them' of God the Holy Spirit. Jesus had spoken of this using the metaphor of baptism (v. 5) after the model of John's immersion rite. Accordingly the enablement will be, at least in its inception, an overwhelming experience of God; a being immersed and overpowered. Jesus had already spoken at some length in the Upper Room of the Spirit's unique enablement of the apostles (John 14:26f, etc), and indeed

38. D. Bosch, *Transforming Mission* (Orbis, New York, 2006), 116. cf. also J.I. Packer, 'The commission to publish the gospel and make disciples was never confined to the apostles...it is a commission which rests upon the church collectively, and therefore upon each Christian individually' (*Evangelism and the Sovereignty of God* [IVP, 1961], 45).

had given them, immediately following the resurrection, a memorable image of the essential nature of this Spirit-impartation by breathing upon them: the Spirit who will come upon them will be none other than the life-breath of the Risen Lord (John 20:22). But what He now promises further enriches that perspective, for the happening of Acts 2 is destined to be not just a special experience of the Spirit, but also a model for the entire mission of the church.

We should note also the corporate terms of this enablement. All the verbs in these verses are plural. It is a 'coming on' the church, the disciple community. The instrument of the mission is the disciples together. The referring of the mission's enablement, and hence its essential realization, to the Holy Spirit through the community, is also a salutary corrective to the erroneous material, political, territorial and ethnically limited view of the kingdom reflected in the disciples' question of verse 6. The kingdom's coming is essentially linked to the Spirit's coming and presence. As Paul would affirm later, 'The kingdom of God is not a matter of eating and drinking (external, material practices and performances), but of righteousness, peace and joy in the Holy Spirit' (Rom. 14:17). We can note the parallel with Jesus' ministry and His empowerment by the same Holy Spirit (1:1; Luke 1:35; 3:21ff; 4:1; 4:14; 4:17f).

(3) *The scope of its reach*: **in Jerusalem, all Judea and Samaria, and to the ends of the earth**. The mission begins locally. It is to be launched where they are, in Jerusalem. Their witness will be borne first in the heart of the nation, in the city of God, the site of the Temple, the place of sacred association for Israel's entire relationship with God. It will begin therefore in a place where the culture is familiar and the language of communication is common to both the witnesses and those witnessed to. But it will not be confined there. It is to move beyond Jerusalem to the whole nation of Israel in its homeland, and then to the morally and spiritually compromised Samaritans with their inadequate theology and separate history and culture. But even that will be no stopping place, for beyond that their concern must carry them on to a witness to the Gentile world, to Israel's scattered diaspora, and to the Gentile nations

themselves with all their cultural, linguistic, historical and spiritual foreignness.

There is discussion of the precise meaning of 'to the ends of the earth'. Is this diaspora Jews, wherever they might be found? or the entire populations of Spain at the limits of the western Mediterranean, or of the Gentile nations generally, or the furthest geographical limits of the world? It is difficult not to miss the Old Testament background here (Isa. 48:20; 49:6; Jer. 10:13). It is perhaps possible to see both an immediate and a more ultimate reference. From the literary standpoint of the book of Acts the goal, in an evident sense, is reached with Paul freely preaching the gospel from his 'prison' in Rome (28:31). Thus the mission culminates as the message is proclaimed in 'the centre of the world',[39] from where it can radiate outwards in every direction. However the occurrence of the phrase in Isaiah (48:20; 49:6) points finally to the global dimensions of the mission, in terms of the redemptive purpose of God through His Servant. The God of Israel, who is witnessed to in Genesis 1 as the creator of the entire earth, now embraces the entire earth in His work of redemption. The disciple community is thus called to share the universal vision of the God who creates all peoples and nations, who holds them all accountable to Him, and who embraces them all in the scope of His salvation achieved through the infinitely costly ministry of His Servant. The church is thus defined at its birth as a global people who will 'go into all the world and preach the good news to all creation', and whose communal life will reflect the diversity and richness of all the world's peoples; a global church of a global God.

Marshall observes the implications: 'These verses spell out God's purpose and the place of the church in it. They postulate that the period of witness and mission must precede the return of Jesus. They were thus in effect warning the disciples not to expect a speedy winding up of history. For Luke's readers some forty years or more later (as to

---

39. Floyd V. Fison, 'The Journey motif in Luke-Acts' in W.W. Gasque and R.P Martin, eds., *Apostolic History and the Gospel: Biblical and Historical Essays* (Paternoster, 1970), 76.

ourselves today) they were a reminder of the ongoing task: the gospel must still be taken to the ends of the earth. At the same time the words contain a note of promise in that the departure of Jesus is compensated for by the coming of the Spirit, given by Jesus himself (2:33).' [40]

The Ascension of Jesus (1:9-11)

The historical reality of the ascension: The period of forty days is drawn to a conclusion by a unique action, the ascension of Jesus. As the disciples look on, He is taken up into a cloud (Matt. 28:16ff; Luke 24:50f). The ascension has been regularly dismissed as a hangover from primitive belief in a three-decker world, with God's home 'above the sky'. But its general historicity is perfectly defensible provided we allow for the Bible's regular use of symbolism in conveying its message.

The disciples' experience of seeing Jesus physically gathered up into a cloud – a memory which would have impressed itself on their minds for the remainder of their lives – taught them three important, highly relevant truths. *First*, its climactic nature at the end of the forty days would have indicated the conclusion of that period. They were not to anticipate further *physical* appearances of Jesus. *Second*, for men immersed in the Old Testament, the cloud was a revered symbol of the awesome presence of God, as for example at Sinai, or in the wilderness (Exod. 40:34, 13:21), at the dedication of Solomon's temple (1 Kings 8:10f), or more immediately of the glory of Jesus on the Mount of Transfiguration (Luke 9:34f); Jesus is 'going' into the very heart and centre of Godhead. *Third*, the movement of Jesus upwards into the cloud (**he was taken up...**) would have conveyed what such elevation does in every age (cf. 'the king ascended to the throne...'; 'she went up in my estimation...'), viz. his exaltation to a place of supreme dignity, respect, and authority.

Taken together these three implications coalesce in an ascension-mediated conviction that Jesus, though now and hereafter to be hidden from physical sight and tan-

---

40. Marshall, 59.

gible contact, is in the very presence of God, and exalted as Lord over all things.

The meaning of the ascension:

(1) *For Jesus Himself:* Ascension means reign, as we noted above. Paul explores this implication memorably in Philippians 2.9f, 'God has highly exalted Jesus and given him the name which is above every other name', viz. the name 'Lord', with all its Old Testament overtones of deity. Thus the risen one can claim, 'All authority in heaven and earth is given to me' (Matt. 28:18). Jesus is therefore the '*Lord* Jesus' (cf. Acts 2:34), the one addressed as 'Lord' in the messianic Psalm 110:1 (cf. Rom. 8:34; Col. 3:1; Heb. 1:13; 1 Pet. 3:22; Acts 10:36).

(2) *For the mission of the church:* We recall that Luke has already given an account of the ascension at the end of his Gospel (Luke 24:50f). There it acts as a fitting conclusion to the story of Jesus' earthly ministry. He who was rejected and exposed to the horrors of crucifixion is not only raised again, the conqueror of death; but is vindicated in His claims, and in His divinely intended self-sacrifice, by being exalted to the right hand of God. So the Gospel ends with the disciples offering Him worship, and being filled with great joy (Luke 24:52).

However Luke repeats the ascension in some detail here in Acts 1, because the ascension is not only the fitting conclusion to the gospel story, it is also the supremely important presupposition and basis of the entire on-going life of the disciple-community, the church. It is in the light shed by the ascension that we are to view the ministry of the Holy Spirit, the whole course of the Christian centuries, and the entire mission of the gospel in the world. 'Christ is ascended, but his abiding presence and energy fill the whole book of Acts, and the whole succeeding story of his people on earth…"He ascended far above all the heavens, that he might fill all things".' [41]

---

41. Bruce: 41-2. So in Acts 1:22; 2:33; 3:19; 4:33; 5:14, 31; 7:54; 8:16; 9:17; 10:36; 11:20f; 14:3; 15:11, 26; 16:14, 31; 17:7; 18:9f; 20:21, 24; 22:17-21; 23:11; 26:15-18; 28:31.

It is on the basis of the ascension that the church goes forth to the world with the gospel. It is His ascended presence which authenticates its testimony, and which again and again renews its life, inspires its servants, establishes its authority, directs its progress, and will culminate its work. 'There is all the difference in the world between going out on mission with the motive of helping Christ to become King, and going out because the King has sent you...The command "go into all the world" has behind it the urge and power of that stupendous affirmation "All authority in heaven and earth has been given to me." The dynamic of the church's unaccomplished task is the accomplished deed of God. Underneath the urgent imperative there rests, firm as a rock, the eternal indicative.' [42]

Calvin notes a further lesson of the ascension: 'He ascended to heaven to remain there until such time as he should come a second time to judge the world. Let us therefore learn...that Christ is not to be sought either in heaven or upon earth other than by faith; and also that we must not desire to have Him present with us bodily in the world. For the man who clings to either of these ambitions often moves further away from Him.'[43]

(3) *For our personal service of the mission of Christ.* More generally, the ascension clarifies the conditions under which Christ is present for us in our personal lives. It is a relationship with Him that is real and living, for He is risen and alive forever. It a relationship which does not depend on sight but rather on faith, listening to His voice rather than straining for His physical presence; 'this is my Son...*listen* to him' (Luke 9:35). It is a relationship of confidence for He reigns in the world. It is a relationship of sympathy, 'for he is not unable to sympathize with our weaknesses', and 'he ever lives to make intercession for us'. It is a relationship of hope because 'he will come again' (11). It is a relationship experienced in the context of mission, the command to be witnesses 'until he comes'. But He who comes will be 'this same Jesus', and hence

---

42. J.S. Stewart, *Thine is the Kingdom* (St Andrew Press, 1956), 27–28.

43. Calvin, 14.

it is a relationship of love as we rest in the revelation of the Gospels and nurture a relationship with Him which is daily enlightened by their witness. Accordingly the ascension is no 'tearful farewell' as at some parting at a deathbed, or before a long journey with the prospect of a yawning separation and no certainty of ever renewing the contact of sight and touch. Hence Luke 24:52...'they returned to Jerusalem with great joy'. The implications of the ascension for Christian living as well as witness, have rarely been more defiantly, or thrillingly expressed, than in a passage in Calvin's fourth sermon on the ascension:

'Since he has gone up there, and is in heaven for us, let us note that we need not fear to be in this world. It is true that we are subject to so much misery that our condition is pitiable, but at that we need neither be astonished nor confine our attention to ourselves. Thus, we look to our Head Who is already in heaven, and say, "Although I am weak, there is Jesus Christ Who is powerful enough to make me stand upright. Although I am feeble, there is Jesus Christ Who is my strength. Although I am full of miseries, Jesus Christ is in immortal glory and what he has will some time be given to me and I shall partake of all his benefits. Yes, the devil is called the prince of this world. But what of it? Jesus Christ holds him in check; for he is King of heaven and earth. There are devils above us in the air who make war against us. But what of it? Jesus Christ rules above, having entire control of the battle. Thus we need not doubt that he gives us the victory. I am here subject to many changes, which may cause me to lose courage. But what of it? The Son of God is my Head, who is exempt from all change. I must, then, take confidence in Him." This is how we must look to his ascension, applying the benefits to ourselves.' [44]

(4) *For the form of our Christian hope*: A final point from these verses is to consider the intrinsic relationship established here between the ascension and the return of Christ.

44. Calvin, *The Deity of Christ and Other Sermons* (Audubon, N.J.: Old Paths Publications, 1977), 238-9. Cited Andrew Purves, *Reconstructing Pastoral Theology* (Westminster, John Knox, 2004), 112-13.

The incarnation of the Son of God was not a temporary phase of His being. His uniting to Himself a full human nature is a continuing reality, and hence, although His physical form remains hidden from us during the age of the church, it is realized in the present through His High Priestly intercession and sympathy (Heb. 4:14–5:10; 7:23-25; Rom. 8:34), and it is destined to reappear for us at His return. 'We shall see him as he is!' (1 John 3:2).[45]

3. Further preparations for the Mission (1:12-26)

(1) The Upper Room company (1:12-14)
The ascension is located on **the hill called the Mount of Olives** (12). In his Gospel Luke makes a similarly general reference to the ascension having taken place **in the vicinity of Bethany** (Luke 24:50), the home village of Mary, Martha and Lazarus, and perched near the brow of the Mount. Following Jesus' ascension the disciple group return to the city of **Jerusalem** extending south and westwards from the walled Temple area, about a kilometre to their west, across the Kedron valley.

Once arrived in the city they gather in an upstairs room, a company comprising the eleven apostles, a number of **women,** and several of Jesus' family members, specifically **his mother and brothers.** It is an interesting group. The apostolic list is identical to that given in Luke 6:14 apart from the obvious absence of Judas Iscariot. This implies a certain fixedness, and that would accord with the evidence of the opening chapters of Acts that the apostles remained a tight-knit group, united by Jesus' choice of them and jealous to fulfil the task given them of being in a special sense Jesus' witnesses.

We should note also however the diversity of the group as a whole. The presence of women reflects Jesus' dignifying of women by including them among those he taught (Luke 10:38-42; Matt. 14:21; 15:38; Mark 15:40f). Jesus' mother is an unsurprising member, as we recall His special care of her to His final breath at Calvary (John 19:26-27). Marshall

---

45. Stott: 50f, considers ways in which the return of Christ will be both like, and unlike His ascension.

notes, interestingly, that according to Jewish law 120 males was the minimum required to begin a new community;[46] though strikingly this Upper Room body is multi-gender. If this is in fact part of the context here, then we need to note that in the new community of the risen Lord women have equal status with men, a feature which Pentecost would soon underline. This is noteworthy in view of the reference to the group in verse 15 as **brothers**, no doubt reflecting the patriarchal traditions of their culture. (The NIV attempts to reduce that by the rendering, **believers**.) The Greek original does imply a deep and important sense of family; however the Spirit would speak a somewhat more inclusive word when he came in power (2:18). As far as Jesus' natural brothers are concerned they had earlier expressed scepticism about His claims (John 7:5). However the resurrection appearances had included a special meeting with James, probably the eldest of them (1 Cor. 15:7), and now at least some of the others, perhaps all three of them, were sharing the conviction of his Lordship and glory.[47]

The room may well have been the site of the last supper (Luke 22:12), and even, possibly, the location of another prayer meeting, for Peter's release, some fifteen years later, though of that we cannot be sure (Acts 12:12). The Gospel account refers to their spending time **continually at the temple, praising God** (Luke 24:53). In Acts they are **together constantly in prayer** (1:14). Stott helpfully notes their 'healthy combination' of 'continuous praise in the temple and continuous prayer in the upper room.'[48]

The praying is particularly notable. Presumably it is prayer, not least, for the needed resources of wisdom, power, and courage, to enable them to fulfil the terms of the commission Jesus had given them; that of being His witnesses to the waiting world, beginning right there in Jerusalem. It was arguably therefore a focussed prayer for the coming of the Holy Spirit, the one Jesus had promised them, who would give them all they needed (1:4; cf.

---

46. Marshall, 64.

47. Mark 6:3 identifies four brothers, probably in order of age.

48. Stott, 52.

Luke 11:13); and a prayer based accordingly on the personal promise of Jesus. Such praying is never inappropriate, for though the Spirit's coming is solemnly promised, He is clearly still to be sought. We note too the spirit of unity in their praying, and its persistence, **they all joined together constantly in prayer**. While our prayer never compels God, it is the unfailing prerequisite for spiritual blessing and renewal, both in Scripture and experience. 'When God intends great mercy for his people, the first thing he does is to set them praying.' (Matthew Henry).[49]

Such praying is surely in every bit as great demand in our day as it was in the first century. *'Veni Creator Spiritus!'*

(2) Matthias replaces Judas (1:15-26)

One further matter needed to be attended to before the life of the disciple community was fully readied for the launch of the mission. They had to revisit, and deal with, the tragic and embarrassing 'business of Judas'. For his betrayal must have continued to linger at the back of all their minds as a dark, even shocking, assault on their fellowship. Even the glory of resurrection could not totally eliminate it from their memories, and with the ascension now behind them, and with it the realization that there would be no further 'meetings' with Jesus, the horror of Judas and his actions would have reasserted itself for them all. It had to be addressed, and they proceeded to confront it.

There is a lesson here for many lives and churches. When the unthinkable happens, and overwhelming moral failure comes crashing into the life of an individual or a group of people close to us, there is the greatest temptation to try to look the other way and distance ourselves from it all. But to pursue that course indefinitely is rarely either wise or helpful. Sooner or later we need to confront the issues, as do the disciples here, and as they would do again in the sad case of Ananias and Sapphira in chapter 5.

---

49. 'From the day of Pentecost, there has not been one great spiritual awakening in any land which has not been begun in a union of prayer, though only among two or three; no such outward, upward movement has continued after such prayer meetings have declined' (A.T. Pierson).

Such 'confronting' should never lack a genuine degree of compassion or a deep empathy, nor the constant and renewed sense of our own vulnerabilities and short-comings. But, at times, judgment, albeit supportive and sensitive, must begin at the house of God. If a breach of the law of the land is uncovered then of course there is no choice in terms of confronting. Christians are upholders of the law, save only where it directly contradicts the law of God (4:19). In other cases generalizations are probably unhelpful; each case has its own nuances and calls for its own sensitive, prayerful handling. However the temptation to ignore is only deferring the day of reckoning. To cite a congregational case, I recall a conversation recently with a Welsh pastor who spoke of the exhausting struggles for a real spiritual breakthrough during his long and eminently faithful ministry, a struggle occasioned largely, as he came to believe, by the entail of a serious moral failure on the part of a church leader during an earlier ministry, which no one had had the courage to confront.

15-20 Appropriately, Peter, Jesus' chosen leader, takes the initiative (Matt. 16:18). There is the larger question of re-establishing the 'group of twelve' which Jesus had formed and which Judas had effectively destroyed by his folly. That will occupy the later part of this section (vv. 21–26). But before coming to that Peter does four things:

(1) *He brings the issue right into the open:* **concerning Judas** (16; cf. 5:3-4 and 8-9). He refers to his **wickedness** and the ensuing judgment that had overtaken him: **he fell headlong** (18b-19). Verses 18-19 are set within brackets in the NIV translation. This is because the editors view these verses as Luke's explanatory aside, rather than part of Peter's speech.

(2) *He sets the failure of Judas within the overruling will of God, but not in a way that exculpates him:* **the Scripture had to be fulfilled which the Holy Spirit spoke long ago.** Despite the deep mystery of Judas' action, and the raw sense of shock and defeat it registered for the apostolic group, God had not been finally thwarted in His purposes. Indeed even Judas' hideous act of betrayal of the love of

Christ for him had been foreseen, and in some sense been taken account of. God remained, and remains, Lord of all, even of desperate acts of failure. Psalm 69:25, the Scripture Peter cites in this connection, a general pronouncement of God's judgment on his enemies, also speaks of a loss of 'his place', '**may his place be deserted...**'(20), which has a certain aptness with respect to Judas' attempt to obtain land; **he bought a field**, from **the reward** of his betrayal (Luke 22:5).

No failure, of whatever proportion, by whatever person, can finally thwart the will of God; He is, and forever will be, Lord of all. This glorious truth, however, does not imply that Judas is thereby excused. His **wickedness** remains the case. 'Judas may not be excused on the ground that what befell him was prophesied, since he fell away not through the compulsion of the prophecy but through the wickedness of his own heart.'[50] This brings us to the frontier of the elusive mystery of divine sovereignty and human free will. For all Peter's clear affirmation of God's sovereign overruling, Judas' culpability remains.

(3) *He acknowledges the deep personal pain for them all, and even, possibly, some lingering sense of responsibility they may have felt.* Judas, after all, had been **one of our number and shared in this ministry.** One of the complicating emotions in facing up to situations like that of Judas is that we are made aware the more sharply of our own weaknesses and lesser failures. Such must not paralyse the instinct to have the sin brought into judgment, but it makes responding to it with full integrity the more difficult.

> *because we are all*
> *betrayers, taking*
> *body and blood and asking*
> *(guilty) is it I and hearing*
> *him say yes*
> *it would be simple for us all*
> *to rush out*
> *and hang ourselves*

---

50. Calvin: 40.

> *but if we find grace*
> *to cry and wait*
> *after the voice of morning*
> *has crowed in our ears*
> *clearly enough*
> *to break our hearts*
> *he will be there*
> *to ask us each again*
> *do you love me.* [51]

But Peter's note of the shared life of the apostolic group also underlines the degree of Judas' culpability, for he had not only betrayed Jesus; he had also betrayed them all, and their trust in him, and betrayed also the astonishingly privileged position Jesus had given him. It is one of the blinding factors which so often operates in moral failure that the party concerned fails to recognize how many others will be impacted by their sin.[52]

(4) *Peter leaves Judas finally to God*: **Judas left to go where he belongs (**25), and finds Scripture, **May another take his place of leadership** (Ps. 109:8), which directs the group forward to action which will move them beyond the tragedy of Judas, and hence able to refocus the responsibilities and possibilities lying ahead of them.[53]

Was Matthias a mistake? Some so argue. They note that the outpouring of the Spirit has not yet occurred and

---

51. Luci Shaw, 'Judas, Peter' from *The Sighting* (Harold Shaw, 1981), 82.

52. cf. the sensitive examination of moral failure on the part of Christian leaders in, Stanley J. Grenz and Roy D. Bell, *Betrayal of Trust* (Baker, 2001).

53. The account given by Luke here of the events surrounding the suicide of Judas is often claimed to be irreconcilable with that offered in Matthew 27:3-5. Before addressing these we should note, with Stott (55-6), the large degree of agreement between the two versions: 'both say that Judas died a miserable death; that a field was bought with the money paid him (thirty silver coins), and that it was called "Blood Field"' (55). Three discrepancies are alleged: how Judas died, who bought the field, and why it was called the 'Blood Field'. As to the reason for his death there is no intrinsic difficulty in Judas' body, after his hanging, having fallen to the ground and ruptured. As to who bought the field, in principle *both* the priests, to whom Judas returned the money, *and* Judas himself, bought the field, since the money was his by all rights having kept his bargain to betray Jesus. And how the name came to be attached to the field thereafter was probably understood in different ways by different parties without there being any contradiction. Marshall actually suggests it is 'quite possible that Matthew or Luke is simply reporting what was commonly said in Jerusalem, and that we are not meant to harmonize the two accounts' (Marshall, 65).

so the disciples, lacking this divine, miraculous energy, resort to a merely human form of appointment involving the superstitious employment of a lot. They also note that no further word is heard of Matthias' ministry; however that carries little weight as the same could be said of many of the other apostles, even some who have quite prominent roles in the Gospels, such as Peter's brother Andrew, or Philip, or Thomas. Others have even suggested that the disciples show an inappropriate hastiness in proceeding in this way since the twelfth apostle was in fact Saul of Tarsus. This latter claim appears to be particularly unlikely as Saul/Paul was not to be converted for some years. Exact dates are not available, but anything from two to five years is suggested. Were the apostles then to enter upon their crucial public witness-bearing role depleted in number, and by their 'apostolic gap' carrying clear and ongoing evidence of the success of a satanic attack upon them?

There is in fact no hint in the text that the disciples, led by Peter, were in any respect out of line in their procedural process. The Old Testament Scriptures carry numerous references to the use of the lot, for example the 'allotment' (!) of the land to the various tribes was done by the use of the lot (Lev. 16:8; Josh. 18:6; 19:51). There is also a New Testament instance which was to have significant impact on the circumstances of Jesus' birth (Luke 1:9). According to Proverbs 16:33, 'The lot is cast into the lap, but its every decision is from the Lord', and 18:18, 'Casting the lot settles disputes and keeps strong opponents apart.' Used with prayer for divine overruling it was a way of putting matters into the Lord's hands, which in verse 24 here surely means 'the Lord Jesus' who was among them. So Jesus is again the one who is electing an apostle.

It is certainly to be noted that there is no further reference to this form of guidance being employed later in the book of Acts, or elsewhere in the New Testament. We may therefore fairly infer that the Holy Spirit's outpoured coming at Pentecost opened the way for more direct and personal forms of divine direction (cf. 13:3). However, recognizing the point in the history of divine revelation in which the disciples found themselves, their action here is not lacking in propriety. 'The church was asking the Lord to make *his* choice of the right man, who was then *enrolled* as an apostle; the church cannot be said to have elected him.' [54]

Study Questions:

1. In what ways does 1:1-11 set the scene for the story of the church? What does 1:1 in particular mean in your life, or the life of your church?

2. Consider Luke's table of contents at 1:8. It presents the vision of a global mission. In what ways does this resonate for our global age? What are some of the things we can do to help our church identify with this vision?

3. What is the significance of Jesus' ascension? James Denney sees it as the key to Christianity...what might he be referring to?

4. What are lessons of the tragic story of Judas? What is to be learned from the way the church handled what had happened to Judas?

---

54. Marshall, 67.

2

Pentecost – the Birthing of the Mission
(Acts 2:1-47)

The outpouring of the Holy Spirit at Pentecost is a critical moment for the book of Acts as a whole. But it is critical also in the history of the self-manifestation of God. Pentecost is one of the epochal moments in a series which runs from the creation of the universe and humanity (Gen 1–2), the call of, and covenant with, Abraham (Gen. 12, 15, 17), the incarnation (John 1:14), the cross (Mark 14–15), the resurrection (Luke 24), and the parousia (1 Thess. 4:16). At Pentecost God Himself drew back the curtain and revealed His glory. At Pentecost He came in person, overwhelmingly affirming Himself as God, intimately and eternally present among us in the Holy Spirit.

a. Pentecost described (2:1-13).
'A Sound from Heaven'

The opening two verses preserve an appropriate balance between human preparation and sovereign divine initiative. The preparation had already been signalled in chapter one in several ways. Jesus' proven resurrection, the completion of His teaching about the Kingdom of God, His heavenly ascension, the communal waiting in prayer, the reaffirmation of the apostolic leadership group, and finally the praying assembly of the whole disciple body 'together in one place', all combined like an accumulating snowbed in the final moments before an avalanche.

This 'internal' preparation of the community is now complemented by a significant 'external' factor, the arrival in Jerusalem of vast crowds of pilgrims from all parts of the Mediterranean world and beyond, for the celebration of the next great Jewish festival following Passover, viz. Pentecost. This was fifty days exactly (*pentecostos*, Gk. for fiftieth) from the sacrificing of the Passover lamb; fifty days, that is, from the festival which enshrined the central moment in all history, the self-offering of the Lamb of God at Calvary. [1]

The Pentecost festival, like the other Jewish annual feasts, commemorated important events in the Old Testament story. Passover was associated with the Exodus; Pentecost, also called the 'Feast of Weeks', was associated with the celebration of the wheat harvest and, more theologically, with God's covenant with Noah, and later with Moses (Exod. 23:16: Lev. 23:15-21: Deut. 16:9-12).

Later Judaism was also to link the festival with the giving of the law on Sinai, which was believed to be fifty days after the Exodus, though this clearly appears to have been a second-century development. Bearing in mind the tradition that the law was promulgated in seventy languages and accompanied by the phenomena of wind, fire and voices, it is tempting in the extreme to assume a connection here; there is, however, no extant evidence to sustain it. In exploring the Jewish background to Pentecost, Bock's comments are responsibly cautionary: 'Luke's lack of appeal to the idea (of the giving of the law) means that the debate over the background for Acts is not of such great significance for interpreting Acts, even though it may have been at work in the cultural backdrop to the event. What Luke sees here is the realization of the divine programme tied to the Messiah's promised work, as Peter's speech makes clear.' [2]

Typically, divine sovereign intervention, while it does not annul human anticipations, nonetheless so suffuses

---

1. Apart from any other consideration the link to Pentecost implies that 'the essential historicity of the incident is firmly assured'. J.D.G. Dunn, *Jesus and the Spirit* (SCM, 1975), 135-6.

2. Bock, 96.

and overwhelms them that the coming of God is marked by its apparent surprise and unexpectedness; cf. **suddenly** (2, *aphno*). When God comes, it is so utterly different, and sheerly supernatural, that all the human preparation which may have authentically anticipated the event is effectively eliminated from consideration.[3] 'Be silent, all flesh, before the Lord, for he has roused himself from his holy dwelling' (Zech. 2:13, ESV).

Some discussion has gathered around the location of this coming of God the Spirit. In our desire to capture the scene in imagination it would be helpful, we feel, to know where it occurred. The text only notes that it happened **in the place where they were sitting** (2). The posture perhaps underlines the 'suddenness'; we might have expected them to be described as prostrate in prayer, or standing with outstretched hands in exulting worship. In fact they were simply seated, perhaps at a meal table or in a moment of relative leisure? **The place** was probably the 'upper room', (1:13), though others have preferred to set it all in the temple courts, which they certainly were frequenting (Luke 24:52). A difficulty with the temple as the location is that Luke invariably in his writing uses the formal term, *to hieron* (twenty-two times), to refer to it and there is no trace of that here. If it occurred in the upper room then one needs presumably to think of the disciples under the impulse of the Spirit's outpouring, subsequently moving out into the surrounding streets to some public place where the thronging crowds were able to be affected by the many-tongued witness, and to a large enough setting for Peter to have opportunity to preach with such effect that thousands were brought immediately to faith.

In all this we cannot do more than conjecture. It was God's moment, of that we can be sure, a moment prepared

---

3. 'Numinous' was a word coined last century to try to refer to such moments (R. Otto, *The Idea of the Holy*, Penguin, 1959). We can helpfully link this divine visitation with other Scriptures: Isaiah crying 'woe is me' (Isa. 6), Job repenting in dust and ashes (Job 42), Daniel (Dan. 9), Ezekiel (Ezek.1) and John (Rev. 1) falling as though dead, Paul blinded (Acts 9). 'God chose the lowly things of this world, and the despised things – *and the things that are not* – to nullify the things that are' (1 Cor. 1:28), and 'the God who gives life to the dead, and calls *the things that are not* as though they were' (Rom. 4:17).

from before the beginning of time; and hence a God-moment for which God did not require specific human conditions; hence 'suddenly....' He came!

Luke mentions three distinct phenomena which were expressed in the following moments as the awesome, mystery and majesty of the divine presence descended upon, and enveloped them all. The first two were externally registered, with their *hearing*, **a sound like the blowing of a violent wind** (2), and their *seeing*, **they saw what seemed to be tongues of fire that separated and came to rest on each of them** (v.3). The third was internally registered as **all of them were filled with the Holy Spirit and began to speak in tongues as the Holy Spirit enabled them** (4).

On the tangibility of the phenomena in general, Calvin aptly observes: 'The gifts had to be visible to stir up the disciples through the bodily senses. For such is our dullness in appreciating the gifts of God that unless He first aroused all our senses His power would pass us by and vanish unrecognized. This therefore was to prepare them and to help them to understand that the gift promised by Christ had come.' [4]

The first, the sound **like the blowing of a violent wind**, draws on the Hebrew ambiguity by which the word for wind, *ruach*, is also the word for 'Spirit' (cf. Gen. 1:2), and has obvious links to Ezekiel's wind which breathed life into the valley of dry bones (Ezek. 37:9-14), and to Jesus' words to Nicodemus (John 3:8; cf. also 2 Sam. 22:16; Job 12:10; Ezek. 13:13). The **like** is important, as is **what seemed to be** with respect to the tongues of fire. The phenomena were not the thing itself but like lenses through which the thing itself was given some point of focus. The 'thing itself' was the disciples being **filled with the Holy Spirit** expressed in tongues of witness (4).

The second, the **tongues of fire**, has links back to God's self-disclosure at the burning bush (Exod. 3:2ff), the pillar of fire (Exod. 13:21), the engulfing 'fire of God' at Mount Carmel (1 Kings 18:38), and Elijah's 'chariot of fire' (and whirlwind; 2 Kings 2:11). More immediately it

---

connects with John the Baptist's witness to Jesus as the one who would baptize 'with the Holy Spirit and with fire' (Luke 3:16). Judgment is a common element in biblical references to divine fire (Exod. 9:24; Deut. 4:33; 9:3; 2 Kings 1:10; Joel 2:3; Mal. 3:2; Matt. 3:11; 1 Cor. 3:13; 2 Thess. :7-8; Heb. 12:29). The present reference, however, appears primarily a pointer to the manifestation of God in His heavenly glory. [5]

In respect of the **'tongues of fire'** the language refers to its **separating and coming to rest upon each of them**. Thus the gift of the Holy Spirit is both corporate and personal. The Spirit comes upon the community to energize its life and mission, but is received individually. He is not so much a general spiritual power or force, as a personal, indwelling companion. Further, His gifting is inclusive of **all** the disciple company, and hence as truly to women (like 'Mary'), as to men (like 'Jesus' brothers', 1:14); as truly to leaders (like Peter, 15) as to 'led' (like the many nameless ones in the one hundred and twenty, 15); as truly to the specially chosen (like Matthias, 26), as to the not so chosen (like Barsabbas, 23). With reference to this final distinction, that between Matthias and Barsabbas, it is important to underline that *not* being called to a particular position, even one we may have had sincere and godly hopes of attaining, in no way excludes us from the personal approval of God, nor from His subsequent blessing in our lives, and through us in the lives of others.

With respect to the third element, the filling with the Spirit and the Spirit-enabled tongues of witness (v. 4), it is to be noted that while this third element continues to be developed in Luke's narrative, and will find further expression in terms of *glossais,* both in Acts and in the New Testament letters (cf. 1:5ff; 10:46; 19:6; 1 Cor. 12:28; 13:1, 8;

---

5. 'In Acts 2:3 the comparison with fire indicates the heavenly origin of the descending Spirit. In the main fire represents judgment in the New Testament, but the divine judgment and the divine glory go together. Fire signifies the whole eschatological denouement, whether in heaven or hell.' F. Lang, TWNT ed. G.W. Bromily (Eerdmans, 1985), 979.

14:1-39), the other phenomena of wind and fire recede from view.

This carries two important implications. First, there is a uniqueness to this Pentecost moment. The presence of the non-recurring phenomena proclaim the unrepeatable core of the event: the arrival of the Kingdom of God. As we noted earlier, the reign of God, the 'last day age' or *eschaton*, came progressively in a critical series of events – the incarnation, the baptism and ministry of Jesus, the death of Jesus, His resurrection, and His ascension. All these are now, as it were, gathered up together and registered for human existence in this climactic moment, as the Kingdom's arrival is signalled for all humanity in the birth of the new community of God's people. Thus understood, Pentecost is in principle an unrepeatable, once-for-all event, just as the crucifixion and resurrection of Jesus on the third day are unrepeatable. However, with the gift of God the Holy Spirit, as with these moments in Jesus' story, the implications of these happenings, and the reception of their blessings, are open to a continual re-appropriation in the lives of God's people, both personally and corporately. Hence Charles Finney was not speaking out of turn when he claimed that though Pentecost itself is unrepeatable, 'the antecedents, accompaniments, and results of revivals are always substantially the same as in the case of Pentecost.' [6]

Second, what critically matters for the arrival of the Kingdom of God is its being proclaimed among the nations (1:8). Thus the outpoured Spirit will, in the following minutes, translate the tongues of fire into the living, supernaturally moving tongues of these human witnesses to the saving acts of God in Jesus Christ, with their glorious global inclusiveness, whereby, **everyone who calls on the name of the Lord (Jesus) will be saved** (2:21).

This leads on to a consideration of this third feature of the glorious manifestation of the descending Holy Spirit: **and they were all filled with the Spirit and began to speak in other tongues as the Spirit enabled them**

---

6. C.G. Finney, *Revivals of Religion*, Cited Wallis, *In the Day of Thy Power* (CLC, 1956), 56.

(v. 4). We should observe the diversity in terminology here, and throughout the New Testament, with respect to the Spirit's work. Jesus had spoken of a coming 'baptism with the Holy Spirit' (1:5), after the pattern of John's water baptism. That was arguably an immersion rite, as was commonly administered to proselytes, and confirmed by John's locating his ministry where there was 'plenty of water' (John 3:23), i.e. of sufficient depth for the responding initiates to be immersed. Jesus' image therefore points to an overwhelming experience in which the Spirit would 'immerse' the persons concerned. Being 'filled' is a similarly comprehensive image, focusing on an inward immersion rather than an external one. As a description of God the Spirit's overwhelming possession of His children there is little to distinguish between the two images. It is accordingly difficult to challenge the view that what Jesus promised and predicted in 1:8 was realized here in verse 4.

Marshall notes a distinction in usage in that being 'baptized with the Spirit' is not used in the New Testament for any subsequent experience of the Spirit (cf. 1 Cor. 12:13), whereas being 'filled with the Spirit' is regularly also used of later experiences of His presence and power (Acts 4:8; 4:31; 13:9). [7]

Baptism is in general an initiation term in the New Testament and hence probably best used with some respect to that origin, and therefore as a way of referring to the regenerating, rebirthing work of the Spirit by which Christians are initiated into the new life of God's Kingdom of salvation. 'Pouring out' is also used (2:17f; 10:45), as is 'receiving' the Holy Spirit (10:47).

Two conclusions appear justified from this diverse usage. First, while Marshall's plea certainly needs to be heard, it is perhaps to be wondered, more generally, whether tidy, 'one size fits all', doctrines of the Spirit's activity in the lives of believers are entirely justifiable, either by biblical language or by actual experience. The Spirit, as Jesus observed, is, in His action, commonly like the wind, 'blowing wherever (He) pleases. You hear the

---

7. Marshall, 69.

sound, but you cannot tell where (He) comes from or where (He) is going' (John 3:8). He is, after all, *the Lord who is the Spirit!* (2 Cor. 3:17). He is not our agent at our disposal, but our Holy Omnipotent God at whose complete disposal we live our entire lives.

Second, the New Testament knows nothing of people claiming particular experiences of the Spirit. Specifically, and this may come as a surprise to many readers, no-one in the New Testament ever *claims* to be filled with the Spirit. That people *are* so filled is not of course in question, to look no further than Acts 2:4! But in every case that reality is noted by others, not claimed by the parties themselves. In other words being 'full of the Holy Spirit' is an observed disposition rather than a claimed possession. Much misunderstanding, and unhelpful division, even ungodly antipathies (in the name of the Spirit whose primary fruit and gift is *agape*-love!) could have been avoided had these simple conclusions been noted. Every Christian believer is called to be a man or woman, or boy or girl, 'of the Holy Spirit'. We, all of us, need the presence and power of God the Holy Spirit at the centre of our lives every single day, particularly so when we are, as were the disciples in Acts, engaged in the witness and service of the Kingdom of Christ. Our part is accordingly to pray repeatedly and earnestly for, and open ourselves daily to, all the blessing of God the Holy Spirit, whatever name others may choose to use of it. To borrow a phrase from an early Report on the Charismatic Movement, 'By Whatever Name…Receive!', and in faith go forth, and live for the greater glory, and glad service of our triune God.

This particular experience of the Holy Spirit enabled the 120 disciples to **speak in other tongues (*glossolalia*)… declaring the wonders of God** (vv. 4, 11). What exactly was this 'enablement'? The later New Testament will refer to a Holy Spirit gift (*charisma*) of tongues (*glossolalia*); most notably in 1 Corinthians 12–14; cf. also Acts 19:6. Is this what the disciples experienced, or was it something different and hence unique to the Pentecost outpouring? There appears ground for seeing the Pentecostal blessing as reproduced, at least in the case of Acts 10:46, in the household of Cornelius since it evoked Peter's comment 'They have received the Holy Spirit *just as we have*'. (See also comment on 8:17.)

Occasional claims are made of people using tongues today in that direct, 'single-step' manner such that, it is claimed, visitors from other places, to their astonishment, hear sentences in their native tongue although that language is entirely unknown by the tongue-speaker. These claims however have not gone unchallenged.[8] As Bloch notes, there was clearly in Acts 2 an ability to use the other languages in a manner which was immediately comprehensible by their hearers, and with significant fluency such that **We hear them declaring…in our own languages the wonders of God** (2:11). This 'one-stage' process appears to be in contrast to Paul's reference in 1 Corinthians 12–14 where a two-stage process obtains, the gift of a tongue, and then a further, supportive gift of a translation (or interpretation) without which 'unbelievers who come in', far from being immediately addressed as in Acts 2:8, 'will say that you are out of your mind' (1 Cor. 14:23). Therefore 'if someone speaks in a tongue…someone must interpret' (14:27). Admittedly in both passages the Greek term is identical; however the contextual description is surely determinative, and there does appear to be something special at work in the Acts 2 (and 10) case.

As far as the audience is concerned, they probably primarily comprised *diaspora* [9] Jews from all over the Mediterranean world who had come to reside in Jerusalem, cf. **staying in Jerusalem** (5),[10] as well as, **visitors** from other places (10). The geographical range is significant, both in its extent, and also for its contribution to our understanding of the Pentecost event and its missiological implication. The list of native homelands in verses 9-11 moves from east to west and then from north-west to south-west. While we cannot press literally Luke's phrase, **from every**

---

8. See the discussion in Stott, 76-8, and the literature cited in his fn. 20.

9. A technical term for the scattered communities of Jews which were to be found all over the ancient world.

10. Hence the references to 'homes' and 'houses' at 2:46 and 4:34.

nation under heaven (5), it can certainly be understood representatively. 'In his own subtle way, Luke is saying to us that on that Day of Pentecost the whole world was there in the representatives of the various nations.'[11] In terms of 1:8 and God's purpose of universal witness, these verses are of immense significance. Here, in this initial act of witness-bearing, is a divine authorization which in principle points to three things.

First, it reverses the curse of Babel, by which linguistic diversity brought about confusion, a loss of communication, and communal dispersion (Gen. 11:1-9). It achieves this through the sovereign creation of a new people of God, bound together across all their diversities in a 'fellowship' in the Holy Spirit (2:42). As David Lyon perceptively, and movingly, remarks, '(Pentecost), this "anti-Babel", denies permanence to "Babel", and offers a profound perspective, a signpost in the mist, that re-orientates those who had mistaken Babel for the terminus.'[12]

Second, it authenticates the missional perspective both of the book of Acts and, more importantly, of the eternal purpose of God throughout the entire period between the two comings of Jesus. The time from the ascension to the parousia is herein established as the era of the global mission of the Holy Spirit-inspired and energized people of God. Stott observes, of this astonishingly wide-ranging ethnic audience, 'Nothing could have demonstrated more clearly than this the multi-racial, multi-national, multi-lingual nature of the kingdom of God.'[13]

Third, the gift of languages points to a God who is concerned that His gospel and its mighty acts of grace in Jesus Christ be heard and responded to by individuals in terms they can immediately understand. It accordingly vindi-

---

11. Stott, 68

12. David Lyon, 'Jesus in Disneyland: The Church meets the Postmodern Challenge,' *ARC* (1994), 32.

13. Stott, 68; cf. also Bock, 103: 'The list appears to highlight the key communities where the Jews of the diaspora congregated and suggests the gospel's universal scope.' Also Bruce, 58, who notes that the very range of the languages spoken, 'suggests that Luke thought of the coming of the Spirit as a preparation for the world-wide proclamation of the gospel.'

cates, even mandates, a missional approach which will take pains, and use means, to ensure that barriers to the gospel's reception are eliminated as fully as possible, and hence that the hearers, from whatever culture, language grouping, age, or other formational background influence, really do have every opportunity to understand and respond to the message of salvation.

Finally, the Pentecost event confronts us with the irreducible reality of supernatural intervention. Or, to put the same point more theologically, it affords ineffaceable evidence that the God who is present and at work in all things as their upholding Lord, is ever able, when appropriate, to act in a sovereignly different manner which unmistakably draws attention to Himself as the Lord in the midst, and which in some particular way furthers His purpose in history. Such was the Pentecostal outpouring of the Spirit.

Not surprisingly the human reaction is **bewilderment** (*sunechythe*, 6), **amazement** (*existemi*, 7, 12), **wonder** (*thaumazo*, 7), and **perplexity** (*diaporeo*, 12). The sounds of their own, and all the other native languages, being fluently used in the soaring praises of God, by Galileans who were universally recognized by their accents (as Peter knew to his cost, cf. Luke 22:59), and dismissed by the sophisticates of Jerusalem as uneducated provincials, pushed them beyond all the limits of their previous experience. They were utterly bewildered and confounded. This was simply inexplicable. **What does this mean?** (12).[14]

Some, unpersuaded of any supernatural source, resorted to mockery, **made fun of them** (13); still a universal refuge for those humbled by divine intervention but unwilling to revise their world-view in the light of it (cf. 17:32, where the same Greek term is used). So the disciples' evident rapture and intoxication of praise evoked an accusation of inebriation: **they have had too much wine** (13). Calvin rightly notes, 'There is nothing too wonderful for men who are touched with no concern about God to

---

14. Longenecker, *Acts*, 272. cf. 'you stupid Galileans,' in b. 'Erub.53b; Bock: 101, fn. 13.

turn to mockery.' [15] In this sense even Pentecost, for all of its greatness, is only an anticipation of that final, climactic self-disclosure when, at the return of the Lord, 'every eye will see him, even those who pierced him, and all the peoples of the earth will mourn because of him'; that day when 'every knee will bow...and every tongue confess that Jesus Christ is Lord to the glory of God the Father' (Rev. 1:7; Phil. 2:11). Then the curtain will fall forever on atheism, and agnosticism, and on 'every pretension that sets itself up against the knowledge of God' (2 Cor. 10:5). There will be no mockery then: only exultant joy and praise on the one hand, or heart-stricken anguish on the other; but no mockery...nor ever again...nor ever again.

b. 'This is that...this is Jesus...' (2:14-36). Peter's Sermon

Peter's sermon, arguably the most significant in the entire 2,000-year history of the church, is in essence a response to the question put by the bewildered crowd – **What does this mean?** (12).

Negatively first, Peter rebuts the accusation of inebriation to explain the extraordinary behaviour and utterances of the Spirit-filled disciples (14-15). Then positively, he announces the true nature and origin of what they were experiencing: (a) This is God's fulfilment of the Old Testament prophecies of the coming of the kingdom of God (16-21); (b) This is the result of the death, rising and exaltation of Jesus (22-36).

The sermon is then followed by the response of the crowd (37-41), and a description of the life of the new community of believers which was immediately created (42-47).

Peter **stood up with the Eleven** (14). By now the Spirit-enabled, multi-language-speaking disciples are in a public area (some commentators suggest the temple precincts) where Peter is able to find a vantage point from which to preach to the assembled, and distracted, crowd. **Fellow Jews and all of you who live in Jerusalem** – Peter first

---

15. Calvin, 55.

of all identifies with his hearers, always a good starting point for a speech or sermon. He appeals to the Jewishness common to himself and his audience, both the locals and the *diaspora* visitors. **Let me explain...listen carefully...** Peter offers to help them understand the Pentecostal phenomena, and summons the crowd to give closest attention to his words.

14-15: What Pentecost IS NOT: **These men are not drunk...it's only nine in the morning!** (15). Despite the obvious fervour and exuberance of the disciples, drunkenness was simply not a credible explanation of their behaviour since it was too early in the day. Sunrise would have beeen followed by morning prayers in the temple; only after that would some food and drink be taken, and the wine shops opened for business. If they were 'under the influence', as it must have seemed, it was not alcoholic spirit that was responsible.

16-36: What Pentecost IS:

A. **...this is what was spoken by the prophet Joel...** Having thus cleared the decks of their inept explanation Peter now reveals the true nature of this Pentecostal outpouring. It is nothing less than the fulfilment of the ancient prophetic promises of the arrival of the new era of the kingdom of God![16]

In essence the kingdom of God is to be understood against the backdrop of Old Testament thought and experience. We have already offered an explanation at 1:3; however some repetition is not out of place here as Peter will amplify the idea in his exposition. The 'kingdom of God' emerges from the interaction of three truths. First, God is King (Ps. 93.1; etc.), He exists as the unqualifiably sovereign one. Second, God's kingship is resisted on this planet, beginning in the Fall at the dawn of responsible human life, and possibly behind that in a

---

16. The literature dealing with this notion is a vast one. In particular we can note, G. Vos, *The Teaching of Jesus concerning the Kingdom and the Church*, (PRPC, 1951); O. Cullman, *Christ and Time* (SCM, 1951); R. Schnackenburg, *God's Rule and Kingdom* (London, 1963); G.R. Beasley-Murray, *Jesus and the Kingdom of God* (Paternoster, 1986); H. Ridderbos, *The Coming of the Kingdom* (Paideia Press, 1992); G.E. Ladd, *Jesus and the Kingdom* (Eerdmans, 1966).

pre-mundane rebellion of the devil and his cohorts. Thus human beings, and certain super-human beings, exist in rebellion against God's rule, a rebellion extending even to His chosen people, Israel. Third, God has promised through his prophets (cf. Joel 2:28-32; Isa. 2:1-5; 11:1-10; 25-26; 40:1-11; 41:17-20; 43:1-7; 44:24-28 46:6-13;65-66; Zeph. 3:15; Zech. 14:9f; Amos 5:18f; Mal. 4:1f; Dan. 2, 7) that this condition will not continue indefinitely: a day is coming when God's reign will be authentically established in the world. That reign, and its appearance, will be the arrival and appearance of 'the kingdom of God'. Peter's claim is simply that that third, long-promised moment has now arrived, through the coming and ministry of Jesus Christ. He actually makes this even more explicit than the prophecy. Joel's temporal reference is to 'afterwards' (2:28), a general future time, but Peter sharpens this to **in the last days** (17), i.e. what in the developed thought of first-century Judaism would have meant the long-awaited days of the kingdom of God.

That which the prophets had anticipated centuries before has now appeared; the day of divine vindication and salvation is at hand, the key turning point in the entire human story has arrived, the time of God's manifest reign has begun! Peter cites from Joel 2:28-32. He might as easily have cited Isaiah 32:15; Ezekiel 34–37, esp. 36:22-32; or Jeremiah 31:31-33. However the Joel prophecy is particularly apt, as we will note below.[17]

It is perhaps in order to ask where Peter learned this wonderfully appropriate Old Testament reference and, without minimizing the possibilities of the immediate inspiration of the Spirit, to consider the ultimate source as Jesus. After all he had taught them intensively during the forty days after his resurrection, and reiterated the promise of the Spirit's coming, surely using Scriptures such as this one to help them grasp what this meant. The same question arises from the early Christian use of the Old

---

17. As well as the direct quotation from Joel 2:28-32 we can note a further phrase from the passage at v. 39, 'among the survivors whom the Lord calls.' cf. also use of this passage in Romans 10:13 and Revelation 6:12.

Testament in these first chapters of Acts (cf. 2:25-28, 34-35; 3:21-26; 4:11, 25-26). It makes every sense to link all this back to Luke 24:25-27, and 24:45-46, where the risen Jesus is recorded as 'opening their minds so that they could understand the Scriptures' (= the Old Testament).

Four features of the Joel prophecy are most evident to the eyes and ears of the Jerusalem audience.

(1) An 'outpouring' of the Holy Spirit (17a). The metaphor, **I will pour out my Spirit**, is that of the tumultuous precipitation of a thunderstorm. It conveys a sense of almost uncontrolled abundance, of overwhelming fullness. There is a raw physicality to the image which should not be overlooked, implying that to be caught in the path of this blessing involves being encountered by sheer supernatural power, and personally and corporately overwhelmed by the glorious and awesome Presence at its heart.

(2) An unprecedented breadth of influence (17b–18). There is an indiscriminating inclusiveness in the blessing. All those in its path are engulfed in its influence. Unlike the days of the Old Covenant when the blessings of the Spirit had been largely confined to prophets, priests and kings, **all people,** including specifically **sons and daughters…young men and old men…both men and women,** will be recipients of the divine blessing, and be equipped to share together in the prophetic witness Jesus had called for. So, **they will prophesy** (17-18, cf. 8).

Both the gender and the generational inclusiveness here must not be missed. Hierarchical discrimination in both these spheres was a prominent feature of the Judaistic culture within which Jesus ministered, and the Pentecostal blessing had erupted. Inclusiveness at both these levels was part of the scandal of the ministry of Jesus (Mark 10:13-16; Matt. 18:3; Mark 9:33-37; John 4:27; Luke 11:27; Luke 10:38-42; John 11; Mark 15:40-41; Luke 8:1-3). Here that same radical equality of spiritual status with respect to young and old, and men and women, is asserted for the relational life of the community of Jesus within the long-anticipated kingdom of God.

This truth does not contradict a proper respect for the value of maturity in the choosing of church leaders (cf. 1

Timothy 3, esp. vv. 4-6), nor a certain husbandly ' leadership' within a Christian marriage (cf. Eph. 5:22-24, 33). But what it surely eliminates, absolutely and forever, is even an intimation of a hint of a suggestion, that in the sight of God the young are, in any degree whatever, less important or less valuable than the old; or that in the sight of God women are, in any degree whatever, less important or less valuable than men. All this is of course nothing other than the plain, unambiguous meaning of the cross, e.g. 'one died for all' (2 Cor. 5:14 = 'for all' without distinction or discrimination). But it is salutary to have it thus taken up and underlined in the coming of the Holy Spirit.

(3) Joel refers to a third feature, the appearing of unusual, even totally unprecedented phenomena **in the heaven above** and **on the earth below** (19). Specifically he instances supra-terrestrial events, **blood and fire and billows of smoke. The sun will be turned to darkness and the moon to blood** (19b-20a). Whereas Joel links the heavenly and earthly 'wonders in the heavens and on the earth' (2:30), Peter notably distinguishes the locations, **wonders** in the heavens, and **signs** on the earth. The heavenly **wonders** are not part of the Pentecostal happening. Their appearance lies in the future when they will anticipate the final act of the drama of human history, **the coming of the great and glorious day of the Lord** (20b). The standard received text[18] in Joel has 'great and terrible' in accord with the note of judgment which will be a major feature of that coming day. Peter's wording, in accordance with the LXX, is 'notable' (Gk. *epiphane*). However the outpouring of judgment is not absent from his thought, cf. verse 40: **he warned them...save yourselves from this corrupt generation**. In Joel's prophecy judgment is expressed in a plague of locusts, a harbinger of fuller judgment in the future (3:1-16). For Peter the present day of the kingdom's arrival anticipates the future day of judgment for all nations and all people. 'Peter is saying that the eschatological clock is

---

18. The so-named Massoretic Text which was the text of the Old Testament edited into fixed form about 500 B.C.

ticking.'[19] Hence, now, while you have opportunity, **'repent and be baptized...for the forgiveness of your sins'** (38). Thus the anticipation of the future day of judgment underlines the urgency of the present day of grace. Peter locates the **signs** on the earth, and his reference here may be to the tongues of witness and the various healing miracles which will occur within the life of the Pentecostal community in the immediate future.[20]

(4) A universal invitation to salvation for **everyone who calls on the name of the Lord** (21). This universalism is about to be modelled in the geographical breadth of Peter's listening audience, and in their astonishing numerical response to the apostle's subsequent appeal (38-41). Behind it of course lies the universality of the terms of Jesus' commission,...**and to the ends of the earth** (1:8).

The linkage of the Pentecostal happening to Joel's prophecy of the coming of the Kingdom of God represents only the first, and in a sense preliminary, part of Peter's positive explanation. The 'outpouring of the Holy Spirit' means that the long-anticipated Day of God and His universal salvation has finally dawned, with all its global implications. But Peter still needs to link all this to his primary point of reference, the coming and ministry of Jesus the Messiah, and the climactic events of His death and resurrection. Pentecost is important, evidentially and experientially impressive, and the point of departure for the crowd ('What does this mean?', v.12); but the real driving centre of Peter and his fellow apostles' convictions is the person of Jesus, and in particular His role as the risen Lord in the entire purpose of God for Israel and the world.[21]

---

19. Bock, 117.

20. Marshall, 74.

21. Barrett: 140. 'Christian preaching begins with the name of Jesus.' It is entirely possible that Peter has already made the transition to a focus on Jesus in the meaning to be attached to the final phrase of his Joel citation. 'Everyone who calls on the name of the Lord will be saved.' In its Old Testament setting of course the meaning of 'Lord' is Yahweh, but Peter's conviction is that that title now belongs also to Jesus, as he will unambiguously assert in verse 36. Bock, 117-19, notes 'If Peter had cited Joel in a Semitic

16-36: What Pentecost IS:

Men of Israel...Jesus of Nazareth (22). Peter's fuller, second answer to the question of the meaning of Pentecost is simply that it is the work of Jesus Christ (= Jesus Messiah). Accordingly he now proceeds to confront his hearers with the fact of Jesus, arguing deliberately towards his great conclusion, in verse 36: **therefore let all Israel be assured that God has made this Jesus, whom you crucified, both Lord and Christ**. He justifies this audacious claim by drawing attention to three supporting evidences, within which he will further clarify the meaning of the Pentecostal outpouring.

In attempting this goal for his message Peter's courage, as well as his moral and rational audacity, needs to be duly appreciated. For this claim for Jesus had to deal head-on with a major piece of counter-evidence in the minds of his devout Judaistic audience: as everyone in Jerusalem knew, a few weeks previously Jesus of Nazareth had died there, on a cross! Our two millennia of crucifixion devotion, 'In the cross of Christ I glory', etc., make it difficult to realize what the fact and circumstances of Jesus' death would have meant in Jerusalem (cf. 1 Cor. 1:23). Firstly, it meant that Jesus in dying had succumbed to the general, universal effect of sin in human experience (Gen. 2:17). More seriously, secondly, he had died on a cross, and hence under the evident curse of the God of Israel (Deut. 21:23). Thirdly, he had died at the hands of the uncircumcised, 'lawless' (23) Gentiles (the hated Roman occupiers). Fourthly, he had been judicially condemned by the great high Council of the Jewish people, the holy Sanhedrin.[22]

---

context in the first century he likely would probably...have used a substitute for the divine name.' This calls into question the assumption of not a little modern interpretation that using 'Lord' for Jesus was a later development of the Hellenistic church. That assumption also fails to face the full implications of the resurrection for an understanding of the person of Christ.

22. One can also note the more general prejudice against Jesus' place of origin, Nazareth. cf. Nathanael, 'Can anything good come from Nazareth?' (Jn 1:46). Judeans in general despised people from Nazareth. It was a 'non-place' in a culture where eminence of origin and lineage was of high significance. 'The residence of Jesus in Nazareth is akin to his birth in a stable; it is part of the offence of the incarnation.' G.R. Beasley-Murray, *John* [Word, 1987], 27.

It says much for the depth of Peter's conviction and the effectiveness of the Spirit's special enablement (Luke 12:12), that he is able, not only to confront their negative prejudice (23), but to undermine and overturn its force by a series of considerations which carry his affirmation of Jesus to triumphant vindication (36), and move several thousand of his hearers to immediate life-commitment to this 'God-cursed' Messiah (41). It is an astonishing sermonic *tour de force*.

Peter directs attention to the life of Jesus in three stages. First, he reminds the audience of Jesus' God-owned, miraculous ministry (22). Second, he asserts His resurrection from the dead, verified by appeal to the Old Testament Scriptures (25-31), as well as the personal witness of the apostles (32). Third, he affirms Jesus' consequent exaltation to the right hand of God (33), which is demonstrated in His initiating the present outpouring of the Holy Spirit (33), which was also anticipated in the Old Testament Scriptures (34-35), and implies that 'this Jesus', who had so recently ministered among them, who had been crucified by them and their leaders, and then raised by God from the dead, is the Messiah of Israel's hopes, and the present Lord of all (36).

1. Jesus' ministry (22)
It has been **accredited by God** as expressed in the supernatural phenomena which had accompanied it.

Peter uses three terms in describing Jesus' ministry: (1) *dynamesi* = **miracles**, more literally, 'works of power' a very common word in Acts. (1:8; 2:22; 3:12; 4:7; 4:33; 6:8; also significantly, Luke 4:14; 4:36; 5:17; 6:19; 8:46); (2) *terasi* = **'wonders'**; (3) *semeiois* **'signs'** = actions 'embodying or signifying spiritual truth' (Stott).[23] Generally this refers to evidences of God's manifest attestation of, and His presence in, the life and ministry of Jesus. He accordingly was **accredited by God...what God did among you through him as you yourselves know**. This claim of Peter is to be historically upheld. It is widely conceded by gospel cri-

---

23. Stott, 75.

tics, even including many who retain reservations about ascribing deity to Jesus.[24]

In particular Jesus believed Himself to have authority over the realm of the demonic. His casting out of demons from the possessed and disturbed had critical significance for His ministry as a whole, in terms of God's presence in it, and its significance within God's historic purpose. 'If it is by the finger of God that I cast out demons, then the Kingdom of God has come upon you' (Luke 11:20). This saying is again widely conceded to be authentic. Significantly, 'later Jewish polemic against Jesus did not deny that he had wrought miracles, but rather claimed that he was a sorcerer.'[25] This all carries significant import in terms of Jesus' person, which is of course Peter's point.

This factual summary of Jesus' three-year Palestinian ministry creates major problems for radical New Testament critics, such as the participants in the so-called 'Jesus Seminar', who reduce Jesus to simply a wise Jewish sage who went about uttering short, cryptic proverbs. Such a Jesus is unrecognizable from the historic figure who again and again impacted His hearers in the most radical manner, and finally so alienated the political authorities as to bring about his judicial execution. The Jesus of the 'Seminar' is a bland, shadowy figure who would never have evoked such reaction, a Jesus 'who would not have alienated the authorities of his day sufficiently to have triggered his execution' – none of them would have bothered! [26] The Jesus

---

24. We can note the testimony of an extra-biblical contemporary, the Jewish historian Josephus in his *Jewish Antiquities*. 18.3.3: '(Jesus) was a doer of remarkable/strange (*paradoxon*) works…' We note Jesus' own awareness of His ability to perform such (Matt. 11:4–5). 'Whatever the "facts" were, Jesus evidently believed he had cured cases of blindness, lameness and deafness – indeed there is no reason to doubt that he believed lepers had been cured under his ministry, and dead restored to life' (J.D.G. Dunn, *Jesus and the Spirit* [SCM, 1975], 60). W.L. Craig claims: 'The miracle stories are so widely represented in all the strata of the gospel traditions that it would be fatuous to not regard these as rooted in the life of Jesus' (*Reasonable Faith*, 2nd edition [Crossway, 2008], 250.

25. Marshall, 75; cf. B. Witherington III: That Jesus was an exorcist is 'one of the most incontestable facts about his ministry' (*Christology of Jesus* [Fortress Press, 1990], 188).

26. Craig L. Blomberg, 'The historical reliability of the New Testament', in *Reasonable Faith*, Wm. L.Craig, 2nd edn. (Crossway, 1994), 225.

of the Seminar turns out to be, in John P. Meier's words, 'A tweedy poetaster who spent his time spinning parables and Japanese koans, a literary aesthete who toyed with first century deconstructionism, or a bland Jesus who simply told people to look at the lilies of the field – such a Jesus would threaten no one, just as the university professors who create him threaten no one.' [27]

Jesus' ministry had reeked of the supernatural, as reflected in His astonishing claims, such as the right to forgive sins, or to teach with the direct authority of God, or to be the arbiter of people's eternal destiny, or, where necessary, to stand over the received teaching of the Old Testament Law, all of which evinced a self-consciousness without precedent or successor. In sum, 'There is absolutely convincing evidence, that Jesus did intend to stand in the place of God himself.' [28]

Peter reminds his Jerusalem auditors of all this, and also reminds us...what *are* we to make of Jesus?

2. Jesus' Resurrection (23-32)
Peter's first line of evidence, though telling in terms of awakening suppressed conviction (cf. John 3:2; 7:31; 9:33; 10:38), required further confirmation. That further witness the resurrection fully supplied. So, Peter moves naturally from Jesus' public ministry to its almost incredible climax.

This man was handed over to you...(23). Peter does not hesitate to lay responsibility for the death of Jesus at the door of his hearers (cf. 3:13-14), though the Jewish leadership is not spared when Peter has opportunity to confront them directly (4:10-11; 5:30). Nor are the Romans entirely exculpated either, **with the help of wicked men** (= lit., 'lawless', 'without the law' = Gentiles; cf. 4:27) **'(you) put him to death'**. In 4:27 the church as a whole affirms the shared responsibility: **Herod and Pontius Pilate...together with the Gentiles and the people of Israel in this city... conspire(d) against your holy servant Jesus**. The deeper truth is that in the end humanity as a race participates

---

27. John P. Meier, *A Marginal Jesus*, 2 vols. (Doubleday, 1991), 177.

28. R.G. Gruenler, *New Approaches to Jesus and the Gospels*, (Baker, 1982), 74.

in the responsibility, as Jesus powerfully argued in the parable of the tenants (Mark 12:1-12). Israel acted in a profound sense on behalf of the race, as Paul will later assert in Romans 11:11-16. That the Jews as a people should have been singled out for blame and subjected to appalling retribution over the centuries is a tragic, shameful chapter in the history of the church, and global culture generally.

This 'handing over', however,[29] was **by God's set purpose and foreknowledge**. Here, in the very first Christian sermon, with reference to the death of Jesus, we meet 'the paradox of divine predestination and human freewill in its strongest form'.[30] This sense of the sovereign overruling of God is a consistent Lukan emphasis. 'All the texts that Luke-Acts (cites) about Jesus' suffering point to the idea that God planned, or knew, that Jesus would suffer.'[31] Peter's reference to the divine will in the death of Jesus is hardly surprising in view of Jesus' post-resurrection teaching – Luke 24:26f: 'Did not the Christ have to suffer these things...And beginning with Moses and all the prophets, he explained to them what was said in all the Scriptures concerning himself'; and Luke 24:44: 'Everything must be fulfilled that is written about me in the Law of Moses, the prophets and the Psalms.'

As might be expected at this point the allusion to the death of Jesus omits any developed doctrine of the atonement, affording a further evidence of the primitive nature of this account of Peter's message. 'But there is already an understanding that through Jesus' death the purpose of God was being worked out.'[32]

The resurrection is then announced '**But God raised him from the dead freeing him from the agony of death...**' Peter adduces a three-fold support for this claim.

---

29. cf. the use of 'handing over' in John13:26; 18:35; 19:11, with 13:3 as its ultimate expression.

30. Marshall, 75.

31. Bock, 120. Bock also notes that the verb for predetermined (*horizo*) appears eight times in the New Testament of which six are in Luke's writing (Luke 22:22; Acts 10:42; 11:29; 17:26, 31; Rom. 1:4; Heb. 4:7).

32. Stott, 75.

(1) *The triumphant power of God.* The presence, and
indeed identity of God with Jesus and His mission, implies
the inevitability of God's action on His behalf in the face
of death. This is asserted directly – **it was not possible
for death to hold him**, and also underlies the reference
to God's **freeing him from death's agony**, which is literally 'loosing him from death's birthpangs (or birthcords)'.
Underlying this is the thought of the realm of death
personified as a pregnant woman unable to restrain the
emergence of the new life stirring within her. 'The Abyss
can no more hold the Redeemer than a pregnant woman
can hold the child in her body.' [33]

(2) *The witness of the Scriptures* (25-31). This appeal, and
its many counterparts in the apostolic witness throughout
the New Testament, to the fulfilling of the Old Testament
in the life and mission of Jesus is traceable surely to the
ministry of the post-resurrection Jesus noted earlier.

Peter here cites David's words in Psalm 16:8-11. This
is generally pertinent in view of the link between David,
as the model king of Israel, and Israel's coming Messiah.
But it has verbal pertinence in David's claim in Psalm 16:9,
my body also will live in hope; cf. verse 31: **you will
not abandon me to the grave nor let your Holy One see
decay**. David speaks here of a bodily (= *sarx*, v. 26) hope
in face of death, one encompassing the entire person. But
patently this hope was not fulfilled for David, in that his
remains were entombed at that moment within the city of
Jerusalem (29). Hence David was speaking prophetically
of someone else, a Davidic capacity particularly present in
the Psalms, as was generally recognized. Peter alludes then
to Psalm 132:11: 'The Lord swore an oath to David…"One
of your own descendants I will place on your throne"'(30).

Peter then compounds the two references by interpreting David's prophecies as referring to the Messiah, who
is Jesus, his lineal descendant. (God has) **not abandoned**
(Jesus) **to the grave nor did his body see decay** (after
death)**,** but **God has raised this Jesus to life!** (32).

---

33. Bertram, *TDNT*, 9, 673.

(3) *The witness of the apostles*: **We are all witnesses of the fact** (32). Here the terms of the commission of 1:8 find obedient fulfilment in the apostolic testimony to the resurrection of Jesus; cf. 1:22, and 4:33: 'with great power the apostles continued to give testimony (= *marturiov*, witness) to the resurrection of the Lord Jesus.' Although the words **of the fact** (of the resurrection) are not part of the original text they are certainly defensible as expressing the force of Peter's claim. It cannot be overstressed both how utterly certain the apostles were of the resurrection, and correspondingly how critical this is for the entire Christian truth-claim. This 'witness' was not so much to having been present at the tomb of Jesus to 'see' his lifeless body physically reanimated and gloriously transformed; nor was it primarily a witness to the emptiness of the tomb, though that certainly had its place in providing supportive evidence (cf. 1 Cor. 15:4). It was witness rather to appearances of the risen Jesus, His various meetings with them over the forty days following the crucifixion.

In assessing the veracity of these experiences and their claim to authenticate the resurrection, it is important to put 'resurrection' in its first-century context within Judaism. J.P. Moreland, in a summary of the thought-world of first-century Judaism with respect to 'resurrection', and hence of the form of any predisposition of the apostles towards this astonishing claim for Jesus, states:

> 'The disciples were not disposed to inventing the appearance stories...and even if they were, the messianic expectations and the concepts of resurrection in first-century Palestinian Judaism would not have led to the belief that Jesus rose from the dead. In this regard four features of first-century Jewish beliefs about resurrection and the afterlife are especially important. First, in Jewish thought, the resurrection of the dead always occurred at the end of the world, and not at some point prior to the end. Second, there was no conception of isolated individuals rising from the dead. The resurrection was conceived as a general resurrection of all mankind. Third, the resurrection was conceived in a crude, physicalist way which involved a reassembling of the parts of the pre-death body. No conception of a resurrection body

fits the (gospels) picture of Jesus' body with the unique features of its behaviour. Fourth, the Jewish understanding of visions contained two elements: they were understood as being visions of people directly translated to heaven and not raised from the dead, and in Jewish tradition, visions were always experienced by individuals and not by groups (cf. 1 Cor. 15:5-7)...Because of these features of Jewish belief, the disciples would not have had expectations or needs for wish-fulfilment which the resurrection of Jesus met. The resurrection was unexpected and it is reported in such a way as to be almost completely out of touch with what these men had been taught to expect from the time they were little boys. Thus they would not have been in a position to have hallucinations, nor would they have made up such a culturally odd concept as the resurrection of Jesus....The most reasonable explanation for the interpretation they do give to their experiences is that Jesus really rose bodily.' [34]

In the often-quoted challenge of C.F.D. Moule: 'If the coming into existence of the Nazarenes, a phenomenon undeniably attested in the New Testament, rips a great hole in history, a hole the size and shape of the Resurrection, what does the secular historian propose to stop the hole with?...the birth and rapid rise of the Christian church...remain an unsolved enigma for any historian who refuses to take seriously the only explanation offered by the Church itself.' [35]

3. The Outpouring of the Holy Spirit (33).
Peter, however, does not confine the meaning of the resurrection to its offering proof of the overcoming of death, with its invariable progressive bodily decay. There are in fact a series of hugely significant further implications.

(1) Jesus is exalted to the right hand of God.[36] The power of God which had raised Jesus from death had

---

34. J.P. Moreland, *Scaling the Secular City* (Baker, 1987), 175-7.

35. C.F.D. Moule, *The Phenomenon of the New Testament*, Studies in Biblical Theology 2/1 (SCM, 1967), 3, 13.

36. The preposition is left to be supplied by the dative *te dexia*. Some prefer an instrumental sense 'by the right hand of God'; e.g. Barrett: 149. Most others incline to a locational meaning 'to the right hand', e.g. Hanchaen: 183, n1. This latter is preferable

also **exalted Him to the right hand of God**. 'The resurrection is not simply a revivification but an ascension.'[37] The right hand was a place of special favour and carried also a note of authority. It is prominent in the Old Testament (cf. Exod. 15:6; 1 Kings 2:19; 1 Chron. 6:39; Ps. 44:3; Neh. 8:4). The New Testament references are all significant in the light of this Acts reference (cf. Jesus in Luke 22:69; also Acts 7:55-56; Rom. 8:34; Eph. 1:20; Col. 3:1; Heb. 1:13; 8:1; 10:12; 12:2; 1 Pet. 3:22). It is difficult to overestimate the importance of this conviction for the entire fabric of early Christian belief. As James Denney trenchantly affirmed: 'The starting point for the writers of the New Testament is the resurrection and exaltation of Jesus. This is the grand illuminative fact from which they all proceed. Not a single New Testament writer, unless he is simply engaged in recording Christ's earthly life, thinks of him as he lived on earth. They all think of him as he lives now, with angels and principalities and powers put under him. His sovereignty in glory is not a thing which may or may not, as one pleases, be added to the religious appreciation of his life on earth; it is the first and last and dominating element in the Christian consciousness of the New Testament.'[38]

(2) He has **received from the Father the promised Holy Spirit**. This promised gift of the outpoured Spirit has Messianic roots (see above on 2:16). It had been further witnessed by John the Baptist in relation to the ministry of the Messiah, whom he identified clearly as Jesus (Luke 3:16-17; cf. John 1:32-34), and Jesus Himself had assured the disciples of this future blessing (Luke 24:49; Acts 1:4-5). The mental pictures evoked here are impressive ones. The outpoured blessing of God, may, for example, be likened to an overflowing harvest, gathered in and laid up in the heart of God awaiting the moment when the doors to the barns of blessing can be thrown open and the rich grain poured forth for a hungry

---

in view of the Psalm 110 reference, and the allusion earlier to 'seating on a throne' (30).

37. Marshall, 78.

38. J. Denney, *Studies in Theology* (Hodder and Stoughton, 1904), 48-9.

and expectant community. The exalted Son receives and shares the promised Spirit.

(3) **He has poured out what you now see and hear**. The empowering ministry of God the Holy Spirit is bound inseparably to the saving ministry of God the Son. Other New Testament witness concurs (Matt. 3:11; John 3:34; 7:37-39; 14:16-18; 14:26-27; 15:26; 16:7-15; 20:22-23; Eph. 4:7-13). 'The Spirit is the earthly presence of the exalted Lord. To say it more precisely: "in the Spirit the Resurrected One is manifested in his resurrection-power."'[39]

We recall 1:1, and Luke's profound linkage there of his earlier account of the ministry of the incarnate Jesus = the Gospel of Luke, to the continuing ministry of the risen and exalted Jesus = the book of Acts.

This connection between the Son's death, resurrection and ascension, and the Spirit's outpouring, may, to employ a further image, be thought of as a 'filling up' through the death and resurrection of Jesus of a vast, immeasurable, dammed-up, reservoir of divine blessing, which, at Pentecost, the exalted Lord proceeded to breach, and thereby unleash a mighty, cascading flood-tide which overwhelmed the 120 in the Upper Room, swept out into the community, and would eventually, in Luke's story, send its ripples to the very heart of the civilized world in Rome, and in subsequent years, to the furthest corners of the planet.

Surveying verses 22-33 together we note that the evidential support for the identification of Jesus as the promised Messiah of Israel moves from His miraculous ministry (22), through fulfilled Scripture (25-28) and accredited resurrection (32), to God's self-witness through the invading Spirit.

In its way Peter's proclamation at this point represents a persuasive summary of the Christian truth claim. While all four forms of testimony contribute, the final element, expressed in the Spirit-inspired Scriptures (25-28), is the ultimate ground of appeal insofar as it represents God's own self-testimony. As Hilary argued in the fourth

---

39. Ernst Kasemann, 'Geist und Geistesgaben im NT' R.G.G., II, col. 1272-1278.

century, 'He whom we can know only through his own
utterances is a fitting witness concerning himself.'[40] Truly,
'When he, the Spirit of truth comes, he will guide you into
all truth' (John 16:13), a promise which was to be further
confirmed in the following moments, **Repent and be baptized every one of you in the name of Jesus Christ for the
forgiveness of sins, and you will receive the gift of the
Holy Spirit** (38).

Peter's claim for Jesus is rounded out by appeal to yet
another Old Testament witness: Psalm 110:1. This is one of
the most frequently occurring citations in the New Testament. It was 'a "fundamental" text of the early church's
preaching.'[41] Jesus had appealed to it during his controversies with the Jerusalem authorities (Luke 20:42-3) in
support of his own unique status. It is similarly employed
here. Again Peter sees the import of the words 'the Lord
said to my Lord "Sit at my right hand..."' as referring, not
to David the writer, but to his 'greater son', the risen and
exalted Jesus. Hence, having laid his foundation through
appeal to Jesus' miracle-strewn ministry (22); His resurrection in fulfilment of the prophetic Messianic Scriptures
(25-31) – an event to which the apostles can provide eye-
witness corroboration (32); and the presently experienced
outpouring of the Holy Spirit (33), Peter now adds his
copestone: **Therefore let all Israel be assured that God
has made this Jesus, whom you crucified, both Lord and
Christ** (36).

The implications of Peter's claim are major ones. Not
only is Jesus to be viewed as Israel's long-awaited Messiah (= Christ), but beyond even that, nothing less is being
claimed for Jesus than a status of equality with God. Such
a position is not directly affirmed in the Old Testament
usage where the Hebrew for 'The *Lord*' is *Yahweh*, the
name of God, while 'to my *Lord*' is *adon* which, though

---

40. *On the Trinity*, I xviii. Reformed epistemology is similarly based. 'The testimony
of the Spirit is more excellent than all reason. For as God alone is a fit witness of himself
in his Word, so also the Word will not find acceptance in men's hearts before it is sealed
by the inward testimony of the Spirit.' Calvin, *Institutes*, I.vii.4.

41. Bock: 133.

often used for God, can also be used of human lords and masters. However it must be recalled that between the psalmist's phrase and Peter's quotation lies the ministry of Jesus culminating in His resurrection from the dead and His exaltation to God's right hand. Accordingly it is surely justified to see here an implicit assertion of Jesus' share in the Lordship of Yahweh, that is, His identity with God. 'In Judaism no person is able to sit permanently in God's presence. God's glory and person are too unique to allow this….Who is holy enough to do so? This description of Jesus' position suggests an intimate connection between Jesus and the Father and an equality between them….Here the title "Lord" has its full, heavenly authority because of Jesus' position.'[42]

Thus, as Bruce aptly notes, 'The first apostolic sermon leads up to the first apostolic creed "Jesus is Lord" (cf. Rom. 10:9; 1 Cor. 12:3; Phil. 2:11).'[43]

It is a commonplace of radical New Testament scholarship that the lofty status claimed for Jesus in the New Testament is the result, over an extended period, of a progressive exaggeration of His person and role, so that what began as a deep respect for a highly unusual man became eventually the veneration of a God-man. This text, along with many, many others eliminates that possibility. Grant the fact of the resurrection (and the supporting historical evidence for it is overwhelming, as we noted above), then everything that is necessary for the claim Peter makes here lies to hand, right on the heels of Easter.

We note however that Peter is not only concerned to assert who Jesus truly is. He is an evangelist as well as a theologian. He is acting under the commission given him by his Lord: 'you shall be witnesses unto me…go and make disciples.' And so he is concerned not only to establish the glory of Jesus' person, but also the ignominy of Israel's response to Him, and not least the culpability of his hearers. So, this Messiah and Lord of Israel is also the one you crucified, **you, with the help of wicked men, put him to**

---

42. Bock, 134–5.

43. Bruce, 73.

death by nailing him to the cross (23). Hence if Jesus truly is who Peter has so masterfully demonstrated Him to be, the long-promised Messiah and the exalted Lord at God's right hand – how terrible beyond all accounting is their position! Incredibly, after all the long ages of waiting, God has fulfilled His covenant promise and has sent His Chosen One among them. They have actually lived in the long-awaited day of salvation, actually seen and encountered the Redeemer. But have they welcomed him? Have they honoured him? Have they given him their allegiance? No, no, no…almost incredibly, as it must now seem, they have wilfully rejected Him, handed Him over to the Gentiles, shouted for His blood, and hounded Him to an appalling death on a cross! It comes as no surprise to read that, in Luke's deeply evocative phrase, **they were cut to the heart** (37).

c. The Response to the Message (2:37-41)

Peter's sermon is profoundly impactful. The sense of guilt in his hearers for their treatment of the one clearly proved to be the Messiah sent by God is deep and palpable. In consternation they ask, on every hand: **Brothers, what shall we do?** It is the response every preacher longs to hear to a presentation of the gospel. Peter, in reply, shares the response which has become in essence the answer to the seeking heart in every generation, in every culture, and in every nation. He calls for two actions: **repent and be baptized in the name of Jesus**, and promises two blessings: **you will receive forgiveness of your sins and…the gift of the Holy Spirit** (38).

With reference to the actions called for, repentance (*metanoia*) is literally a change of direction; 'a spiritual right-about-turn.'[44] A similar call had been prominent in John the Baptist's preaching (Luke 3:3), and been echoed by Jesus (Mark 1:15; Luke 13:1-5). In this context repentance would have involved a change of view of Jesus, and the establishing of Him and His Messianic ministry at the centre of their subsequent relationship to God, and probably also a thoroughgoing moral about-face in terms not

---

44. Bruce, 75.

dissimilar to those called for by John (Luke 3:7-14). The change of view of Jesus would find natural expression in their being **baptized in the name of Jesus**.[45]

At the very least, this would have meant a humbling acknowledgement of the ongoing, personal Lordship over their lives of the one they had rejected, and the belief that He and His ministry, including His death and resurrection, were critical to their subsequent relationship to God. The act of baptism, arguably like John's an immersion rite after the model of Gentile proselyte baptism, would have powerfully affirmed the washing away of their guilt, even the unthinkable horror of Messianic rejection, in the gift of forgiveness through Jesus. It also brought the promise of the Holy Spirit, God's living presence in their lives, and their consequent incorporation into the new era of the divine Messianic kingdom. As becomes explicit in the following paragraphs, it also brought commitment to the new Messianic community.

The link between baptism in Jesus' name and the gift of the Spirit is not exhaustively explored in this verse other than in terms of a promised blessing and the instrumental means of its reception. The promise, however, is wonderfully expansive, being extended to all who will be called by God from henceforth, beginning with immediate family (**your children**), and extending to those **afar off** (39). While this geographic expansion possibly had immediately in mind the far-flung parameters of the Jewish diaspora, the Spirit would in time lead Peter (and the whole church) to see the promise as including all the Gentile nations (cf. 10:9-48).

Luke clearly wants his readers to know that his account of the sermon is only a summary of its primary themes. So, **many other words** are spoken (40). The fervency and urgency of the appeal is however stressed in conclusion; **he warned them and pleaded with them.** This is a note that all of us who carry the responsibility for preaching the gospel need to take to heart, however little we may

45. 'In (or 'into') the name of…' has the force of 'dedication to…for the sake of'. G.R. Beasley-Murray, *Baptism in the New Testament* (Macmillan, 1963), 100.

feel drawn to it. As Peter clearly discerned, and as his citation from Joel makes very plain (cf.19-20), the dawning of the day of salvation, the opening of the door of grace, whereby 'everyone who calls upon the name of the Lord will be saved' is only one aspect of the arrival of the kingdom of God. As in the day of Joel, refusal of offered grace leads inevitably to future judgment. Today's widespread adoption of the unbiblical error of universalism, whereby everyone will be saved in the end, has led inevitably to a muting of the warning note, and a general loss of urgency in the conduct of evangelism. Peter's faithfulness here needs to be recovered. Salvation is not only by and to grace, but also from judgment, and not all will escape it. The **corrupt generation** is still with us, and people need to be saved from its inevitable future destruction.

The harvest of Peter's sermon is finally noted, a magnificent one. **Three thousand were baptized** and became part of the new Messianic community of the believers in Jesus. This represented a markedly larger ingathering than that recorded at any point in Jesus' ministry; more indeed in that one day than from His three years of labour. It is pertinent therefore to recall, as does Bruce, Jesus' promise in John 14:12: that the disciples will perform 'greater things than these...' Here surely are 'greater things'. Why? '... because I am going to the Father'; going, that is, through death and resurrection to the Father's right hand from whence He would send the Holy Spirit in power to provide authentic divine attestation to the human words of the Christian preacher, enabling thereby the miracles of regeneration in the hearts and minds of those moved to repentant and believing response to this crucified, risen and eternally reigning Lord.[46]

d. The New Community of Jesus (42-47)

The transition from verse 41 to verse 42 cannot be sufficiently underlined. Verse 42's opening word is **they were**, *esan*, a plural verb. To respond to the invitation of

---

46. Bruce, 79.

the exalted Jesus, through repentance and baptism, and receive His gifts of forgiveness and new life in the Holy Spirit is to be brought into community. The New Testament, no less than the Old, knows nothing of solitary religion. Individual, personal faith is no doubt necessary, to appropriate God's gift of Jesus Christ, and to be the vehicle of God's gracious salvation in each recipient's heart. But the act of God in saving us immediately and eternally sets us in the community of the Spirit, the body of Christ, comprising all those in every place and in every time who own him as Lord.[47]

Pentecost birthed a community, not a collection of persons each claiming a new spiritual experience. While it would be strictly speaking wrong to refer to Pentecost as 'the birth of the church', if by church we mean the divine community of faith – that had patently begun 2,000 years before with Abraham and his successors – it would not be wrong to speak of the initiation of a new common life in the Holy Spirit of all those who own Jesus Christ as Lord and Saviour.

The common life of this new community is described in the following verses. Verse 42 uses a verb (*proskartereo*) commonly translated **devoted**. It has the idea of persistence in an activity. Luke probably intends us to understand the following summary as reflecting ongoing features, not simply happenings of the first day or two. Five such are to be noted.

(1) *The apostles' teaching.* As Stott helpfully points out, the experience of Pentecost was no anti-intellectual 'gig' which despised the place of teaching; nor did it give any support to the notion that the indwelling Holy Spirit was sufficient for the believer's enlightenment, and their understanding of God and His will, thereby dispensing with the need for the Spirit's human pedagogues.[48]

---

47. This is a particularly needed truth in Western society, and perhaps especially in North American cultures with their rampant individualism. cf. *Habits of the Heart*, R. Bellah and others (Berkeley, 1985); Charles W. Colson, *Against the Night* (Servant Publications, 1989), 97ff and passim.

48. Stott, 82.

Rather, from the outset, the community submitted to Jesus' personally chosen and endowed leaders, the apostles, **they devoted themselves to the apostles' teaching**. Since the **'apostles' teaching'** comes to us today in the Spirit-inspired words of the New Testament, submission to their teaching continues to be a fundamental feature of the community of Christ, as we joyfully receive, and diligently submit to, the New Testament as the Word of God, alongside the earlier Old Testament Word of God.

The apostles were also endowed with the ability to perform **many wonders and miraculous signs** (43); which neatly echoes the combination of these ministry features, 'doing and teaching' (1:1), begun in Jesus' own ministry, but to be continued through His living presence in the new company of the faithful.

(2) *Fellowship* (*koinonia*). Its root meaning is a 'belonging together in something'. The legacy of the Pentecost experience was of a whole new sense of 'life together' as the determining centre of experience. They saw themselves as wrapped up together in a new way of life, dominated by an awareness of being parts of a larger, living whole. The three occurrences of **together** in the following verses help flesh out something of what this new mutuality involved.

First, **all the believers were together and had everything in common** (44). **Selling their possessions and goods, they gave to anyone as he had need** (45). Care is needed here lest we read more into these verses than the text permits. The 'everything' which was had in common may simply be a general reference to a deep sense of shared identity, a further explanation of **they...were together**. If understood in this way, the reference to how this affected their attitude to material possessions arises only in the next verse (45), as a specific area in which this **fellowship** found expression. It was realized as, **selling their possessions they gave to anyone who had need**. The entire verse needs to be read together here and need not mean more than that the selling was in response to specific needs as they arose, rather than having been an 'across the board' practice, even a requirement for membership. That there was a huge sense of caring for one another is certainly not to be doubted, and a caring which did not hesitate to give sacrificially to one another as needs were recognized. But the notion that universal 'community of goods' was practised does not appear to be clearly stated, and this would accord with the fact that in the tragic case of Ananias and Sapphira in 5:1-11 it is their collusion in lies, rather than their withholding of a part of their property, which falls under judgment. Peter in fact explicitly states, 'after your property was sold, wasn't the money at your disposal?' (5:4). This interpretation accords too with the more general acceptance in Scripture of the right to private property, albeit always under the constraint of sacrificial giving to the needs of the neighbour after the example of Jesus (2 Cor. 8-9). Such a reading of verse 44 and 45 would also make sense of the apparent reference in verse 46 to their continuing to own homes. But in making this clarification we dare not evade the challenge to give to the needy, and it is perhaps not out of order to note additionally that giving sacrificially to the poorest should not forget giving to those among the poor who are our brothers and sisters in Christ in needy areas of the world (Gal. 6:10).

The larger, underlying challenge, however, is real, and ever pertinent. How do we view material possessions? Where does acquiring riches and their benefits come in our scale of life's priorities? What Luke depicts here is a company where the material had become suddenly of secondary significance in the light of the blessing of God the Holy Spirit; a community where spiritual realities had come to override the desire for a comfortable, secure material environment.

Second, **every day they continued to meet together in the temple courts (46)**. The 'fellowship' involved regular gatherings, interestingly in the 'temple courts'. Clearly recognizing Jesus as the Messiah promised to Israel, and through Israel to the world, did not mean that the believers cut themselves off from the Jewish community and their central worship shrine, the Jerusalem temple – 3:1 implies that this continuing association did not exclude the daily prayer services. Clearly their recognition of Jesus as the Passover lamb of God slain for sin, which Jesus had unforgettably taught at the Last Supper, and which was embodied in the offer of forgiveness of sin which Peter had preached (2:38), implied an altered understanding of the temple sacrifices. However at least in the initial period confession of Jesus as Saviour and Lord did not mean the abandonment of their heritage in the old covenant, nor of its ongoing worship. That Jesus was the Saviour of the Gentile world beyond Israel did not obscure the truth that He was also the fulfiller of the promise to Israel, and hence the one in whom God's ancient people were also summoned to find their salvation.

Third, **they broke bread in their homes and ate together with glad and sincere hearts** (46). The reference to common meals probably included some around which an early form of the Lord's Supper was observed. We will note this further under the third head of 'worship'. The shared meals in homes, however, carrying as they would the strong sense, continued in the Middle Eastern cultures to this day, that such shared table fellowship implied profound mutual acceptance, were no doubt an important practical expression of their new common life. Sharing a home continues to be a significant way of expressing a deepening fellowship. 'Given to hospitality' is a clear New Testament Christian virtue.

(3) *Worship*...**to the breaking of bread and to prayer... praising God** (42; 47). As could hardly surprise us, worship was a further watermark of the new Messianic community of Jesus. God had 'done great things' for them and they were correspondingly glad and celebrative. The commentators differ on how to understand this 'breaking of bread'. While it may be too much to assume this to be a full Lord's Supper celebration, such as Paul would later describe in 1 Corinthians 11:23ff., it is equally difficult to believe that what Jesus had so clearly commanded to be done 'in remembrance of me' in the Upper Room did not significantly inform their practice. The praise (47) had already preceded Pentecost as Luke records it in 24:52. Returning from the ascension experience they had 'worshipped him (Jesus) with great joy and...stayed continually at the temple, praising God.' But the outpouring

of the Holy Spirit would now be bringing yet greater richness, depth and fullness of joy to their worship.

The **prayer**, since the connection with the temple is generally asserted in verse 46, and given quite explicit reference in 3:1, would presumably have included both formal prayers linked to the temple, enriched probably by Jesus' teaching of the model prayer 'Our Father...', and more spontaneous personal and Spirit-inspired utterances. Pentecost had broken upon them in answer to a prolonged period of prayer (1:14). It is hard to believe that a continual waiting upon God for yet more of His blessing did not characterize their ongoing life, as 4:23-31 appears clearly to confirm.

(4) The *favour of all the people* (47). This is a significant feature. 'This is not an isolated, private club, or a hermetically sealed community. Their reputation with outsiders also is good.'[49] Clearly such favour is not inevitable, nor an invariable result of Christian community. Jesus had warned, 'If they have persecuted me, they will persecute you' (John 15:20), and had taught all the apostles, and particularly Peter, about a cross yet to be carried (John 21:18–19). History would vindicate these warnings. However it is significant that the Spirit's arrival brought the disciples abounding joy, and mutual and sacrificial caring, and it radiated out inevitably into the surrounding population. It is a plain fact that when such favour is obtained evangelistic fruitfulness commonly follows, as noted here. We are called to be faithful before being popular. But the combination of the two is often more available than we imagine, and its results are commonly, what McCheyne referred to as, 'the honour of God in the salvation of souls.' People were made for community and to discover a congregation bound together in the love of the Holy Spirit is often the key to their being persuaded to join it. The Billy Graham organization, in common with all other research into the key to people's committing themselves to Christ, refer to 86 per cent of those thus won to Christ attributing the primary influence being that of the friendship of an individual believer or a

---

49. Bock: 154.

group of Christians. 'People do not go where the action is; they go where the love is' (Jess Moody).

(5) *Mission,* **the Lord added to their number daily those who were being saved.** This final feature follows naturally on from the fourth. A Spirit-inspired, Spirit-filled church will be a growing church. We note that this took place in a regular ongoing manner, **daily.** While we can perhaps read too much into this reference, it is good to remind ourselves that evangelism in special efforts, while it may augment and give special focus to the church's mission, can never replace the regular witness of a congregation whose members are living lives of loving obedience to Christ on a daily basis, or whose communal life is committed to regular, ongoing efforts to bring the good news to its neighbourhood, and indeed to the world.

We should also give due place to Luke's clear stress on God's role in people finding salvation, **the Lord added daily.** This is a common emphasis in Luke, as we noted earlier (cf. 2:39; etc.). While human responsibility is never neglected, as is made very clear here in Peter's appeal: 'Repent and be baptized...the promise is to you and to all...**save yourselves**,' there is no ignoring of the necessary, irreplaceable role which God plays in people finding His salvation. Salvation is of God. As Jesus informed a seeker in John 3, 'except a person is born again (or from above), they cannot see the kingdom of God...The wind blows wherever it pleases...So it is with everyone born of the Spirit' (vv. 3, 8). Do we then simply sit around and wait for God's invading grace? No, we 'call upon the Lord' (2:21); we seek grace to 'repent'...and, renounce the 'corrupt generation' (38, 40); we '**receive the message**' of the gospel (41), with conviction that the gospel is for us, that Christ died in our place and brings us forgiveness and new life; we '**are baptized**' (38, 41). But we do all this in the confidence that we are not saving ourselves, but with empty hands we are embracing Christ whom God is pleased to impart to us as we cast ourselves upon Him, and in that moment also gives us new spiritual life in the Holy Spirit. And then we bless God for His great, and gracious salvation.

Finally, we take to heart Stott's warning, 'Tens of thousands of sermons have been preached on Acts 2:42, which well illustrates the danger of isolating a text from its context. On its own verse 42 presents a very lopsided picture of the church's life. Verse 47b needs to be added....Those first Jerusalem Christians were not so preoccupied with learning, sharing and worshipping that they forgot about witnessing. For the Holy Spirit is a missionary Spirit who created a missionary church.' Stott quotes the highly pertinent words of Harry Boer: 'The (book of) Acts is governed by one dominating, overriding and controlling motif. This motif is the expansion of the faith through missionary witness in the power of the Spirit...Relentlessly the Spirit drives the church to witness, and continually churches rise out of the witness. The church is a missionary church.'[50]

Study Questions:

1. Pentecost was unique in certain respects, but not in others: what are its continuing implications? What can you identify at this precise time of the Holy Spirit's ministry in your church? In what ways is the Holy Spirit at work in your own life?

2. Identify the three phenomena which accompanied the coming of the Spirit (2:1-12). Find where you can anticipations of these phenomena elsewhere in Scripture, and apply them to your life and to your church.

3. Consider the primary evidence of the Spirit's coming, viz. the effectual preaching of the gospel (2:14-41). What is the implication of this for the global and local church of today?

4. Identify the principal points of Peter's sermon (2:14-41). How does present-day preaching measure up against it? Are there any notes struck in Peter's address which we may be in danger of missing today?

---

50. Stott: 86; H. Boer, *Pentecost and Missions* (Lutterworth, 1961), 161-2.

5. State the five features of the first church (2:42-47). What here (a) challenges (b) encourages you? As you compare these features with the life of your own church today, what may we do to help the two 'churches' be more clearly aligned with each other?

3

'Witnesses in Jerusalem'
(Acts 3:1–5:42)

3:1-10: A miracle of healing in Jesus' name

Luke adopts the same basic pattern in chapters two and three. There is first a miraculous event (the outpouring of the Spirit/a miraculous healing), second an explanatory sermon by Peter, and third the consequences (a new community and its life/the new community persecuted, praying and sharing).

The healing miracle has clear links back to Jesus' ministry as Luke recorded it earlier (Luke 5:17-26; 9:1-6), and hence underscores Acts 1:1, understanding of the ministry of the church as the continuing ministry of Jesus.

The newborn Christian community has not yet cut its deep inherited ties to Judaism and to the temple worship with its daily liturgical life in particular. So **Peter and John**, a relationship already noted (John 20:3-8), **were going up to the temple at the time of prayer**, to share in the daily, afternoon prayer service (1). This may reflect the early Christian habit of ministering in pairs, a practice traceable back to Jesus (Luke 9:1-6). Behind that again may be the Old Testament law which required legal testimony to be by two witnesses if it was to carry weight (Deut. 17:6, 19). On their way into the worship area they are hailed by **a man crippled from birth** who was being carried to his accustomed begging place, at **the temple**

gate called Beautiful (2).[1] The noting of the seriousness of his condition may reflect a medical interest by Luke (Col. 4:14). The man **asked them for money** (3).

The giving of alms to the needy was an important duty for Jews seeking to live godly lives. We recall Jesus' challenge to the lawyer seeking eternal life to 'sell everything you have and give to the poor' (Luke 18:22); and His teaching in the Sermon on the Mount on the lifestyle of the Kingdom of God, 'when you give to the needy...' (Matt. 6:2). We note the *when* which is not an *if*; it is assumed that all His disciples will give alms.

Verses 4-5 describe in vivid terms a clear, visual interaction with the physically challenged man on the parts of both the apostles, who **looked straight at him**, and the beggar in his turn who **gave them his attention** on hearing Peter's welcome summons to **Look at us!** Peter initially dashes the beggar's hopes: **Silver or gold I do not have** (6) – the church is boasting of its bankruptcy! The great medieval theologian and philosopher Thomas Aquinas, once happened to call upon Pope Innocent II while the latter was counting a large sum of money. 'You see Thomas,' said the Pope, 'the church can no longer say "Silver and gold have I none."' 'True, holy father,' replied Thomas, 'and neither can she now say, "Arise and walk."'

But penniless Peter has another gift in mind, and one of infinitely greater value, since it would at a stroke affirm the man's dignity, transform his prospects in all kinds of ways, and eliminate forever his need to live off charity: **In the name of Jesus Christ of Nazareth, walk** (6). We note again the 'Christ' reference, and the echo from the Gospel (Luke 8:54). The arrival of the Spirit, the end-time blessing of the inaugurated kingdom of God (which is also signalled by the lame leaping like deer, cf. Isa. 35:6) is nothing other than the inaugurated reign of the exalted Jesus Christ, as Peter had carefully explained at Pentecost (2:33).

---

1. This is viewed by most authorities as today's Nicanor Gate; cf. discussion of the options in Marshall, 87.

Peter helps the lame man to his feet using his **right hand** (a nice eye-witness touch, received no doubt from one of Luke's apostolic sources). **Instantly** (perhaps echoing 2:2's 'suddenly'), the former beggar does what he has never previously been able to do at any time in his forty odd years (cf. 4:22), he **began to walk**! Indeed, and again the eye-witness feature is evident, he begins in his sheer delight to **leap** and bounce around in frenzied elation, all the while **giving praise to God** (8). It is important, however, to note the added feature – **he went with them into the temple courts** (8). For this was also something he had never ever done before. As a person with his degree of physical challenge he would, by the dictate of the law (Lev. 21:18-19, which actually specified a 'crippled foot'; cf. 2 Sam. 5:8), have been barred from the inner courts of the temple and hence from any sense of full acceptance by the God worshipped there.[2] Day after day, month after month, decade after decade, he had wistfully sat by the entry gate watching the worshippers and pilgrims crowding into the temple, and he all the while shut out, excluded: but no more, nor ever again!

The fact that the healed man's first act is to go into the temple is fraught with significance. This is what the experience of the healing power of Christ in salvation necessarily does for all who encounter it – it leads us into worship. Whenever we may have had the privilege of helping someone commit themselves to Christ we are naturally anxious in the following days to see evidence of their change of heart. Witnessing to others, getting involved in Christian work and service, are two time-honoured confirmations. But worship is surely even more significant. For meeting Christ and, by grace, submitting life and destiny to him,

---

2. A provision of the Old Testament law designed to underline the holiness of God, and hence the need for proper fitness and reverence in approaching Him. It might be rightly wondered whether our entirely proper elimination today of such provisions relating to physical imperfections, may possibly blind us to the *intent* of this law, and its continuing relevance. For 'Holiness to the Lord' is still engraved on the turban of our Great High Priest who welcomes us to worship (Ex. 28:36), and no less on the harness of the horses which convey pilgrims to the inner presence of the Almighty (Zech. 14:20). We are called to come before the Lord, 'just as we are' and certainly without fear, but nonetheless with proper reverence (Heb. 12:28).

brings us to the heart of God. We now cry 'Abba, Father'; we are made worshippers. Duncan Campbell expresses this memorably: 'Salvation just means that the Spirit of God has brought me into touch with God's personality, and I am possessed and thrilled by something infinitely greater than myself.'[3] I become a worshipper; I enter the temple of God.

The effect of all this is predictable, and reminiscent of the Pentecostal outpouring: **wonder and amazement** (2:6, 7, 12). A crowd immediately **came running** (11), since the man, through his long life of begging, would have been something of an institution at the temple, and hence possibly, in this sense, one of the best-known personalities in the entire city; **they recognized him** (10). They are now at **Solomon's Colonnade,** which is sited near the Nicanor Gate, a famous location for commerce and discussion. Jesus had taught there (John 10:23), and the disciples would soon make it their regular place of meeting (Acts 5:12). The exalted Jesus now speaks again there, as Peter seizes the opportunity to preach the good news to the assembled crowd. This is the first of three sequels to the miracle.

3:11-26: A sermon explaining the miracle: it is Jesus; it is the kingdom come.

Once again the point of departure is twofold: the supernatural action of God, and His human instruments.

In general this sermon is an important statement of the core convictions which had birthed and continued to motivate the new community of Jesus. It is notable not least for its pervasive Christo-centrism. 'Signs and wonders' may be in the air through the powerful presence of the Holy Spirit, but the Spirit's ministry is ever to exalt Jesus, and so it is to Him that the apostles point continually. There is never the danger for them, a danger unfortunately not always avoided by His later followers, of Christianity as a religion of supernatural phenomena, instead of a religion of Christ-glorification. This is not to eliminate the 'signs and wonders', and in our materialistic generation

---

3. Duncan Campbell, *God's Answer:Revival Sermons* (Pickering and Inglis, 1972), 35.

there is hopefully a respected role for these in pointing to supernatural reality. But they are to be understood, as are all the other less spectacular, more mundane and everyday works of the kingdom of God, as works of the risen, exalted Christ, and hence as important only insofar as they exalt and magnify Him.

The sermon can be loosely described as a journey of four steps; an imagery with a certain propriety from its association with a man who had just begun to step for the first time in his life.

Step one (12-16): Explaining the miracle. Peter, as at Pentecost, has an obvious starting point in the miraculous intervention. **Why does this surprise you? Why do you stare?** Again he uses a 'what this is not/what this is' dialectic (2:15ff).

Negatively, this is *not* explicable in merely human terms. At Pentecost, 'they are not pickled' – 'these men are not drunk as you suppose' (2:15); here, 'they are not pious' – **as if by our own power or godliness we had made this man walk** (12). It is instructive how consistently throughout Acts the apostles vehemently disavow their own worth: cf. 10:25f; 14:14f; (13:25; and contra – 12:21-23).

Positively, *this is God*: **The God of Abraham, Isaac and Jacob, the God of our fathers...**But, critically, it is not an arbitrary divine act of power of the covenant-God of Israel. It is a sovereign act of Israel's God *which is rooted in His recent prior act* – that of having **glorified his servant Jesus** (13a)! It is the act of their familiar God of the Old Testament, the God of Israel, who, however, requires to be henceforth *defined in a new and fuller way*: as the God who raised and exalted Jesus.

In other words, here Peter faces his hearers with the central claim of the entire apostolic witness, and of the book of Acts from end to end. It is still the central claim of Christianity: that God, the one God, the universal creator, has come into our space-time world in person in Jesus Christ. All else hangs upon and flows from this central truth. With it Christianity stands or falls. This is the stumbling block still for Judaism, and for Islam, and for all who dream of a synthesis of world religions. God, the one true and living God, cannot be understood or truly confessed except as the God, supremely and definitively, revealed and known in Jesus Christ. By this Christians live; for this they have been, and will be, again and again, willing to die.

Peter's title for Jesus is striking. Not surprisingly it is one drawn from the Old Testament Scriptures – the prophecy of the obedient and suffering Servant of the Lord of Isaiah (Isa. 52:13–53:12), which opens with the words, 'See my **servant**...he will be raised and lifted up and highly exalted.' This designation was first declared at Jesus' baptism by the Father's voice (Luke 3:22), and a major theme surely of the risen Jesus' forty-day seminar ((Luke 24:44f). Bruce rightly notes that 'No passage of OT prophecy has made so deep and plain a mark on NT thought and language as this.'[4]

Familiarity with this identification of Jesus as the Servant of the Lord must not blind us to the astonishing paradox at its heart. The one so uniquely exalted and acclaimed is one who lived the life of an obedient servant, one who consciously renounced the externals of glory and honour, and chose the lowliest place. The great hymn of Philippians 2:5-11 is probably the fullest and most adequate commentary on this verse. If such a reversal, whereby the one who renounced glory was in the end crowned with it, has resonance in our world, it had even greater impact in the classical world of the first century. For there the attaining of eminence, power and honour was almost universally assumed as a primary life-goal. Jesus here radically rewrites the ethical code of antiquity, and also that of today. The exalted life, the honoured life, is the servant life. The implications for the life of the church, and its leaders in particular, is profound. In oft-cited words, 'In the kingdom of God service is not a stepping-stone to nobility; it *is* nobility, the only kind of nobility that is recognized.'[5] Or again, 'The lure of power

---

4. Bruce, 88; cf. also Marshall, 91, who observes that this suggests 'a primitive understanding of Jesus', since it is surprisingly absent from later New Testament writings.

5. T.W. Manson, *The Church's Ministry* (Hodder and Stoughton, 1948), 27.

can separate the most resolute of Christians from the true nature of Christian leadership, which is service to others. It is difficult to stand on a pedestal and wash the feet of those below.'[6] 'The kings of the Gentiles lord it over them...*you are not to be like that*...the greatest among you should be... the one who serves' (Luke 22:25-26). God has exalted a servant Messiah.

The walking and leaping of the lifelong cripple was further evidence of this divine affirmation of Jesus, and the explanation of it. **Faith in** this exalted and glorified servant **Jesus** had been the means to his **complete healing** (16).

Step two: The guilt from having rejected Jesus (13b–15a). Peter employs here a 'What you did/what God did' dialectic (cf. 4:10; 5:30) to bring out the appalling implications as far as his audience was concerned.

What God did: He had glorified Jesus (13), and raised Him from the dead, an historic fact of which the apostles were the totally convinced **witnesses** (15).

What you did: They, representing the Jewish people, but ultimately our whole race, had **handed him over to be killed** (13), **disowned him before Pilate** (13), **disowned the Holy and Righteous One** (14), **asked for a murderer to be released** (14), **killed the author of life** (15).

Even with regard to an ordinary individual this series represents a catalogue of infamy. But Jesus was no ordinary individual. He was the **Holy One**, an ascription of Jesus which Luke had noted in his Gospel, used not least by the demons He exorcized (Luke 4:34; also 1:35); He was the **Righteous One** (a Messianic title, 2 Sam. 23:3; Isa. 32:1; 53:11; Zech. 9:9); He was the **author of life**, possibly in the sense of 'Originator' (Heb. 2:10).

Thus, as with his Pentecost sermon, Peter confronts his hearers with their overwhelming guilt. The irony was astonishing, had it not been so terrible. After centuries of waiting for the **Christ** (Messiah) (18), He had at last arrived among them, in their time and their place. They

---

6. Charles W. Colson, *Kingdoms in Conflict: An Insider's Challenging View of Politics* (Morrow-Zondervan, 1987), 272.

were the uniquely privileged generation, from the dawn of time to the present moment. Into their hands the Holy and Righteous One had been given. But they had failed to recognize Him when He came; worse, they had disowned Him; worse still, they had handed Him over to the Gentile Roman overlords; yet worse again, they had chosen to liberate Barabbas, a murderer, rather than God's Messiah; worst of all, almost unthinkably, they had *killed Him!* They had murdered the Messiah, disowned the divine one, slain the Son of God, killed the King of Glory!

Step three: The way to be saved (17-20, 26). Peter mercifully tries to mitigate their culpability as best he can. **Brothers** he calls them, and acknowledges that they **acted in ignorance** of the full implications of their deed (17). He notes further that God's purpose was not thwarted thereby since **he had foretold through all the prophets that his Christ would suffer** (18). All that, however, does not absolve them. Nevertheless there is hope, even for Messiah-slayers, such as they now knew themselves to be.

First, they must **repent**; they must freely and fully acknowledge their deed of shame, renounce it, turn wholeheartedly from it, and **turn to God** and seek His mercy. Though Peter does not here explicitly link forgiveness to Christ's coming and death as clearly as he did at Pentecost, and as he would on other occasions (2:38; cf. 4:12; 5:31; 10:42-43), it is certainly implicit, not least in the reference in the previous sentence to the necessity of Christ's sufferings. So he offers the wonder of forgiveness, **that your sins may be wiped out** (19). The allusion is a telling one: 'Ancient writing was upon papyrus, and the ink used had no acid in it. It therefore did not bite into the papyrus as modern ink does; it simply lay upon the top of it. To erase the writing a man might take a wet sponge and simply wipe it away.'[7] Nothing less is held out to them with respect to their sins, and also ours.

If we assume that baptism would have been performed on all who responded, after the model of Pentecost, and elsewhere in Acts (2:38, 41; 8:12; 8:36f; 9:18; 10:47f; 16:33),

---

7. Barclay, 32.

and surely we may, the use of water, and its associations with cleansing would be deeply meaningful, as is no less the case today. The author is vividly reminded of a prostitute from our Vancouver community who came to Christ, and after her baptism, when I asked her, 'How do you feel now?' she replied, movingly, 'For the first time in my life I feel really clean!'

> *What can wash away my sin;*
> *Nothing but the blood of Jesus...*

Step four: Full salvation (19b–21). The wiping away of their guilt is linked by Peter to God sending **times of refreshing** (19). In a real sense the phrase describes what those responding to Peter's invitation would experience at that moment, salvation, modelled in the healed man; lifelong limitation and its accompanying exclusion from God's presence now gloriously banished forever. But the following verse moves that reference on to a wider plane as Peter refers to the **sending** again **of Christ** from His present location **in heaven** (20-21). This re-sending will happen **at the time for God to restore everything, as he promised long ago through his holy prophets** (21).

Thus, while Luke gives enormous stress, both in the Gospel and Acts, to the fact and achievement of the first coming of Christ, he never loses sight of the future horizon and the final fulfilling of God's purposes at Christ's coming again. For Peter's hearers their invitation to repent and believe, and receive forgiveness, did not mean salvation was confined to a merely personal experience in the immediate present. Rather their repentance and faith in Christ would bring them into an entirely new sphere of being, the long-promised kingdom of God, and hence to a full participation in its final, culminating realization when the ascended Lord would be the descending Lord, 'with power and great glory', as he had himself promised (Luke 21:27); a fullness in the terms presented in the Old Testament prophets (cf. Isa. 65–66; 34:4; 51:6; Jer. 15:18-19; 16:15; 23:8; 24:6; Ezek. 17:23). The verb **restore** points to a transformation which will at the very least recover the pristine character of the original creation.

Peter rounds off his message by noting several such prophetic anticipations. He mentions **Moses** in Deuteronomy 18:15, 18, 19, referring to the **Prophet like me** who was to come (22-23; cf. 7:37). He notes **all the prophets from Samuel on** (24), foretold **these days**. In Samuel's case there is a probable reference to his close ties to David, and the Davidic kingship which was a template of Jesus' reign in certain regards. Finally Peter reaches back to the father of the nation, Abraham and the primal covenant with him in Genesis 22:18; 26:4, that **all peoples on earth would be blessed** through God's having **raised up his servant** (26). This promised blessing has now come to them first among 'all peoples', a blessing in terms of moral renewal, the **turning of each of you from your wicked ways** (26).

Peter's message has several features which remain significant for the preacher of today.

1. *The authenticity attained by the healing/salvation of the cripple.* Peter's proclamation is generated by the need to explain the phenomenon of a transformed life. The fact that the cripple was well known in the community only extended the opportunity. Today dramatic, instantaneous miracles of this physical nature are infrequent, and even when approached with the sincerity and sensitivity they demand, can create pastoral dilemmas, both at the time and subsequently. However there remains the life-transformation which is widely celebrated in the New Testament and which is devoid of these liabilities. Jesus called for it: 'Let your light shine before men, that they may see your good deeds and praise your Father in heaven' (Matt. 5:16). Jesus clearly holds out the possibility here, to those who enter the kingdom of God, of so living in the public sphere ('seen by men') that people 'out there' are brought to acknowledge, and even 'praise your Father in heaven'. We dare not minimize the evangelistic potential of a godly, outgoing Christian life, renewed by the Holy Spirit. The hard statistical evidence of the overwhelming proportion of people professing faith in all known cultures, because

of the friendship and persuasive witness of such lives, makes this Acts passage perennially relevant.

2. *The focus on Jesus Christ*. 'The speech is one of the most Christologically rich addresses in Acts', writes Bock, and he does not exaggerate.[8] Peter refers to **the name of Jesus**, which means His person, as the source of the healing (16). The entire message effectively unpacks what the name of Jesus encloses. He is the **Servant** of the Lord (13, 26); He is the **Holy One** (14); He is the **Righteous One** (14); He is the **Author of Life** (15); He is the **Risen** One (15, 26); He is the **Healer** and the source of the powers of the kingdom of God (16); He is the **Sufferer** appointed by God through whom sins may be **wiped out** (18-19); He is the long-promised **Messiah** (18); He is the Returning One, through whom God will finally **restore everything** (20-21); He is the **Prophet** foretold by Moses (22-23); He is David's promised **heir** as foretold by Samuel (24); He is the **offspring of Abraham through whom all peoples of the earth will be blessed** (25)…It is all **Jesus**! One is reminded of a great passage in Calvin's *Institutes* in similar vein:

'We see that our whole salvation and all its parts are comprehended in Christ (Acts 4:12). We should therefore take care not to derive the least portion of it from anywhere else. If we seek salvation we are taught by the very name Jesus that it is "of him" (1 Cor. 1:30). If we seek any other gifts of the Spirit, they will be found in his anointing. If we seek strength, it lies in his dominion; if purity in his conception; if gentleness, it appears in his birth. If we seek redemption, it lies in his passion; if acquittal, in his condemnation; if remission of the curse, in his cross (Gal. 3:13); if satisfaction, in his sacrifice; if purification, in his blood; if reconciliation, in his descent into hell; if mortification of the flesh, in his tomb; if newness of life, in his resurrection; if immortality, in the same; if inheritance in the heavenly Kingdom, in his entrance into heaven; if protection, if security, if abundant supply of all blessings, in his Kingdom; if untroubled expectation of judgment, in the power given to him to judge. In

---

8. Bock, 165.

short, since a rich store of every kind of good abounds in him, let us drink of our fill from this fountain, and from no other.'[9]

'Sir…we would like to see Jesus' (John 12:21) is still the unuttered cry of every listening congregation. We are to 'preach Christ'. This means of course preaching Him in all the Scriptures, since it takes a whole Bible to reveal a full Christ. Peter, we should note, is (necessarily) confined to the Old Testament in this glorious exposition of Jesus' person and work, and it patently does not hinder him.

3. *The range of the sermon.* Peter's canvas is exceedingly broad. Historically he relates salvation to the entire age-long, redeeming purpose of God. Although that does not mean he refers at length to every stage of it, his hearers are given a vision of a God who 'works all things out according to his will', a God who is gloriously sovereign over all things, and a God who has a great purpose of love moving forward to triumphant conclusion and all-embracing victory in Jesus Christ.

Geographically, Peter refers to the God who reaches out to 'every family of the earth'. In other words, Peter's understanding of salvation is mind-blowing, comprehensive and exhilarating. We will note at a later point a comment of John Stott on Paul's amazingly comprehensive sermon to the pagan philosophers in Athens, that 'Many people are rejecting our gospel today, not because they perceive it to be false, but because they perceive it to be trivial.' We need a big gospel today, wide-ranging and all-embracing, and Peter mirrors that here.

4. *The moral appeal.* Peter is unapologetically drawn to address the consciences of his hearers. **You handed Jesus over to be killed…you disowned him…you asked for a murderer…you killed the author of life.** Peter's message is not afraid to awaken guilt. Calvin comments, 'It is impossible to bring them truly to God unless they were first brought to a knowledge of their sins.' [10]

---

9. Calvin, *Institutes*, II, xvi, 19.

10. Calvin: II, 98.

Jesus is, among other things **the Holy and Righteous One**. The call issued is first of all a call to **repent**. They are warned most solemnly of the implications of rejecting the **Prophet who should come** (22), that of being **cut off completely from among his people**. In other words to dismiss the claims of Christ, and refuse to submit to Him as Lord and only Saviour, brings eternal divine judgment. And the whole goal of the work of Christ is, according to Peter's final comment, **to bless you by turning each of you from your wicked ways**.

The reference to blessing his hearers is important. Peter's moral preaching is based on a moral interpretation of human existence, by which the supreme reality is a God of gracious righteousness, 'holy love' if you like, and hence for the creatures of such a God the greatest possible blessing lies in attaining an identical righteousness before Him. The whole ministry of Christ is a grand, divine means to that. And the blessings of attaining that righteousness exceed any others. Hence it is the holy love of God which motivates the gift of salvation, and it is the holy love of the preacher for the hearers which underlies the appeal to them to embrace it. Nothing in earth or heaven is conceivably a greater, fuller, more satisfying, or more permanent blessing, than to have repented of our sins, and embraced Jesus Christ as our only Lord and Saviour, and hence to have set out with Him on the road to final, entire likeness to the Righteous One.

Study Questions:

1. Consider the apostles' habit of joining in the continuing religious life of the Jewish people, and its temple worship in particular (3:1, 9). What was 'right' about that, and what were its dangers?

2. What are the lessons of this healing miracle (3:2-9)?

3. Peter's sermon here (3:12-26) is predominantly Christ-focused. Identify all the points he makes about the Lord Jesus Christ in his message. Which

are most relevant to your life today? Which are most relevant to your church's life and witness? Which of them is your surrounding culture needing most urgently to recognize?

4. Identify ways in which the sermon addresses Peter's hearers' (a) in their minds? (b) in their knowledge of Old Testament Scripture? (c) in their wills? (d) in their consciences? (e) in their emotions? (f) in their longings and imaginations?

5. Go carefully and prayerfully through the sermon and worship the Lord Jesus Christ at each point where His worthiness is affirmed.

4:1-22: A Trial

The healing and the sermon gather a significant crowd at the Nicanor Gate, and also attract the authorities who move to deal with it. **They seized Peter and John** (3). This is another critical moment in the story of the church: the beginning of its long history of persecution.

The opposition is led by **the captain of the temple guard** (1); as number-two man in the temple he was responsible among other things for maintaining peace and order within and around its sacred precincts. An over-the-shoulder glance at Rome stoked this concern (cf. John 11:47-48). The main responsibility for this assault on the apostles lies, however, with **the Sadducees,** one of the key sects of Judaism.

The Sadducees traced their origin to Zadok, son of Aaron, the high priest under Solomon. In political terms they were a very influential group, aristocratic, and materialistic, within the limits of that profoundly religious culture. Their political policy called for appeasement with Rome, which of course undergirded their position of continuing influence within the Jewish state. Seeing themselves as the disciples of Moses, they denied any teaching which was not clearly upheld in the Books of Moses, Genesis to Deuteronomy. In particular they denied life after death in any form; 'the doctrine of the Sadducees is that souls die with bodies.'[11] It is further testimony to how central the hope of resurrection was in the apostles' message that it is the Sadducees who are identified as leading the opposition at this point. The apostles are taken into custody pending trial (3).

But many who heard the message believed…(4). Here is a wonderful adversative. You can imprison preachers, you can silence preachers, you can kill preachers, but you cannot imprison, silence or slay the word of God.[12] So, while the apostles languish in jail the message they have preached is actively at work in the hearts of its hearers, and to such effect that **the number of men grew to about five thousand.** The commentators divide over whether the 'men' here is generic. Clearly Luke intends an impression of significant further growth, so one may well be intended to reckon on a significant number of women besides. Clearly the 120 men and women in the Upper Room at prayer (1:15) have grown and multiplied dramatically.

Having imprisoned the apostles, the authorities must needs bring them to trial. The remainder of the passage covers the proceedings. The Jewish court was known as the Sanhedrin (15, though the actual word does not occur in the passage at any point; however see 5:21, 27, 34, etc.). It consisted of seventy-one men covering the highest levels of political, social, academic, religious, and ecclesiastical life within the Jewish state at this point in time. This was the court which a few weeks previously had been hastily assembled in the early hours of a Friday morning to try another prisoner whose ministry had been similarly clouded in controversy, though adorned with multiple, evidences of divine, supernatural attestation.

---

11. Josephus, *Antiquities*, 18: 1, 4. cf. Calvin, 112, who speaks of the 'monstrous confusion…that so profane a sect should have such authority…for what godliness could remain when the immortality of the soul could be counted as a fable.'

12. cf. Luther, famously, 'I simply taught, preached, wrote God's Word: otherwise I did nothing. And while I slept, or drank Wittenberg beer with my Philip or my Amsdorf, the Word so greatly weakened the papacy that never a Prince or Emperor inflicted such damage upon it. I did nothing. The Word did it all.' Henry H. Mitchell, *The Recovery of Preaching* (Hodder and Stoughton, 1979), 124.

Verse 6 notes some of the leading figures, particularly the high-priestly connection. The reference to **Annas** needs comment. A former high priest, from A.D. 6–15, before being deposed by Pilate's predecessor, no fewer than four of his sons had held the office in the succeeding period, and the current incumbent, **Caiaphas**, was a son-in-law. Annas remained through all this period the real power behind the throne, even being capable, as here, of being actually identified as the high priest. Luke elsewhere refers to 'the high priesthood of Annas and Caiaphas' which gets it about right (Luke 3:2; John 11:47-48; 18:12-27).

Peter and John are brought before them. The charge is formulated in a question: **by what power or what name did you do this?** (7). In the Greek text the **you** is at the end of the question, giving a sense, 'What power or authority gave this right to you, insignificant nobodies?'[13] Peter is spokesperson, as we might expect; however, this gives some cause for concern, recalling the last occasion he was publicly confronted concerning his relationship to Jesus (Luke 22:54-62). But this is a new Peter, no longer dependent on his own, notoriously unreliable, personal resources. He is a **filled-with-the-Spirit** Peter; the power and evident presence of the Risen Lord Jesus is upon him.

Peter first unpacks the charge: what is 'this'? (7); actually **an act of kindness shown to a cripple**, by which he has been **healed** (8). Here is a striking moment – the Church of Christ on trial for its kindness! Would that it had ever been so throughout its years. Having thus clarified the charge, Peter proceeds to respond to it with astonishing courage and forthrightness. **Know this…it is by the name of Jesus Christ of Nazareth, whom you crucified, whom God raised from the dead…**(10). We note again the stark contrast between the attitude to Jesus represented by the Jewish authorities, and that of the Lord God of Israel. Peter is in effect in this sentence reversing the roles in the judicial process; he, the accused, becomes the accuser; the judgment seat of the Sanhedrin is transformed into the judgment seat of God! The referencing of

13. Bock: 190.

Jesus' place of origin is probably not accidental. For Nazareth was despised by these effete elitists in Jerusalem, and would have been an element in the contemptuous dismissal implicit in the form of the charge noted above. But Peter is not finished: he proceeds to support his claims for Jesus by an aptly chosen citation from the Scriptures: **He is 'the stone you builders rejected which has become the capstone'** (11). This text from Psalm 118:22, with its 'reversal' motif, was widely acknowledged as a Messianic prophecy (cf. Matt. 21:42; Mark 12:10; Luke 20:17; 1 Pet. 2:4, 7).[14] Scholars debate whether *kephalen* here refers to the corner-stone, the main oversized stone, which holds up two adjoining walls, or the capstone which crowns an archway. The former, reflected in the NIV text, appears, on balance, more likely.

The implications of this claim are immense: Jesus is therefore declared by God as the promised Saviour, not only of all Israel, and by implication all those listening members of the Sanhedrin, and beyond that again, of all people everywhere, and hence: **Salvation is found in no one else, for there is no other name given to men by which we must be saved** (12). Here die all universalistic dreams. 'Peter is no advocate of modern notions of religious pluralism.'[15] There is one way to salvation, and only one, the way that passes through Jesus Christ. His own claim is confirmed here: 'no one comes to the Father except through me' (John 14:6). For those who lived in ages before, notably within the covenant-community of Israel, salvation was also through Jesus, as His coming and self-sacrifice was anticipated. For all living subsequently salvation is by a trusting reliance upon Him and His atoning sacrifice on Calvary. There is no further option on offer. While for us today the virtue of the cross is projected forward, in the case of the Old Testament saints it is projected backwards (Matt. 8:16f; Luke 2:38; John 3:4f; 8:56; Rom. 4:25; 10:11-13; 1 Cor. 5:7; Heb. 9:15; 10:12-14;

---

14. Here again one surely sees the hand of Jesus, during his post-resurrection seminar, in the apostles' choice of highly appropriate OT prophetic witnesses.

15. Witherington, 194.

1 Pet. 1:18f). For them, no whit less than for us, atonement, ultimately considered, is by the blood of Christ.

However, the thrust of Peter's words here is not merely on affirming the exclusiveness of Christ's salvation, but also its glorious *in*clusiveness, for it extends to all who come to Christ irrespective of their religious tradition and practices, or even their entire lack of them. It would, however, take the full course of the Book of Acts to convince the church of this global inclusiveness, which had of course been established in the terms of Jesus' commission: '...and to the ends of the earth' (1:8). But they would get there in the end, under the leadership of Peter (eventually! chs. 10–11), and Paul (chs. 13–28). This positive dimension is nicely expressed in Peter's final phrase: **by which *we* must be saved**. He places John and himself in the identical position of those whom he has newly accused of Messiah-slaying: for all distinctions are rendered void at the cross. There we are all equally helpless sinners, whether apostolic saints or adversarial Sanhedrin, and are all equally welcome there, to full and final salvation.

When Peter had finished his defence one can, without much imagination, presume a silence in the Sanhedrin. This body was not accustomed to being thus addressed, even instructed, particularly so by a group of **unschooled, ordinary men** (13). We note again the element of contempt for 'ordinary' people. The only observation they could make in explanation was their having met this unofficial, unauthorized pretension in the one they had been, until lately, led by – Jesus the Nazarene: **they took note that these men had been with Jesus**. It is surely the church's greatest hour when that association is noted in the lives of its members, as the only credible explanation of our conduct or spirit. But all the while the Sanhedrin's discomfort was only increased by the visible presence in the court of the lifelong cripple, who was doing there before their very eyes the one thing which he had been unable to do for all of his forty-odd years – **standing!** (14).

Baffled, even speechless, they do the only thing remaining to them – they clear the court of these embarrassing people: **So they ordered them to withdraw from the San-**

hedrin and then conferred together (14-15). **What are we going to do…to stop this thing from spreading any further?** (16). It is a moment of beautiful irony and significance.

It is, further, of huge and continuing importance to note what they do *not* do. Bruce explains, 'It is particularly striking that neither here on this or on any subsequent occasion (so far as our information goes) did the Sanhedrin take any serious action to disprove the apostles' central affirmation – the resurrection of Jesus. Had it seemed possible to refute them on this point, how readily would the Sanhedrin have seized the opportunity! Had they succeeded how quickly and completely the new movement would have collapsed! It is plain that the apostles meant a physical resurrection when they said that Jesus has risen; it is equally plain that the rulers understood them in this sense. The body of Jesus had vanished so completely that all the authority they had at their command could not produce it.'[16]

The plain fact of history is that when one reflects on this supreme court in Jerusalem, and recognizes their entire command of that Jerusalem society, all of its people and all of their movements, and that the period of their command encompassed, most critically, the immediate days and weeks around and following the date of the alleged resurrection of Jesus in the very location where it was claimed to have occurred, their demonstrable failure to successfully refute the apostolic claim is arguably a piece of evidence in support of the resurrection of hugely impressive weight. It surely outweighs any and every so-called 'disproof' offered by any modern sceptic, formulated two thousand years later, and on the other side of the world in most cases, quite irrespective of the sceptic's intellectual or scholarly credentials. At this point faith appears to score what looks remarkably like a winning goal! 'It is true! The Lord has risen' (Luke 24:34).[17]

---

16. Bruce, 103.

17. This conclusion is further buttressed by the only piece of historical testimony which *has* come down to us, Matthew 28:11-15, which very neatly undergirds our (and Bruce's) point concerning the authorities' desperate need to find some contrary evidence, and the equally desperate limits they were apparently driven to when nothing of significance became available – the evidence of sleeping soldiers!! (Matt. 28:13). One

What then *do* they do? They recall the apostles and inform them that they are **not to speak or teach at all in the name of Jesus** (18). One is reminded of King Canute of England, reputedly seated on his throne, commanding the incoming tide to recede![18] Poor fools they, to imagine that they in the Sanhedrin still retained the reins of spiritual and moral authority in the land. They were in effect appealing to an old order which had passed out of existence with the death and rising of Jesus. They had yet to wake up to the new world which had dawned, a world in which people marched to an entirely different beat, and took their orders from an entirely different throne.

Peter's response is predictable, but deeply significant, and deserving of being quoted in full. **Judge for yourselves whether it is right in God's sight to obey you rather than God**. At one level this is an epochal statement of the rights of the individual conscience over against the collective, coercive will of the state. But the larger point is that the claims of God necessarily take precedence over, and command a higher allegiance than, that to be accorded to any human court or tribunal. The obligation to obey God stands above and supersedes submission to every religious and political system.

We cannot but speak of what we have seen and heard (20) presumably refers to the evidence of their meetings with the risen Jesus, and His teaching of them, after the cross. As we will note again and again in these chapters there is a sheer, bedrock conviction throbbing through these 'men and women of the resurrection', which defies explanation other than on the basis of the reason they themselves consistently gave for it – that it had really happened.

The authorities are baffled but, faced with the public acclaim at the healing, and the indomitable spirit of the apostles in their midst, they can only fall back upon threats

---

would simply love to be present with these soldier 'witnesses' under cross-examination by a Perry Mason, or a Rumpole of the Bailey!!

18. In fairness to the said monarch, it should be recognized that he apparently resorted to this memorable ruse in order to try and impress on some of his over-demanding courtiers the limits of his royal power. He made his point; as in a real sense did the Sanhedrin make their 'non-point' here.

of more severe reactions for any further breach of their demand that the apostles cease their activities forthwith. **So they let them go** (21).

There are two predominant lessons from this passage. The first is the subtle and yet terrible danger of the religion of the Sanhedrin. For nothing can eliminate the sheer fact of history that these were profoundly religious men, who daily participated in acts of communal prayer and worship, and supplemented that piety with study of the Old Testament Scriptures, and sacrificial almsgiving. Yet, for all those religious trappings, with few exceptions, they perpetrated the most heinous act of injustice in the entire human story, the judicial condemnation and execution of history's one utterly innocent individual, and here, and in subsequent chapters, the persecution of His dedicated followers. What explains this? Its accounting lies in the way in which the lure of influence, and power over others, can seduce and finally dominate human personality, especially when bolstered by entrenched mutual loyalties, to the point that higher human values of sensitivity, compassion, and justice are routinely overridden. Once this reversal is in place, the point is quickly reached where everything becomes dispensable in the interests of the preservation of these all-consuming, ego-serving, interests and goals.

The second lesson lies in the way this passage lays bare the ultimate secret of biblical Christianity: the presence of the risen, reigning Jesus Christ in the midst of His church. For, in merely human terms, this passage describes a contest which should never have been permitted: it was simply too one-sided. On the one side there was the Sanhedrin, all seventy-one of them, embracing all the political, military (with Roman approval), social, religious, moral, administrative, intellectual and scholarly authority available within the Jewish state of the period. On the other side there stood Peter and John, two 'unschooled, ordinary men' totally lacking all of the Sanhedrin's multiple credentials and paraphernalia of power. Yet, against all the odds, the apostles triumphed. How can we possibly explain this astonishing outcome? It lies surely in the two sides' respective relationships to Jesus.

For their part, the Sanhedrin imagined that they had dealt with Jesus. He had been deeply, disturbingly, troublesome to their power-lusts and ambitions, but they had won in the end; Jesus was dead. No doubt they had gone home on Good Friday evening with a deep sense of satisfaction, after having, in many of their cases, mocked and derided the dying Jesus on the cross. Once home we can perhaps in imagination see them entering their studies, switching on their personal computers, and bringing up the file entitled 'Jesus of Nazareth', and then applying the 'delete' command, with a warm sense of satisfaction and achievement. They were the people! They had proved a match for Jesus! Jesus would cause them no more trouble! Jesus was history! Jesus was gone!...Yet, in actual fact, His presence dominates this account. Jesus is the real determiner of the events; His name, and the claims made for Him, ripple through the entire story. Jesus is the source of the healing miracle which precipitated the whole scene, and His presence is the key to the astonishing inspiration, naked courage, and empowerment of the apostles.

But such has continued to be the case over all the centuries since, as the various persecutors of Jesus and His church have learned to their cost. This, the presence of the living Christ, is the only finally satisfactory explanation for the preservation of the Christian faith through the last two thousand, turbulent years, and it is the reason why Christianity is destined finally to conquer the world. It is not because Christians are wonderful people; in fact they are routinely demonstrated to be deeply ordinary and flawed. *But they are not alone, the Risen and Reigning Lord is among them. That is the faith, and that is its certain Victory!*

A Prayer Meeting (4:23-31)

Fresh from their triumphant encounter with the Sanhedrin Peter and John report back to the disciple community, engagingly described as **their own people** (23). The depth of mutual engagement needs to be noted; quite simply these earliest Christians are already bound together in a sense of belonging which transcends anything previously experienced. Their life together in Christ is their defining identity. The apostles report the threats now hanging over them all. The reaction is instructive – **they raised their voices together in prayer** (24). Turning to God in prayer, the spontaneous cry of 'Abba, Father' is perhaps the deepest reality of the regenerate heart, not least when faced by any form of peril.[19] The great model prayer which follows (24-30) has a number of significant features.

First, we observe its *corporate base*: **they raised their voices together**. Corporate prayer gatherings have been a marked feature of the life of God's people through the ages, not least as a precursor to, and an expression of, times of Holy Spirit revival. Against this background and the widespread experience of today's 'southern' churches, the relative prayerlessness of modern Western Christianity is troubling. When we bemoan, as we commonly do, the incursions of secularism and the marginalization of Christianity, we may not need to look much further than this for one of its primary causes. 'You have not because you ask not' (James 4:2). While individual intercession is obviously a fundamental part of the church's praying in every age there is also the coming together to seek God's face, as was the case before Pentecost (1:14), and again here. It is worth recalling that the model prayer of Jesus, '*Our Father…*' cannot, in one sense, be prayed on one's own. 'From the day of Pentecost, there has not been one great spiritual awakening in any land which has not begun in a union of prayer, though only among two or three; no such onward upward movement has continued after such prayer meetings have declined.'[20] 'If my people who are called by my name will humble themselves *and pray and seek my face*, and turn from their wicked ways I will hear from heaven and will forgive their sin, and will heal their land' (2 Chron. 7:14).

Second, we note *its view of God:* **Sovereign Lord**. The God on whom they call is the Lord God Almighty, the

---

19. J.I. Packer writes, 'What is a Christian? The question can be answered in many ways, but the richest answer I know is that a Christian is one who has God for his Father'. *Knowing God* (IVP, 1973), 181.

20. A.T. Pierson, cited Arthur Wallis, *In the Day of Thy Power* (CLC, 1956), 112.

Reigning and Infinite One, who is sovereign over all; the one whom Gabriel would describe as the God for whom 'nothing is impossible' (Luke 1:37), and Paul as 'him who is able to do immeasurably more than all we ask or imagine' (Eph. 3:20). This is the God who revealed Himself to Abraham, facing the 'impossibility' of a son in Sarah's and his own great age, 'Is anything too hard for the Lord? I will return to you at this time next year and Sarah will have a son' (Gen. 18:14). It is the God who, with Jerusalem, and all Judah with it, facing imminent destruction by the encircled Babylonian army, tells Jeremiah to buy a field in the local district of Anathoth, because 'I am the Lord, the God of all mankind. Is anything too hard for me?' (Jer. 32:27). It is this conviction of God's infinite ability which is implicit in all sincere prayer, and which alone makes prayer a reasonable, meaningful and worthy activity.

For these Jerusalem believers God's almightiness is expressed in creation. He is the one who **made the heaven and the earth and the sea and everything in them** (24). Our modern appreciation of the numbing vastness of the macro-universe beyond us 'out there', and the incredible, almost unbelievable complexity and interactive subtlety of the micro-universe beneath us 'down here', surely affords even greater creation-generated ground for approaching the 'Sovereign Lord' with confidence.

Third, we identify *its use of Scripture*; the prayer is based upon, and finds its intercessory fulcrum in, divine revelation; in this case Psalm 2. In a way this simply extends the recognition of God's sovereignty to the sphere of revelation. In revelation, He is the God who **spoke by the Holy Spirit through the mouth of your servant, our father David** (25). The blending of both the human and the divine elements should be noted, under the supervising control of the Spirit, so that the product in the form of the words of Psalm 2, is the very Word of God. It is a Word which is old, having been composed a thousand years before, and yet ever new, as it finds fresh application to the situation in which the infant church finds itself. This transference is made possible because of the striking parallel between the confederation of God's enemies identified by the Psalmist: 'the raging **nations**, the plotting **peoples**, the marshalled **kings and rulers**, drawn up **against the Lord and against his Anointed One'**, and the confederation of antipathy represented by the conspiracy of **Herod, Pilate, the Gentiles** (Romans), and **the people of Israel**. The Messianic reference, 'the Anointed One', was so understood as early as the mid-first century B.C., and had been specifically cited by the Father at Jesus' baptism (Luke 3:22, cf. Ps. 2:7). The triumphant and defiant spirit of the Psalm is memorably reflected in the words immediately following those quoted: 'He who sits in the heavens laughs' (Ps. 2:4); the laughter of God! There can be few things more energizing to the believing heart than to catch the echoes of that heavenly dismissal of every assemblage of opposition, demonic or human, individual or corporate, from earth or hell. This laughter does not of course imply any diminution of the tears of God over a rebellious world, nor his utter identification with those who weep among all the nations. But there is a place too for his triumphant discounting of His enemies. He is Lord; He is ever so, world without end; blessed be His name. Importantly God's lordship is seen also in this very conspiracy of opposition to Jesus which ended in the cross (28); it was **what your power and will had decided beforehand should happen** (cf. Luke 24:26, 46; a consistent theme in the early apologetic: Acts 2:23; 3:18).

Fourth, we celebrate *its courageous petition*: It faces the threatening opposition, by asking God to **consider their threats**; but it petitions, not, as we might have expected, for the removal of the opposition through a supernatural routing of their enemies, but for the enablement to **speak your word with great boldness** (29), and for God's supernatural attestation to the truth and divine origin of their words by the stretching forth of God's hand **to heal and perform miraculous signs and wonders through the name of your holy servant Jesus** (30). The focus of the petition is salutary, and well expressed by Bock: 'The early church knew that its key priority was the mission of preaching Jesus to a needy world....Their prayer is not for individual, personal needs, as in many places in the

Psalms, but for their needs as a community in terms of their mission. They call on God to support them with spiritual provision for that mission.'[21]

The prayer also embraces a petition for divine attestation to the preaching of the gospel by **signs and wonders**. In principle this call for God's confirming of His Word is always appropriate. Further, that He may do so in a manner which is in markedly intensified terms, such as in healings where the more regular healing processes of the body are directly activated by special divine action, is again never an inappropriate petition, having an eye to the primary concern here, which is the spread of the gospel of grace. 'Signs and wonders' are never outside the possibilities of a sovereign God. Campbell Morgan's observation is unchallengeable: 'granted the truth of the first verse of the Bible, there is no difficulty with the miracles.'

There are, however, undoubted theological and pastoral issues which also bear on this issue. John Stott raises these most sensitively, and with typical fairness, in an excursus in his commentary on Acts which, although written nearly twenty years ago, continues to reward reflection. He concludes, 'If we take Scripture as our guide we will avoid opposite extremes. We will neither describe miracles as "never happening", nor as "everyday occurrences"…. When a healing miracle is claimed we will expect it to resemble those in the Gospels and the Acts and so to be the instantaneous and complete cure of an organic condition, without the use of medical or surgical means, inviting investigation and persuading even unbelievers.'[22]

We also again note the primitive nature of the reference to Jesus – **your holy servant Jesus**. Luke is reflecting, with great faithfulness, the earliest Christology. The source he is drawing upon for this report of the prayer's contents is clearly an authentic one; to say nothing of course of the inspirational possibilities of the same, sovereign Holy Spirit who had worked through David centuries before.

---

21. Bock, 202-3.
22. Stott, 100-4.

Fifth, we are moved by *its remarkable response*: it was threefold. Firstly, **the place where they were meeting was shaken**; secondly they were again **all filled with the Holy Spirit**; thirdly they **spoke the word of God boldly** (31). Their prayer was heard and answered; God powerfully and awesomely manifested His presence anew among them so that the very meeting place trembled. While we dare not ignore the uniqueness of these earliest days of the church's life, nor the importance of a special divine enablement of that initial witness, for the sake both of the waiting world, as well as the multiplied ages yet unborn (not excluding our own); nonetheless the hand of God, which was 'stretched out' in answer to this united prayer (30-31), is not shortened in our day. He is ever able to give the seal of His abounding blessing to the witness of His servants.

'Oh, that you would rend the heavens and come down, that the mountains would tremble before you…come down to make your name known! Will you not revive us again? We stand in awe of your deeds…renew them in our day, in our time make them known; in wrath remember mercy' (Isa. 64:1-2; Ps. 85:6; Hab. 3:2).

Study Questions:

1. What are the implications of the authorities' arrest of Peter and John (4:1-3)? Can you identify other New Testament texts which refer to the inevitability of opposition for faithful witnesses to Christ? What forms may that opposition assume today? Is our lack, commonly, of similarly overt persecution something we should be concerned about?

2. What are the implications of 4:12 (a) for our personal lives? (b) for Christian witness in our locality? (c) for Christian witness globally? Reflect on the fact that the Sanhedrin do not challenge the apostles' central claim that Jesus has been raised from the dead (4:2, 10, 20). What might this imply?

3. What was driving the sense of compulsion reflected by Peter in 4:20? Is this recoverable today? What encouragement do you derive from this story in general?

4. List the lessons of 4:23-31 for the prayer life of the church today. Are there things here which we can use to encourage a richer prayer life, both personally, and in our local church?

Community: Realized and Compromised (4:32–5:11)

(1) *Community Realized (4:32-37).* The next two paragraphs are separated in the received text by an unfortunate chapter division. The theme in both is the same, viz. the communal life of the new movement, presented in the form of a contrast between its positive expression in the noble person of Barnabas, and its sad contradiction in the less than noble persons of Ananias and Sapphira.

Stott sees this section from 4:1–6:7 as a series of demonic counter-attacks on the infant church, already presaged in the rising tide of persecution (4:1-22 and 5:17-40), surfacing here in the deceit practised by the hapless couple (5:1-11), and further expressed in the following chapter in the threatening, and potentially divisive distraction of the complaints over the food distribution (6:1-7).

The scene opens most positively, **all the believers were one in heart and mind** (32). This irenic communal life is captured in an engaging phrase, **much grace was upon them all** (33). It is perhaps surprising that this is the first occurrence of 'grace' in the book of Acts; however its reality is present everywhere in these early chapters. The undeserved love of God, which is what grace essentially consists in, underlies the continuing ministry of the risen Jesus with which the book opens; it is the basis of the outpouring of the 'gift' of the Holy Spirit at Pentecost. It is the theme of Peter's first sermon, since both the arrival of the kingdom of God and the exaltation of Jesus, the Son of God, are works of God's infinite mercy. Grace is expressed in Peter's offer of salvation to those responsible for the rejection and slaying of Jesus, and in the blessings of forgiveness and the Holy Spirit which His death has won for all who receive Him. Grace shines through the act of baptism whereby sinners find cleansing and a new life in the people of God. Grace alone explains the healing of the lame man outside the temple and his entry into it, and grace for the guilty is the theme of Peter's second message, a grace received through Jesus Christ. Enabling grace infuses the apostles' triumphant encounter with the Sanhedrin. And finally, the heavenly response to the communal cry of the church is nothing other than the outstretched hand of a gracious God who wills the saving of lost and needy people through the church's rekindled witness. In all of this, the loving, merciful heart of God is the driving source. All this is grace unleashed.

The continuing presence of this gracious God in the nascent church is doubly expressed. First, it is reflected in a spirit of sacrificial generosity: **no one claimed any of his possessions was his own, but they shared everything** (32). Some of those owning property were willing **from time to time** to sell up and give the money to the apostles for use within the community. As a result **there were no needy persons among them** (34). We observe that the text falls short of stating that this was either mandatory or universal. The right of private property was retained, as will be seen in interpreting 5:4, and the evidence of continuing house ownership elsewhere (e.g. 12:12). We should, however, not ignore the New Testament witness to the importance of the gift of hospitality (Rom. 12:13; Gal. 6:10; Col. 4:10; Philem. 22). Even if not sold so as to increase our giving to God's work, our homes and properties are not be hoarded as if 'only ours'. The Christian duty of hospitality is perhaps most clearly stated in 1 Peter 4:9: 'Practise hospitality ungrudgingly to one another', a reference which interestingly occurs in the context of teaching on the gifts of the Holy Spirit (cf. v. 10). Thus we can never complain of the lack of a gift of the Spirit if we have been given a home into which we can welcome people. A home is a gift from God which He wants us to invest in the interests of the kingdom of God. Jesus immortalized this ministry, 'I was a stranger and you invited me in' (Matt. 25:35). 'We must have hearts harder than iron if we are not moved by the reading of this narrative. In those days the believers gave abundantly of what was their own...love made each man's own possessions common property for those in need.'[23]

Second, the grace of God was manifested in their effective ongoing witness, as led by the apostles: **with great power the apostles continued to testify to the resurrection of the Lord Jesus** (33). The persuasiveness of that testimony continues to be a significant argument in support of its truth. As we noted above, contradictory evidence, had it existed, could hardly have been suppressed in the very location in which the resurrection, involving the total disappearance of a body, and repeated visual, even tangible encounters with the recently executed person, were claimed to have happened.

The generosity expressed in the sale of property to augment the communal purse was modelled in particular by **Joseph...from Cyprus** (36) **who sold a field he owned and brought the money and laid it at the apostles' feet** (37). Thus an important Acts figure makes his first appearance. We are given his nickname, one which he was to thoroughly earn, **Barnabas (which**, in Aramaic, **means Son of Encouragement)**.

For all the gulfs of difference which stretch between Christian churches of today and the one described here in Acts 4, effective ministry still calls for many of the identical ingredients. We too need powerful prayer meetings, waiting upon God and calling upon Him for His enabling blessing. We too need the outstretched hand of God to fill us with His Spirit, and confirm His Word in ways that embolden our witness. We too need a spirit of mutual care expressed in sacrificial financial generosity so that there are no needy persons among us. We too need powerful and persuasive preaching of the good news of a risen Jesus. We too need congregations peopled by sons and daughters of encouragement.

---

23. Calvin, 130.

Community Compromised (5:1-11). The seemingly triumphant progress of the work in Jerusalem experiences a
serious setback in this section. We need to commend the
honesty of Luke's portrayal. The outpoured blessing of
God ensured a good, even glorious course in the opening period, but within the inaugurated kingdom of God
human hearts remain a mixture of good and evil, old
habits can retain a foothold, even among the godly, and we
are reminded here, as throughout Acts, that we are dealing with the church of this age, not yet with the church
of glory. Nor can we fail to note the activity of the evil
one (5:3); even within vivid memories of Pentecostal blessing, loving fellowship, and supernaturally shaken prayer
meetings, we remain at war.

The tragic story of the sin of Ananias and Sapphira is
often paralleled to the Old Testament account of the sin
of Achan (Josh. 7). So Bruce: 'The story of Ananias is to
the Book of Acts, what the story of Achan is to the Book
of Joshua. In both narratives an act of deceit interrupts the
victorious progress of the people of God.'[24]

There is a clear flow into this account from the previous passage with its strong affirmation of the depth of
mutual commitment being experienced in the church, and
the model of the sacrificial generosity of Barnabas. We
are now introduced to two other members of the community, **a man named Ananias with his wife Sapphira, who
also sold a piece of property** (5:1). However, in contrast
to Barnabas there is in Ananias' case a conscious limit to
his wholeheartedness; he **kept back part of the money
for himself** (2). Ananias then brings the remaining portion to the apostles in a show of similar overwhelming
sacrificial generosity; but his duplicity is discerned by
Peter. An important new dimension is added to the mix at
this point, viz. the reference to **Satan** who is perceived as
having **filled** Ananias' **heart** (3). The verb used for 'filled'
here is the same as used for the filling with the Spirit in
4:31 and elsewhere.

---

24. Bruce, 110.

Satan, the devil, is a mysterious and yet deeply real spiritual agency in Scripture. Jesus was often conscious of his opposition (Luke 4:1-13, 33-35; Matt. 13:37ff;16:23; Mark 4:15; John 8:44; 12:31), and Paul regularly unmasks his malignant activity (Eph. 6:10-20; 2 Cor. 4:4; 2 Cor. 10:3-5; 11:14f; cf. also 1 Pet. 5:8f; I John 3:8; 5:19; Heb. 2:14; Rev. 12:9). Perhaps Peter's later picture of the devil as a 'roaring lion' on the prowl for someone to devour, probing for the most vulnerable animal in a herd which he can make his prey, reflects a truth learned from Ananias' sorry fall.

The nature of Ananias' sin: We need to note Peter's precise words in unmasking Ananias' duplicity. It is not the sin of failing to give all. Peter makes that clear: **after it was sold was not the money (still) at your disposal?** (4). Rather Ananias had deliberately presented his gift *as if* it was the full payment for his property, no doubt relishing the praise, and the moral and spiritual kudos, which accrued to him in the eyes of the community; but in fact all the while he had duplicitously kept back a portion of the total for his own use. In other words he had deliberately tried to deceive the apostles and the church fellowship. He had lied, to men, and worse, to God: **What made you think of doing such a thing?...You have lied...to God**. Bock notes that the real thrust of Peter's question, is: 'How *could you* do such a thing? How *could you* with deliberate, premeditated intent despise God by publicly lying to Him?'

The resultant judgment: **When Ananias heard this he fell down and died** (5). It is to be recognized that the actual cause of Ananias' death is not stated in the text. Clearly God is involved: His judgment is expressed. Yet we may not doubt that the special atmosphere of the community at that point, experiencing the awesome sense of God's living reality in the midst, would have contributed to the overwhelming sense of guilt, self-judgment and internal disintegration which Ananias experienced.

Sapphira is absent and ignorant of her husband's fate. When she returns some hours later Peter is naturally authorized to raise the issue of the sale, and the amount of the gift with her (7f). He quotes the numbers given by her husband,

and clearly provides her with a full opportunity to correct Ananias' lie, and to tell the truth of the matter. Sadly she repeats her husband's deceit. Peter then confronts her with the real moral situation. She has colluded with her husband **to test the Spirit of the Lord** (9). As Peter predicts, a similar overwhelming sense of guilt comes upon her, and she too falls under life-terminating judgment. We are not at all surprised to read **that great fear seized the whole church and all who heard about these events** (11).

Our modern sensitivities, with their easy tolerance of moral failure, are no doubt somewhat offended by this story. Peter here appears in the guise of the divine judge apparently expressing little mercy for what was, by general present-day standards both outside the church and within it, an understandable act of weakness. Such a conclusion, however, is certainly peremptory for an incident of which we are given only sketchy details. More generally, our trouble is that we are too quickly and easily detached from the biblical revelation of the nature of God, the seriousness with which He views human sin, and the solemn implications for the community and their critical mission responsibilities if open, colluded deceit such as this were permitted to go unrebuked.

The corrective to the first two of these considerations lies at the cross. To see the blessed Son of God hanging there, impaled upon the tree, and crying out in the darkness, 'My God, my God why have you forsaken me?' as, in infinite love, He is 'made sin' for us – *that* is to begin to comprehend the terrible nature of sin and evil, and God's implacable resistance to them. It is to discover 'how great a weight sin is' (Anselm). If God in dealing with human sin must endure the cross in His divine trinity, then clearly sin is no passing peccadillo but a monstrous contradiction of His nature and purpose. Viewing the cross at this point also enables us to understand, with Scripture from Genesis to Revelation, why there is, inevitably, a far more fearful judgment still to come for all who refuse to part from sin, or who willingly, even eagerly in many cases, trample underfoot the promptings of conscience, and sell themselves into sin's destructive slavery.

But the communal context of Ananias' and Sapphira's sin also needs to be noted. The open, unadulterated, mutual fellowship of that community was utterly critical to its fulfilment of the mandated task of global witness. That task would never be a possibility if this kind of public deceit was casually tolerated.

Henri Nouwen's observation with respect to sexual sin has relevance across the board: 'Often we think about sexuality as a private affair. Sexual fantasies, sexual thoughts, sexual actions are seen as belonging to the private life of a person. But the distinction between the private and the public sphere of life is a false distinction....In the Christian life the distinction between a private life (just for me!), and a public life (for the others), does not exist. For the Christian, even the most hidden fantasies, thoughts, feelings, emotions and actions are a service or a disservice to the community. I can never say, "What I think, feel or do in my private time is nobody else's business." It is everybody's business.'[25]

Thus early the church learned the lesson which Paul would later underline: 'Don't you know that you yourselves are God's temple and that God's Spirit lives in you? If anyone destroys God's temple, God will destroy him; for God's temple is sacred, and you are that temple' (1 Cor. 3:16-17). The 'you' in these verses is plural; it has reference to the temple of the corporate body, the church. 'Paul meant, not that the Spirit dwelt in each of them, true as that would be for him (6:19), but that the Spirit of God "lives in your midst."'[26] These are solemn truths for our churches, today and in every day. They are particularly so for all who by conscious sin compromise a church's fellowship, or by a contentious spirit deliberately rend its unity.

The effect on the church of these events is entirely predictable: **Great fear seized the whole church and all who heard about these events** (11). The reaction is not unlike Isaiah's centuries before, who was suddenly awakened to the awesomeness of having God actually present 'in the

---

25. Henri Nouwen, *Journey to Daybreak* (Maryknoll, 1980), 168–9.
26. Gordon D. Fee, *The First Epistle to the Corinthians* (Eerdmans, 1987), 147.

midst' as 'the Holy One of Israel' (6:1-4), and responded, 'Woe to me! I am ruined! For I am a man of unclean lips and I dwell amid a people of unclean lips; and my eyes have seen the King, the Lord Almighty.' Often, as we gather for worship, and invite God to 'show Himself', and to 'come among us', we may be thankful that He does not answer that prayer in its fullest terms, for, as Malachi pertinently asks, 'Who can endure the day of his coming? Who can stand when he appears?' (3:2). Yet, the prophet is nonetheless able to continue, 'for you who revere my name, the sun of righteousness will rise, with healing in its wings' (4:2). We may be entirely confident that had Ananias and Sapphira found the courage to publicly acknowledge their sin, and repent of it, they too would have found shelter beneath these wings of mercy.

Two final comments may be in order. First, it is perhaps notable that the word for church here in verse 11 is *ecclesia*. This is the first appearance in Acts of the commonest word for church in the New Testament. Thus 'church' makes its appearance on the occasion of this deeply sad exposure of its human weakness and ongoing vulnerability to the enticements of sin and the assaults of the devil. Since none of us are ever free of these the moral of this story is clear: to cry from the heart, 'there but for the grace of God go I', and to cast ourselves once again upon His mercy.

The second comment is offered by missiologist, David Bosch: 'We can be utterly disgusted at times with the earthiness of the Church; at other times we can be enraptured by the awareness of the divine dimension in the Church. Usually however, it is the ambivalence that strikes us: the Church as a community of people – good people, weak people, hesitant people, courageous people – on their way through the world, dust-stained but somehow strangely illuminated by a radiancy from elsewhere.'[27]

---

27. D. Bosch, *Witness to the World* (Marshall, Morgan and Scott, 1980), 93.

Study questions:

1. Consider the stewardship of these first Christians (4:32-37). What about it challenges us today?

2. Contrast the examples of Barnabas (4:36-37); and Ananias and Sapphira (5:1-11). What principles of biblical stewardship are surfaced by these positive and negative models? Are there changes which these principles are calling for in your own case?

3. What was Ananias' and Sapphira's sin? What might explain the seriousness of God's judgment on them?

Signs and Ministry (5:12-16)

Luke, perhaps in conscious relief from the last section, gives us at this point another of the series of summary paragraphs which dot his story (cf. 2:42-47; 4:32-35; 9:31). The texture is noticeably brighter. The **signs and wonders** requested in the prayer at 4:30 are being experienced through the agency of the apostles (12). The community continues to meet regularly within the temple precincts at **Solomon's Colonnade**, the site of one of Peter's earlier sermons (3:11). The text expresses the ambiguity of this period by noting the hesitancy on the part of the general populace to join the disciples, **no one else dared join them** despite their being **highly regarded by the people,** a hesitancy fuelled no doubt by the widely spread news of Ananias' and Sapphira's fates (13).

Yet, despite this, there is report of the continuing growth as **more and more men and women believed in the Lord and were added to their number** (14), an increase which would bring new challenges, as the following chapter will report (6:1-7). Miracles of healing are particularly noted, Peter being identified as the chief instrument. The final verse, stating that **crowds gathered from the towns around Jerusalem, bringing their sick and those tormented by evil spirits, and all of them were healed** (16), is closely paralleled by similar accounts of the ministry of Jesus in Luke's Gospel

(Luke 4:31-44; 5:17-26; 6:17-19). This is not accidental of course, for Acts is the story of what Jesus 'continued to do and teach' (1:1). Note should also be made of the distinction drawn between sickness and demon possession (16). They are not identical (cf. Luke 4:40-41; 6:17-18; 7:21; 13:32).

We can observe also that the healing ministry is closely linked to the evangelistic one. Crowds are gathered from the surrounding area, while more and more are believing in the Lord (Jesus). The church's prayer in 4:30 is being answered; the healings are fulfilling their role as authentications of the apostles' preaching, particularly its primary claim: that Jesus is Messiah and Lord. The geographical breadth means that the apostolic witness is spilling out beyond the confines of Jerusalem into Judea. (1:8). We can also observe the gender breadth, as **more and more men and women believed in the Lord**. The attraction of the new movement to women in particular is documented here. Judaism saw women as inappropriate candidates for discipleship. Jesus broke that mould (Luke 10:38-42; 23:27f, 49; John 4:1-30); He continues to.

Persecution Again (5:17-42)

It is some time since we heard from the Jewish authorities. Their demand for silence on the part of the apostles, and for ceasing all activity 'in the name of Jesus' had been dismissed by Peter and John during their trial, and so it should have come as no surprise to the authorities that it had been dismissed in the apostles' subsequent practice. Despite a satanic counter-attack the church continued to advance both in general spiritual power and impact, as well as in numbers of adherents. Further opposition was inevitable, and it is described in this section.

The leadership of those opposing the church is similar to that which surfaced in chapter 4, **the Sadducees,** with Caiaphas and Annas **and their associates** predictably to the fore (17). Although no doubt the contempt shown towards their orders would have fuelled this next wave of opposition, along with the apostles' vexing habit of laying the blame for Jesus' death at their door (v. 28), Luke cites

a deeper motive, **jealousy**. Quite simply the new movement of 'the Nazarenes' (as the disciples were popularly
known) was universally respected in the city and being
widely seen as a legitimate expression of Israel's ancient
faith. In other words people had modified their loyalties;
for many the Sanhedrin no longer commanded primary
allegiance. The Nazarenes, not the Sadducees, were the
flavour of the month!

The authorities had good intelligence as far as the
believers were concerned and recognized correctly that
the apostles were the key figures; so they **arrested them
and put them in prison** (18). The opposition is, however, a
much more formidable force than the Sadducees appreciate – **an angel of the Lord** frees the apostles during the
night (19). This of course not only underlines the authorities' impotence; it clarifies whose side God is on.

The angel's message is a highly significant one: **Go...
and tell the people the full message of this new life**
(20).[28] Thus heaven acts to enable the gospel to continue to
be proclaimed. The message is defined as, literally, **all the
words of this new life** (20). The gospel is not life without
words, nor words without life; it is life-imparting words.
True doctrine and life-changing salvation belong together;
'what God has joined together, let no one put asunder...'
Once again the base text of 1:8 is echoing in the background...mission, mission, mission.

The apostles waste no time in obeying the messenger's
words. So **at daybreak they entered the temple courts, as
they had been told, and began to teach the people** (21).
This sets the scene for a marvellous piece of ironic theatre,
though of course it is also so deadly serious.

The Sanhedrin, **the full assembly of the elders of Israel**
(21), gathers in its council chamber, probably at another location within the temple buildings. They are of course attired
in all their finery with the symbols of their authority to the
fore. One can almost overhear the murmur of voices...'time
to deal with this bunch of ignorant, upstart fanatics...we've

---

28. The word 'angel' literally means 'messenger' and so this may not necessarily be
a supernatural visitant, though that is certainly most likely, cf. 12:6-10; 16:25-6.

waited long enough…we'll show them who is in charge here…let's finish them here and now.' So…the chairman's call to order, the intoning of an opening prayer, a quick dispatch of the minutes, the approval of the agenda – there is only one item. Then the order to the temple police – 'Go get them, and bring them in!' **They sent to the jail for the apostles** (21). Perhaps they listened to the treasurer's report while they were waiting, or maybe just took a coffee break!

Then, suddenly, consternation! The police return with their report, 'We have been to the jail, and everything is as it was left last night…**the jail securely locked, with the guards standing at the doors**; but when they opened up… **we found no one inside**!!' Yikes! (23). While they are trying to make some sense of this, suddenly a messenger bursts in: 'You are not going to believe this…but right now, this very minute, **the men you put in jail are standing in the temple courts teaching the people!**' (25). One would have loved to have been a fly on the wall at that moment, especially a fly with access to the Sanhedrin's inner thoughts. For in that moment of truth a terrible thought must have hovered for an instant on the edge of at least some of their minds '…my goodness…perhaps it's true…perhaps these Nazarenes are right…even, maybe, just maybe…Jesus of Nazareth really was the Messiah…no, no, no…that can't be…that *mustn't* be!' The significance of the moment was certainly not lost on at least one Sanhedrin member, as we shall see (vv. 34-39).

So the apostles are '**brought**', not rearrested; the police sense the crowd's mood (26), and besides the sense of supernatural agency is very evidently in the air. The Sanhedrin, having recovered a bit of its composure and sense of authority, proceeds to address them. They remind the apostles of their earlier **strict orders not to teach in this name,** orders which have clearly not been respected; and their continuing nasty habit of **making us guilty of this man's blood** (28).

Peter is again the spokesperson; he is in no mood for backtracking or apologies. He lays it out again in a series of seven points:

1. **We must obey God rather than men!** (meaning, 'than you who claim to be leaders in Israel') (29).

2. 'Therefore we need to continue to testify to the resurrection of Jesus, because it is a fact; however unexpected and unprecedented, it has actually happened; and **we are witnesses** (32), we met with Him, touched Him, and spoke with Him after He rose again.' As has been noted previously (4:16), all this is asserted without the slightest fear of contradiction, in the public presence of the group who were better placed than any other in history, before or since, to challenge this claim if there was any evidence which would have refuted it. The Sanhedrin's silence is eloquent, as is, of course, the apostles' vocal, public, faith-claims, and their willingness to die for them.

3. The resurrection was an act of God, the God of our fathers, the **God** of Israel; *he* raised **Jesus from the dead** (30).

4. By contrast you, the Sanhedrin, **killed him**, **by hanging him on a tree** (30).[29]

5. The resurrection means that Jesus **is exalted at God's right hand**, as Lord over all, and is therefore the **Saviour** we in **Israel** have been for generations waiting to appear (31).

6. If we **repent** by God's help, we all, even including you Messiah-slayers, will receive **forgiveness of sins** from Jesus and through him (31).

7. These things we are utterly sure of; but confirmation of all this is available from **God the Holy Spirit** if we are open to **obey him** (32).

This is too much for the Sanhedrin, particularly its main Sadducean element. Despite the evidences provided by the miracle of their deliverance from prison, and the palpable evidence of the apostles' transformed lives and radiant conviction, they explode in fury, and demand the death penalty for the apostles (33).[30]

---

29. This is a clear echo of Deuteronomy 21:23: 'cursed is everyone who hangs upon a tree' – implying that the cross is being understood already as the means to salvation by virtue of its being an event in which the curse of sin was borne by Christ for us. Cf. Paul in Galatians 3:10-14.

30. The word for 'fury' carries a sense of 'sawn asunder'; they were 'split open' in rage.

Gamaliel's Counsel (34-39). The Sanhedrin's boiling anger is, however, suddenly stayed by one of their number. Asking that the court go into closed session, Gamaliel then addresses them. He was a widely respected teacher at the time (counting among his prize students one named Saul who had left his home in Tarsus to study at Gamaliel's feet).[31] A follower of the legendary Hillel, and renowned for his personal piety, Gamaliel belonged to the Pharisaic party within the mosaic of Jewish first-century religious and political life. This group were the zealots for the law and its fulfilment. In contrast to the worldly, materialistic Sadducees, the Pharisees believed in the sovereignty of God, resurrection, and spirit agencies such as angels and demons, and also in the authority of oral traditions alongside the written Scriptures.

Gamaliel calls for caution (35). He then reminds them of a series of movements over the recent period led by self-appointed leaders. When these leaders were killed their movements collapsed.

Of the two cases he particularly identifies, the first has raised some issues from the historian's viewpoint. It was led by one, **Theudas,** supported by some four hundred men (36). Josephus mentions a Theudas, but dates him too late to fit Gamaliel's reference. Josephus may have his dates wrong (it would not be the first time); however Theudas was a common name, and these were times of considerable turbulence throughout Palestine. The movement at any rate ended with the leader's death. The second case, **Judas the Galilean,** has a more specific dating at the time of the census (37). He revolted with his followers against the taxation imposed by the Romans around the census of Quirinius in A.D. 6 or so. He too was killed and this brought his movement to an end.

Gamaliel's point is a simple one; if this Nazarene movement is of merely **human origin** it will inevitably come to nothing, just as happened in these historical examples (38). **However if it is from God you will not be able to stop these men; you will only find yourselves fighting**

---

31. cf. 22:3; cf. Gal. 1:14; Phil. 3:6.

against God (39). It is an interesting, and weighty perspective, clearly reflecting something of Gamaliel's Pharisaic conviction concerning God's sovereignty. Unfortunately history has not quite borne out this principle, unless one paints with the broadest of brush-strokes. Many movements which can hardly claim divine origin or enablement have continued long after their leader's demise and their moral and spiritual limitations been thoroughly exposed. Yet, we can certainly note that if applied to the apostles, which was the specific case before the Sanhedrin, Gamaliel's test of authenticity has been broadly upheld. Today we are looking back on more than 2,000 years of Christianity, a faith which is today, as never before, a global phenomenon of approaching two billion adherents, with the genuine prospect, despite all the problems and challenges of our time, of representing, even on conservative projections, a worldwide community of something of the order of 2.6 billion by 2025.[32]

Gamaliel's wise counsel prevailed. The Sanhedrin agreed to back off from their blood lust, for the present at least. So their verdict was delivered to the apostles, along with a repeat of the demand **not to speak in the name of Jesus**, and a flogging, probably the requisite Jewish punishment of forty lashes less one (cf. 2 Cor. 11:24). This was no merely token beating. However if the Sanhedrin hoped this administration of corporal punishment would silence the apostles, or cover them with shame, they were sadly mistaken, as they appear to have regularly been about many things. The apostles left, **rejoicing because they had been counted worthy of suffering disgrace for the name of Jesus** (41). And, predictably, the mission of Jesus in the proclaiming of **the good news that Jesus is the Christ** continued unabated, both **in the temple**, and interestingly, also **from house to house (42)**.[33]

---

32. Philip Jenkins, *The Next Christendom* (Oxford University Press, 2002), chapter 5 and passim.

33. This is the first appearance in Acts of the primary verb in the Greek New Testament for preaching the gospel, *euangellizomai*.

Thus, once again the Lord enables the apostles to stand firm, even to triumph, and in the process to show great wisdom, and to even experience a joy which prevails over severe physical suffering. The story of this last section, verses 40-42, could be repeated almost endlessly from the history books of mission all over the world. While it is true that not all disciples have been able to hold firm on every occasion, the record shows that the vast majority of Christ's witnesses, no matter the violence perpetrated against them, have been ready to follow their crucified and risen Lord into the dark valley of suffering, and, in millions of cases over the centuries, to be enrolled finally, often even with great joy, in 'the noble army of martyrs', for the sake of Him who loved them and gave Himself for them.

Let one example, described by Dr David Yonggi Cho, of Seoul, suffice:

'The Communists were vicious to the pastors. One pastor's family were captured in Inchon, Korea, and the Communists put them on a "People's Trial"…They dug a large hole, putting the pastor, his wife and several of his children in. The leader then spoke, "Mister, all these years you have misled the people with the superstition of the Bible. Now if you will publicly disclaim it before these people, and repent of this misdemeanour, then you, your wife, and your children will be freed. But if you persist in your superstitions, all of your family is going to be buried alive. Make a decision!" All of his children then blurted, "Oh Daddy! Daddy! Think of us! Daddy!"'

'Think of it. If you were in his place, what would you do? I am the father of three children, and would almost feel like going to hell rather than see my children killed.

'The father was shaken. He lifted his hand and said, "Yes, yes, I'll do it. I am going to denounce…my…" But before he could finish his sentence his wife nudged him, saying, "Daddy! Say NO!" "Hush children", she said, "tonight we are going to have supper with the King of kings, the Lord of lords!" She led them in singing "In the Sweet By and By," her husband and children following, while the Communists began to bury them. Soon the children were buried, but until the soil came up to their necks they sang, and all the people watched. God did not deliver them, but almost all the people who watched this execution became Christians, many now members of my church.' [34]

Study Questions:

1. What echoes of Jesus' ministry do you detect in 5:12-16; (cf. 1:1)? What points of application should we be making to our churches today?

2. Identify the divine priorities reflected in 5:20, and apply them to your own life, and to your church's priorities and programmes. Is there need for some change of focus?

3. Which specific truths have led to 5:29-32 being described as a 'summary of apostolic Christianity'?

4. What is the 'Gamaliel counsel' (5:33-39)? Can you think of specific situations where it might be applicable today?

5. What are the lessons for us all of 5:40-42?

---

34. *The Fourth Dimension* (Plainfield, New Jersey: Logos International, 1979), 103-4.

4

The Ministry of Stephen
(Acts 6:1–8:1a)

1. A Conflict Resolved (6:1-6)

We have already noted Luke's mention of the continuing growth of the movement (4:4; 5:14). This growth, as is commonly the case, surfaced a new set of issues for the infant church. We can usefully refer again to Stott's claim to see behind the scenes the counter-attacks of Satan, through persecution in chapters 4 and 5, moral subversion in the case of Ananias and Sapphira in chapter 5, and now distraction in chapter 6. This should not surprise us. There has never been a work of God in any place or at any time which has not encountered at some point or another the malignant hand of the enemy, and this is true not least when that work has manifested evidences of advance and blessing. It is a call to constant vigilance, but not to craven fear, for the devil is ever, as Luther asserted with typical daring, 'God's devil.'

The issue is one of **complaint** (1) concerning the daily food distribution. The responsibility to care for the poor is asserted regularly in both Old and New Testaments.[1] We have marked earlier the early church's large public purse created by the generous, sacrificial giving of many of its

---

1. cf. Deut. 14:29; 24:17; 26:12; Isa. 1:17, 23; 10:2; Jer. 7:6; 22:3; Ezek. 22:7; Mal. 3:5; also I Tim. 5:9-16; James 1:27.

members (2:45; 4:32-37). This enabled significant food donations on a day-by-day basis to the poor among them, not least widows. It was now claimed that this daily distribution was being done unfairly. This was the presenting problem. Its seriousness, however, lay in its surfacing a potentially divisive interface in the community, that between **Grecian Jews** and **Hebraic Jews** (1).

This distinction was one the church had inherited from Judaism. In the centuries preceding Jesus' ministry, Greek language and culture had come to penetrate the entire civilized world. Greek by this point was the *lingua franca* of the entire eastern Mediterranean and, interestingly, would accordingly most probably have been understood and spoken by Jesus and many of His disciples. The situation was further impacted by the 'Jewish diaspora', the existence of close-knit Jewish communities within all the main centres of population around the Mediterranean. These elements all spilled over into the church, from the day of Pentecost onwards (cf. 2:5-11). Hence the church inherited representatives from both of these fairly distinct expressions of Jewishness. Specifically, the 'Hebraic Jews' (1) would have been, typically, Jews (now disciples of Jesus Christ) who were natives of Palestine and profoundly shaped by its culture and traditions; who primarily spoke a Semitic language, probably Aramaic, and in addition in many cases a smattering of Greek. 'Grecian Jews' (1) would have been, typically, disciples of Jesus drawn from the diaspora, and subject to significant Hellenistic influences; who had come to Palestine from elsewhere, and whose primary language was Greek, though who also probably had a smattering of Aramaic. The reference to **widows** is significant as apparently many widows in the dispersion came to Jerusalem to spend their final days, and obviously had in many cases become believers in Jesus.

The potential for serious ongoing division was obvious and had to be addressed. One can again applaud the honesty of Luke here. Despite his 4:32 assertion of the significant unity 'in heart and mind' of all the believers, he is not unable to present moments of tension, as here.

In a sense the issues here would simmer, in a different but related form, all the way through to the Consultation called in Jerusalem in chapter 15, when the fundamental and irreducible spiritual, cultural, and racial unity of all God's people would be clearly established.

A relevant pastoral issue here should be noted. Acts 6:1-6 describes a potential division in the church which had its roots in the distant past; the church inherited it. All who are called to ministry leadership in established congregations require to take this passage to heart. Every congregation we inherit has a history, and that history will usually go a long way in determining potential present and future points of conflict. Apart from the more obvious generational differences, there often lie long-standing family rivalries, or differences between those who have grown up within the church and those who have only recently become part of it. Another potential for difference lies with members who had previous leadership in the congregation with resulting differences of opinion and their legacy among those who were hurt, or perceived themselves to be so. Increasingly today ethnic diversity is an already well-established feature in many churches carrying similar possibilities of misunderstanding, even division. The possibilities here are multiple, even within a relatively harmonious congregation.

Patently we were not responsible for these potential dis-connects. But we will be naïve if we assume that our coming to a congregation has wiped them all away. We need accordingly to get to know a congregation's history, to spend time listening to long-standing members, and, as best we can, become informed concerning what has transpired here over the years. There is no need to view this negatively. It simply means that the congregation we have come to serve in the Lord's name, and to love with all our hearts, is a special and unique people of God. Just as in loving people individually, so in loving God's people corporately, getting to know them, their story, their successes and failures, their defeats and their victories, their strengths and their weaknesses, their fears and their dreams, is critical to a mature and fruitful relationship in the present and future.[2]

Returning to the text, we should observe that although it does not actually state that the apostles were directly involved in this daily food distribution programme they clearly saw themselves as ultimately responsible for it.[3] Their response was a salutary one; it consisted of three elements.

First, they assembled the whole community, **the Twelve gathered all the disciples together** (2). For all the specialness of the apostles' role in the witness and leadership, as well as their being the focal point of the persecution, they disavow any attempt to resolve the issue on their own, but instead bring the whole disciple community together to deal with the matter. There is no hierarchical spirit here. Jesus' lessons on leadership had not been forgotten: 'The kings of the Gentiles lord it over them… but you are not to be like that…the one who rules should be like the one who serves…I am among you as one who serves' (Luke 22:25-27). What a different Christian history we would look back on today had that become the charter of the church. There are no 'ordinary' Christians. The same God is in all, and at work through all.

Second, the apostles clarified their own ministry and its priorities. **It would not be right for us to neglect the ministry of the Word of God in order to wait on tables** (2). The verb, 'be right' (*aresko*), can also be translated 'pleasing', and hence here, 'pleasing to God'. God is pleased when we retain the priorities that He has called us to. We should

2. We may note that this passage in Acts 6, and the potential division which it highlights, has been a rich vein for critical scholarship on the Book of Acts and the New Testament generally over the last two hundred years. Thus we are presented by some scholars with the picture of a deeply divided Christian movement almost from the first, with a Hebraic-Palestinian wing and a Hellenistic-Graeco-Roman wing, championed by Peter and Paul respectively, and openly at logger-heads; and with people like Luke trying desperately to paper over the cracks in his Gospel and the Acts. Those wishing to explore this are referred to the article by Dr I. Howard Marshall in *New Testament Studies* 19: 1972-3, pp. 271-87, where he exposes the severe limitations of the case made in support of this alleged, far-reaching divide in the church, as well as the highly tenuous nature of the interpretations which have been based on it.

3. Coverdale's 1533 version of the NT refers rather delightfully to the 'dailie hand-reachinge'.

not imply from this apostolic statement that 'spiritual' ministries such as teaching the Word of God and prayer are superior, in the sense of being more important to God, than 'practical' ministries such as distributing food. *Both* activities are referred to here by the identical Greek term, *diakonia*, = 'service' (2, 4).[4] The Reformation doctrine of 'vocation' is reflected here. This affirmed the sanctity of all legitimate callings. As Luther expressed it: 'Those who are called spiritual; that is priests, bishops, and popes are neither different from other Christians nor superior to them, except that they are charged with the administration of the word of God and the sacraments, which is their work and office.'[5]

Third, the apostles proposed a way of handling the contentious issue. **Brothers, choose seven men from among you who are known to be full of the Spirit and wisdom… turn this responsibility over to them** (3). We note that the selection is delegated to the whole body. Again there is a renunciation of any appeal to special privilege; the opening word **brothers** says it all. This is family, not hierarchy. Not surprisingly this action with its implicit affirmation on the capacity and dignity of the whole body is warmly affirmed, **this proposal pleased the whole group** (5). The number seven corresponds to the tradition in Judaism of appointing a board of seven to deal with *ad hoc* tasks.

Several further points are to be noted:

1. *The apostles' special responsibilities*: **We will give our attention to prayer and the ministry of the Word** (4). These surely remain the staples of apostolically authorized ministry in every day. We note that prayer is added to the teaching of the Word mentioned in verse 2. Prayer and the

---

4. cf. Leon Morris, 'It is significant that the characteristic word for the work of Christian ministry in the NT is *diakonia*. The basic idea in this term is the service of the table waiter, but it came to be used very generally of service of a lowly kind…(The Church) took a term in common use for the most ordinary kind of service and made that its characteristic word for ministering.' *Ministers of God* (IVP, 1964), 34-5.

5. Martin Luther, *Weimarer Ausgabe* (1883–), vol. 44, 130. William Perkins puts it even more sharply: 'The action of the shepherd in keeping sheep is as good a work of God as is the action of the judge in giving sentence, or of a magistrate in ruling, or a minister in preaching.' *The Work of William Perkins*, Courtney Library of Christian Classics, ed. Ian Breward (Sutton Courtney Press, 1970), 458.

Word are inseparable. The prayer ministry is simply non-negotiable. It is this which allows God to preside over a church. When He is waited upon, sought and depended upon, He will speak His Word with power, and the congregation will be spiritually prepared to hear and respond to it.

Samuel Chadwick's words are as relevant today as when he first penned them: 'Satan dreads nothing but prayer. His one concern is to keep the saints from praying. He fears nothing from prayerless studies, prayerless work, prayerless religion. He laughs at our toil, he mocks our wisdom, but he trembles when we pray.' One is reminded of the reported comment of a South Korean leader who was recently taken on a tour of some 'successful' mega-churches in North America, but was surprised to discover in the course of it how little prayer featured in these congregations, either in the multiplicity of ministries being undertaken, or in the services of public worship. When his hosts asked him at the conclusion for his impression he apparently responded: 'I am astonished at how much you folks are able to do without God!'

2. *The qualifications of the 'seven'*: They are to be **known to be full of the Spirit and wisdom**. Being people **of the Spirit** is the first and, arguably, the primary quality. We recall that the task in hand is to supervise and probably participate in distributing food to needy people. But known spiritual quality is critical to its pursuance. Again we observe the refusal to separate 'spiritual' ministry from 'practical' ministry. Every task undertaken in a church is a 'spiritual' ministry and calls for heart dedication to the Lord, and lives wholeheartedly open to His Spirit. We can also note that this 'spiritual' characteristic is to be recognized by others; being 'filled with the Spirit', as we saw earlier, is essentially a quality of life which others recognize, rather than one which people may claim for themselves.

Wisdom was likewise required. Zeal without knowledge can be a dangerous combination. Spiritual commitment needed to be blended with mature people-skills, an ability to sensitively handle a situation where delicate and deep human susceptibilities were involved. The meaning here may be illustrated in Stephen's reference to Joseph at 7:10: 'He gave Joseph wisdom and enabled him to gain the goodwill of Pharaoh King of Egypt.' We can also note a not dissimilar combination of qualities in the appointment of Joshua (Num. 27:16-20).

Their being 'of good reputation' [6] is worth underlining. Scripture at one point even calls for Christian leaders to have earned a warm commendation from those right outside the community of faith, cf. 'a good reputation with outsiders' (1 Tim. 3:7). During my career I spent ten years on a seminary faculty which involved regularly sharing the demanding task of assessing candidates for ordination. In the spirit of this text we customarily required that at least one of the references supplied should be from a non-Christian employer, or their equivalent, and generally afforded these references considerable weight.

3. *The nature of their appointment*: Was this action in verses 5-6 the establishing of a distinct and continuing 'office' of deacon? There exists a long tradition across the centuries that this was the case; however the evidence appears less than convincing. The term used for their service here employs, as we noted above, the basic New Testament word for service, *diakonia* (1). However this term is used also for the 'ministry' = 'service' of the Word of God in verse 4; and in very many other places in the New Testament it is used with no direct association with an order of ministry (e.g. Luke 4:39; John 12:26; 2 Cor. 11:8). The 'seven' listed in 6:5 are nowhere actually referred to as 'deacons' (cf. 21:8, where it might have been expected if an 'order' had already been established). Again, when a food distribution issue resurfaces in 11:30 the matter is entrusted, not to 'the deacons', but to 'the elders'. Further the list of qualities drawn up for the seven in 6:5 is not replicated in the list of the qualities to be sought in deacons in 1 Timothy 3:8f; the Acts list is notably more demanding. What we *can* assert is that clearly the *kind of function* addressed by the seven here, if not necessarily intended

---

6. Bock, 260, his rendering of 'known to be…'

to be present in every congregation, was nonetheless to prove a recurring one. It is therefore unsurprising that we do meet an official deacon office later in the New Testament (Phil. 1:1; 1 Tim. 3:3-13, which probably includes deaconesses, v. 11).

4. *The ethnic origin of the names of the seven*: They are all Greek, and therefore primarily drawn from the Hellenistic element in the church, the quarter from which the complaint had arisen. It is true that occasionally 'Greek names were used by Palestinian Jews but, apart from Philip, these are unlikely names for Palestinians.'[7] This is extremely meaningful. Those who had a sense of being wronged were the ones primarily entrusted with putting matters right. The marginalized were trusted with leadership power. There is a deeply important point made here with relevance for all congregations, especially those made up, as was the Jerusalem church and so many of our congregations today (and tomorrow), from diverse and relatively distinct sub-cultures. It is when people are trusted with power, and not till then, that they are truly included. This author recalls the appointment to a significant leadership role in our congregation in Vancouver, of a representative of a growing ethnic minority within our social mosaic. From the Sunday of his appointment the representatives of that minority present in worship increased exponentially; they had been trusted with power: they now truly knew they were welcome! This has application right across the board: to women, youth, seniors, new attendees, the physically challenged, different ethnic groups, and whatever corresponds to these in our specific situation. How all this works out is for each congregation to address within their own context and traditions, but the principle is unassailable and corresponds to the message of the cross: there are no second-best disciples of Jesus. It is beautifully underwritten here in Acts 6.

5. *The act of ordination*: The men chosen are 'ordained' in the sense of having hands laid on them with prayer. This will be repeated later in Acts for another solemn moment

---

7. Marshall, 127.

of dedication (13:3). It has its roots in the Old Testament, for example in Moses setting Joshua apart as his successor (Deut. 34:9). 'The rite indicated a conferring of authority, and the accompanying prayer was for the power of the Spirit to fill the recipients.' [8]

6. *The role of effective structure*: We observe how a structural modification enabled the avoidance of a potentially serious division, and permitted continuing advance, as the following verse indicates. Structural propriety can never serve as a substitute for spiritual power and grace, but when it facilitates the addressing of a potential conflict, and the release of new and appropriate ministry, as it clearly did here, it is certainly not to be regarded lightly.

Overall, the community faced its relational crisis with spiritual wisdom, humility and sensitivity to both of the parties involved. It thus allowed both sub-communities to feel affirmed, and to recover their mutual focus on the great things which united them in Christ and His gospel mission (v. 7), rather than on the things which differentiated them. But further, by uniting the Grecian and Hebraic wings of the church they were able to make a prophetic statement to the wider Jewish culture of the unique significance of Jesus Christ, and the way in which He offered a new quality of mutual relationships which transcended all distinctions and separations.

This is a prophetic statement which we are most surely called upon to make in our congregations today, with greater urgency than ever before in human history, for we confess the faith and bear our witness to it in a world where unprecedented diversity, with its threatening potential for social conflict, is a marked and deepening reality. Today it is in the church, among those who own Jesus Christ as Lord of all, more than in any other sub-community in the surrounding society, that there ought to be, and by His grace can be, the richest and deepest experience of authentic human community. Jesus' words to the disciples, and later to the Father, are timeless in this context: 'By this shall all people know that you are my disciples, if you love

---

8. Marshall, 127.

one another…My prayer is…that they may be one as we are one…may they be brought to complete unity to let the world know that you sent me, and have loved them even as you have loved me' (John 13:34-35; 17:20, 22-23).

2. Continuing Growth (6:7)

Luke shares another of his summary reflections at this point. The setting, however, is significant. Effectively dealing with a troubling threat to the church's unity leads immediately to further growth.

Luke uses three verbs to indicate the progress: **the word of God 'spreading', the number of the disciples 'increasing'**, and the numerous **priests 'obeying'**. The last-named group would have been drawn from the large body of part-time, auxiliary temple priests in and around Jerusalem, estimated along with Levites at 18,000. They apparently served by strict rota, for two weeks every year. The incursion of a large number of them into the church was, in its way, a not insignificant indication that the case the apostles had made, and continued to make, for the Messiahship of Jesus, not least His bodily resurrection, had largely won the day; the 'other side', who would have had access to contradictory evidence, were that available, were no longer uniformly sceptical, but were now being persuaded, in significant numbers, of the validity of the Christian claim.

The reference to their response as 'obedience' touches an abiding feature of saving faith. Christianity is no doubt much more than obedience to the God who has met us in Jesus Christ. But it is not less than that. It is, in the end, confessing that Christ is Lord (of all), and hence by implication Lord of our personal lives in all meaningful senses; as Hebrews 5:9 notes, Christ is 'the source of eternal salvation for all who obey him'. The call of the gospel is certainly a wooing invitation to cast ourselves upon the mercy of God revealed for all time in the indescribable gift of Jesus and His dying love at Calvary. But it is simultaneously also a *summons* to believe; it is the demand of our Lord and Maker to recognize His claim upon our lives. Negatively it is a call to cease from the dishonour we do, and have done, to the triune God by our many breaches of His holy law and the idolatrous worship we have offered to a variety of no-gods through our days. Positively it is the insistence that we repent of our disobedience and live henceforth, by His grace, for His glory. Robert Reymond writes appropriately in this context of 'the confrontational character of the gospel' [9] (cf. 10:36; Rom. 10:9; 2 Thess. 1:8; John 20:28; Luke 6:46).

3. Stephen's Impact and Arrest (6:8-15)

In terms of Luke's 1:8 perspective, the story of the church has reached a critical point of transition. 'Jerusalem' has, in broad terms, been evangelized (2:1–6:7), but a whole world awaits beyond the borders of the holy city and its old covenant populace. Christianity as a global faith, proclaiming a global God and a global saviour and salvation, has still to clearly appear.

Before this expansion beyond Jerusalem could effectively occur two developments were required. The first was *theological*. There was needed a new understanding of the gospel as a message of truly global significance, so that what was given in promise in the Old Testament was understood as having reached fulfilment in the New Testament. Put another way, there was needed a full realization of the global implications of the exaltation of Jesus Christ to the 'right hand of God'.

The apostles had to this point drawn upon Messianic prophecies, such as Psalm 110:1 (2:34), which certainly saw Jesus as the exalted Lord, the Prince at God's right hand (5:31). He was moreover the Servant of the Lord (Isa. 52:13–53:10; cf. 3:26; 4:27; 4:30), the vicarious sufferer, and hence the Saviour (5:31), the capstone to God's purpose of salvation (4:10), a salvation offered to all who were ready to repent and believe in Him, signalled and sealed by baptism in his name (2:38). Hence the larger global dimensions were not entirely missing, for the promise of new life in the Spirit through Him was also 'to all who are afar off' (2:39), and as the fulfiller of the ancient prom-

---

9. Robert L. Reymond, *Paul: Missionary Theologian* (Christian Focus, 2000), 85f.

ise to Abraham he would bring blessing to 'all peoples on earth' (3:25). Yet these wider geographical horizons may have been largely viewed in terms of the diaspora of Israel, rather than the far-flung Gentile nations, or if reaching beyond that, in terms simply of proselyte conversion to Judaism (cf. Matt. 23:15). The theological categories which would face the church with the reality of an entire 'second people of God' from among the Gentiles, and hence with the all-inclusive worldwide implications of Jesus and His ministry, were still dormant in the Old Testament. In particular they lay latent in the Son of Man image of Daniel chapter seven, of the one who will return in glory at the end of history to receive the obeisance and worship from 'all peoples, nations and people of every language' (Dan. 7:14). This clearly universal category had been already embraced by Jesus as His favoured self-designation (Luke 6:5, etc.) but that connection had still to resurface in its fullest terms in the apostles' minds.[10]

The second was *geographical*. There was also required a centrifugal force to push the witnessing church beyond its Jerusalem birthplace, and out into the maelstrom of Gentile life and culture beyond the boundaries of Palestine.

Both of these critical developments were to be contributed by Stephen; the *theological* by his insightful instruction, culminating in his dying vision of the glorified Lord as Son of Man (7:55-56); the *geographical* by his inadvertent instigation, through his ministry and death, of a violent persecution of the church in Jerusalem which would scatter it not only throughout Palestine, and beyond Judea into Samaria (8:1), but eventually also to Antioch and authentic Gentile territory (11:19-21), with startling results.

Thus, almost single-handedly, or as a single instrument in the hands of the Holy Spirit, Stephen laid the highway which was to lead Christianity out of the dangerous, potentially stifling mental and geographical confinement of a mono-ethnic, mono-cultural enclosure in Jerusalem,

---

10. See the important essay, 'The Son of Man' by C.D.F. Moule, *The Origin of Christology* (CUP, 1977), 11–22.

to become what it was always intended to be in the mind of God, a faith for all peoples, and all places, and all times. Further, in the process of opening this road, Stephen touched the heart and conscience of the man who was claimed by Christ through Stephen's self-sacrifice, and who was destined, more than any other, to give leadership to this world-embracing development, Paul the apostle to the Gentiles.

In this sense, Stephen is a classic illustration of how the assessment of a life can never be limited to matters of mere duration, or immediate historical impression. This is surely one of the reasons why we are bidden to 'judge nothing before the appointed time, before the Lord comes' (1 Cor. 4:5). Only the entire context of history, and by implication the final context of eternity, can provide the perspective for the true evaluation of any life. All our present estimates of lives and ministries are accordingly provisional at best. It is not accidental in this context that the saying of Jesus which is most often repeated in the gospels is, 'the first shall be last, and the last first' (Luke 13:30; Matt. 19:30; Mark 10:31). In other words, we are all going to get it wrong. In grasping this lies our peace.

Stephen first appears in the text here as pre-eminently a 'man of the Spirit' (6:3, 5, 10); an instrument prepared and anointed by God; an anointing which touches both his deeds – great wonders and miraculous signs (8); and his words – they could not stand up against the wisdom and the Spirit by whom he spoke (10). This testimony marks the first time in the narrative that someone other than an apostle is spoken of in such terms.

This triumphant ministry report is shadowed, however, by the appearance of opposition (9). The Synagogue of the Freedmen was a chain of Jewish synagogues running across the Mediterranean world. They had their origin historically in Pompey's decision in 63 B.C. to imprison and enslave many Jews. Their liberated descendants came together to form these synagogues in expression of thanksgiving for their freedom. Insofar as a distinction between a Hebraic and a Hellenistic wing within first-century Judaism is defensible, the 'Freedmen' would have been aligned with the latter. Clearly there were such Judaistic disciples in Jerusalem,[11] and traces have been found of similar synagogues in North Africa, Cyrene, Alexandria and Egypt, as well as in Tarsus in the eastern Mediterranean, and the Roman province of Asia. The link to Tarsus raises the fascinating possibility that Paul belonged to this group in his native Tarsus, and that he was among those bested in argument by Stephen in Jerusalem, a fact which, if true, might go some way to explain Paul's violent antipathy to the Christian movement.

Stephen, at any rate, with the help of the Spirit, as promised by Jesus – 'I will give you words that none of your adversaries will be able to resist or contradict' (Luke 21:15; 12:11-12) – comprehensively defeats the Freedmen in public debate; they could not stand up against his wisdom or the Spirit by whom he spoke (10). Few experiences are so destabilizing to one's self-worth and identity, or so evocative of a longing for revenge, than to be comprehensively routed in public dialogue. We faced a tragic case in my last pastorate where exactly this experience led directly to a suicide.

Having been thus exposed and humiliated in discussion, these opponents in Jerusalem resort, such is fallen human nature, to less worthy channels for their revenge. They suborn false witnesses, secretly persuading some men to accuse Stephen of propagating blasphemous views; specifically of speaking **words against Moses and God** (11). Their plot succeeds, the general populace of the city, and more importantly their leaders, are stirred up (12); and so Stephen finds himself forthwith unceremoniously seized and brought before the Sanhedrin. The witnesses appear before the court, alleging: **This fellow never stops speaking against this holy place** (the temple) **and against the law** (13). They additionally bring a charge which clearly echoes and draws upon the charge presented against Jesus, that Stephen has claimed that Jesus will **destroy the temple, and change the customs Moses handed down to us** (14; cf. Mark 14:58: John 2:19; Matt. 26:61; Mark 15:29).

---

11. The Greek construction in v. 9 suggests that there were two in the city.

The essential charge is one of blasphemy – an exceedingly serious offence in that, and other such, fanatically religious societies. Deuteronomy 13:1-11 had spelled out in chilling terms the fate of anyone 'even your own son or daughter, or the wife you love, or your closest friend, who secretly entices you saying, 'Let us go and worship other gods'...Show him no pity. Do not spare him or shield him. You must certainly put him to death...stone him to death.' Stephen is also accused, as we noted, of having taught subversion of the law of Moses, and of the destruction of the temple – both, allegedly, at the instigation of Jesus. The parallels to Jesus' arraignment are clear, though interestingly Luke does not include these charges in detail in his account of Jesus' trial. This is the first of a series of striking parallels to Jesus in this section.

It is clear from this account that there were features of Stephen's teaching which triggered a hostile reaction among the Jewish faithful, an antipathy which the apostles' teaching had apparently not done to the same degree, although of course we need to constantly retain the fact that the accounts of their teaching in the previous chapters are rarely given in full. We should not underestimate either the emotional reaction generated by being trounced by Stephen in the synagogue debates. At the very least, however, these opponents had found material in Stephen's teaching which they were able to twist into a perceived disrespect for, and even dismissal of, the law and the temple. Further the identification of Jesus as a source of their anger is also important, for Jesus had certainly made reference to the temple being destroyed (John 2:19-22), unambiguously so in his eschatological discourse (Luke 21:5-6, 20-24; 14:58; 15:29).[12]

---

12. cf. B. Gartner: 'We have behind the texts at our disposal a historical nucleus in which Jesus, criticizing the temple and teaching its replacement, referred to his own person. He represented the new dimension of fellowship with God which was to outdistance the old cultus. In its negative aspect this meant a sharp criticism of the actual temple and its worship; in its positive aspect, it meant a new fellowship with God, centred on himself and replacing the temple.' Marshall observes, 'If this line of thought was grasped by Stephen, it is easy to see how it could...provide an obvious basis for a charge of attacking the temple' (Marshall, 130).

Further, with respect to the law, Jesus in the Sermon on the Mount explicitly contrasts His teaching with that of the 'teachers of the law' (Matt. 7:28), and later in the Sermon, recorded in Matthew 5:31-32, quotes Moses' teaching on divorce in Deuteronomy 24:1-4 and opposes it with His own teaching. In general, to cite Witherington, 'Jesus seems to assume an authority over the Torah that no Pharisee or OT prophet assumed – the authority to set it aside.' [13] If Stephen was drawing upon these elements in Jesus' teaching it is not difficult to understand why an unscrupulous opponent could claim that he was 'speaking against' Moses, the temple and God.

Dramatically, as Stephen faces his accusers his very face is transfigured like the face of an angel (15). It is hardly beside the point that the only other occasion of a 'radiant face' on their religious landscape was that of their hero, Moses, after his receipt of the law on Sinai (Exod. 34:29-35; cf. Luke 9:29). This unearthly countenance is nothing less than a divine vindication of Stephen. So heaven stoops to affirm one who will shortly pass into that divine society. God does not forsake His servant as he approaches 'the valley of the shadow of death'.

We can note more generally, as Luke's account gathers momentum, the clear escalation of the opposition to the Christian faith within the ranks of Judaism. A warning in chapter four, moves on to further solemn warnings and a flogging in chapter five, then here in chapter six, a general rising of the populace against the Christians, which will climax in Stephen's martyrdom.

Study Questions:

1. The roots of the division which threatened the unity of the church in 6:1-6 were cultural and geographical. In our multi-cultural societies how can we guard against these kinds of tensions arising in the church?

---

13. B. Witherington III, *Christology of Jesus* (Fortress, 1990), 65.

2. What lessons about Christian ministry can we learn from verses 1-6?

3. Identify the qualities sought in the 'seven' (3). Comment on their relevance to ministry leadership today.

4. Note the way the church overcame the potential division (6:1-6): which continuing principles for preserving congregational unity do these verses illustrate?

5. In 6:7 Luke shares an overview of the church at this point, perhaps three years after Pentecost. What were its strong positive qualities? What were its limitations?

6. Consider Stephen as we meet him in 6:5-15. What are the lessons of his life to this point?

4. Stephen's Defence before the Sanhedrin (7:1-53)

Having been thus accused, Stephen faces the question put by the Sanhedrin chairperson, Caiaphas: **Are these charges true?** (1). So Stephen presents his defence, in the course of which he will attempt to refute the charges, and also clarify and reaffirm his commitment to Jesus as the long-promised Messiah. This second element, his pointing to Jesus, has to be somewhat inferred since Stephen was cut off in mid-course by the eruption of murderous rage which ended his life. It is no doubt an indication of Luke's faithfulness to his source(s), and of the source(s) itself, that we lack that climactic section of his speech; however it does, unfortunately, leave us arguing from silence to some degree. This is only one of a number of questions which arise at this point, which we can only note in general. The literature dealing with Stephen's apology is notably vast.

Another introductory issue which has puzzled expositors over the ages is why this speech is reported at such length. Of the nineteen speeches scattered through the book of Acts this is clearly the longest, by some way. Its fifty-two verses contrast, for example, with the twenty-two of Peter's Pentecost sermon, or the nine verses, both of Paul's Areopagus address, and of Peter's message in the home of Cornelius.

The length may have been influenced by Luke's unwillingness to tamper with his source(s). That would necessarily have been some person, or persons, who were members of the Sanhedrin. Nicodemus comes to mind as a possible candidate, and since he was referred to by Jesus as 'the teacher of Israel' (John 3:10; the definite article here is supported by the Greek text), we may justifiably assume that he would retain a very full and reliable memory of both the historical allusions and theological nuances of Stephen's exposition. But Paul (then known as Saul) may also have been a member of the Sanhedrin, and as Luke's later companion and confidant would have been an obvious primary human source. In this of course we dare not eliminate or minimize the possibilities inherent in the Holy Spirit's inspiration.[14]

As far as the source(s) are concerned views have ranged all the way from those who believe that Luke faithfully transmits what Stephen said to the Sanhedrin, to those who believe that Luke created the entire discourse. In support of the former view we can cite Bock, 'There is nothing here that would be unlikely for someone such as Stephen to say.' [15] Marshall adds, 'The speech as recorded in Acts fits admirably into what we know about Stephen from the surrounding narrative.' [16]

Respect for Stephen may also have figured in accounting for the length and, as an extension of that, Luke's recognition of Stephen's importance for the global spread of the gospel. As we noted above we are here at a critical watershed as far as the commission of 1:8, and the remaining story of Acts is concerned, and Stephen and his convictions are clearly pivotal in ushering in the new chapter which immediately follows.

---

14. On Paul's possibly having been a Sanhedrin member, see 26:10
15. Bock, 278.
16. Marshall, 133.

A further more general perspective which might also explain the fullness of the account is to recognize its role in charting a road from Old Testament promise to New Testament fulfilment. Our 'reading' of Acts and the history of early Christianity today is deeply affected by the overwhelming dominance of the Gentile wing of the church which has obtained ever since the destruction of Jerusalem in A.D. 70. It is accordingly difficult for us to recover the crisis represented by the issue of Jew-Gentile relationships which dominated the horizon in Luke's lifetime. Even though it is likely that Jewish Christianity was something of a spent force by the time Luke was writing, Luke, himself a Gentile, nonetheless conveys a remarkable understanding of, and sympathy for, the church's significant debt to the people of the old covenant.

David Bosch expresses it appropriately: 'It was Luke, the Gentile, who saw the need for rooting the Christian church in Israel. He did this in a bold way: Jesus was first and foremost the Messiah of Israel and precisely for this reason also the Saviour of the Gentiles....There is for Luke, no break in the history of salvation. The church may therefore never in a spirit of triumphalism arrogate the gospel to itself and in the process turn its back on the people of the old covenant.' [17]

Seen from this perspective Stephen's speech represents for Luke a critical watershed, which affirms the blessings of God's relationship to Israel, but, alert to the inherent limitations of that relationship, points forward to a new work of God in Jesus Christ which re-forms the Old Testament faith so as to make it accessible to the Gentile nations, who were always the destined object, along with Israel, of the saving purpose of God.

The form used by Stephen, a historical recital, has precedent in the Old Testament, in Psalms 78, 105 and 106. It was a common method in rabbinic instruction; Paul takes a similar course in the synagogue in Pisidian Antioch (13:13-41); and Jesus, to some degree, in the synagogue in Capernaum (Luke 4:16-27). It certainly served Stephen

---

17. David J. Bosch, *Transforming Mission* (Orbis, 1991), 115.

well as showing him to be innocent of any radical rejection of Judaism.

Following other commentators, we can note two primary themes: (1) Throughout Israel's history God has raised up leaders, such as Joseph (7:9-16), and Moses (17-44), to deliver His people, but they were consistently rejected. (2) God gave the tabernacle and the temple (39-43), but people mistakenly believed God actually resided in the temple (44-50).

Accordingly: (1) Stephen is not against the law and the temple; both are from God. Rather is he confronting Israel's regular unfaithfulness to both, expressed in disobedience and idolatry. (2) God Himself declared that He transcended both the tabernacle (which moved from place to place), and the temple. Therefore the idea of a new place to worship God, in the Messiah Jesus, is in keeping with the Old Testament revelation.

Thus Stephen accomplishes three things by his defence: (1) The charges do not stand up; he is innocent. (2) The nation is culpable for having repeated its history by now rejecting the Messiah He has sent them. (3) This failure opens the way for the church to turn to the Gentiles.

Various divisions are offered by the commentators. We will follow a five-part division: 1. Abraham (2-8); 2. Joseph (9-16); 3. Moses (17-44); 4. David and Solomon (45-50); 5. Application/accusation...Jesus Christ (cut short, 51-53).

1. Abraham (2-8)
Stephen's opening words, **Brothers and fathers, listen to me! The God of glory appeared to our father Abraham,** showed appropriate respect for his audience and, in the reference to God, an ascription hardly compatible with blasphemy! His reference to God as 'the God of glory' also in an important manner establishes the doxological perspective of Stephen's defence, and of his faith. Thus the closing moments of Stephen's testimony will embody the identical perspective, 'he saw the glory of God..."I see heaven open...and the Son of Man standing at the right hand of God"' (55).

These doxological brackets establish Stephen's theological and personal vision. The Sanhedrin had succumbed to a form of religion in which humanity, in the shape of revered traditions, human acts of piety, ethnic superiority, and the manipulation of political and ecclesiastical power, had become the dominating centre; the wood had become hidden by the trees. Stephen sees beyond all that to the glory and the service of the living God, the infinite 'I AM' who is forever present in the midst, the glorious and ever-blessed One, the God not just of His covenanted people Israel, but of the entire cosmos and all peoples.

Viewing Abraham as the starting point of Israel's special relationship with God, **the God of glory appeared to our father Abraham** (2), was also certainly no innovation, though it is probably significant that Stephen places the initial revelation at Ur, in pagan Mesopotamia (2).[18]

After the death of his father, God sent him to this land (4). The place and time of Terah's death differs from Genesis 11:32 and 12:4, but reflects other Jewish writers. 'It is probable that Stephen is following a well-known tradition that his audience knows.'[19] However any apparent difficulty here is eliminated if God in fact called Abraham on two occasions, first in Ur, and then again in Haran after his father Terah died. There is clear biblical precedent in the case of Paul (Acts 9:15 and 13:2). Isaiah may well be a similar case of a two-stage calling if we accept that his early prophetic work, reflecting an initial call, is recorded in the opening five chapters of Isaiah, dated as '*during* the reign of Uzziah...' (1:1); and that at the time of Uzziah's death he received a second call in the Jerusalem temple, as memorably recounted in 6:1-13. Christian biography would furnish many other examples.

In referring to God's promise of the land of Canaan to Abraham and his successors, to **possess** (5), Stephen notes the later Egyptian 'exile' and return to **worship me in 'this**

---

18. Although Genesis 11:31–12:1 sets the initial command in Haran rather than Ur there was Judaistic tradition which placed it there (Gen. 12:1, which can be rendered 'The Lord *had said*...': cf. Josh. 24:3; Neh. 9:7.

19. Bock, 284; see his discussion.

place' (7), which probably means 'this land'. Egypt falls under judgment for mistreating God's chosen people (7). All this teaching carries no hint of blasphemy! Nor does the recognition of the divine command to Abraham to institute the **covenant** ceremony **of circumcision,** and its transmission to his successors (8), contain any suggestion of a rejection of Israel. It is possible that Stephen is using this first part of his apology to simply establish the false-hood of the blasphemy charge.

2. Joseph (9-16)
This brings Stephen to **the twelve patriarchs,** and to Joseph in particular, and introduces a principal element of his critique of Israel, and of the Sanhedrin in particu-lar. Though **God was with him** (9) and had sent him, Joseph was, in jealousy, rejected by his brothers, and **sold as a slave into Egypt**. Thus God's chosen messenger was cast out by God's people. Despite this, God's purpose pre-vailed and culminated in the entire family being rescued and securely established in Egypt, before returning even-tually to Canaan. The extended details of the Joseph story appear somewhat extrinsic to Stephen's primary thrust; however they build towards the introduction of the major figure of Moses. The detail afforded here may also in part reflect Stephen's own reflection on the massive vindication of the redeeming providence of God in the Joseph story. Here, as vividly as any story could portray it, the one who was rejected truly became the Saviour of the rejecters, and hence afforded a lucid anticipation of the earlier words of Peter, 'This man was handed over to you by God's set purpose and foreknowledge, and you...put him to death by nailing him to the cross. But God raised him from the dead....Therefore let all Israel be assured of this: God has made this Jesus, whom you crucified, both Lord and Christ' (2:23, 36).[20]

---

20. Diversities exist at two further points of detail, in v.14 relating to the number who went into Egypt, and in v.16 in relation to the exact details of who was buried and where. A variety of Jewish traditions exist for both of these; and in any event Stephen may well have been telescoping the story. For discussion see Bock, 288-9.

3. Moses (17-43)

This is the longest section. It retells the Moses story in faithful detail, beginning with his being **born** in Egypt during the time of oppression (18-21), his education within Pharaoh's court **in all the wisdom of the Egyptians** (22), his sense of identity with the Israelites (23a), his dawning sense of God's call to him to liberate his people (25), and the abysmal failure of his early attempt to express it (23b-29). Again the note is struck of a leader sent by God being rejected by those he was sent to lead; the reconciler, **why do you want to hurt each other?** is denied his role – **Who made you ruler and judge over us?** (26-27).

At the end of another forty-year span God takes the initiative and summons Moses at the **burning bush** (30-34; Exod. 3:1-10), **holy ground** (Exod. 3:5) in spite of its location in the 'foreign' Mt Sinai desert. **So, this same Moses whom they had rejected with the words, 'Who made you ruler and judge?' was sent to be their ruler and deliverer by God himself** (35).[21]

Next comes the miracle-strewn 'contest' with Pharaoh, the mighty deliverance at the Red Sea, and the forty years of desert wandering during which Moses received the revelation of the law, impressively referred to as **living words to pass on to us** (38). No one could accuse Stephen of 'speaking blasphemy against Moses' (6:11), or of 'speaking against the law' (6:13), from these expressions of profoundest respect for both the law and its human mediator.

Stephen here inserts the great Mosaic Messianic prophecy of Deuteronomy 18:15 (cf. 3:22-23), **This is the Moses who told the Israelites, 'God will send you a prophet like me from your own people'**. By implication Stephen's commitment to Jesus is justified here, and in the same breath absolved from any stain of blasphemy; Jesus is 'the one prophesied by Moses', and hence, at the very least, Moses' equal.

---

21. The parallels to Jesus are multiple here. Barrett (1994), 362-3 identifies six. cf. Bock, 295.

Again the inveterate tendency to reject God's messenger arises – the people **refused to obey him** (39), instead, indulging in the worst form of pagan idolatry by worshipping **an idol in the form of a calf** (39-41). This drew forth divine judgment as **God turned away and gave them over to the worship of the heavenly bodies** (42), a sequence of idolatry and judgment which was tragically re-enacted, as Amos had prophesied, in the Babylonian exile some seven hundred years later (42b-43; Amos 5:25-27). Barrett's comment is to the point: 'Never had a people been so privileged, or a people who had so completely negated their vocation.'[22]

4. David and Solomon (44-50)

Stephen's final section steps back into the period of the settlement under Joshua and the establishing of the monarchy under David and Solomon, which had been overstepped by the reference to the exile (43). Here he chooses the topic of sacred worship places. This is the second theme of his address as we noted above. The first, the ever-repeated rejection of God-given leaders, he has amply demonstrated, and will return to in his conclusion. The second is the transcendence of God, and its implication for attitudes to worship places.

During Israel's history God had given **the tabernacle of the Testimony** (44) as a worship centre (44-45; Exod. 25–27; 36–38). It was a portable shrine, moving around with the tribes as they travelled. It gave place eventually to the temple of Solomon (45b–47), built **as a dwelling place for the God of Jacob** (46); and by implication, on the same Jerusalem site, the Second Temple where they are actually gathered for this trial. However, Stephen warns, care is needed in how these shrines are perceived. He cites Isaiah 66:1 which has God speaking through the prophet: **Heaven is my throne, and the earth is my footstool. What kind of a house will you build for me? ...have not my hands made all these things?** Solomon had actually spoken in similar terms at the dedication of the First Temple, 'Will

---

22. Barrett (1994), 360.

God indeed dwell on earth with men? The heavens, even the highest heavens, cannot contain you. How much less this temple I have built' (2 Chron. 6:18). It is critical to note Stephen's designation of God which prefaces this citation from Isaiah, **the Most High**, which emphasizes God's sovereign majesty and uniqueness (cf. Gen. 14:18, 19, 22; Deut. 32:8; Ps. 46:3). He therefore **does not live in houses made by men** (48). Here Stephen is underlining a point made through his entire narrative: God is a pilgrim God, meeting Abraham in Mesopotamia, Joseph in Egypt, Moses in the desert of Midian. God transcends the specificity of a single place, since He fills all places and all things. He meets with His people wherever they are. He accordingly meets with the church as it gathers 'in the name of Jesus'; however, that implication has to be drawn by present readers since Stephen does not state it. In effect Stephen is rejecting what Witherington refers to as a 'God in a box' theology.[23]

With regard to the actual temple Stephen's point is a nuanced one. He is not criticizing the temple as such, but how it is perceived. However, that distinction may well have entirely failed to register with many, if not most, of his hearers, for whom their worst fears concerning Stephen's heterodoxy would have been amply confirmed at this point.

5. Application and accusation (51-53)

Stephen has presented his case. In his own eyes he is not guilty of the charge of blasphemy. He is not 'against Moses or God'. Neither is he dismissing the law, or calling for the destruction of the temple. He *is*, however, summoning Israel to recognize that God, the pilgrim God, who had chosen Abraham and his historic successors as His covenant people; the God who truly revealed Himself in Old Testament Scripture, not least in the law revealed to Moses; the God who as the infinite creator transcends all places and things; that God has fulfilled the ancient promises, and sent the promised one, Jesus of Nazareth. Jesus is

---

23. B. Witherington, III, 1998, 273.

'the prophet like Moses', whose coming has inaugurated the last day, the time of fulfilment of the Old Testament faith, the final blessing and goal of which was shared with Abraham at its inception, the 'blessing of all the families on earth'.

But Stephen's survey has surfaced another critical feature of Israel's history, the continual rejection of those whom God sent to them. So Stephen in conclusion applies that darkest of threads in their history directly to his hearers. He turns on his Sanhedrin audience, charging them with having repeated that historic rebellion and wickedness. **You stiff-necked people, with uncircumcised hearts and ears! You are just like your fathers.** The Messiah has come, **and you have betrayed and murdered him** (51-52). The slaying of the prophets who brought the Messianic hope to Israel, **predicting the coming of the Righteous One,** had been serious enough. But the Sanhedrin had sunk beneath even that treacherous perfidy – they had engineered the murder of the Righteous One Himself, the Holy Messiah. The accused becomes the accuser!

Stiff-necked means stubborn. It implies that Jesus was not killed in ignorance. They had consciously **resisted the Holy Spirit** (51). Like those who received the law from God they have deliberately **disobeyed** God's will. **Uncircumcised hearts and ears** means, 'you have behaved just like Gentiles'. In other words your behaviour is so out of line with the character and calling of God that you have called into question your belonging to His covenant people at all; a shocking indictment, even insult. Stephen's final charge is of their having **not obeyed the law which was put into effect through angels** (53). The notion that angelic intermediaries were present on Sinai is not exactly stated in Exodus, though may perhaps be alluded to in Deuteronomy 33:2. It was, however, a firmly established Jewish tradition and Christian writers appear willing to accept it (Gal. 3:19; Heb. 2:2). The point Stephen is making is that they, the supremely privileged recipients of God's very Word and law, had committed the blasphemy of disobeying it in the murder of Jesus. This saying alone was actually conclusive evidence that any charge of dismissing the law in Stephen's case was completely unfounded. But by this point the Sanhedrin are beyond caring about the niceties of legal charges and process.

Before turning to the moving account of Stephen's death, two other observations are appropriate. First, the trial of Stephen marks the ending of any prospect of rapprochement between Judaism and Christianity. The coming of Jesus Christ (= 'Jesus, Messiah') faced Judaism with an inescapable choice. They had to decide *either* to accord with the view of the early Christians and accept that God's purposes had been gloriously fulfilled; the Messiah, as promised, had been given, first to Israel, and then beyond Israel to the entire Gentile world, *or* to reject it as a blasphemous error. In all conscience acceptance would have called for change, almost beyond imagination. But it would have allowed Israel the supreme vindication of its age-long faith, and the prospect of multiple future enrichments and fulfilments as it embraced this new, further, and greatest of all the redeeming works of God. But Israel would not countenance it. The implied loss of its exclusive status; the modification, even abandonment, of many of its hallowed worship forms; the new openness to grace; the acceptance of Gentiles who would not in the process become fully accredited Jews within the covenant people; the acknowledgment of their historic failure to embrace the Messiah when He came; these, and many other more personal barriers, proved insuperable. So, beginning with the martyrdom of Stephen, the church was opposed; and to this day, despite thankfully improved relations at some points, helped not least by the church's long overdue acknowledgment of the shame of its own tragic, historic antipathy, the gulf remains.

Second, there is a very different, more personal, but not unimportant pastoral application. Stephen, in all probability, never completed his presentation to the Sanhedrin. The omission of a concluding proclamation of Jesus as Messiah and Lord is otherwise inexplicable in the case of one who was so utterly committed to Christ, as his dying vision makes evident, and one moreover whose eloquence and effective evangelistic impulse was so marked. This 'inadequacy', as far as Stephen's presentation was concerned, did not, however, prevent God's blessing being wonderfully expressed in a heavenly vision, nor did it prevent, as we will note in following chapters, the impact of his message producing the effect which he in retrospect would most dearly have wished, the effective promotion of the gospel among all the Gentile nations.

There is a great lesson here for all Christian preachers and communicators. The perfect sermon has never been preached; the perfect presentation has never been made. A lifetime of preaching has taught me that every sermon has its inadequacies, whether in content, or in delivery, or in reception, or in all three. Perfection, in this, as in all aspects of our Christian response, is never a possibility in this life. However, and here is the great encouragement of this passage, the fact that we never fully realize our ideal does not mean that the living God, by His Holy Spirit, cannot do for us, in grace, what He did for Stephen here – use what we offer Him, in its imperfection and incompleteness, for the glory of His name, for the good of others, and for the blessing of our own hearts. In the case of the first of these, the glory of His name, Calvin comments aptly: 'Even if the result may not always correspond to our wishes let us realize that firmness in declaring the teaching of godliness is a sweet-smelling sacrifice to God.'[24] In the third issue, the blessing of our own hearts, that may simply be our being cast back again and again in helplessness, upon the boundless mercy of a God whose grace is still sufficient for each of His servants, and whose strength is still made perfect in weakness. But that too is blessing; so…we do not lose heart!

5. The Death of Stephen (7:54–8:1a)

The Sanhedrin had heard enough. Stephen's closing accusation was the detonating charge. **They were furious and gnashed their teeth at him** (54). The verb 'were furious'

24. Calvin: I, 217.

(*dieprionto*) literally means 'they were ripped, or sawn, in their hearts' (cf. 5:33). Bock speaks of 'a visceral, emotional reaction of anger', an all-consuming rage which is about to explode in murderous violence.[25] But before coming to that Luke directs attention back to Stephen as he stands before the Council.

He is **full of the Holy Spirit**; we note again that this characteristic is attributed by others rather than claimed by the party concerned. The holy power and presence of God radiates forth from him. He **looked up to heaven and saw the glory of God** (55). As Stephen raises his gaze above the masks of naked hatred transfiguring the faces all around him, he is permitted a visionary penetration to the presence of the glory of the Lord. He receives a 'throne vision' such as Isaiah had glimpsed centuries before in Solomon's temple (Isa. 6:1-5), and John, would also be afforded some years later, on Patmos (Rev. 4:1–5:14). It was the outshining of the divine majesty, the discerned, but finally indescribable, manifestation of deity, with, at its very centre, none other than **Jesus standing at the right hand of God.** It naturally overwhelms Stephen, completely capturing his attention and drawing forth his spontaneous testimony to this most awesome of sights – **Look, I see heaven open, and the Son of Man standing at the right hand of God!** (56).[26]

We focus the highly significant content of the vision. Two features in particular call for comment.

First, we observe who it is that Stephen discerns; he sees the divine glory, but at the heart of it is Jesus, whom he immediately describes as **the Son of Man.** This was of course the title Jesus chose for Himself during His ministry. The name carried a clear link to His suffering, cf. 'the Son of Man must suffer' (Luke 9:22). In particular he must suffer being 'rejected by the elders, the chief priests, and the teachers of the law', that is, suffer at the hands of this very court, the Sanhedrin, '…and he must be killed'

---

25. Bock: 310.

26. Marshall helpfully refers to 'the glory that hides God from view', 148.

(Luke 9:22). So Jesus comes to Stephen as he follows in His holy steps, and suffers unto death.

But the definite article which Jesus consistently attached to the title is also critical to its explanation. 'The Son of Man' = the Son of Man you already know about, which can be none other than the Son of Man of the prophetic vision of Daniel, the one who will appear at the end of time: 'there before me was one like a son of man, coming with the clouds of heaven. He approached the Ancient of Days and was led into his presence. He was given author- ity, glory and sovereign power: all peoples, nations, and men of every language worshipped him. His dominion is an everlasting dominion that will not pass away, and his kingdom is one that will never be destroyed' (Dan. 7:13-14). The appropriateness of this designation for Stephen and the truth he has newly testified to, needs no underlining. We can do no better than quote a passage from William Manson, cited by Bruce: 'This represents the only instance in the NT of the apocalyptic title "Son of Man" being found on any lips but those of Jesus. This remarkable fact is not one to be undervalued or ignored. It is, on the face of it, a very distinct piece of evidence that, actually and historically, *Stephen grasped and asserted the more-than-Jewish-Messianic sense in which the office and significance of Jesus in religious history were to be understood*....Whereas the Jewish nationalists were holding to the permanence of their national historical privilege, and even the "Hebrew" Christians gathered round the apostles were, with all their new Messianic faith, idealizing the sacred institutions of the past, "continuing steadfastly in the temple", "going up to the temple at the hour of prayer" which was also the hour of the sacrificial service, sheltering under the eaves of the Holy Place, *Stephen saw that the Messiah was on the throne of the Universe.*'[27]

It was this theological understanding of the person and work of Jesus as universal Lord, which the church stood in urgent need of in order to justify and motivate its global mission. It was this Christology, which Jesus had

---

27. Wm. Manson, *The Epistle to the Hebrews* (London, 1951), 31f; cited Bruce, 166.

himself enunciated in His words of commission in Matthew 28:18: 'All authority in heaven and earth is given to me. Therefore go and make disciples of all the nations.' It was this Christology, which Peter would assert in the home of Cornelius, 'Jesus Christ, who is Lord of all' (Acts 10:36), and which would find its fullest development in the teaching of the apostle Paul (Phil. 2:5-11; Rom. 1:4; 10:9; 1 Cor 8:6; 12:3; 2 Cor. 4:5; Eph. 1:20-23; Col. 1:15-20). It was this Christology which was to find its latest expression biblically in the vision of John on Patmos: 'Then I saw a Lamb, looking as if it had been slain, standing in the centre of the throne...then the four living creatures and the twenty-four elders fell down before the Lamb... and they sang a new song: "You are worthy to take the scroll and to open its seals, because you were slain, and with your blood you purchased men for God from every tribe and language and people and nation....Then I heard every creature...singing, "To him who sits upon the throne and to the Lamb be praise and honour and glory and power, for ever and ever"' (Rev. 5:6, 8, 9, 13).

At this point Stephen effectively directs the community of Jesus on to the theological freeway that would lead the church out of Jerusalem, beyond Judaism and the diaspora, and endlessly on, to all the roadways of the world, both of the first century and of our own.

Second, there is the matter of Jesus' posture: He is **standing.** The imagery of the vision, with its reference to the 'right hand of God' (= the place of supreme authority over all) clearly echoes the words of Psalm 110:1, a well-known Messianic prophecy as was conceded by Jesus' opponents, and which He Himself drew upon in his debates with them (cf. Luke 20:41-44). But there the posture is different: 'The Lord (Yahweh) said to my Lord (the Messiah), "*Sit* at my right hand until I make your enemies a stool for your feet."'[28]

Several explanations of a 'standing Jesus' have been offered. Possibly the most persuasive is that which argues

---

28. This passage is cited more than any other in the NT as a Messianic anticipation; cf. Matt. 22:44; 26:64; Mark 12:36; 14:62; Luke 20:42f; 22:69; Acts 2:34f: Heb. 1:13.

for a judicial association. Jesus appears standing as Stephen's advocate in his defence against his accusers, as the Son of Man of the coming final judgment (Dan. 7:10, 'The court was seated, and the books were opened' (Dan 7:10).[29] Jesus stands as the vindicator of Stephen and his claims. But also, by implication, as the judge of his accusers, hence Stephen's prayer: **Lord, do not lay this sin against them** (60).

Jesus' stance may additionally signal His rising to welcome His faithful witness into God's nearer presence. If so, there can be fewer more attractive images of the homegoing of a child of God than this one. Marshall observes, 'The individual Christian finds that Christ comes to him or her in the moment of death.'[30]

> 'The opening heavens around me shine,
> With beams of heavenly bliss,
> If Jesus shows his mercy mine,
> And whispers I am his.
>
> My soul would leave this heavy clay,
> At that transporting word;
> Run up with joy the shining way,
> To meet my dearest Lord.' [31]

However there may just be another explanation. For a 'standing Jesus' is of course an active Jesus, and that is the critical perspective, as we have repeatedly noted, of Luke's entire presentation, 'what Jesus *began to do and teach*…'. It is perhaps confirmatory of this possibility that in Paul's vision of the Lord after his harrowing Sanhedrin appearance in 23:1-10, we read, 'The Lord *stood near* Paul and said…' (23:11). We can further undergird this proposal by referring to Paul's testimony to the Lord's enabling at his appearance at Caesar's tribunal, 'the Lord *stood at my side* and gave me strength…' (2 Tim. 4:17), and note finally the 'throne vision' of Revelation 5:6 cited

---

29. cf. also, John 5:27 'The Father has given the Son authority to judge because he is the Son of Man'.

30. Marshall, 149. cf. Calvin, 'From this we can derive the general encouragement that God will be no less present to us if we leave the world behind us.' Calvin, I, 218.

31. Isaac Watts.

above: 'Then I saw a Lamb, looking as if it had been slain, *standing* in the centre of the throne....He came and took the scroll from the right hand of him who sat on the throne...' The scroll is a 'document relating to the destiny of mankind.'[32] Christ appears here as the slain Lamb of God, but also as the present, active Lord who 'is authorized to execute the judgments which conclude this age and initiate the kingdom which belongs to the new age.'[33] In this sense it is arguable that 'Jesus *standing*' is the characteristic posture of the Lord in the Book of Acts, and the New Testament as a whole. But if that be true, then bearing in mind the unfinished nature of Acts, we can go on to affirm that 'Jesus standing' is His essential posture for this day and this hour, and for each one of our lives. He is still involved, the 'standing Christ', still actively at work, the Lord of human history, the initiator of the kingdom and salvation of God, and the living, present Lord of the mission of the church, today and tomorrow: 'Jesus *stand* among us...' He does.

As far as the Sanhedrin was concerned this claim to see the Risen Lord at God's right hand was the final straw: for Stephen to claim for Jesus this place of ultimate honour was sheer, unmitigated blasphemy. And of course, by implication, were it true, it expressed unambiguously both their personal and collective culpability and blasphemous error in rejecting and crucifying him, and additionally exposed the utter futility of their opposition since Jesus was now triumphantly alive and with the Father.

So, **they covered their ears** (to reduce their exposure to the blasphemy) **and yelling at the top of their voices** (presumably to drown out any further words from Stephen) **they all rushed at him, dragged him out of the city and began to stone him** (57-58).

This moment, as we noted above, marks 'The parting of the ways between Judaism and what became Christianity, centred on the status the believers in the new faith

---

32. G.R. Beasley-Murray, *The Book of Revelation*, NCB (Marshall, Morgan and Scott, 1983), 120.

33. ibid., 126.

assigned to Jesus. Stephen's vision and the crowd's violent reaction exemplify this difference.'[34]

The question is fairly raised as to what all this represented at the judicial level. There are semblances of legal process here. The Sanhedrin assembles in its role as a court of justice, and lays charges following the testimony of witnesses (6:12-14). The chairman, Caiaphas, as High Priest, then invites the accused to defend himself (7:1, 'are these charges true?'). Another hint of proper process surfaces in the final act of stoning (the law's prescribed form of execution for proven blasphemy, cf. Deut. 17:2-7), and the apparent role of the witnesses, noted in the placing of their clothes at the feet of a young man named Saul (58). On the other hand, there is notable omission of the pronouncement of any formal verdict at the conclusion.[35] There is the additional issue of the fact that the Romans had withdrawn from the Jews the right to execute, as of course surfaced over the execution of Jesus. Nevertheless there appears some possibility that Stephen's death occurred during an interregnum as far as official Roman procurators were concerned, and this perhaps allowed the Jewish authorities to dare to take matters into their own hands.

The consensus of the commentators, however, is that Stephen's execution, while preserving certain features of judicial process, was essentially an act of mob violence. The Jewish leadership were frustrated by their repeated inability to deal with the Nazarene movement, deeply angered by its continuing unwillingness to respect the

---

34. Bock, 313.

35. *The Mishnah*, the oral traditions which the Pharisaic party viewed as equally authoritative alongside the law and had been recorded in the 2nd century B.C., give details of the execution procedure. So this would have been known to the Sanhedrin. It states, in *Sanhedrin* vi. 1–4: 'When the trial is finished the convicted man is brought out to be stoned....When ten cubits from the stoning place say to him, "Confess... and everyone who confesses has a share in the world to come". Four cubits from the stoning place the criminal is stripped...the drop is twice the height of a man. One of the witnesses pushes the man from behind, so that he falls face downward. He is then turned on his back. If he dies from the fall that is sufficient. If not, the second witness takes the stone and drops it on his heart. If this does not cause death than he is stoned by all the congregation of Israel.'

authority of the Sanhedrin, irritated beyond measure by the disciples' repeated attempts to lay the blame for Jesus' death at their door, and finally provoked, beyond any capacity to control themselves, by the boldness, acumen, and the blasphemous claims made by Stephen. To use a popular phrase: at this point they 'completely lost it', and fell upon him with murderous intent.

Even amid the hellish hatred which was unloosed all around Stephen in these moments Luke neatly interjects a beautiful counter-point: **they dragged him out of the city and began to stone him...Meanwhile the witnesses laid their coats at the feet of a young man called Saul.** (58) For this young man, as we all know, through the spell laid upon him by Jesus of Nazareth, and, among other influences, his witness Stephen (22:20), would become in the following decades the heroic leader of the Christian mission to the Gentile world; a mission through which the Nazarene movement would become in time arguably the largest single, shaping influence in the future history of humanity. Further this 'young man's' inspired writings would be translated into the majority of the languages of the entire world and be a major driving force in propelling the good news of the Lord Jesus Christ to the furthest corners of the earth. The Sanhedrin's triumph would be ephemeral and momentary; Christ's, and Stephen's, would be imperishable and eternal.

In the account of Stephen's death there are a number of unmistakable parallels to the death of his Master. Like Jesus, Stephen faces the venomous wrath of the Jewish Sanhedrin, where he too has to endure the damaging testimony of false witnesses; like Jesus, his final moments are imbued with prayers, for the forgiveness of his murderers, **while they were stoning him Stephen prayed, 'Lord, do not hold this sin against them'** (60), cf. Luke 23:34; and then for the committal of His spirit into the hands of God, **'Lord Jesus, receive my spirit'** (59), cf. Luke 23:46. Yet there is a critical difference in Stephen's case. Jesus offers prayers to the Father; Stephen offers prayers to Jesus; so 'Lord Jesus, receive...', 'Lord (Jesus) do not hold this sin...'

As Bock notes, this implies 'a high Christology'. Stott does not over-state, 'This puts Jesus on a level equal with God.'[36]

On the prayer of committal, Calvin writes: 'As long as we remain in this world... it is right for us to commend our spirit into the hands of God every day...so that God may snatch our lives out of all danger. But when we are called to certain death, we must have recourse to this prayer, that Christ may receive our spirit. For he himself committed his own spirit into the hands of the Father, expressly so that he may keep ours forever.' [37]

So...**he fell asleep** (60): 'An unexpectedly beautiful and peaceful description of so brutal a death, but one which fits the spirit in which Stephen accepted his martyrdom.'[38]

So Stephen becomes the personal lightning-rod of fallen humanity's unceasing rebellion against the ever-blessed God who made, sustains, and loves us all, and who at infinite cost has made it possible for all to return to His waiting arms and yearning heart, in full salvation. 'If they persecute me,' Jesus had warned, 'they will persecute you also' (John 15:20). 'Those who would come after me, must deny themselves and take up their cross and follow me. For those who want to save their lives will lose them, but those who lose their lives for me and the gospel will save them' (Mark 8:34-35, NIVI). The terms of discipleship could not be more starkly expressed; let every follower of Jesus take heed. Not all will pay the price of the martyr, but the very Greek word for 'witness', that key term in Jesus' commission (1:8), is *martus* ; so it must not surprise us if many already have, nor if many more in future will.

We live in the day of the martyrs of Jesus. It was reliably computed that during the bloody decades of the twentieth century 26,625,000 died for Christ's sake, all around the globe, making that century the greatest century of martyrs since the first.[39]

---

36. Bock, 315; Stott, 142.

37. Calvin, I. 222.

38. Bruce, 172.

39. 'The world of Figures', David B. Barrett and F.K. Jansen, paper presented to Lausanne II in Manila, July 1989, 13-14. 'Martyrs in the 20th Century' (1900–1990).

More recent statistics support the view that last century's rates continue today; which generates a projection that around 1 in every 200 Christians worldwide will die for Christ in this century, if the Lord's Return continues to be deferred. 'When Christ calls a man or woman, he bids them come and die.' [40]

> *Afraid? – of what?*
> *To feel the Spirit's glad release?*
> *To pass from pain to perfect peace,*
> *The strife and strain of life to cease?*
> * Afraid – of that?*
>
> *Afraid? – of what?*
> *Afraid to see the Saviour's face,*
> *To hear his welcome, and to trace*
> *The glory gleam from wounds of grace?*
> * Afraid – of that?*
>
> *Afraid – of what?*
> *A flash, a crash, a pierc'd heart;*
> *Darkness, light, O Heaven's art!*
> *A wound of His a counterpart!*
> * Afraid – of that?*
>
> *Afraid – of what?*
> *To do by death what life could not –*
> *Baptize with blood a stony plot,*
> *Till souls shall blossom from the spot?*
> * Afraid – of that?* [41]

What might Stephen have accomplished in his extended lifetime had he been spared a martyr's death? We can but speculate. Certainly the range and wealth of his gifts, and his sheer Spirit-enabled dynamism held promise of very great things. Yet, in the event, his brief life was to prove, in the providence of God, astonishingly fruitful.

For one thing, that messenger of the murderers, the young man from Tarsus, was never to forget the trium-

---

40. Dietrich Bonhoeffer, *The Cost of Discipleship* (SCM, 1959), 99 (adapted).

41. E.H. Hamilton, cited Frank Houghton, *The Fire Burns On* (Overseas Missionary Fellowship, Lutterworth, 1965), 190-1.

phant passage of this fair prince of the covenant. Here surely was a primary element in the 'goads' which finally brought Paul to his knees outside Damascus, as, in the blessed ordering of the Lord, he fell under the spell of Stephen's vision of a global kingdom, and grasped the torch which fell from his dying hand.

More generally, as we noted earlier, the missional programme as expressed in the commission of the risen Jesus (1:8), required a break-out from Jerusalem, and that in turn required the development of a global theology and the application of a centrifugal force. Both of these were provided by Stephen. We can salute him therefore today, across the battlements of the centuries, not only as the church's first martyr, but also, arguably, its first global theologian and missionary.

Stephen's life is a timely reminder also that the object of existence here lies not in living long, but in living well; a salutary truth in a generation when nothing appears to be more dreaded than the marks of ageing, whether physical or mental. The quest for longevity has become for many a virtual idolatry. But a thousand years from now how little will it matter how long our lives have stretched; but how much will it matter whether, like Stephen, we have been welcomed into eternity by the risen Lord, and heard, as Stephen surely did, 'Well done, good and faithful servant.'

Biblical religion is a social phenomenon; salvation takes us out of individual isolation into authentic community in the one body of Christ. Pentecost signalled that at the very outset of the church's life, 'they devoted themselves to...fellowship...all the believers were together' (2:42, 44). However that corporate life-reality never eliminates the possibilities of an individual ministry of peculiar significance, within the calling of God. Stephen's life, brief though it may have been in temporal terms, among other things, challenges us afresh personally, to dare to step out from the crowd, to push wide our vision, to dream large dreams, and, with William Carey, to 'Expect great things from God'; and 'attempt great things for God.'

Study Questions:

1. Stephen's defence before the Sanhedrin is given at considerable length. It has many detailed points of application: what can we learn from his account of (a) Abraham (7:2-8)? (b) Joseph (7:9-16)? (c) Moses (7:20-38)? (d) God's 'dwelling-place' (7:44-50)? (e) the Sanhedrin (7:51-53)?

2. Stephen's final vision (55-56) is critical for the entire storyline of the book of Acts. In what ways is it still significant to Christian vision today?

3. John Stott refers to 'several parallels between the death of Stephen and the death of Jesus'. What might they be?

4. Stephen is honoured as the 'first Christian martyr'. It is clear from Jesus' teaching and the New Testament generally, that many more Christians are likely to die for their faith before Christ returns. Have you considered that you may be called upon to die for Christ? What are some of your reactions to such a prospect?

5. What makes this chapter 'one of the critical turning points for the church's global mission'?

5

Witnesses in Judea and Samaria
(Acts 8:1b–9:31)

1. Persecution and Scattering (8:1b-4)

Stephen's martyrdom had two immediate effects. First it provoked **a great persecution.** The fragile tolerance of the church shown by the Sanhedrin and their allies was abruptly ended, the thin layer of civilized conduct torn aside. The persecution was now openly visited upon the entire **church at Jerusalem**, with the sole exception of **the apostles** (1). The stated result that **all** the believers were forthwith dispersed (1) may be, as Calvin suggests, a hyperbolic generalized reference to a widespread assault, as arguably is the case in the use of the same word in 9:35 for the response to the gospel in Lydda and Sharon. Certainly, not long afterwards, Peter reports on his experience in the home of Cornelius to a clearly significant group of 'the circumcised believers' gathered in Jerusalem (11:2), and the crucial Consultation in Jerusalem on Gentile inclusion (15:2, 4) offers a clear impression of a significant Christian presence still there in the city.

Without unnecessarily overstating the Judaistic/Hellenistic division, there may well have been some awareness on the part of the authorities of a diversity of view among the 'followers of the Way' (22:4). The believers of more radical tendency, identified with Stephen, clearly bore the brunt of the persecution (11:19). This may also partly explain the apostles being left intact as a group, if they were to this point maintaining their earliest practice of continuing identity with the temple and its worship (3:1; 5:12, 42), while nonetheless of course completely unanimous in their belief in Jesus' redeeming Messiahship, and His being worthy of worship. The deeper reason for the apostles being permitted continuing liberty was probably palpable fear. There had been more than sufficient evidence of special powers being activated through the apostles to cause any God-fearing, or simply self-respecting, person in Jerusalem to hesitate before raising their hands against them (3:7-8; 5:12-16, 25).

The second effect of Stephen's death was the disciples being **scattered throughout Judea and Samaria.** Those among Luke's readers with a good memory would immediately detect here an echo of the terms of the risen Lord's commission: 'Witnesses in Jerusalem, and in *all Judea and Samaria*....' In this they would surely be justified. Luke's is a carefully crafted composition. He tells his story from the standpoint of the gospel's spread, and 1:8 is his table of contents, as we have earlier argued. The phrase also anticipates the contents of the next section of Acts: 8:5–11:18.

So here the second great stage of God's purpose for and through the church is reached; here, in a real sense, begins 'chapter two'. At one level at least Stephen's tragic death can be viewed in the same terms as those Paul was to express years later concerning his imprisonment in Rome: 'What has happened to me has really served to advance the gospel...and because of this I rejoice' (Phil. 1:12, 18). The church finally breaks out from the confines of the city, and the angels dance in heaven!

It is a common error among the people of God in every generation, not least our own, to lapse into the belief that God is really not as concerned for worldwide evangelization as some of our more earnest brothers and sisters. But such is Luke's God, the God of the Acts; a God whose entire purpose for this planet involves the global spread of His message of salvation. Is He not also the God whom Jesus proclaimed, for whom the finale of history awaits just such a global mission? 'This gospel of the kingdom will be preached in the whole world as a testimony to all nations, and then the end will come' (Matt. 24:14; cf. Matt. 28:18-20). Accordingly, if we have lost sight of this clear biblical reality, we may discover to our discomfort, as did the believers in Jerusalem, that God is perfectly prepared to treat our personal schemes of domestic security, self-fulfilment, financial aggrandizement, and career development with a cavalier disinterest if they stand in the way of the realizing of His heart-concern, the spread of the gospel through the world.

Further, if God was prepared to countenance the destruction of the church in Jerusalem in the interests of an expanded mission (3), then we have cause to fear for our little Jerusalems today. By any standard the church in Jerusalem was a great one. It was apparently a church which had everything – powerful God-anointed preaching; great local evangelistic effectiveness; rich and devoted fellowship; miraculous Holy Spirit gifts and demonstrations; amazingly sacrificial stewardship; powerful prayer ministry; and yet, in the end God blew it away! Why? Because it lost sight of a lost world. It is a lesson which has been repeated again and again over the centuries. It is not too much to claim that 'Every movement of spiritual renewal in Christian history has issued in evangelism or has withered on the branch.'[1]

One of the clearest developments in mission practice around the world in the last fifty years has been the enthronement of holistic ministry. It needs no special justification since all of life comes to us from the hand of God and accordingly, at every level, is a sphere for His being glorified. Further, Jesus specifically taught the pre-eminence of neighbour-love, and embodied it in His ministry to the hungry, diseased and marginalized. But that did not prevent His constant proclamation of the coming of the kingdom of God, and the need to personally repent and believe in order to enter it and become recipients of eternal life. Jesus did not make that final journey to Jerusalem to embrace the cross with its indescribable costliness other

---

1. David Phypers, *Renewal Magazine*.

than because of His burning conviction that He must lay down, sacrifice His life, to redeem lost sinners from the judgment their sinning had brought upon them. Social ministry or soul ministry? It is always a both/and. We are responsible for helping people to live better in this world, as well as be readied to joyfully enter the world which is to come. Hence sacrificial compassion for the needy will always well up in the hearts of those who know and walk with God. But the soul-needs must not be neglected in this process, albeit always responded to with great sensitivity to local conditions. 'This gospel must first be preached to the whole world…' To lose that concern is to lose touch with the God of the Bible.

The deep pain and sense of loss of the church at Stephen's death is not hidden: **Godly men buried Stephen, and mourned deeply for him** (v. 2). There is notably no attempt to hide the deep heart-grief of the believers. Sometimes the Christian attitude to bereavement is seen as a willing acquiescence, even calling at times for a celebrative cheerfulness. Deep and open grieving, especially if prolonged beyond the immediate aftermath of the loss, may even be frowned upon as a lack of faith. 'Your loved one is with the Lord, which is "far better", so cheer up, and dry your tears.' People's expressions of mourning are, of course, as diverse as their personalities, the specific circumstances of the death, and the depth, quality and tone of the relationship which has been severed. But stoic, 'stiff upper lip' acceptance gets little encouragement from Scripture – witness the **godly men** who carried Stephen's broken body to its resting-place. Godly men can 'mourn deeply'! Woe to the Christian leader, or the Christian congregation, which has not learned to 'weep with those who weep'.

But Saul began to destroy the church (3). The verb here for 'destroy' (*lymaino*) refers, Barclay claims, to 'bloody and sadistic cruelty'. The contrast between the actions of Stephen and Paul at this point can hardly have been greater. The one gives his life for the church's well-being, the other falls upon it for its destruction. To the impartial observer there could be little doubt as to who had won. And so it has often appeared across the centuries, and does today, in many places and in many personal circumstances…to the impartial observer. 'Why have you rejected us for ever, O God? …Your foes have burned your sanctuary to the ground; they defiled the dwelling place of your Name…. Why do you hold back your hand?' (Ps. 74:1, 7, 11). But the eye of faith sees further and deeper: 'When you pass through the waters, I will be with you'; 'I will build my church, and the gates of hell will not prevail against it' (Isa. 43:2; Matt. 16:18).

Saul's violent rage against the believers knows no limits. **Going from house to house…he dragged them off…and put them in prison** (3). It reads like the horrors of Nazi SS sweeping up Jews for the holocaust, or the knock on the door in the night during Stalin's pogroms, or their many subsequent repetitions, in too may places, at too many times. Nor are any humane values permitted: **men and women** are snatched. Paul would later refer to himself at this point as a 'blasphemer, a persecutor and a violent man' (1 Tim.1:13). He did not exaggerate. It was a phase of Paul's life he was never to forget (22:4; 26:10; 1 Cor. 15:9; Gal. 1:13, 23; Phil. 3:6). While Stephen's death is highlighted he was not the only martyr of this wave of persecution as the plural verbs in 22:4 and 26:10 clearly imply. The fanatical anti-Christian on his way to Damascus had much blood on his hands.

Nonetheless, the Lordship of the God of the gospel is undisturbed. For **those who had been scattered preached the word wherever they went** (4). The brutal murder of Stephen did nothing to reduce the believers' evangelistic zeal. Like Peter and John before them they 'cannot but speak' of what they had heard and come to believe (4:19). So suddenly the persecution, for all its pain and bloodshed, begins to make sense in terms of God's plan, an outcome immediately confirmed in Philip's Samaritan mission (5-25), and the Gentile mission in Antioch (11:19-21). In what would be a regularly repeated tactical error on the part of the enemies of the gospel, both demonic and human, they overreach themselves, and so what appears to be a defeat for the cause of the gospel becomes the basis of a huge new evangelistic advance. One need but contemplate the miracle of the church of Jesus Christ in China today to see that truth etched in present history. What was estimated as a Christian community of between one and two million in China in 1949 when the Maoist revolution fell on the nation, and not least upon the church, is today a Christian community of anything up to a hundred million. Indeed one optimistic growth projection even speaks of the possibility of up to a third of China as Christian by 2025.[2] Not that the cost was anything less than terrible; some twenty million are estimated to have died in the Maoist repressions including many, many Christians.

Jesus, as we noted above, had of course warned of such costliness. '"No servant is greater than his master." If they have persecuted me they will persecute you.' Nate Saint, Christian pilot and former US airman, refers to the lesson he quickly learned during his military training – that he was personally expendable if involved in a military conflict. It was a lesson he was to directly experience personally some years later as a missionary soldier of Christ to the savage Auca Indians of the Ecuadorean jungles.[3] But every Christian needs to face up to it also. The Lord can certainly ask for that if it should serve His mission, and He may.

2. Philip evangelizes in Samaria (8:5-25)

The 'scattered' include Stephen's fellow deacon, Philip (6:5). Although the identification is not explicitly made, the fact that Luke introduces Philip here without further explanatory or biographical note makes the identification highly likely.

Philip travels north to **a city of Samaria**. The manuscript evidence hovers between the presence and absence of a definite article before 'city'. But, as Bosch rightly observes, 'its identity is not important for Luke. That Samaria is the location is all Luke wishes to note.' [4] Stott does not understate the implication: 'It is hard for us to

2. David Aikman, *Jesus in Beijing* (Regency Publishing, 2003), 285, and passim.

3. Elizabeth Elliot, *Through Gates of Splendour* (Harper, New York, 1957).

4. Bosch: 325.

conceive the boldness of the step Philip took in preaching the gospel to Samaritans.' [5] Jews and Samaritans were bitter enemies, and this was no passing antipathy. The hostility reached back to the division of the monarchy after the death of Solomon in the tenth century B.C., when the ten northern tribes had formed the separate confederacy of Israel (1 Kings 12; 2 Kings 17). The Assyrian annexation of Israel in 722 B.C., and its forced repopulation by foreigners, added to the sense of disconnection. In the fourth century B.C. the antagonism was further hardened by the dedication of a rival, Samaritan temple at Mount Gerizim, and the Samaritans' formal repudiation of the Old Testament, other than the Pentateuch.

By the time of Jesus, the Samaritans were despised as unfaithful, defecting half-breeds (cf. Luke 17:18). Indeed for nationalistic Jews, Samaritans were worse than Gentiles. The hatred was mutual, exemplified as Samaritans refuse Jesus and the disciples accommodation, calling forth James and John's imprecation (Luke 9:51-55). All this throws into surprising relief Jesus' ministry to the Samaritans in John 4:1-42, and the high honour extended by Jesus in His parable which history has entitled 'The Good Samaritan', a title which would have been, for Jesus' audience, an impossible contradiction. For Jesus' hearers the Samaritan represented profanity, even non-humanity; he was an enemy, not only of Jews, but also of God. 'Jesus' audience, including his disciples,' notes Bosch, 'must have found this parable unpalatable, even obnoxious.'[6] But Jesus had explicitly identified them as appropriate recipients of the good news (1:8), and Philip is clearly aware of it. So, to the Samaritans he goes, **and proclaimed** (*kyrusso*) **the Christ** (= Messiah) **there** (5). The effect is remarkable.

Luke describes Philip's reception in two stages; first in general (vv. 6-8); and then, second, in relation to a specific, highly significant, Samaritan figure (vv. 9-13).

In general, the ministry was astonishingly effective. Philip stands before us in these verses, as in the broader

---

5. Stott: 147.

6. Bosch, 90; cf. also Luke 17:11-19.

perspective of this chapter, as one of the great Christian evangelists of all time. The cumulative impact of his ministry is memorably caught in verse 8: **So there was great joy in that city**. In terms of content there was an impressive combination of persuasively proclaimed word, and deeds of power. The **crowds 'heard . . .and saw.'** They heard **the good news of the kingdom of God and the name of Jesus Christ** (6, 12), and they **saw the miraculous signs that he did**, involving both healings and exorcisms (6). The combination of 'hearing' and 'seeing' is always impressive. When the church becomes an authentic expression of the gospel it proclaims, there will always be fruit borne, as was the case in Samaria.

So, **they all paid close attention** to Philip's message and embraced it (12), in the process forsaking Simon the Sorcerer, whom they had earlier revered, exclaiming – **this man is the divine power** (10). Instead they turn to Philip, whose divine credentials so evidently outshine those of Simon. In Philip's case, as with Elijah centuries before him, being 'a man just like us' did not exclude the possibility of being also the instrument of heavenly powers (James 5:17-18), nor need it be even for us. James' reference to Elijah in the previous verse as 'a righteous man', is not to be overlooked; but here, as ever, grace reigns: 'our sufficiency is from God' (2 Cor. 3:5), the God who delights to use 'the foolish things of the world to shame the wise, and the weak things of the world to shame the strong, and the lowly things of this world and the despised things – and the things that are not – to nullify the things that are' (1 Cor. 1:27-28).

The content of Philip's message importantly combines two great biblical concepts: **the kingdom of God** and the **name of Jesus Christ.** Here was the heart of the early Christian claim: the ancient Old Testament promise of God's future reign was fulfilled in their very time – in the person and ministry of the Messiah, Jesus! The last day had arrived, the time was realized, the great new day of universal salvation had broken across the darkened sky of human history. Thus the central component of Jesus' preaching ministry, the kingdom of God, finds continuity in the apostolic community's witness to the fact and ministry of Jesus. Luke's perspective in 1:1 is being worked out clearly here (cf. Luke 9:2). There is hence the clear conviction that 'the kingly power of God was being manifested in their own time through the mighty name of Jesus.' [7]

The Samaritans had their own form of the Messianic hope (cf. John 4:25), based on Moses' prediction in Deuteronomy 18:15ff of 'the prophet like unto me'. Known as the *ta'eb*, or 'restorer', he would essentially be a teacher rather than ruler or redeemer. Philip was obviously able to draw upon that latent preparation, but in the process to fill the anticipation with glorious new content, such that **they were baptized** in the name of this true Messiah, Lord, and Saviour. Luke also notes the gender inclusiveness both of the gospel's invitation and its rite of response: **both men and women** were becoming disciples, a happy balance to 4:4, and significant in that patriarchal culture. The gospel is already loosening traditional estimates of personal value. The content of what today would probably be referred to as Philip's 'charismatic ministry' is given in some detail. **With shrieks, evil spirits came out of many, and many paralytics and cripples were healed** (7). In general we should note the continuity motif in play once again. Here is Jesus 'continuing to do…' what he had previously done (1:1; cf. Luke 4:31-41; 5:17-26).

It is probably worth recording also that the reference to **great joy** echoes the response of the 'seventy-two' to the similar results of their own ministries when they were sent out by Jesus in preparation for His coming (Luke 10:1-17). They 'returned **with joy** and said, "Even the demons are subject to us in your name"' (10:17). The ground of this delight was the same, and identified by Jesus, 'I saw Satan fall…' (10:18). Jesus Himself is also impacted by the mood, 'At that time, Jesus, full of joy through the Holy Spirit, said, "I praise you Father, Lord of heaven and earth, that you have revealed these things to little children"' (10:21).

The arrival of 'the kingdom of God' through the ministry and Easter conquest of Jesus, which Philip preached

---

7. Marshall, 156.

in Samaria, was never, and is never, a mere idea or concept, nor is it simply a marker point in religious history. It is the declaration of an almighty divine victory. It is the proclamation of the glorious triumph of the living God. It is joyful news of 'Satan fallen like lightning from heaven'. Such 'signs following' Satan's downfall are at times both intellectually perplexing, and pastorally problematic – as this former pastor would have to concede. Despite this, the church is called to minister in the aftermath of that divine triumph, and hence to exercise the spiritual authority and effectiveness which Christ's victory makes available for its mission to the broken and enslaved lives that litter our local communities and global highways.

Having looked in verses 5-8 and 12 at the account of Philip's ministry to the general Samaritan community, we turn in the remaining verses, 9-11 and 13, to his relationship with a particular individual there, **Simon** the Sorcerer (or Simon Magus as he was generally known), though this change of focus does not alter the general theme of spiritual warfare. There are a number of references to Simon in later literature, some evidently apocryphal. However he clearly was a man of some influence and importance, derived from his practicing magic arts. Several of the later Christian references identify him as the originator of the Gnostic heresy in the period subsequent to his encounter with Philip described here. Another has him later corrupting the Christians in Rome and being responsible for the authorities becoming ill-disposed towards them.

His sorcery had deeply impressed the Samaritans so that he had risen in their estimate to be something of an august, even divine figure. **All the people, both high and low, gave him their attention and exclaimed 'This man is the divine power known as the Great Power'.** However all this changed with the arrival of the Christian evangelist. The people turned from Simon to Philip, or better, from Satan to Christ, and were baptized. Simon is deeply impressed. Rather like Pharaoh's magicians in Egypt (Exod. 8:18-19), he is forced to recognize the presence and operation of what clearly is spiritual authority of a significantly different order than he had exercised himself.

Eventually **Simon himself believed and was baptized, and followed Philip everywhere, astonished by the great signs and miracles he saw** (13).

To this point the Samaritan mission appears a model of evangelistic and full-gospel conquest; significant numbers have turned to the Lord and been baptized, the bondages of the evil one had been broken in many lives, many diseased and physically impotent folks had been cured, a major enemy of God had apparently turned to Him, and the entire community was rejoicing in a glorious new day of salvation. However there is more to be reckoned with here; for the seemingly triumphant story of the mission to Samaria immediately throws up the serious question of its essential authenticity, both with respect to the response of the general populace, and the response of Simon in particular. There are differences between these two cases as we will note; however both have created disagreement among interpreters, particularly so with respect to the general Samaritan response.

Luke arrives at these two issues in turn in the following paragraphs (14-24). As far as the authenticity of the general Samaritan response is concerned, Luke notes that the news of their having **accepted the word of God** reached the apostles back in Jerusalem and prompted the group to **send** the two senior apostles, **Peter and John**, to examine the work at first hand (paired again as they had been in chapters 3 and 4; and in an Easter Day footrace! John 20:3-4). On their arrival in Samaria, we are not a little surprised to read that the apostles **prayed for them that they might receive the Holy Spirit** (15). The explanation given, rather than expelling our confusion only deepens it – **because the Holy Spirit had not come upon any of them; they had simply been baptized in the name of the Lord Jesus** (15-16). Marshall does not exaggerate in describing these words as 'perhaps the most extraordinary statement in Acts'.[8]

Luke concludes his account of this surprising development by noting that the apostles then **placed their hands on them, and they received the Holy Spirit** (17). What

---

8. Marshall, 157.

are we to make of this? The account of the Samaritan response up to this point has seemed entirely congruent with responses to the gospel noted earlier in Acts; so what differentiates this? What was it that they lacked? Apparently, they lacked the Holy Spirit, according to verse 17. How are these verses to be interpreted? We will briefly note the main approaches which have been offered, and finally argue for our own proposal, though no single view is likely to prove conclusive; a timely reminder that the task of biblical interpretation is always a work in progress this side of Christ's return.

1. The first way of understanding verses 15-16 takes the words at their face value: only under the ministry of the apostles, Peter and John, did the Samaritans, for the very first time 'receive' the Holy Spirit. In support of this interpretation, note is taken here of the prominence of Philip in the account in verses 5 and 6, leading some to understand the reference in verse 12 to their 'believing Philip' as implying that his whole ministry in Samaria was 'in the flesh' and not a true work of God's Spirit. However this way of accommodating the verses in question appears to pay too high a price in terms of its raising uncertainty concerning the integrity of Luke's account of what happened when the gospel was shared, both here in Samaria, and earlier in Jerusalem.

As far as Samaria is concerned, how could their turning to the Lord after paying close attention to the preaching of the Word, renouncing a satanically inspired leader, accepting the gospel of the kingdom of God and the name of Jesus Christ, being liberated from demonic oppression and major physical illnesses, being baptized, and experiencing great joy, all have been possible without any influence of the Holy Spirit (vv. 5-8, 12)?

Further, does this rather negative appraisal of Philip's work not stand in clear contradiction to what we would have expected from a leader chosen in 6:5 for his being, with others, a 'man full of the Spirit and wisdom' (6:3), 'full of faith and the Holy Spirit' (6:5), a companion of Stephen, and clearly powerfully moved by the Spirit at other points (8:29, 39; 21:8)?

As far as the accounts earlier in Acts of the effects following the sharing of the gospel are concerned, how is what happened in Samaria, as described in verses 5-8 and 12, which apparently were not 'in the Spirit', to be distinguished from e.g. 2:38-41; 3:19; 4:29f; 5:14 where the Holy Spirit *was* apparently involved?

In other words the implication of taking this line of interpretation is apparently to call into question the perspicuity of Scripture.

2. Others take verses 16-17 as teaching that while the ministry of Philip *was* enabled by the Spirit, the further ministry of the apostles implies a second experience of the Spirit in the Samaritan case. This appears the correct route to follow. But it opens a further point of division, between (a) those who see the Samaritan experience as normative in some sense for all Christian experience of the Holy Spirit, and (b) those who believe it to have been unique to the circumstances in Acts chapter eight.

(a) Among those favouring a normative understanding would be those holding to a two-stage Christian initiation process. Roman Catholic and Anglo-Catholic interpreters teach that salvation is communicated in these terms: stage one being infant baptism, stage two being confirmation carried out with the imposition of the hands of a bishop in historic succession to the apostles. Thus the two stages of the reception of the Spirit in Samaritan experience is fairly precisely reproduced in that approach.

Somewhat similarly, many Pentecostal and charismatic teachers uphold a similar two-stage experiential normativity, teaching a regenerational, first-stage experience of the Holy Spirit in a personal faith-response to the gospel, followed subsequently, at a later stage, by a definitive 'second blessing' or 'Holy Spirit baptism'. Quite apart from the problems raised by the understanding of apostolicity which underlies the Roman and Anglo-Catholic view, these interpretations will not carry convincing force with those who find Christian experience, both in Scripture and in practice, to defy such 'one size fits all' approaches.

(b) This leaves the approach which accepts the two-stage coming of the Spirit in Samaria as explicable in terms of the uniqueness of that particular first-century context. Calvin, and others who follow him here, note a distinction between the work of the Spirit in the emergence of faith, and the Spirit's ministry in terms of the impartation of 'extraordinary gifts and graces'.[9] Further, Calvin notes the importance of the long history of division between Jews and Samaritans, and hence the danger of that history fostering a divided Christian community now that Samaritans had come to faith. Accordingly God, in order to 'foster the unity of his Church' allows Philip's ministry – their being brought by God to saving faith 'by the Spirit of adoption' – to be complemented, because of the unique historical background operating in this case, by the ministry of Peter and John representing the 'first church', a ministry which was primarily that of the impartation of the Spirit in terms of His 'further gifts'. This appears to offer the most satisfactory line of interpretation; however, it would appear capable of being developed still further in a way which binds it more closely to the actual wording of verse 16, and which also takes fuller account of the larger context of the book of Acts as a whole.

As far as verse 16 is concerned we note the verb *epipipto*, translated 'come upon' in the NIV (ESV, 'fallen on'). This is a critical word since it defines what it was that the Samaritans were lacking. It is an intensive form of the commoner verb, *pipto* (meaning 'to fall'), and is hence best rendered by a meaning such as, 'fall all over'. It appears twelve times in the New Testament, nine from the pen of Luke. It is the word used, for example, for the father's reception of the returning prodigal: '...he ran to his son and *threw this arms around* him' (Luke 15:20, *epepesev*). It is used for Paul's being embraced by the weeping elders of Ephesus (Acts 20:37, *epipesonses*), or in the same chapter for Paul 'throwing himself upon' young Eutychus as he embraced him and sought to revive his life (20:10, *epepesev*). In all these cases the verb expresses an abundance of emotion and its physical expression, an 'over the top' kind of reaction, a 'falling all over'. What the Samaritans up to this

---

9. Calvin, I, 236.

point had *not* received was not the general regenerating, renewing, even supernaturally gifting work of the Holy Spirit, but rather the all-embracing 'falling all over' of the Spirit, which of course the apostles had earlier experienced at Pentecost. But this intensive meaning is thrown into even sharper relief when we set Philip's Samaritan ministry in the context of Luke's fundamental story-line, expressed in his table of contents. So we go back once again to 1:8, and the three concentric rings of the gospel's expanding spread: first, 'Jerusalem and all Judea', the world of Judaism; second, 'Samaria', as here; and finally, third, 'the ends of the earth', the Gentile world. The first outbreak is sealed from heaven by a Holy Spirit 'falling all over' in the shape of Pentecost; the third (to anticipate a little) is sealed at the home of Gentile Cornelius by a Holy Spirit 'falling all over' which Peter crucially describes as *'just as'* = 'the same as' '…on us at the beginning' = Pentecost (11:15); and here in 8:16-17 a similar sealing from heaven by a Holy Spirit 'falling all over' at Samaria, thereby authenticating the Samaritan response as a heaven-born entry into the one family of God.

Thus at these three critical moments of gospel boundary -breaking, God sets His divine seal and supernaturally demonstrates His approval by this 'extra', 'all over embrace', in a Holy Spirit outpouring. So Acts offers us, I would argue, *three* Pentecosts, three critical 'outbreaks' of the gospel into human social experience. Admittedly there is not in this second case the explicit mention of tongue-speaking. But clearly there was something visible and tangible because of the way Simon reacts to its effect (18). Hence Bruce is not overstating when he remarks: 'The context leaves no doubt that their reception of the Spirit was attended by external manifestations such as had marked His descent on the earliest disciples at Pentecost.'[10]

The critical factor in each case was not so much a particular gift of the Spirit but the overwhelming, evident,

---

10. Bruce, 181. Cf. G.W.H. Lampe, 'There occurs a Samaritan "Pentecost" at least to the extent that visible signs are manifested of the outpouring of the Spirit.' *The Seal of the Spirit* (London, 1951), 72.

awesome, self-disclosure of the Living God. In its way this was as significant as the voice from heaven at Jesus' baptism, and on the Mount of Transfiguration, and bore the same essential message: then it was 'this is my Son!'; now it is 'these are my people!'

What is undoubtedly achieved by this view of these verses is the unequivocal binding of the Samaritan church to the apostolic church in Jerusalem, as would be the case later with the nascent Gentile church in Caesarea. The lesson was there for all to see and experience as the church moved ever outward in the purpose of God – *one* people of God, *one* body of Christ, *one* community of the Holy Spirit, the fruit of *one* indescribable act of divine self-sacrifice by *one* Lord Jesus Christ, issuing in *one* glorious gospel of grace. The unity with Samaria was demonstrated, not because the apostles took the initiative to check Samaria out, but because God took the initiative to get the apostles to Samaria to be there to see and experience it for themselves as the Spirit was 'poured all over'. But additionally, what an encouragement this must have represented to the Samaritans, the half-breeds, the apostates, the non-people, who were now one, in acceptance, dignity, and status, with all the other people of God! For all this the blessed Spirit 'fell all over' them at Samaria.

Simon again (18-24)
In our absorption in the events surrounding the apostolic visit we are perhaps in danger of almost forgetting Simon the Sorcerer; however Luke brings us back to earth with a fairly pronounced bump as Simon returns to the centre of the narrative. Simon is deeply impressed by this special, expanded manifestation of the Spirit which has accompanied Peter and John's ministry (18a). He covets the ability for himself; **he offered them money and said, 'Give me also this ability so that everyone on whom I lay hands may receive the Holy Spirit'** (18b-19). So, simony, the sin of selling offices in the church, makes its entrance into human vocabulary, taking its name from the confused and avaricious Simon Magus. Simon of course makes here the most fundamental of mistakes, identifying spiritual power with

material wealth. He imagines that God's holy gifts, specifically **the gift of God** the Holy Spirit, God Himself, **could be bought with money** (20). He stumbles against the unbreakable, inescapable law of the spiritual order: as Jesus had identified it – 'whoever tries to keep his life will lose it, and whoever loses his life will preserve it' (Luke 17:33). Spiritual power and authority is for those, and only those, who renounce it; spiritual fulfilment comes to those, and only those, who are prepared to die for it. On that immovable rock Simon shatters. He has **no part or share in this ministry** because his **heart is not right before God** (21).

Peter's reaction is uncompromising, even vehement. The phrase in verse 20 is actually (accurately) translated by J.B. Philips, 'to hell with your money!' For someone who lives, like Peter, at the white-hot centre of the divine presence, the intrusion of such crass and shameless self-seeking is inevitably intolerable, utterly repugnant. But he holds out to Simon a hope of escape from **the captivity of bitterness and sin** nonetheless; if he will **repent of this wickedness and pray to the Lord** (23).

Was Simon then no true disciple? Peter's rebuke points to that for many commentators. 'It is clear from Peter's judgment that Simon is still unregenerate'.[11] Barrett even sees Peter as voicing a threat of a curse on Simon.[12] Calvin is prepared to be a bit more generous, seeing Simon in his concluding plea – **Pray to the Lord for me so that nothing you have said may happen to me** (24) – as 'turning to the mercy of God and commending himself to the prayers of the church'; and hence giving grounds for us to 'conjecture that he did repent.'[13] However, as Calvin concedes, the subsequent evidence leaves that as unlikely, since later tradition paints a consistent picture of Simon as a persistent opponent of Christianity, and an arch-heretic identified with Gnostic views.

More generally for the cause of Christian evangelism, it is not inappropriate in the light of the Simon story to

11. Bruce, 223.

12. Barrett, 414.

13. Calvin, 242.

observe that prominent public figures who profess conversion bequeath at times an ambiguous legacy. On the positive side their coming to faith lends, in the short term, significant authenticity to the gospel and its claims in the eyes of the general populace, and may well open new doors and wider opportunities. An obvious example is the series of significant household names in Los Angeles who professed faith during Billy Graham's historic mission there in 1948. There is little doubt that their testimonies catapulted Dr Graham on to the public stage in the USA; a position he was to retain, with remarkable grace and humility, for the next fifty years. Yet gangster and crime-boss Jim Vaus, probably the best known among them, would later renounce his Christian commitment, having found the cost of repentance, in his case, too high. He apparently entertained the hope that he might be able to function as a 'Christian gangster'! [14] The Vaus story is regrettably not unique. The call to a lifelong obedience along the 'narrow road' with Jesus is demanding enough for any of us; that any of us pursue it to the end is only by a miracle of grace. But among those who set out on that road having had to renounce the widespread popular stardom of earlier years, there are, perhaps inevitably, some who find, as arguably in the case of Simon here, that the loss of that acclaim is more than they can cope with.

The Apostles Return to Jerusalem (25).
The segment is rounded off with the apostles' return journey and its extension of the Samaritan ministry as they are occupied in **preaching the gospel in many Samaritan villages**. The lesson of the 'Samaritan Pentecost' has been absorbed. It is accordingly not surprising that we read a report in 9:31, that **the church throughout Judea, Galilee *and Samaria* enjoyed a time of peace. It was strengthened; and encouraged by the Holy Spirit, it grew in numbers, living in the fear of the Lord.**

The complex interpretive issues raised in this section must not be permitted to distract us from the immensity

14. Charles W. Colson, *Loving God* (Zondervan, 1983), 81-92.

of what is conveyed here. We can well summarize by adapting words from a similarly significant breakthrough moment not long afterwards, 'so then God has granted *even the Samaritans* repentance unto life!' (cf. 11:18). While this section is chock-full of human endeavour and human responses, the real story is of 'God's granting'; *His* divine initiative, and *His* decisive intervention. The growth, expansion, and the opening of new frontiers in the story of the church are always His before ours, and ours only because already, and always, His. That is the glory of this passage, and its perennial significance. For here we find ourselves within earshot of the throbbing heartbeat of God as He yearns for a world that has turned its back upon Him, and we sense again His irresistible determination in spite of that, 'to take from the nations a people for himself' (15:14) – including from among the despised and vilified Samaritans, and all their present-day cousins and equivalents. 'I will build my church and the gates of hell shall not prevail against it' (Matt.16:18 ESV).

3. An Ethiopian finds Salvation (8:26-40)

The profession, and later defection, of Simon will shortly be more than outweighed by the even more remarkable conversion of another enemy of the truth, Saul, whose subsequent mission career will occupy the centre of the stage for virtually the entire remainder of Acts. Before we come to that, Luke shares another fascinating and attractive chapter from Philip's mission diary.

It begins with a surprising summons. **An angel of the Lord said to Philip, 'Go south to the road – the desert road – that goes down from Jerusalem to Gaza.'** God has a rich panoply of instruments who convey His will. As well as direct verbal instructions, often attributed to the Holy Spirit, Scripture additionally records dreams, visions, voices, human intermediaries of a wide variety of types and circumstances, and not infrequently 'angels'. The words translated 'angel' in both Hebrew and Greek retain such breadth of meaning that it is not in every case clear whether a human or divine agency is to be understood. In this case an angelic being appears correct. The message is surprising indeed, for it plucks Philip from the heart of an urban revival to a lonely assignment in the middle of a desert.

Several considerations might have made Philip hesitate. Surely he was deeply needed in Samaria? Apart from the fact that Simon was still around to trouble the new-made saints, there was surely a clamant need for further instruction in the faith in the case of people who had until so recently been steeped in, what was at best, a very limited understanding of God and His redeeming purpose. Many times such considerations are to be heeded. Evangelism which scorns the painful, slower, 'follow-up' ministry of discipleship has been a massive hindrance to mission worldwide over the centuries, and it continues to be so. Our Lord's vision for His disciples, that they would bring forth 'fruit that remains' (John 15:16), needs to be engraved on every missional agenda. But there are exceptions, not least in terms of the instruments God would use in this discipling. Patently, despite appearances, Philip's work in Samaria was done. That this was so is reflected in the very positive estimate of the church there at 9:31 which we noted a little earlier, a situation obviously achieved without Philip's continuing involvement. The deeper challenge was perhaps in the heart of Philip himself; was he able to leave it? It speaks volumes for his dedication to the Lord that he was.

Missionary statesman of the last generation, E. Stanley Jones, shares his encounter with this principle during his final years, after a debilitating stroke had left him in a care-home, immobile and virtually speechless. He mentions a conversation there with another resident, a retired bishop: 'When he was no longer in the limelight of the bishopric he was frustrated and he told me so. He wanted to know the secret of victorious living. I told him it was self-surrender. The difference was in giving up the innermost self to Jesus. In his case when the outer strands of his life were broken by retirement, the inner strands were not enough to hold him. Apparently it was a case of "limelight-itis" instead of a case of surrender to Jesus. Fortunately, with me, surrender to Jesus was the primary thing, and when the outer strands were broken by this stroke, my life didn't shake.' [15]

'Limelight-itis' remains a threatening virus among God's servants. It is when the supporting props of public ministry and acclaimed Christian service are knocked out from our lives that we discover who we truly are, and what essentially motivates us. The discovery can be quite devastating. The secret of victory here, which we all do well to absorb in preparation for that coming day of obscurity, is identified by Stanley Jones, and is seen in practice here in Philip. It is caught in his message, **Philip proclaimed the Christ there** (8:5).

> *'Christ! I am Christ's! and let the name suffice you;*
> *Ay, for me too He greatly hath sufficed...*
> *Christ is the end, for Christ was the beginning,*
> *Christ the beginning, for the end is Christ.'* [16]

So Philip started out, and on his way he met an Ethiopian eunuch ... humanly the setting could hardly have been a greater contrast to what he had so recently faced in Samaria; from urban mission among the city masses to a rural, seemingly happenstance meeting, with just one individual; from city-wide proclamation to a one-on-one encounter; from mass evangelism to personal evangelism; from huge personal attention to total personal obscurity. Yet in both settings Philip appears as a Christ-surrendered, Spirit-enabled, skilful and effective servant of the Lord.

What follows is the first of three individual conversion stories, of the eunuch (8:26-39), Saul (9:1-19), and Cornelius (10:1-48), as the gospel moves out from its Jerusalem birthplace; until, in Paul's ministry, it finds its essential ambience in the Gentile world, arriving finally in Rome (13–28).

In his presentation Luke typically stresses the initiative of God, which finds realization through His servant's availability and obedience to the Spirit's promptings.

---

15. E. Stanley Jones, *The Divine Yes* (Abingdon, 1975), 68.

16. Frederic W.H. Myers, *Saint Paul*.

The result is a situation of extraordinary, supernaturally ordered opportunity. The command 'go south' translates a Greek word (*eremos*), which is more usually rendered 'noon', making Philip's angelic instruction a concern with time rather than place. Noon was not a common time to be travelling due to its intense heat, which inclines many commentators and translators to prefer the geographical reference; however the point may be that a temporal instruction would probably have singled out the eunuch's transport from others on the road. We cannot be certain. What is clear is that the destined encounter took place, as **on his way he met an Ethiopian eunuch, an important official in charge of all the treasury of Candace, Queen of the Ethiopians**. Ethiopia was today's Sudan; the traveller's skin pigment was very likely to have been black. The description 'a eunuch' probably points to a castrated man, a type not uncommon in the Ethiopian court, having charge of the harems, and often serving as treasurers. The Queen was regarded as a heavenly person, a child of the sun, and hence not to be expected to discharge the secular functions of royalty. Alternatively, however, the title may simply have been a general way of denoting royal officials in Ethiopia.

This question, however, touches on the religious status of the eunuch as one who has travelled to Jerusalem to share in worship there. (This was no small journey; about five months' travelling each way.) Was he physically a eunuch, as Stott and others judge to be the case? If so, since such were excluded from temple worship according to Deuteronomy 23:1, he could not have been a full Gentile proselyte (convert to Judaism), but rather have been among the Gentile 'God-fearers' who were widely attracted to Jewish religion, attended synagogue services and who, as we will soon discover, formed a fruitful source of conversions as the apostolic movement spread out into the Roman provinces. One of the prophetic hopes for the coming of the kingdom of God was of its removing such barriers: 'To the eunuchs who keep my Sabbaths, who choose what pleases me and hold fast to my covenant – to them I will give within my temple and its walls a memorial and a name better than sons and daughters…' (Isa. 56:4-5). Perhaps Luke, as Marshall attractively suggests, is presenting the eunuch's conversion in terms of that kingdom promise, now fulfilled in Jesus, and part of his subsequent joy (v. 39) consequently lay in the fact that he who had been excluded for so long from the temple and the inner shrine of Judaism, was now at last included at the very centre, in Christ. This same joy is still experienced today by many, who, like this author, struggle over a long period to find true assurance of salvation, but at last find themselves embraced and brought in. It is joy indeed!

If, on the other hand he were a true Gentile proselyte then, as Christopher Wright perceptively observes, Luke can be seen consciously widening the 'gospel net' as we move 'from Jerusalem Jews to Samaritans, to a proselyte Gentile (the Ethiopian), then to a God-fearing Gentile (Cornelius), and finally to the real Gentile world of Greeks and other nationalities (Antioch).' [17] From another perspective, in terms of the major branches of the human family as expressed in the sons of Noah, 'with this man's conversion the gospel reaches south into Africa, the land of Ham. It was already reaching the lands of Shem. And soon, under Paul, it would go north and west to the lands of Japheth.' [18] The gospel is 'good news' for *all* the world!

The Ethiopian's status is to be noted, **in charge of all her treasury,** which prompts Marshall's observation: 'this was no insignificant convert.' [19] This is an entirely proper comment in passing; the gospel is already penetrating the higher reaches of human societies. From another perspective, of course, the same words can be used of every conversion in every generation, and in every place. Abraham Lincoln once observed, 'God must love ordinary people, he made so many of them!' Which, of course, is helping us learn from Lincoln's magnificent, all-embracing humanity – there *are* no ordinary people! Correspondingly, there are no 'ordinary Christians!' Discovering that

17. C. Wright, 516.

18. C. Wright, 516.

19. Marshall, 162.

in practice is one of the endless joys of Christian service. One other feature of the Ethiopian's situation is noted, he was **reading the book of Isaiah the prophet** (28); not the first traveller to find the enforced leisure of a long journey providing opportunity to consider life's larger issues.

Philip now receives his 'fine-tuning' instruction, this time attributed directly to the Holy Spirit; the Spirit said, **Go to that chariot and stay near it** (29). Only those who, like Philip, are fully surrendered to 'the Lord who is the Spirit' (6:3) can identify with this kind of lifestyle. The dangers of self-delusion here are real, but not insurmountable to such a Lord. Philip, obedient as ever, **ran up to the chariot and heard the man reading Isaiah the prophet** (30). This was made possible by two factors. First the chariot was probably not travelling much faster than walking pace, and second, in the ancient world, people read out loud. The reason was partly that in written texts the letters tended to be all run together, making speed of reading very difficult. Interestingly it was apparently not until the fourth century that bishop Ambrose, Augustine's spiritual mentor in Milan, was the first to be noted for his silent reading style. In these early cultures, a library was clearly the *last* place one would go for quiet study!

A golden opportunity presents itself, and the evangelistic heart of Philip leaps up and grasps it appropriately. **'Do you understand what you are reading?' 'How can I unless someone explains it to me?'** (31). The verb translated 'explain' (*hodegeo*), is used of guiding people who need to be pointed in the right direction, commonly of leading the blind (Matt. 15:14; Luke 6:39). This little piece of dialogue can be repeated endlessly from every corner of the world in our time. Whether in the context of the biblical illiteracy which characterizes much life in the Western world, both outside and inside the church, or among the host of the newly converted or the genuine seekers in the developing world, there is a clamant and global need today for 'Bible guides'. Obviously written materials such as this commentary series, radio broadcasts, films, internet connections, and other contemporary media forms, all contribute to meeting this need. But there is also, as a primary element, the critical role of the human guide and conversation partner who will 'come alongside' and journey with these new converts or seekers, both young and old, listening to their questions, and sharing the true meaning of God's Word. 'How can I understand unless someone explains it to me?' is a heart-cry today, from the neighbourhoods, and the nations, of the world. Readers of this commentary may well be among those needing to make themselves available to respond to that yearning, as God opens doors of opportunity, whether through our local congregation or in more informal settings. For some it could become a life-calling; is there any greater?

Philip climbs into the chariot at the Ethiopian's invitation, and, seated beside him, begins his instruction. The Scriptural passage he is reading is Isaiah 53:7–8: **He was led like a sheep to the slaughter, and as a lamb before the shearer is silent, so he did not open his mouth. In his humiliation he was deprived of all justice. Who can speak of his descendants? For his life was taken from the earth.** 'With what Scripture could any evangelist have begun more appropriately in order to preach Jesus to one who did not know him?'[20]

The passage, of course, speaks powerfully and movingly of an innocent sufferer brought to the place of slaughter and unjustly executed. The reference to his 'descendants' may allude in fact to his future 'generation', or to the wicked generation of his oppressors.

Who is the prophet talking about? (34). Here the Ethiopian asks a highly pertinent question for first-century Judaism. In general, Jewish scholars did not know what to make of this strange figure, the 'suffering servant of God' who appears in the later chapters of Isaiah (42:1-9; 49:1-13; 50:4-11; 52:13–53:12). Three broad alternatives were proposed. First, that it referred to the prophet himself as a rejected mouthpiece for God, and hence a vicarious sufferer on the Lord's behalf; second, that it referred to another prophetic figure; or third, that it referred to the entire nation of Israel, whose sufferings are

---

20. Bruce, 189.

to be thought of as in some sense expiating their national sins. What is supremely significant is that the rabbis and other teachers at no point connected the suffering servant to the Messianic hope. As Bruce notes: 'There is no evidence that between the time of the prophet and the time of Christ anyone had identified the suffering servant of Isaiah 53 with the Davidic Messiah of Isaiah 11, or with the Son of Man of Daniel 7:13.'[21]

The reasons for this failure are not hard to appreciate. The Messiah was essentially a royal figure, the living, personal representative of the Almighty, heir to the throne of David, whose ministry would be to overthrow the Gentile nations, elevate Israel, and introduce the worldwide reign of God. How could all that be squared with this humiliated, pathetic, discarded, and unjustly condemned figure in Isaiah's visions? Strikingly it was the voice of the Father at Jesus' baptism which was the great turning point in the history of Old Testament interpretation at this point. At Jesus' baptism (Matt. 3:17) the Father laid His hand, as it were, upon these two strands of Old Testament prophecy, the Kingly Son, 'This is my Son' (Ps. 2:7), and the Suffering Servant, 'with whom I am well pleased' (Is. 42:1), and fused them together. So Jesus is designated, and goes forth into His mission, as the 'Servant King' the one who will attain God's sovereign salvation for the world through suffering (cf. Luke 24:25-27, 44-47). As Bruce aptly adds, 'How difficult it was to understand the prophecy before it was fulfilled; how easy, once the fulfilment is known.'

Philip does not miss this heaven-sent opportunity. He **began with that very passage of Scripture and told him the good news about Jesus** (35). 'Began' is no doubt an important indicator, as Philip used his own knowledge of the Old Testament, and his awareness of the numerous traditions of Jesus' life and ministry which were already circulating, to fill out the Isaiah passages. As the journey continued the Ethiopian's mind and heart no doubt fell increasingly under the spell of the One who had come from God's heart into the world, lived, ministered and

---

21. Bruce, 188.

finally offered Himself in sacrifice for our sins, before rising triumphantly on the third day and ascending, now reigning, one day to return. And most amazingly of all – that this meant the present offer to sinners and seekers like this Ethiopian friend, of cleansing from all sin and the gift of the living Spirit; a full, free and endless salvation within the new community of the believers in Jesus Christ – 'good news' indeed!

The Ethiopian is convinced; so why delay? **Look, here is water. Why shouldn't I be baptized?** So it happened; **Philip and the eunuch went down into the water and Philip baptized him** (38). So this 'outsider' pilgrim from North Africa steps into the everlasting family of God. The 'going down' may reflect an immersion form, as appears to be similarly indicated in John the Baptist's ministry (Matt. 3:16; Mark 1:10; John 3:23); however the amount of water involved is hardly a primary concern compared with the greatness of the blessings promised in baptism, and the greatness of the grace of the God it proclaims.

This whole account is a beautiful demonstration of the sovereignty of God in human redemption. As we will see a little later, in the remarkable ordering of circumstances which brought Peter to a waiting Roman household in Caesarea, God works in multiple ways in multiple lives to orchestrate an encounter with Christ. In this sense Philip was only the final link in a chain of circumstance which brought this searching African to the end of his search for salvation and to experience its joy. One sometimes muses that when heaven is entered, every one who arrives there will be found at some point encircled by a signifi-cant group of praising people, comprising all those who contributed in any way to that individual's salvation – all those who prayed for them; all those who reflected Christ to them; all those who cared for them; all those who helped them to believe; all those who taught them some aspect of the gospel, whether through books written, or movies or videos created; all those who witnessed to them; all those who preached the good news to them; all those whose sac-rifices and service made possible the ministries which at particular moments influenced them towards Christ; from their earliest days till their final moment of commitment. Nor can we forget all those through whom the Word of God came to be created, recorded, transcribed, printed, translated and made available, often at incredible cost. Every conversion, as we commonly affirm, is a miracle of grace; but it is also a miracle of divine orchestration and human complementariness and community. It is a huge encouragement to all of us, no matter how untutored or, as we may feel, ungifted, to, like Philip, make ourselves available day by day to God the Holy Spirit, so that we may, in ways very often entirely unknown to ourselves, become a link in a chain of redemption. Heaven will be, among many other things, a place of wonderful surprises.

That the baptism created utter astonishment to the Ethiopian's entourage can hardly be doubted, to say nothing of any other passing travellers. But when God is in control, and His Spirit abroad, we need to be ready at times for the surprising and the unexpected.

At this point the Western text supplies us with a piece of the baptismal liturgy. Philip states the condition for admission to baptism: 'if you believe with all your heart you may'; and the eunuch's response is shared: 'I believe that Jesus Christ is the Son of God.' Hesitation around the Western text is indicated by the setting of these words in a footnote in many English versions. However even if that reservation is appropriate we are clearly here in touch with very early standards for baptismal practice.

What is not in any doubt is the effect on the eunuch. **He went on his way rejoicing** (39). And well he might. Attracted to the faith of Israel, perhaps from boyhood, he studied its holy books and sought its enlightenment. In his zeal he had undertaken a lengthy, time-consuming, and costly journey to its holiest shrine in Jerusalem. And yet at the end he had been left with unresolved questions. But the God who discerns the seeking heart (4:10; 17:27) had intervened in mercy, and suddenly a servant of God had appeared at his side, a 'Bible-guide' who, in an hour or two there in his chariot, had answered his questions and shown him from the Scriptures the way to salvation, in the crucified and risen Saviour, Jesus Christ. Now at last he had answers, he had a new life, he was forgiven and new-born. He had Christ! It meant joy – inexpressible and glorious! (1 Pet. 1:8).

In 1654, as brilliant French philosopher and physicist Blaise Pascal was reading his Bible the room was suddenly illuminated. 'Monday 23rd November, Eve of St Chrysostom, from about half past ten in the evening till about half past twelve. Fire...Certainty. Feeling. Joy. Peace. God of Jesus Christ...' He wrote down a full account of this conversion experience and sewed it into the lining of his coat. His life was transformed from that moment onward. Like the eunuch, **He went on his way rejoicing.** But that joy is discoverable today. A student from the north of England who had been brought up in spiritism came to Christ. He testified: 'I cried out in despair to Jesus Christ to save me. He really came to me. I felt actual, real love, I can't describe it. It was just pure beauty and serenity. And despite the fact that I knew hardly anything about salvation and sin, and what they meant, I just knew I was forgiven. I was unbelievably happy.' He too, **went on his way rejoicing**. It is still happening, this very day, all around the world.

Philip meanwhile is gone – **the Lord suddenly took Philip away** – and he is next noted, still by the Mediterranean coast, to the north at Azotus, not far from Caesarea where we will meet him again in 21:8. The account here reads somewhat dramatically; however it may simply reflect Philip's own sense that, with the eunuch's baptism and continuing journey back to Ethiopia, this chapter of his own ministry is closed; but a new one beckons him to the north. When God closes a door he has the happy habit of regularly opening another one.

Study Questions:

1. One positive result of Stephen's death was that it got the church out of Jerusalem, where God never intended it to stay (cf. 1:8).

   Would you agree that we often face a similar temptation in the church today? How do we get 'out of Jerusalem'; or, to use Jesus' metaphor, how does the salt get out of the salt-cellar of the church into the waiting world beyond it? How are we faring in this regard in our own congregation at present? Are there new initiatives which might be taken?

2. We note the church's mourning deeply for Stephen (8:2), as did Jesus, apparently, for Lazarus (John 11:35). What does it mean in practice to 'mourn with those who mourn' (Rom. 12:15)?

3. Trace the effects of Stephen's ministry in getting the message of the gospel out from Jerusalem into Samaria (8:1-4); into the great Gentile centre in Antioch (11:19-21); and winning Paul, 'the apostle to the Gentiles' for Christ (Acts 22:20, 26:14). Consider ways in which God may want to use your life to assist the global mission of Christ.

4. What are the primary qualities of Philip's ministry in Samaria (8:5-13)? What do we learn from the Spirit's outpouring in Samaria (8:17), and from Simon's request of Peter (8:19)?

5. What important qualities does Philip illustrate in his willingness to leave his work in Samaria and minister 'in the desert' to the Ethiopian? Have you had a similar experience? Are we able to accept such a change of context and setting in God's service if He calls us?

6. Study 8:26-39 and identify the ways in which Philip models effective personal witness. Which of these ways do we find especially relevant to ourselves?

4. Paul's Encounter with the risen Lord (9:1-19)

Chapter nine brings us to an event of massive consequence for the storyline of Acts, i.e. for the global expansion of the Christian mission. The coming to faith of the apostle Paul, the leader of the extension into the Gentile world, and the largest single contributor to the New Testament, was an event of almost incalculable significance.

In the terms of Luke's presentation we have noted the ending of the initial phase of the mission, 'in Jerusalem' (1:8), modelled by Philip's ministry to Samaria and Ethiopia (by implication). While the full concentration on the Gentile 'to the ends of the earth' phase will not arrive until chapters ten and thirteen, it is given a highly significant precursor by the event covered here, in the first part of chapter nine.

We noted in chapter eight the development of a wider, theological perspective in the Hellenistic wing of the Jerusalem community – a perspective led and embodied by Stephen. With his death a leadership gap emerges, the need for someone who, while utterly conversant with the life and faith of Judaism, is equipped to mesh that with a compassion for, and identity with, the spiritual needs and longings of the Gentile world beyond the geographical and mental boundaries of Palestine and the Jewish diaspora. That person is Saul.

On the surface, **breathing out threats and murder against the Lord's disciples**, he could hardly have been a less promising candidate. The idiom is vivid. Alexander speaks of 'an allusion to the panting and snorting of wild beasts'.[22] Paul himself would later refer to his 'raging fury' (26:11). This covered a significant period of time, 'Many a time I went from one synagogue to another to have them punished' (26:11). Reflecting on Saul's later career in the light of this description Calvin aptly notes, 'But God's wonderful hand was openly shown, not only in such a cruel wolf being turned into a sheep, but also in his assuming the character of a shepherd.'[23]

Not content with his violent assault upon the church in Jerusalem Saul's fanatical determination to extinguish the Nazarenes sends him to the high priest to authorize the apprehending and **taking as prisoners to Jerusalem, any who belonged to the Way, whether men or women**, in other places, where there were significant Jewish popula-

---

22. Alexander: 355.

23. Calvin: 266.

tions, such as Damascus in the Roman province of Syria to the north. To this point there has been no reference to the fact that there was a church in Damascus, though that is the case, as we will shortly discover (10-25). Luke is clearly being (necessarily) selective in his account of the church's growth.

There is a question as to what rights Paul, or Caiaphas for that matter, would have had with respect to law and order issues in a Roman province. The high priest, as president of the Sanhedrin, was head of the Jewish state as far as its internal affairs were concerned. The Romans respected that authority, however it was unlikely to have included right of arrest and subsequent capital punishment. Possibly there were some additional rights concerned with strictly religious issues, such as heretical teachings. Alternatively, Hanson may be right in suggesting that Paul simply sought and received 'authorization from the Sanhedrin to injure and even kidnap leading Christians, if he could with impunity.'[24]

So Saul, sets off for Damascus, a journey of around 150 miles, and of perhaps a week's duration, a circumstance which would have allowed extended opportunity for inner reflection. He is accompanied by an entourage who would have guarded any apprehended followers of Jesus on the return journey. About noon, as the party nears Damascus, it happened! **Suddenly a light from heaven flashed around him. He fell to the ground and heard a voice say to him, 'Saul, Saul, why do you persecute me?'** (3-4). **Suddenly** is indicative of the obtrusive initiative of God (cf. Pentecost, 2:2). God breaks miraculously into Saul's consciousness, 'vertically from above', without so much as a 'by your leave'! It is a patently sovereign action, prepared as it no doubt was by the pressures of conscience (cf. 'the goads', 26:14) expressing the ministry of the Holy Spirit (John 16:8-9). Though the words conveyed by the voice are private to Saul, the physical phenomena are apparently also registered by the others; 'My companions saw the light, but did not understand the voice of him who

---

24. Hanson, 112.

was speaking to me' (22:9). This, as Bock notes, 'excludes a merely private vision'.[25]

We can surely speak here of a glorious epiphany such as was presented to the three disciples on the Mount of Transfiguration, or would later overwhelm John on Patmos (Rev. 1:12-17). Like others thus confronted, Saul falls to the ground (Ezek. 1:28; 3:23-24; 43:3; Dan. 8:17; Rev. 1:17). The voice addresses him in repetition of his name, **Saul, Saul**, indicating intense emotion on the part of the speaker, and the deeply personal nature of the whole experience as far as Saul was concerned (cf. Gen. 22:11; 46:2; Exod. 3:4; 1 Sam. 3:10; 2 Sam. 19:4; Luke 10:41; 22:31). The Risen and glorified Lord, He who even in the days of His earlier earthly ministry ever 'knew what was in a man' (John 2:25) now questions Saul, **Why do you persecute me?** (4). 'Persecuting...you? But, **who are you, Lord?** (22:8; 26:15). The title, 'Lord', (Gk. *Kurios*) had a range of meaning running all the way from a polite, 'Sir', to the term used in the Greek LXX for 'Yahweh', the unutterable name of the Almighty Himself (cf. Ezek. 1:1, 26, 28). Surely Saul's meaning here would have inclined towards the latter end of that scale, as he lies flat on his face, suffused in the glory of the heavenly light, and in the presence of a clearly supernatural personage. 'The word must already have begun to acquire the theological overtones it was later to have in Paul's letters.' [26]

Saul's question is immediately answered: **I am Jesus, whom you are persecuting** (5). 'I am Jesus', a sentence which in an instant both shattered and re-formed Saul's entire world. All the self-erected walls of resistance and rationalization; all the fermenting, driving anger burning in his spirit against these hated, heretical Nazarenes, all collapsed and disintegrated into a thousand pieces before the bedrock fact which now broke upon his consciousness with the force of a sword – Jesus is alive! Jesus is in divine glory! 'These Christians...Stephen...they're right after all; they've been right all along! Jesus truly *is* the Messiah... and we rejected and killed him! The Nazarenes' way

25. Bock, 357.
26. Stott, 173.

is right; it's God's way; it is the fulfilment we have been waiting for all these centuries. We cannot oppose it and succeed. I've been utterly mistaken! This is the truth…I must embrace it! But what have I done? "Persecute *me*!" Horrible, terrible thing…Jesus is with them and in them; the Nazarenes are His precious people, and I've been killing and imprisoning and hurting them – hurting *Him*!'

The later account of the encounter, in 22:10, has Saul asking the question at this point, 'What shall I do Lord?,' which anticipates Jesus' answer in verse 6, **Now get up and go into the city and you will be told what you must do**, a command which will be amplified in Damascus by **a vision** of **a man named Ananias,** who will **come and place his hands on him to restore his sight** (12). Saul obeys, and struggles to his feet, but finds that his eyes no longer function, his sight has gone; he can **see nothing,** his physical condition now humiliatingly epitomizing his spiritual darkness and helplessness.

So they led him by the hand into Damascus (8). What an astonishing *contre temps!* The proud zealot for Yahweh; the rising star of Judaism; the scourge of the Nazarenes; sweeping triumphantly into Damascus to root out the vile heresy…actually enters the city, stumbling blindly along on the arms of his assistants! And there he rested, sight, for all he knew, permanently gone, all appetite drained – he **did not eat or drink anything** (9) – his whole life-course abruptly and radically shut down. The raging bull of Jewish zealotry has been, by a single, overwhelming manoeuvre, comprehensively enveloped in the net of the divine Hunter from Nazareth.

A few observations are in order.

Due to the enormous importance of Saul's conversion for the entire Christian movement in the first century, and in every century since, the accounts of the event in Acts have been subjected, not surprisingly, to intense historical criticism. Since Saul's encounter with the Risen Jesus has some superficial echoes of divine encounters referred to in the inter-testamental books of the Maccabees (2 Macc. 3:13-40 and 4 Macc. 4:8-14), some liberal interpreters suggest this represents an earlier literary source for

Luke's story of Paul's conversion experience. In the former passage, a horseman with two angels strikes down a man called Heliodorus, in judgment for his having tried to steal from the temple in Jerusalem; in the second, another individual, Apollonius, is halted by angels on horseback and by flashes of lightning, as he attempts to steal from the temple treasury. The differences between these legends and Luke's account are patent. The encounter between Jesus and Saul is a means of salvation not judgment; there is no temple theft anywhere in sight, nor angelic horsemen. Bock rightly finds this claimed linkage, simply 'not credible.' [27]

More commonly, the fact of slight differences in detail between the three versions of the Damascus Road experience in Acts (cf. 9:1-18; 22:4-16; 26:9-18), are claimed to undermine their historical reliability. In fact they far more likely confirm the reliability of Luke's account, as would be readily admitted by anyone who has been asked on a number of occasions to 'give their testimony' of how they came to faith. Minor details inevitably are told in different words, or are omitted and then reinserted, often influenced by the specifics of the occasion and the audience being addressed. But none of this in the slightest degree requires calling into question either the reality of our conversion, or our personal integrity, any more than it does for Saul in these Acts accounts. Luke, ever the faithful historian, having 'carefully investigated everything', tells it as it was, so that we can 'know the certainty' of what we have been taught (Luke 1:3-4).

Much more relevant is to note that Jesus in effect sends Saul to the church. It is through the ministry of Jesus' people that he will be brought to a full realization of the salvation he so desperately needs, and through them be united with the community of the Risen One, within whose loving bonds he will live and serve for all his remaining days. Saul's conversion has often been held up as the classical model of how people become Christians. There is some truth there, but it lies not in the details of

27. Bock, 357.

Saul's life nor, most emphatically, in the manifestly super-natural dimensions of his meeting with Jesus – Jesus' later words to Ananias concerning Saul, 'This man is my chosen instrument' (15; cf. 26:16-18) underline the uniqueness of this whole experience; Damascus Road conversions stopped at the Damascus Road! The real points of universal application lie firstly, in Paul's own estimate, 'I was shown mercy so that in me, the worst of sinners, Christ Jesus might display his unlimited patience as an example for those who would believe on him and receive eternal life' (1 Tim. 1:16). A second universal reference lies in the command, 'Go into the city' = go to church! Christianity is a communal religion. Our relationship with God is fulfilled, nurtured and normatively expressed in the fellowship of the body of Christ. Authentic conversion is out of isolation into community. Christ is still, and always will be, the Christ encountered in and with His body; 'why do you persecute *me*?'

A final note, which also impinges on the question of the historicity of the event, is the impressive evidence of the permanent change which this Damascus Road encounter effected. From this moment on, Saul was, in his mental and spiritual world, in virtually every sense a 'new man'. His convictions about Jesus and Christianity, his understanding of the significance of the Christian movement, his view of God and God's historic purpose of salvation, his view of Israel and her place within that purpose, his interpretation of the Old Testament, his view of himself and humanity generally, all of these changed in a manner which was radical in its scope, and which would remain essentially unaltered through the remaining thirty years of his life. In particular Saul, or Paul as he became known in his 'Christian' years, remained unshakeable in his understanding of the Damascus Road experience as being an authentically objective, historical encounter with the Risen Jesus Christ in His glorified form. No amount of suffering, persecution, criticism or opposition – and his next thirty years were one unrelieved catalogue of all of these (cf. 2 Cor. 11:12-28) – evidence the merest shadow of doubt concerning this cardinal fact, 'he appeared to me' (1 Cor. 15:7; cf. 1 Cor. 9:1; 2 Cor. 4:6; Gal. 1:11-17; 2 Tim. 1:12-14). Bearing in mind the breadth and depth of his mind – Paul's blending of Judaism and the new faith in Jesus Christ represents by all criteria one of the mountain peaks in the history of the human intellect – we find ourselves drawn to the eighteenth-century observation of Baron George Lyttleton, that the conversion of Saul was in itself, aside from other arguments, 'a demonstration sufficient to prove Christianity to be a divine revelation.' We can also note, in similar vein, the recent conclusion of N.T. Wright after a detailed examination of Paul's teaching on the resurrection as well as the Acts conversion accounts. He refers to '...the clear understanding that Paul believed he had seen the risen Jesus in person. Attempts to undermine this conclusion by appeal to "what really happened" at Paul's conversion, on the basis of Acts or of other passages in Paul, carry no conviction.'[28]

The evidence of divine sovereignty is further expressed as **a disciple named Ananias** enters the picture. Described later by Paul as 'a devout observer of the law and highly respected by all the Jews living there' (22:12) and a Christian, he is afforded a visionary conversation with the risen Jesus. Ananias is told where to find Paul, **Go to the house of Judas on Straight Street, and ask for a man called Saul...he is praying** (11). 'Straight Street' is still a major road in Damascus, known today as Derb Al-Mustaquim. The 'house of Judas' is traditionally located near the western end. Saul himself has apparently been prepared for this meeting by a vision which has promised him healing of his blindness as a result (12). Ananias' submissive confession, **Lord!** is put to immediate test by Jesus' instruction. Why so? Because **I have heard many reports about this man and all the harm he has done to your saints in Jerusalem** – Saul was by now a widely feared persecutor, the purpose of whose visit to Damascus was already only too well known by **all who call on your name** (14). **Saints** is the first time this designation is used for Christians in

---

28. N.T. Wright, *The Resurrection of the Son of God* (Fortress, 2003), 398. cf. also, Lee Strobel, *The Case for the Real Jesus*, Zondervan, 2007, 120–45.

Acts. It carries the richly positive sense of people who are 'holy', in the sense of being 'set apart for God's special use and possession'.

Ananias' fears are understood and addressed, **Go! This man is my chosen instrument to carry my name before the Gentiles and their kings and before the people of Israel. I will show him how much he must suffer for my name** (15-16). This represents a highly impressive summary of Saul's future mission, and one no doubt subsequently conveyed to him by Ananias. Johnson refers to a 'programmatic prophecy of Paul's career.' [29] **Chosen instrument** (Gk. *skeuos*, means 'a vessel that is selected... having a special function to perform'),[30] carries a very strong sense of the divine predetermination as far as Saul's salvation and career are concerned (Rom. 1:1, 5; Gal. 1:15; Eph. 3:7-11; 1 Tim. 1:12-16). Did Saul then have no choice in the matter? This touches the much debated issue of the relationship between divine sovereignty and human responsibility. Both are clearly taught in Scripture. There is inevitable mystery here, as is the case at all the points of interface between the divine and human. 'In faith two characteristics are inherent: it is worked by God and willed by man.'[31] Here the divine action is given the major prominence. **Carry my name** is a vivid expression of our missional responsibility in every age and every situation. Incredibly, and perhaps overwhelmingly, God has committed 'His Name', meaning His character and honour in the world, to us, His people. Well should we pray: 'Hallowed be your Name!' and then offer ourselves as the answer to our own petition, an answer which will carry at its heart our making ourselves available for God's mission to the world. *Kurie elayison!*...'Lord, have mercy!'

Note the scope of Saul's task. Appropriately the mission to the **Gentiles** is mentioned first as being the primary

---

29. Johnson, 165.

30. Bock, 361.

31. A. Schlatter, *Der Glaube im Neuen Testament* (Stuttgart, 1905), 267. cf. also K. Barth, 'The Real Church', SJT., vol. 3, 1950, 341; James Denney, *The Christian Doctrine of Reconciliation*, 1918, 169.

focus; but **Israel** is also included. The range of people to be witnessed to is also notable, including **kings** such as Agrippa (25:23–26:23), and then Caesar (25:10-12). The final sentence, however, immediately balances any sense of rarified or discriminating privilege: **how much he must suffer!** We note that the Greek word here, *dei*, rendered 'must', carries a sense of strong compulsion (cf. 'Did not the Christ *have to* {= *dei*} suffer these things and then enter his glory', Luke 24:26; see also Acts 23:11; 2 Cor. 11:30; Col. 1:24; Phil. 1:29). Here is seeded one of the dominating themes of Saul's ministry, and of his understanding of the costly call to discipleship, as a summons to sacrificial identification with the crucified; 'I have been crucified with Christ..., etc.' Calvin's observation is typically to the point: 'This verse shows us that nobody is fit to preach the Gospel in a hostile world, unless his mind has been prepared for suffering. Therefore if we are to prove ourselves faithful ministers of Christ, not only must we ask Him for the spirit of knowledge and of wisdom, but also for the spirit of steadfastness and of courage, so that we may never be broken by desperate suffering, for it is the lot of the godly.'[32]

Ananias obediently proceeds to find Saul at Judas' home (17). As he lays his hands on him his first words are endlessly memorable – **Brother Saul**. 'If it be true that the Church owes Paul to the prayer of Stephen, it is also true that the Church owes Paul to the brotherliness of Ananias.'[33] How unthinkable that phrase would have been only a day or two before! Yet this is what Christ is ever able to do; turn enemies and persecutors into sisters and brothers. Barclay adds the testimony of a black girl testifying to what an evangelistic campaign had meant to her: 'Through this campaign I have found Christ and he made me able to forgive the man who murdered my father.' That claim could be echoed from every Christian age. *Jesus* can, only Jesus!

But if the raving, bloodstained persecutor can become a meek and humbled brother, as Saul here, then another great lesson of Paul's conversion lies open before us –

32. Calvin: I, 266-7.
33. Barclay: 72.

nobody is safe! No matter how violent their antipathy to Christ and His family, no matter how secure they may imagine themselves to be from his truth-claims and summons, whether they be an acclaimed leader of the 'new atheism', or the imam of an Islamist mosque, or a brutal prison torturer of Christian inmates; they are not safe; they are never safe; no one is safe!

> 'Just when we are safest, there's a sunset touch,
> A fancy from a flower-bell, someone's death...' [34]

Ananias notes his source, **The Lord – Jesus…has sent me, so that you may see again and be filled with the Holy Spirit.** The healing miracle follows directly as **something like scales fell from Saul's eyes**, and as he receives the needed empowerment of the Spirit for his future ministry. We should note that the Spirit is here imparted through a non-apostolic medium.

Supernatural healing, supernatural anointing, and then, finally, Saul is also **baptized**. The indication that baptism was already a recognized practice in Damascus is further evidence of a significant continuing expansion of the faith. But herein surely lies the greatest miracle of all, supernatural grace – the washing away of all his guilt, and his reception into the very body of Christ which so recently he had poured his energies into rending, bloodying and destroying. 'Amazing grace, how sweet the sound…'; indeed!

5. Paul's Post-Conversion Ministry (9:20-30)

This mid-chapter section follows Paul as he begins his ministry, first in Damascus itself, and then after Jewish opposition forced his withdrawal, his eventual appearance in Jerusalem. There, after some hesitation, he was accepted, thanks not least to the advocacy of Barnabas. Paul then moves on to Tarsus, his home city. The church throughout the entire region experiences a time of relative peace and growth.

---

34. Robert Browning, *Bishop Blougram's Apology*.

The account of Paul's movements, and the timing of the various periods of ministry, appear at first reading to create some difficulties in relation to his own accounts of his early ministry period as recorded in Galatians 1:11-24, and, more briefly, 2 Corinthians 11:31-33.[35]

Bruce suggests that the 'immediately' in Galatians 1:17 should not be taken too literally, 'the more so since Luke has nothing to say of the visit to Arabia.'[36] Paul's concern in this section of Galatians 1 is to assert his independence of the other Jerusalem-based apostles, as far as his message is concerned. This certainly need not have precluded an initial ministry in Damascus, which is in any event inherently likely. Nor is it at all impossible that at some point he left Damascus for Arabia and later returned there before his 'basket' escape. Luke's silence on the period in Arabia is unsurprising, granted his relatively single-minded focus on the growth of the Christian movement. The 'after many days' threat to Paul's life, while sourced in the Jewish community, may conceivably, as a public order issue, have had backing of the civic ruler, King Aretas.

Saul continues there **in Damascus** for an indefinite period of **several days,** with Ananias and his fellow believers. However the zeal which moved him to action as an anti-Christian now stirs him as a newly convinced follower. He begins to **preach in the synagogues** (19-20). The form of the synagogue service, where visitors might be invited to expound the law and the prophets, was ideal for his purpose. It is surely striking that Saul is already clear enough on who Jesus is; not only the promised Messiah, but also **the Son of God.** This is the only occurrence of this title in Acts. Apart from being implicitly Messianic, as for

---

35. We can set this out as below, with a proposed resolution in the text. Acts 9 Galatians 1–2…Several days' in Damascus (19)…'Immediately' after his call 'did not… preaching in synagogues…consult with man', but goes to Arabia (16f)…'After many days' threat to life;…After 'three years' to Jerusalem (18ff);…disciples get him away in a basket…sees Peter and James only. Tries to join disciples in Jerusalem;…Later, to Syria and Celicia (21)….Barnabas helps him be accepted (27)…14 years later to Jerusalem again…Debates 'Grecian Jews' (29); sent…(2:1-10); spheres of mission, and…for own safety to Tarsus (30)…remember the poor…2 Corinthians 11…In time of Aretus, lowered from window in a basket and escapes from Damascus.

36. Bruce, 202.

example its use in Psalm 2:7 (cf. 13:33: also Mark 14:61; Luke 22:67, 70), the title also proclaims Jesus' unique relationship to the Father. This is a primary element in its use in Paul's letters (Rom. 1:3-4; 8:29, 32; Gal. 4:4; Col. 1:13-20; 1 Thess. 1:10). The blinding glory of the Damascus Road figure has not left him, nor would it ever: 'with unveiled face beholding the glory of the Lord...for God who said "let light shine out of darkness" has shone in our hearts to give us the light of the glory of God in the face of Jesus Christ' (2 Cor. 3:18; 4:6).

The reaction in the Jewish community in Damascus is predictable; they are **astonished. 'Isn't he the man who raised havoc...among those who call upon this name?'** Well, 'Yes he is', and, 'no he isn't'! 'Yes, he is the same man, Saul from Tarsus, Hebrew of Hebrews, Gamaliel's prize student, Pharisee, Nazarene persecutor.' But 'no he isn't the same man' – he is a baptized Christian, a preacher of the gospel of Jesus, a 'new man in Christ'.

Saul's effectiveness is noted, he **grew more and more powerful...proving that Jesus is the Christ** (22). The reference to 'proving Jesus to be the Messiah (Christ)' would have reflected the burden of Saul's synagogue preaching which would have been directly based in the Old Testament and represents a very early form of the kind of proclamation found in his address in the synagogue of Pisidian Antioch some years later (13:14-41). There Psalm 2:7, Isaiah 55:3 and Psalm 16:10 would be combined to support the declaration that 'God has brought to Israel the Saviour Jesus Christ' (13:23), and the further claim that through the crucified and raised-again Jesus, 'the forgiveness of sins is proclaimed to you...(and) everyone who believes is justified from everything you could not be justified from by the law of Moses' (13:38-39).

After many days had gone by (arguably after Saul had left the city for Arabia and then returned) Jewish antipathy reached breaking point and a plot was hatched, with the local ruler Arterus' blessing, to have Saul arrested and killed. The city gates were accordingly put under constant watch. The prophecy of Saul's 'sufferings for Christ's name' has already begun to find fulfilment (16). The plot was leaked, however, and so **his followers took him by night and lowered him in a basket through an opening in the wall** (25).

The reference to **followers** is evidence of the fruitfulness of Saul's earliest ministry. Jesus' commission, not just 'as a witness of what you have seen of me' (26:16) but also 'to open their eyes and turn them from darkness to light, and from the power of Satan to God' is already being honoured (26:18). Saul was to be many things to many people in the years which followed, but he was always, and not least, an evangelist, a servant of Christ with that peculiar Holy Spirit gift – 'He gave some to be evangelists' (Eph. 4:11) – which again and again moved men, women, boys and girls who heard him preach, to yield their lives and destinies to Christ. Saul would later urge his son in the faith, Timothy, to 'do the work of an evangelist' as part of his 'discharging all the duties of your ministry' (2 Tim. 4:5). Part of God's call to His church in this day, as in every other, is to not only bear witness to the gospel and its truth, but to take specific initiative in urging the hearers to repent of their sins and actually commit themselves to Him. Some are uniquely gifted for such evangelistic ministry, both in public preaching and in personal conversation, as Saul here; and, as he exemplifies, that gift will usually come to the surface early in our ministries. But it continues to be a critical mandate within the mission of Jesus, as the Timothy case illustrates. The circumstances and the means will vary immensely, but the goal is the same: that specific folk known to us, whom we love in Christ's name, and who are to our knowledge without a saving relationship with Jesus Christ should, at a specific time and place, by God's mercy, embrace Jesus Christ as their own, personal Lord and Saviour, for time and eternity.

The means of Saul's final exit from Damascus, being smuggled out after dark like a postal package in the night-mail, had clearly been deeply humiliating as he reflected back on it years later. Perhaps the circumstances of his exit were in such contrast to the dignity of his new ministry as an ambassador of Christ, the Risen and Reigning Lord of all; or perhaps so out of keeping for one who had sacrificed his eminence as the rising star of Judaism in order to preach the gospel; or again so unbecoming to one who was already experiencing such marked blessing in his ministry; we do not know. What is clear is that in its context in 2 Corinthians 11:30-33 Paul sets it in conjunction with his much more celebrated discussion of his 'thorn in the flesh' in 2 Corinthians 12:7-10. The 'basket in the night' and the 'thorn in the flesh', in Paul's mind clearly belong together, as humiliating experiences which God had used, to teach him a great, enduring lesson, that God's power in ministry is 'made perfect' not in human strength, but in human weakness, leading him, 'for Christ's sake', to learn to 'delight in weaknesses, in insults, in hardships, in persecutions, in difficulties', for 'when I am weak, then I am strong.' The lesson continues to be a core course offering for all who would enrol in His service, and to the church corporately as it seeks to engage His mission in our time.

Jim Cymbala, pastor of Brooklyn Tabernacle N.Y., shares his discovery of this truth, which was to transform his ministry. Going as a young man without theological training to a dwindling, depressed, discouraged and nearly closing old church, situated in a rundown, drug and gang-dominated district of New York, he writes: 'On one of those Sunday nights early on, I was so depressed by what I saw – and even more by what I felt in my spirit – that I literally could not preach. Five minutes into my sermon, I began choking on the words. Tears filled my eyes. Gloom engulfed me. All I could say to the people was "I'm sorry...I...I can't preach in this atmosphere...I don't know what to say – I can't go on...Carol, would you play something on the piano, and would the rest of you come to this altar? If we don't see God help us, I don't know..." With that I just quit. It was embarrassing, but I couldn't do anything else. The people did as I asked. I leaned into the pulpit, my face planted in my hands, and sobbed. Things were quiet at first, but soon the Spirit of God came down upon us. People began to call upon the Lord, their words motivated by a stirring within. "God help us" we prayed. Carol played the old hymn "I need Thee, O I need Thee", and we sang along. A tide of intercession arose. That evening when I was at my lowest, confounded by obstacles, bewildered by the darkness that surrounded us, unable even to continue preaching, I discovered an astonishing truth: God is attracted to weakness. He can't resist those who humbly and honestly admit how desperately they need him. Our weakness in fact makes room for his power.'[37]

Paul's next port of call is Jerusalem where **he tried to join the disciples, but they were all afraid of him, not believing that he really was a disciple** (26). It is difficult to know how to understand this reaction. It is important to keep before us that this was a world without telephones, or a regular mail system, or cell-phones, or e-mails, or Facebook or Twitter. It is also relevant to raise the time-frame question. If we need to fit in a three-year period in Arabia as well as whatever length of time he spent overall in Damascus following his encounter with Jesus, then it would not be unlikely that Saul had simply dropped off the radar screen as far as his new ministry-life was concerned. His sudden appearance in Jerusalem of all places, where any remaining memories of him would have been of the raging persecutor, and his collaboration in the slaying of the renowned and still fondly remembered Stephen, make the suspicions perhaps not totally surprising. Paul himself throws light on this, as he notes in Galatians 1:22-23, that during this period he was 'personally unknown to the churches of Judea that are in Christ. They only heard the report: "The man who formerly persecuted us is now preaching the faith he once tried to destroy".' Well, they did have the report, so perhaps we are still rather surprised at the response. But apostles are human too, and have their moments of failure; no small comfort that to the rest of us; and mercifully there was a more generous and trusting spirit in the company: Barnabas, the 'Son of Encouragement', living up to every inch of his nickname (4:36).[38] Barnabas **took Saul and brought him**

37. Jim Cymbala, *Fresh Wind, Fresh Fire* (Zondervan, 1997), 18-19.

38. Bock, 368.

to the apostles. **He told them how Saul on his journey had seen the Lord, and that the Lord had spoken to him, and how in Damascus he had preached fearlessly in the name of Jesus** (27). **So Saul stayed...**What, one is perhaps permitted to wonder, if he had been finally turned away? The repercussions for the future of apostolic Christianity might have been grave indeed. But the Lord remains Lord, and the situation is saved, by a man of large heart. Every church needs such people!

So Paul stayed, **and moved about freely in Jerusalem, speaking boldly in the name of the Lord** (28). In a sense this completes the outworking of Saul's repentance, as he preaches Christ in the very place where he had previously denied him and persecuted his disciples. His mode of operation was probably no different from Stephen's before him (6:9-10), exploiting the opportunity afforded by the synagogue services to teach from the Scriptures the fulfilment of the Messianic promises in Jesus of Nazareth, which brought him into contact, as had also been so for Stephen, with the **Grecian Jews**. The result is also no different; **they tried to kill him**. Saul appears here as 'Stephen *redivivus*'. This prompted the Jerusalem **brothers** to take **him down to Caesarea** on the north-west coast (where he was later to spend two years as a prisoner: 24:27); and then on to his native city of **Tarsus** (30). It is perhaps not accidental that Caesarea was the Roman metropolis in Judea and the residence of the Roman procurators. Its population was a mixed one, and overall a much more Gentile city than any in Judea. Perhaps the brothers in Jerusalem felt that Saul was less likely to create murderous opposition there. Saul was probably quite a hot potato for the Jerusalem church which was apparently able to retain the tolerance of the wider Jewish community. The reference in the next verse to the **peace** which was enjoyed after Saul's departure is hardly accidental. For Saul's part this first 'Christian' ministry in Jerusalem does not appear to have been markedly successful, however there can be no doubt that God was training him through these various early endeavours for the synagogue debates and the more general evangelistic labours that lay ahead throughout the Gentile world.

Appendix:
Chronology of the Life and Ministry of the Apostle Paul
(DATES APPROXIMATE IN MANY CASES)

32–33   Paul's conversion

32–35   Early evangelistic ministry in Arabia and Damascus

35–36   First post-conversion visit to Jerusalem

36–45   'Silent years' in Syria/Cilicia

45–46   Ministry in Antioch with Barnabas

46   'Famine relief' visit to Jerusalem

47–48   First mission journey: to Cyprus and South Galatia

48–49   *Letter to the Galatians*

49   Jerusalem Consultation

49–50   Second mission journey: to Macedonia and Achaia via Galatia and Asia

50   *Letters to the Thessalonians*

50–52   Ministry in Corinth

52   Brief visit to Jerusalem

52–55   Third mission journey: to Ephesus, Achaia and Macedonia via Galatia

55–56   *Letters to the Corinthians*

56–57   Journeys in Macedonia, Illyricum and Achaia

57   *Letter to the Romans*

57   Final visit to Jerusalem and arrest there

57–59   Imprisonment in Caesarea

60   Arrival in Rome

60–62   House arrest/imprisonment in Rome

60–62   *Letters to Colossians, Ephesians, Philemon and Philippians*

62–63   Release, and final mission journey to Crete, Ephesus, Macedonia, Nicopolis, Troas, Corinth, Miletus

62–63   *First letter to Timothy, and letter to Titus*

63–64   Rearrest, and second Roman imprisonment

64–65   *Second letter to Timothy*, and Paul's martyrdom in Rome.

6. A Time of Peace and Progress (9:31)

Luke pauses at this point to interject one of his 'progress reports' on the Christian movement (cf.4:32-33; 5:12-14; 5:42; 6:7).

Then the church throughout Judea, Galilee and Samaria enjoyed a time of peace. We note again Luke's selectivity. To this point we have heard nothing of any witness, or emerging communities of faith, in Galilee. But recalling that this was the location of Jesus' own birth and upbringing, and of the larger part of his early years in ministry, the emergence of Galilean disciples was always to be anticipated. The Sower had sown his Word-seed widely there and some had surely fallen on good soil. The use of **church** in the singular is also noteworthy. The multiplication of distinct groups of disciples throughout Judea following the initial emergence of the Nazarenes' in Jerusalem, does not imply a loss of their unique mutual relationship. They are still one people of God, indwelt by the one Holy Spirit, and united to, and following, the one Lord Jesus Christ.

This **time of peace** was accompanied by, and perhaps contributed to, the church being **strengthened**.[39] The sense of God's initiative in this is underlined by the reference to the Holy Spirit. **Encouraged** (*paraklesei*) has the same width of meaning here as in its use in the Spirit-promises of Jesus (John 14-16), and as referred to the ministry of Barnabas (4:36-37).

Two other features are mentioned. The first is a growth **in numbers** – not merely in general spiritual strength. Ideally and commonly these two forms of growth occur simultaneously; growing Christians are attractive Christians. Again the divine action is underlined, here by the passive mood, = 'were being multiplied'. Secondly, there was a sense of **living in the fear of the Lord.** This should not be too quickly passed over. Those who study the primary expressions of spiritual awakenings note this as a fundamental indicator: 'the spirit of revival is the con-

---

39. 'This participle almost has the force of a result': Bock, 373.

sciousness of God'.[40] We can perhaps whet our appe-
tites with Jonathan Edwards' often-quoted note on the
revival in Northampton, Massachusetts, 'In the spring and
summer of 1735, the town seemed to be full of the presence of God. It was never so full of love, nor so full of joy,
and yet so full of distress, as it was then.' [41]

'The fear of the Lord was the secret of the early church…
Odd. Fear of the Lord would not rate particularly high
on the list of modern church growth strategies. But in
the early church it birthed multitudes of believers…We
can feel that awe pulsating throughout the pages of Acts.
The sense of worship and reverence, the conviction that
Christ had risen and would return, the vibrant absolute
joy of their faith. So filled were they with this awe that
they could face a hostile world with holy abandon. Nothing else mattered, not even their lives. For the church in
the west to come alive…more than anything else it needs
to recover the fear of the Lord. Only that will give us the
abandon that will cause us to be the church no matter
what the culture around us says or does. The fear of the
Lord is the beginning…' [42]

Study Questions:

1. In what respects is Saul's conversion a universal model of how people become Christians (cf.
   1 Tim. 1:12-16)? In what respects is Saul's conversion *not* a universal model?

2. What are the implications of Saul's being told
   to 'go into Damascus' (9:6) in order to discover
   God's will for his future?

3. Consider the respective contributions of Ananias
   (9:10-19) and Barnabas (9:26-28) to Saul's conversion and his future ministry? In what ways can

---

40. Arthur Wallis: *In the Day of Thy Power* (CLC, 1956), 65.

41. ibid, 68.

42. Charles W. Colson, *The Body* (Word, 1992), 393-4.

we assume their mantle in our Christian and church contexts today?

4. Observe the features of the church noted by Luke in 9:31. What do you understand by being 'encouraged by the Holy Spirit', and 'living in the fear of the Lord.'? How can we encourage these realities in our church life today?

6

Peter and Antioch
(Acts 9:32–12:25)

1. Aeneas and Dorcas (9:32-43)

Having described Saul's triumphant conversion to the faith he was in the process of destroying, and then seeing him eventually off to Tarsus, Luke returns his attention to the other apostles, and specifically to their appointed leader, Peter.

Three 'Peter stories' follow; a 'double-miracle' story (Aeneas and Dorcas), 9:32-43; a 'conversion story' (Cornelius), 10:1–11:18; and an 'escape story' (from Herod), 12:1-19.[1] In terms of Luke's critical focus (1:8), the pre-eminently significant event here is the coming of the gospel to the Gentile household of Cornelius, and hence Christianity's crossing of the third major bridge on its journey in the service of the gospel, its entering the Gentile world. Indeed the account of Peter's ministry to Aeneas and Dorcas appears to be a lead-up to it by providing the circumstances which got him to the region of Caesarea where Cornelius was (unknown to either of them) awaiting him. This pre-eminence of 10:1-48 is further underlined by the Cornelius story being immediately followed by the direct evangelization of Gentiles in Antioch, and the resultant church there (11:19-30). While the issue of Gentile salvation would continue to give trouble, certainly until the

---

1. So Stott: 181.

Consultation in Jerusalem in chapter fifteen – and for Paul until the end of Acts (28:23-28) – it is in these next paragraphs that we see the Holy Spirit effectively bringing the church into the final dimension of its missional mandate – 'to the ends of the earth'.

Lydda, where **Aeneas** resided, was a community about twenty-five miles to the west of Jerusalem, on the main highway to the Mediterranean coast. Peter is described as going to **visit the saints** (32; cf. 9:13), no doubt for their encouragement, and for further evangelizing and discipling. We are not told whether Aeneas was yet a 'saint', though there can little doubt that he was so by the end of Peter's visit. The reason he comes to our attention is his being **a paralytic** (33) and **bedridden for eight years** (the Greek term may conceivably mean that he had had the condition since he was eight years old). Peter in the name and authority of the risen Jesus proceeds to heal Aeneas. Luke's wording is striking – **'Jesus Christ heals you. Get up and take care of (**or **"take up") your mat.' Immediately Aeneas got up.** The repetition of Jesus words to the paralytic in Luke 5:24-25, Mark 2:11-12, and Matthew 9:6-7, are unmistakable. Thus, again, Acts 1:1 is finding fulfilment: Jesus is continuing His ministry! The evangelistic impact is profound: **all those living in Lydda and Sharon saw him and turned to the Lord** (35). The Sharon region stretched northwards along the coast and was the home of many Gentiles. Even allowing for some natural hyperbole in the **all** it is difficult to think of the Gentile community being entirely unaffected: but on this, more anon!

The connection established here between evangelism and physical healing opens up an issue that has been struggled with in the churches over many years. We can trace its roots to the ministry of Jesus Himself (Matt. 4:23-25), and to the terms in which He commissioned His disciples (Luke 9:2). The matter continues to divide believers of undoubted maturity and sincerity of faith. Perhaps this Acts passage can be best seen as a simple(!) factual observation: Peter's act of healing in the name of Jesus prompted many to seek salvation in Jesus. A similar cause-effect pattern clearly continues to occur in many parts of the world today, particularly in contexts where there are no other medical resources to draw upon. In general, as far as healing miracles are concerned, we dare not set limits to the power of God, though we must rightly retain a concern that God's honour be always pre-eminent, a recognition of the need for wise pastoral response, and the recognition that the supreme 'healing' is always that of rebirth in the Holy Spirit.

A further twelve miles westwards lay the town of **Joppa** (36), where there was also a Christian community. The spread of the faith throughout Judea is clearly extensive by this point. Joppa is the home of one, **Tabitha** (the Aramaic form of her name, the Greek form being **Dorcas**; in both languages it means 'gazelle'). She is a woman of outstanding character, **always doing good and helping the poor**. Almsgiving, to which her 'giving to the poor' refers, was strongly affirmed in Judaism. Jesus clearly assumes that all His followers will practise it, just as He assumes they will also all pray: cf. Matthew 6:2, 'When you give to the poor…', *not* 'should you happen to give…'; and identically at 6:5, 'when you pray…', *not* 'should you happen to pray…'.

However **about this time, Dorcas became sick and died**, causing understandably widespread grief to the believers there. Hearing of Peter's presence in the region **they sent two men to him and urged him, 'Please come at once!'** (38). This is clearly a qualitatively more serious case than that met at Lydda, but **Peter went with them**. On arrival he is **taken upstairs to the room** where Dorcas' body had been washed in preparation for burial (39). Here he meets the widows of the congregation who are **crying**, and who display the clothes she has made, presumably for the needy.

The placing of the body in the room was unusual and possibly indicates an embryonic faith that even now God may work miraculously through Peter to restore her to them. It may alternatively, or additionally, reflect something of the common notion at the time that the soul only departed from the body, and hence made death irreversible, after three days (cf. John 11:6, 17). Peter clears the room of the mourners. He has been here before and seen his Master raise the dead in a room similarly cleared

(Luke 8:51; Acts 1:1). Peter falls on his knees, a token of the understandable intensity of his praying, but he has seen this too...in Gethsemane (Luke 22:41f). He then gives a command: **Tabitha, get up**. Again the echo is unmistakable: in Luke 8:54, to Jairus' daughter – '*Talitha kumi!*', and here in Joppa, '*Tabitha kumi!*' And again an astonishing miracle – **She opened her eyes, and seeing Peter she sat up** (40). Peter **helped her to her feet**, and then **he called the believers and the widows and presented her to them alive**. It comes as no surprise whatever **that this became known all over Joppa and many people believed in the Lord** (42). Here we are moving in the realm of the unashamedly and irreducibly supernatural. Again there are precedents in Jesus' ministry (Luke 7:11-17, 22; 8:49-56; Matt. 10:8; 11:5; John 11:1-44), as there would be later in Acts (20:7-12).

In its way this association of resuscitation after death with effectual preaching is prefigured in the Old Testament story of Jonah. That preacher of righteousness, at Joppa, the very same place where Peter was now ministering, fled from his commission to call Nineveh to repentance. However, after three days in the belly of the great fish, he returned to his calling, as a man effectively raised from the dead; and as a resurrected preacher was the instrument of a gracious and widespread work of salvation (Jonah 3:1-10). It remains true that it is men and women 'back from the dead', who bear in their lives the marks of crucifixion with Christ, that most effectually proclaim the saving gospel of the crucified and risen Lord.

Peter remains in Joppa but, most significantly, stays in the home of **a tanner named Simon** (43). Simon's profession, since it involved working with the skins of dead animals, was, for more scrupulous Jews like the Pharisees, a despised, 'unclean' trade. Peter is being prepared, small step by small step, for the next great chapter of his ministry career; one that would involve a radical revision of Jewish religious exclusiveness, and carry him, with the church on his shoulders, into the global order of his, and our, global God.

Bearing in mind the immensity of the gulf being crossed, the transition into the third phase of the 'Great Commission' '…and to the ends of the earth', is unsurprisingly a gradual one. In a sense it began as early as Pentecost in chapter 2 with the wide geographical range of the Jewish *diaspora* representing effectively a 'roll call of the nations' (2:8-11). The presence of 'Nicolas from Antioch', very probably a Gentile proselyte, among the 'deacons' in 6:5, was a further straw in the wind, and it resonated again in the theology of Stephen (7:1-50) in his vision of a God who transcends any single location, and who is constantly moving forward to embrace new horizons. It is obviously present in the inclusion of the Samaritans in God's family, signalled, as we argued, by their own Pentecostal outpouring of the Spirit (8:17), and by the conversion of the Ethiopian who was most probably a Gentile 'God-fearer'. The 'third phase', however, really picks up momentum with Saul's dramatic conversion and his commission from the risen Jesus to 'carry my name before the Gentiles' (9:15).

Peter had himself laid a fundamental theological foundation for it in arguing, in his second recorded sermon in 3:25, that God's covenant with Abraham, and its global scope ('through you shall all the families of the earth be blessed'), was fulfilled in the person and ministry of Jesus Christ, who is accordingly the sole medium of salvation, both for Israel and the world (4:12). We have noted Peter's further inching towards Gentile association in the last few paragraphs. But he has some way still to go: 'a lifetime lived within the rules of Jewish food laws and the paradigm of segregation they symbolized was not easily set aside.'[2] In a real sense Peter is still engaged in an identity struggle in his own heart and mind. Stott, along with others, rightly observes that the principal subject of these next chapters is 'not so much the conversion of Cornelius as the conversion of Peter;'[3] or as Bakke aptly names it, 'Peter's second conversion.'[4]

While the anticipations noted above are all important in setting the scene, chapter 10, and its sequel in chapter 11,

---

2. Christopher Wright, 515.

3. Stott, 186.

4. *A Theology as Big as the City* (IVP, 1997), 144.

is in many senses the 'pivotal' point at which the bridge to Christianity as a recognizably global faith is crossed.[5] 'This scene is the turning point of the Book of Acts. From here the gospel will fan out in all directions...across a vast array of geographical regions as Paul's three missionary journeys will underscore.'[6]

2. The Conversion of Cornelius (10:1–11:18)

Luke's epochal account of the reception of the gospel by Gentiles in Caesarea divides broadly into two parts, the gospel received in the home of the Gentile, Cornelius (10:1-48); and Peter's Jerusalem defence of his actions (11:1-18). The first, crucial part of the story is developed in a series of 'scenes' in which the sovereignty of God is unmistakably underlined.

Scene 1: *The House of Cornelius in Caesarea* (10:1-8)
As we remarked earlier, **Caesarea**, of which significant remains can still be viewed, was a very important, largely Gentile, centre. Situated on the north-east coastline of Palestine, and built by Herod the Great as the site of his palace, it was Rome's provincial headquarters. Here its legions were garrisoned, and the Roman Procurator had his permanent home there. **Cornelius** was a **centurion,** in charge of 100 men, in the Roman **Italian Regiment**. This was the third rank in an army which consisted of numerous legions, each comprising 6,000 men, and in turn sub-divided into 6 'cohorts', or regiments, each of a 1,000 men, and each cohort in turn further sub-divided into 10 'centuries' each of a 100 men. Cornelius' modern equivalent would be a captain or non-commissioned officer. The Italian Regiment was generally stationed in Austria but their deployment in Palestine at this time has been confirmed in Roman sources.

Cornelius was **devout** (*eusebes*) **and God-fearing,** qualities shared by **his family** (2). He appears as a particularly admirable representative of the significant numbers of 'God-fearers' throughout the Empire who were attracted

---

5. Wright, 515.
6. Bock, 380.

to the Jewish religion by its monotheism and its strong ethical stress. However they remained on the fringes of synagogues because of the impassable gulf which separated Jews from Gentiles.

Not that Old Testament religion taught such; in it God's purposes clearly include all families and nations (Gen. 12:1-4), and the psalmists and prophets repeatedly speak of God's light and blessing coming to all peoples through the ministry of His Messiah (e.g. Ps. 2; 72; Isa 42:6-7; 49:6-7; Dan. 7:13-14). Israel however had taken its special, privileged role in God's plan as a platform for her own pride, and the ground for full-scale rejection and hatred of Gentiles, separation from whom at every level of life became a basic tenet of their religion.[7] Thus no orthodox Jew would ever enter the home of a Gentile, not excluding the most devout of God-fearers, or have a Gentile of any stripe cross his own threshold. 'All familiar intercourse with Gentiles was forbidden' and 'no pious Jew would have sat down at the same table as a Gentile.'[8] In the case of God-fearing Cornelius, his devotion is noted to be additionally expressed in giving **generously to the needy** and **prayer to God regularly**.

Now, at exactly the time that Peter was ministering to Dorcas and the church in Joppa, Cornelius was at home some thirty miles further up the coast at Caesarea. As he was offering his afternoon prayers he experienced a vision in which he **distinctly saw an angel of God**. The angel addressed him by name, **Cornelius**, and then informed him that **his prayers and gifts to the poor** had **come up as a memorial offering before God** (4). Cornelius is then instructed to send down the coast to Joppa to bring back from there **a man named Simon who is called Peter**, and an address is supplied. Recovering from his understandable **fear** at this encounter, Cornelius immediately called

---

7. William Barclay, 'The Jew had an immense contempt for the Gentile. The Gentiles, said the Jews, were created by God to be fuel for the fires of hell. God, they said, loves only Israel of all the nations he has made.' *Letters to the Galatians and the Ephesians* (Saint Andrew Press, 1958), 195.

8. A. Edersheim, *Jewish Social Life*, pp. 25-9; cited Stott: 185.

two of his servants and a devout soldier...and sent them to Joppa (8).

Scene 2: *The House of Simon the Tanner in Joppa* (10:9-23)
Meanwhile...down in Joppa (though by the time the trio from Caesarea arrive there it is actually the next day) Peter also takes to prayer, on the roof of Simon's house. This location was a commonly sought place for quiet. Peter's prayers are disturbed, as many intercessors over the centuries since would concur, by distracting desires, in this case for food. While the meal is in preparation, he falls into a trance. The word used (*ekstasis*) is different from *horama*, which was used for Cornelius' 'vision' (v.3), implying something more visual. Peter apparently **saw heaven opened and something like a large sheet being let down to earth by its four corners** (11). The sheet contained **all kinds of four-footed animals, as well as reptiles...and birds.** The creatures in the sheet were in many cases specifically proscribed in Leviticus 11, and 20:25, as 'unclean' and hence non-kosher for a faithful law-abiding Jew like Peter. It is 'evidently a mixture of clean and unclean animals calculated to disgust any orthodox Jew.'[9]

Peter is commanded by a heavenly voice to **Get up... kill and eat** – a shocking order. He reacts with the revulsion of any self-respecting, God-fearing Jew – **Surely not, Lord!** The Greek word *medamos* is a very strong one = 'absolutely not!' The entire statement, however, is internally contradictory; its two terms are in impossible conflict: *either* 'not so' *or* 'Lord' must prevail. One recalls Peter's similar reaction to Jesus' announcement at Caesarea Philippi of His impending suffering, rejection and death – 'Never, Lord!' (Matt. 16:22). On that occasion Jesus had had to publicly rebuke Peter, though acknowledging the tempter's presence behind him (Matt. 16:23). In this further case 'the Lord' will again prevail, though it will take Peter some time to admit it, and indeed some further time to work out the full implications of that surrender, as Paul was to discover (Gal. 2:11-14).

---

9. Stott:187.

Peter here resorts to trotting out his impeccable record in observing Jewish food laws, **I have never eaten anything impure or unclean** (14). This elicits a further response, one of far-reaching significance: **Do not call anything impure that God has made clean**. The sheet is then withdrawn, only to be let down a second time with the same command, and then the whole thing is repeated for a third time before the sheet is finally removed (16).

The saying, **Do not call anything impure that God has made clean**, carries several important implications. *First*, it confronts Peter with the one to whom he is speaking, the one who is Lord! Peter is therefore implicitly reminded of his proper attitude towards Him; that of complete submission. But not Peter alone! 'Why do you call me "Lord, Lord" and do not do what I say?' (Luke 6:46). No follower of Christ can evade the challenge here. 'Not so, Lord!' is no more acceptable on our lips today than it was on Peter's lips these centuries ago. As the old maxim has it: 'If he is not Lord of all, he is not Lord at all.' While it will not be until the renewal of all things that any of us will be able to fully attain this, it remains our daily challenge. Truly understood, however, the summons to entire obedience is not an imposition but a liberation, for this 'Lord' who claims our total allegiance is the one who loves us with an infinite and endless love; 'his service is perfect freedom!' (Augustine).

> 'How little worthy of any love thou art!
> Whom wilt thou find to love ignoble thee
> Save only Me?
> All which I took from thee I did but take,
> Not for thy harms,
> But just that thou mights't seek it in my arms.
> All that thy child's mistake
> Fancies as lost, I have stored up for thee at home:
> Rise, clasp my hand and come.' [10]

More specifically, for the issue of clean and unclean foods, it is the assertion that God, who instituted the ban on eating 'unclean' foods, has the right, inherent in His

---

10. Francis Thompson.

divine sovereignty, to lift or alter it, as and when He may please.

Second, the statement has major implications for the entire relationship of Jews and Gentiles. At a stroke it eliminates all food regulations as a ground of social or religious distinction. If we uphold the early tradition that Peter's reminiscences underlie the text of Mark's Gospel, then we can be confident that Peter, certainly at a later point, was to recall Jesus' saying recorded in Mark 7:18-19: 'Don't you see that nothing that enters a man from the outside can make him "unclean"? For it doesn't go into his heart but into his stomach.' The obvious implication is immediately drawn by the evangelist: 'In saying this, Jesus declared all foods "clean."' Thus, what had separated Jews from Gentiles for centuries ceases to be applicable: 'The vision (in Acts 10) shows the arrival of a new era.'[11] Hence, in the immediate context, 'it frees Peter from any scruples about going to a Gentile home and eating whatever might be set before him.'[12]

Third, the saying, **do not call anything impure that God has made clean** can be applied to every Christian heart in terms of our appropriation of forgiveness on the basis of Christ's atoning sacrifice. When we believe in this Saviour we affirm that all our sins, past, present and future, were, in their entirety, assumed by Him in His own person offered up for us on the cross. In His death He took upon Himself the full and entire penal implications of our sin, for both time and eternity (1 John 1:8–2:2; Heb. 10:5-17). Amazingly, sinners though we be, we are pronounced *clean* in God's sight and presence. 'There is therefore no condemnation for those who are in Christ Jesus' (Rom. 8:1).

It is a regular fact of Christian experience, however, that our assurance of 'peace with God' is disrupted by a lingering sense of shame and failure, and by the memory of specific sins which we may have fallen into. Accordingly so many Christians, in spite of our free justification by the Lord, live with an ongoing sense of guilt and self-reproach,

---

11. Bock: 389.

12. Marshall:186.

and are as a result often unattractive to non-Christians, and less than a delight to those who share our daily lives.

The words of the Lord to Peter here are perfectly suited to our burdened consciences: 'Do not call impure' – your heart, your spirit, your person – 'what God has made clean', by the atoning sacrifice of the Lord Jesus Christ for these very sins at Calvary. In a deep sense by so affirming and believing we are simply allowing God to be God! We are letting Christ be the full, complete and all-sufficient Saviour He claims to be. Correspondingly, by a continued state of guilty self-reproach, we are in effect reducing and limiting the fullness of His work for us; we are diminishing Calvary! So, let God be God! Give Him the glory, honour and praise which is His due! Let Him fully redeem, save and justify you! Celebrate His *boundless* mercy! Celebrate, and crown this *complete* Saviour! **Do not call impure what God has made clean!**

Peter, no surprise here, is caused to **wonder** about the meaning of the vision. And in the midst of his musings, at that precise moment, the doorbell rings! (17-18). The **three** (Gentile) **men,** sent by Cornelius have arrived at Simon's door and are asking for Peter. We note how perfectly over these hours God dovetailed the actions, and the multiple impressions, reactions and movements of Cornelius and Peter. Since Peter's scruples are still not fully in harmony with the larger plot-line here, the Holy Spirit takes the initiative and informs him directly: **While Peter was still thinking about the vision, the Spirit said to him: 'Simon, three men are looking for you** (does Peter notice the relevance of the number?). **So get up and go downstairs. Do not hesitate to go with them, for I have sent them'** (20).

Peter introduces himself, **I'm the one you are looking for. Why have you come?** (21). The messengers identify their master, and add further testimony to his worthiness: **Cornelius is a righteous and God-fearing man, who is respected by all the Jewish people. A holy angel told him to have you come to his house so that he could hear what you have to say (**22). Peter agrees to go, the Mishnah's prohibition: 'the dwelling places of Gentiles are unclean', notwithstanding. Since it is already too late in the day to make the journey to Caesarea before nightfall, hospitality is offered; the 'unclean' Gentiles are invited into the house for the night; already 'the idea of fellowship is implicit.[13] Peter is getting it!

Scene 3: *Peter arrives at Cornelius' home and introduces himself to the gathered audience* (10:23b-33)
The following day Peter and his party, comprising the three Gentile emissaries along with an additional group of **six brothers** from the Joppa church (11:12), set off for **Caesarea**, arriving **the following day** (24). Cornelius meanwhile has assembled a company of **his relatives and close friends**; Gentiles all, we may safely presume. On Peter's arrival, Cornelius, influenced no doubt by the angelic identification of Peter as the source of a message from God, and perhaps also by the Greek traditions of 'divine men', falls at Peter's feet in obeisance (25), but Peter immediately rejects it, **Stand up, I am only a man myself** ('I'm a human being like you': NLT).

Peter then enters the large inner room of the house and finds the assembled crowd (27). He makes a crucial introductory statement clarifying the proprieties of his visit, and laying open the basis of the unprecedented Jew-Gentile *détente* which is being engaged before their eyes (28-29). **You are well aware** (it was as common knowledge as the air they were all breathing) **that it is against our law for a Jew to associate with a Gentile or visit him**. The word Peter uses for 'against our law' (*athemiton*) has the force of 'disgusting'. Peter uses it again in 1 Peter 4:3, the only other New Testament occurrence. This was an emotive issue, no mere legal quibble. Bruce suggests 'taboo'[14] as an appropriate translation. Peter then uncovers the reason for his having at that moment, as a devout Jew, consciously flouted that sacred, centuries-old, prohibition. **God has shown me**...Peter is no doubt alluding to the overwhelming events of the last hours...but nothing less than a direct divine command would have sufficed...

13. Bock, 392.
14. Bruce, 259.

that I should not call any man impure or unclean. This is such a critical statement that there is a compelling case here for a gender-inclusive reading: 'that I should not call *anyone* impure or unclean.'[15]

Put another way: there are no second-class people in God's world! There are, in fact, no 'ordinary' people, anywhere, or at any time. Calvin reached this truth by way of recognizing the image of God in all people: 'We are not to consider what (people) merit of themselves, but to look at the image of God which exists in all, and to which we owe all honour and love.'[16] Paul provides another demonstration of this irreducible equality; recognizing others as those 'for whom Christ died' (Rom. 14:15). The ground is endlessly level at the cross.

Dr Sheila Cassidy writes prophetically from her immersion in hospice ministry to the dying: 'If I as a doctor spend an hour of my clinic time talking to a woman who has only a few weeks to live, I am making a clear statement of her worth. I am giving her time that could have been spent with people who will get better, who will be able to contribute again to the common good. I am affirming the worth of one individual person in a world in which the individual is at risk of being submerged, or valued only for his strength, intellect or beauty. It is a prophetic statement about the unique value of the human person, irrespective of age, social class, or productivity. It is an affirmation that people matter just because they are people, because God made them and loves them, just as they are, not because they are good or witty or physically beautiful.'[17] 'We lost twenty thousand men,' once stated a leader of armies, 'but no one of importance'. From the perspective of Peter's statement here, and its larger biblical base, that is, quite simply, a sentence from hell.

Returning to the flow of these verses, Stott makes the apt observation; 'Whether consciously or unconsciously, Peter had just now repudiated both extreme and opposite

---

15. So NLT rendering of D.A. Carson and R. Mohrlang; also that of the NIVI.

16. Calvin, *Institutes*. III:7:6.

17. *Sharing the Darkness* (Orbis Books, 1991), 60-1.

attitudes which human beings have sometimes adopted towards one another. He had come to see that it was entirely inappropriate either to worship somebody as if divine (as Cornelius had tried to do to him), or to reject somebody as if unclean (which he would previously have done to Cornelius). Peter refused both to be treated as if he were a god, and to treat Cornelius as if he were a dog.'[18]

Peter, having clarified why he has come **without raising any objection** (29), asks Cornelius to explain why he has sent for him. Cornelius then recounts the vision, with a precise time-reference, **at three in the afternoon**, confirming the objective nature of the experience, and then mentions the angel, **a man in shining clothes**, his message, and the instruction to send for Peter. He ends invitingly – **Now we are all here in the presence of God to listen to everything the Lord has commanded you to tell us** (30-33); thrice happy the preacher for whom these words express the attitude of his waiting congregation, and thrice happy the congregation whose hunger for God is authentically echoed here.

Scene: 4: *Peter's message, and the reaction* (10:34-46)
The sermon has two parts: (a) The principle of equality before God: 34; (b) The good news about Jesus Christ: 35-43.

Peter begins by reiterating the equality principle of verse 28, **God does not show favouritism**; though here the negative is followed by a positive, **but accepts men from every nation who fear him and do what is right**. The word for 'showing no favouritism' (*prosopolemptes*) occurs only here in the New Testament. It renders a Hebrew phrase 'lift (up) the face of'. The image is a vivid one: 'God lifts all faces' without discrimination. The **from every nation** is stressed in the following verse, hence underlining the ethnic implications in particular. External criteria such as race or religious pedigree are now irrelevant: Jews and Gentiles are on the same playing field in the search for God. Specifically **those who fear him**

---

18. Stott: 189.

and do what is right, presumably such as Cornelius, are noted by God wherever their location or whatever their nationality or tradition. Paul teaches no differently in Romans 2:6-10, which concludes identically: 'God does not show favouritism' (2:11). Of course neither Peter nor Paul are implying that individuals of this character, like Cornelius, can thereby secure their standing with God by their meritorious religious and moral practices. Paul immediately follows the passage in Romans 2 with citations from three Psalms, 14:1-3 ('There is no-one righteous, not even one'), Psalm 53:1-3, and Psalm 36:1, all grounding his conclusion, 'no one will be declared righteous in God's sight by observing the law'; 'all have sinned and fall short of God's glory' (Rom. 3:10-18, 20, 23). A similar qualifier applies here, as Lenski pertinently observes: 'if this honest pagan's convictions had been sufficient, why did he seek the synagogue? If the synagogue had been enough, why was Peter there?'[19] To argue, as some do, that the statement, **God accepts (***dektos***) from every nation men who fear him and do what is right** (35) means their having attained thereby an entire righteousness before God, i.e. their eternal justification, requires us, on the basis of an alleged meaning of one biblical text, to set aside the entire biblical account, promised in the Old Testament and fulfilled in the New Testament, of salvation through Jesus Christ alone. For Scripture, 'A good life is acceptable in God's sight only when it leads to recognition of its own inadequacy, and to acceptance of the gospel.'[20] Peter himself could not have been clearer on this very point, 'There is no other name under heaven (than Jesus) by which we must be saved' (4:12). Calvin rightly dismisses this self-justifying understanding of Peter's statement as 'an exceedingly childish error'.[21]

The context (as in Romans 2) points to the correct exegesis here: 'God does not show favouritism', and hence the previously assumed superiority of Jews over Gen-

---

19. Lenski, 419.

20. Marshall, 190.

21. Calvin, 288.

tiles in the eyes of God can no longer be sustained. Jesus' often-repeated saying, 'whoever has will be given more' (Matt. 13:12; 25:29; Mark 4:25; Luke 6:38; 8:18; 11:9; 12:48; Matt. 7:7) is to the point here. Cornelius had responded to what light had been given him, and hence was given more light. With the coming of Jesus a new era has dawned for humanity in which 'every nation' stands on equal foot-ing outside the door to salvation, an era in which, as Paul would later teach the Athenians, every person may 'seek him and perhaps reach out for him and find him...who is not far from each one of us' (17:27). More generally Peter models here the instinctive courtesy and regard which we are to show towards the adherents of other religious tradi-tions where they are patently productive of general moral goodness. Their continuing need to repent and embrace Jesus Christ for their salvation, which is not in question, should not inhibit a genuine, even warm human respect.

Peter now moves to **the good news of peace through Jesus Christ**; only now is salvation brought within reach (36). This is a message which **you know**. 'Jesus was a topic of public discourse.'[22] Moreover it is **the message God sent to the people of Israel**. The Jews had been the deeply privileged, yet simultaneously the fearfully responsible bearers, of the message – salvation *is* 'from the Jews' (John 4:22), but from the Jews *for every nation*.

Peace here is primarily with God, as Peter will reiter-ate at verse 43, the peace which accompanies, and is the fruit of, forgiveness of sins (cf. Isa. 52:7; Nahum 1:15). But the peace brought through Jesus is also critically so in the presence of this particular audience. 'God brings various ethnic groups into one in Christ. This message is impor-tant in Acts. Jesus brings reconciliation not only with God but also between people. The new community will be diverse in make-up, equal in status, and called to reflect peace with one another (Eph. 2:11–22).'[23] **He is Lord of all** represents the basis of the claim for Christ's peace-bring-ing, in both the divine and human spheres. As 'Lord of all'

---

22. Bock , 397.
23. Bock, 410.

He is one in being with the universal Creator, the personal presence of the moral Lord to whom all people are finally accountable, and through whom alone salvation and eternal peace can be obtained (Matt. 28:18-20). As 'Lord of all' He is the exalted ruler of all the nations and hence the one who alone can unite them in peace within His kingdom, and under His gracious rule.

Having thus declared the significance of Jesus Christ in general terms, Peter develops it in three further paragraphs, dealing in turn with Jesus' ministry (37-39a); his death and resurrection (39b-41); and the implications for humanity (42-43).

Jesus' ministry (37-38): Peter's summary begins with **the baptism John preached**, and Jesus having been **anointed with the Holy Spirit and power**, an inclusive reference probably to His baptism at the Jordan and the continuing supernatural accompaniments of His ministry. This reality of **God with him** (cf. John14:10–11; 10:37f; 5:19) is evidenced by His having **gone around doing good**, and **healing all who were under the power of the devil** (38). This 'very much parallels Mark's presentation of Jesus' ministry.'[24] This is no surprise, since according to the tradition of Papias, recorded by Eusebias (c.265–c.339): 'Mark, who was the interpreter of Peter, wrote down accurately all that he remembered, whether of sayings or doings of Christ, but not in order…he accompanied Peter, who adapted his instruction as necessity required…So then Mark made no mistake when he wrote down thus some things as he remembered them; for he concentrated on this alone – not to omit anything that he had heard, nor to include any false statement among them.'[25] Peter affirms the authenticity of this portrayal, **we are witnesses of everything he did in the country of the Jews and in Jerusalem** (39). The outline here is also reflected in Luke's own Gospel account (cf. 3:1-20, 21-22; 4:1-13, 16-18, 31-44; 7:22-23; 8:26-39; 11:17-23; 13:16). Luke's historical method is hence directly affirmed here (Luke 1:1-2).

---

24. Bock, 397.

25. Eusebias, EH 3.39.

On Jesus' 'going about doing good' (AV), the celebrated Japanese Christian leader Kagawa made the pertinent connection with all our lives: 'I read that "Jesus went about doing good"; this bothers me – because most of the time I just go about!'

Jesus' death and resurrection (39b-41): Here is the core of the gospel: there is no 'good news' without it. **They killed him by hanging him on a tree**. The language here has clear resonances of Deuteronomy 21:22-23: 'If a man guilty of a capital offence is put to death and his body is hung on a tree…be sure to bury him that same day, because anyone who is hung on a tree is under God's curse.' As with the similar language in Acts 5:30 and Galatians 3:13, we are clearly encountering an atonement theory here. Jesus died as the vicarious bearer of the curse of God upon our sinning. Our familiarity with this truth must not blind us to the almost incredible claim at its heart. The 'hanging on a tree' of the corpse of the condemned was to signal their being morally polluted in the sight of both God and man. They are 'lifted up' so as to be in a vivid sense 'separated' and hence no longer a source of moral contamination to the community. In the cross Jesus takes our pollution upon Himself and becomes a pollutant on our behalf! At Calvary *we* treat *God* as a contaminant! In face of truths such as this, the observation of the seventeenth-century Scottish churchman Robert Leighton finds entire justification: 'The whole world in comparison with the cross of Jesus is one vast impertinence.'

But God raised him from the dead on the third day and caused him to be seen (40). The resurrection is not merely an inward conviction, but an inward conviction created by an external, space-time event 'on the third day'. It was further authenticated by subsequent visual encounters: **he was seen, by witnesses whom God had already chosen – by us who ate and drank with him after he rose from the dead** (41). Here the audience in Cornelius' assembly room enjoy the unique privilege of a face-to-face encounter with one of the chief witnesses of the resurrection of Jesus; they are literally within touching distance of the interface of human history and divine super-history.

It is increasingly difficult to dismiss this testimony as ancient fable from a prehistoric time, or the projection of frustrated ambition or wish-fulfilment on the disciples' part. Not least, as we noted at an earlier point, there is the difficulty of how we account for this resurrection claim on the part of Peter and the other apostles. For there was no precedent anywhere in their experience of precisely this configuration of what happened to Jesus after the cross. Judaism, which was their common religious milieu, did know of resurrection, but nothing like this. The resurrection was either of all Israel at the end of history, or of all the righteous within Israel at the end of history. That is, it was only understood as a part of the cataclysmic end of human society, and only as a corporate experience of a mass of the dead. Nowhere in Peter's life to this point had he ever come across the notion that a single individual would be raised again after death to new, 'heavenly' life as the precursor, but only that, of the arrival of the end of history, at some still unidentified future point. Where did the disciples get this obscure, unprecedented, notion of an individual resurrection, which none of the celebrated rabbis or revered theological scholars of the time had championed or taught? Further this notion was propagated with unwavering conviction and unflinching courage, not by representatives of the scholarly class whose supreme authority in religious matters was axiomatic, but by a mixed bag of artisan lay-folk who had been denied the rarefied echelons of religious education. When all this is weighed, the only explanation that does justice to the facts is the one provided by Peter here: 'He was seen by us…after he rose from the dead.'[26]

---

26. cf. Prof. C.D.F. Moule: 'I find it difficult, if not impossible, to believe that the disciples had, in the Old Testament Scriptures and in the life and teaching of Jesus and their own circumstances, all that was necessary to create Easter-belief. Granted that they were thrown into an ecstasy of astonishment by what Jesus was and did, something more is needed to lead to the conclusion that Jesus had been not merely a superlatively great prophet, nor simply a man of the Spirit, nor just Messiah (the latter is an almost impossible conclusion, anyway, after the Crucifixion), but that he was alive in a unique and hitherto unexplained way, and therefore Son of God in a far more than Messianic sense, and "Lord," and the climax and coping stone of the whole edifice of God's plan of salvation…One is bound to recognize here something startlingly novel, and to ask

The implications for humanity (42-43): There are four: (1) *The proclamation of the gospel.* **He commanded us to preach to the people** (42). Peter rounds out the ministry of Jesus by alluding to his post-resurrection commissioning of the apostles to proclaim the gospel through the world (cf. Luke 24:47). Whereas the terms of the commission as recorded in Acts 1:8 were in the indicative mood –'you will be my witnesses...' this format is in the imperative: **he commanded us**...To come under the rule of **the Lord of all** means the obligation to obey His direct commands, not least this one: to participate in the proclamation of the gospel. Peter is discharging that responsibility in an epochal manner in this very sermon. The verb here is the classical New Testament one for preaching, *kerysso*. Barth's definition effectively expresses its force: 'Preaching is human speech in and by which God speaks, like a king through the mouth of his herald.'[27]

(2) *The future judgment of all people by Jesus Christ.* **He is the one appointed to judge the living and the dead** (cf. 17:31; John 5:22-30; Rom. 2:16; 2 Cor. 5:10; 2 Thess. 1:7-10; Rev. 14:14-20; 20:11-13). Present universal responsibility implies future universal accountability.

This is one of the most important ideas in biblical religion, and in Christianity's truth system. Unfortunately it is only rarely today given the prominence it occupies in Scripture. Our inveterate desire not to appear judgmental, and to avoid 'turning people off', far too often mutes our witness at this point. The loss is far-reaching, as it arguably contributes to a domestication of God and a consequent lack of depth in the experience of conversion and in subsequent allegiance to him. That we will all one day be called upon to give an account of our lives is, however, not only a universal truth of biblical religion, but also a virtually universal instinct of the human conscience, and consequently a major engine driving unbelief. As Dinesh

---

what there is to account for it. And the answer seems to be a most powerful and original mind, and a tremendous confirmatory event.' 'The Resurrection: A Disagreement.' *Theology* 75 (April 1972): 515.

27. K. Barth, *Church Dogmatics* (T and T Clark, 1975), I.1, 52.

D'Souza pertinently observes: 'Contrary to popular belief, atheism is not primarily an intellectual revolt, it is a moral revolt. Atheists don't find God invisible so much as objectionable…But this is something we can all identify with… We want to be saved, but not from our sins. We are quite willing to be saved from a whole host of social evils, from poverty to disease to war. But we want to leave untouched the personal evils, such as selfishness and lechery and pride…This is the perennial appeal of atheism: it gets rid of the stern fellow with the long beard and liberates us for the pleasures of sin and depravity. The atheist seeks to get rid of moral judgment by getting rid of the judge.'[28]

One specific testimony will suffice, that of atheist Aldous Huxley: 'I had motives for not wanting the world to have meaning: consequently I assumed that it had none…For myself, as no doubt for most of my contemporaries, the philosophy of meaninglessness was essentially an instrument of liberation. The liberation we desired was… liberation from a certain system of morality. We objected to the morality because it interfered with our sexual freedom.'[29] This is not, of course, to imply that all atheists live immoral lives, but it *is* to imply that viewing them (or anyone else) as simple, unbiased 'seekers after truth' is to be fundamentally misinformed.

But the designation of Jesus as the instrument of that inevitable coming judgment is additionally replete with implications as far as His person is concerned. For the Old Testament, God alone is judge (Deut. 32:4; Ps. 99; Isa. 5:16). Final judgment is therefore His sole prerogative (Dan. 7:9f; Eccles. 12:14; Joel 2:31). As the Judge of all, Jesus is consequently one in essence with the Father. As the risen one, Jesus is the Man of the Last Day, the one who holds the ages in His hand and to whom they are all accountable. He was 'declared with power to be the Son of God by his resurrection from the dead' (Rom. 1:4). We may note how totally this overturns the notion, much touted in liberal New Testament interpretation over the last two centuries,

---

28. Dinesh D'Souza, *What's So Great About Christianity?* (Regency, 2007), 272.

29. Aldous Huxley, 'Confessions of a Professed Atheist,' *Report*, June 1996.

that Jesus was essentially a unique human individual who over time grew ever larger in the minds of his followers until by the late first century they were disposed to attribute deity to him. On the contrary, worship of Jesus, and hence His identity as the divine judge of all, was present from the beginning, as Luke notes in his Gospel (24:52), and as is reflected by implication here.

(3) *Jesus is the fulfilment of the Old Testament Messianic promises*: **all the prophets testify about him** (43). Luke had recorded words of the risen Jesus, 'This is what I told you…everything must be fulfilled that is written about me in the Law, the Prophets and the Psalms. Then he opened their minds so they could understand the Scriptures' (Luke 24:44-45). The Old Testament is to be interpreted in terms of its pointing forward to Jesus' life, ministry, death, resurrection and return.

(4) *Believing in Jesus brings forgiveness of sins*: **everyone who believes in him receives forgiveness of sins through his name**. The 'everyone' is the critical new dimension. The gospel emerged in a world where 'salvation' was on offer in a variety of forms; but each was hedged around by limitation: it was salvation only for some. Salvation was on offer in Judaism, but only for those who would share in the coming Messianic age, which meant those who were born Jewish, had been duly circumcised, who took upon themselves the yoke of the law, and were participants in the ongoing cultic worship. There might also be salvation for non-Jews provided they submitted to the rites of proselyte conversion and made a like commitment to respect and follow the Torah. The Essenes were a monastic community by the Dead Sea who essentially limited the hope of salvation to those who would renounce the world and enter their community. The Roman Empire offered 'salvation', but only to those who sought it through their own efforts, whether by mastering magic arts, or by acquiring special knowledge, or engaging in philosophy, or by participation in secret rites of initiation. In every case it was salvation for some. But the 'good news' of Jesus Christ broke the mould; it offered nothing less than salvation for 'everyone without any exception'; it was the breakthrough to a universal gospel offering a universal pos-

sibility that the final judgment can be faced without fear for all who believe. Sin, no matter how often repeated, no matter how terrible, no matter how long-standing, can be totally pardoned and eternally forgiven. Truly Peter is 'telling the good news' (36). Can there be any better? And it is for the *whole world*!

Scene 5: *The reaction to Peter's sermon* (10:44-46)
This heading potentially misleads in two ways. First, we should note that to imply any time lag between the sermon and the response is a mistake. **While Peter was still speaking these words…**Things began to happen even while Peter was in full flight in his message. He will later report, 'As I began to speak…' (11:15). This is an over-precise translation, but it underlines that the coming of the Spirit was clearly initiated before Peter had concluded. Second, to imply that the response was initiated in the listeners would also misrepresent what happened… **the Holy Spirit came on all who heard the message**. The reaction in other words was divine before it was human. God 'came down' upon that listening company in the glory and power of His Holy Spirit's overwhelming, outpoured presence. The verb here translated **came on** is *epepsen,* from *epipipto,* an intensive form of the verb, *pipto* = 'to fall' which we earlier argued is best rendered by 'fell all over' (cf. discussion at 8:17).

Astonishment is registered by the 'six from Joppa' who had come with Peter, the six Jewish believers who had dared to join Peter in his groundbreaking identification with the Gentiles in Cornelius' home. For what they were witnessing was unmistakably Christian – **the gift of the Holy Spirit**. They were **speaking in tongues and praising God – even on Gentiles** the Holy Spirit had fallen! But for Peter there is a further astonishing connection – 'They have received the Holy Spirit, *just as we…*' The verb is implicit, but 'just as we *did*' is surely correct (So AV, NLB, REB). As Peter makes quite clear in his report of these events to the Jerusalem church in 11:15, 'The Holy Spirit came on them as he had come on us *at the beginning.*' In other words he sees this outpouring as identical in its primary features to the outpouring at Pentecost. 'Just as the first Jewish believers had received the Spirit and praised God in other tongues on the day of Pentecost, so now these Gentiles had received the identical gift of God.'[30] It was 'The Pentecost of the Gentile world.'[31]

We may then identify three 'Pentecosts' in Acts, in chapters 2, 8, and 10; three special giftings, three 'falling all overs' of the Spirit, at the three critical boundary points in the church's ever-widening expansion in its proclamation of the gospel, as mandated by Jesus in Acts 1:8: *'Jerusalem, Samaria,* and "the ends of the earth",' *the Gentile world.*

The implication of all this is so simple and yet so profound; whether we be 'Christian insiders', born and raised through our whole lives within the fold of the church (like the Jews); whether we be part of a 'Christian society' with some distant Christian memory but without any Christian practice (like the Samaritans); whether we be people from right outside Christian influences or beliefs (like the pagan Gentiles) – when we commit ourselves to Christ we are all equal. All Christians are one people of God; all are reborn by the 'coming upon' of the same Holy Spirit; all are reconciled to, and received by, the same Almighty Father; all are justified and pardoned through the same atoning sacrifice of the Lord Jesus Christ; all are equally valuable; equally important; equally loved. The point of these three exceptional visitations of the Spirit was to underline that this was *God's* eternal purpose, *God's* personal initiative, *God's* good will. God authenticates the gospel of Jesus Christ as the means of entry to the new community of the people of God in which religious, historical, cultural and ethnic distinctions are finally irrelevant, and all are 'one in Christ Jesus' (Gal. 3:28).

Accordingly, Peter' bows to the overwhelming evidences of God's sovereignty both in the engineering of the meeting in Cornelius' home, and even more so in the dramatic divine imprimatur expressed in the Spirit's descent in Pentecostal glory. These Gentiles are clearly fully endorsed members of the body of Christ, and hence

---

30. Marshall: 194.

31. Bruce: 1990: 264.

they should immediately receive the universal Christian rite of admission: **Can anyone keep these people from being baptized? ... So he ordered that they be baptized in the name of Jesus Christ** (47, 48). The use of water here, while of course symbolic of moral and spiritual cleansing, would have carried a special pertinence, since the Gentiles had been previously viewed by Peter and his fellow-Jews, not just as having the wrong ethnicity, but as 'unclean'.

Hardly surprisingly Peter agreed to **stay with them for a few days**. Since there is no indication that any member of Cornelius' household or circle of friends were Christians prior to these moments, Peter had on his hands a church entirely composed of brand-new converts. Discipleship was desperately needed in that circumstance, but the blessings and benefits of this 'Gentile Pentecost' would have continued to accrue no doubt, not only to these spiritual 'new-borns', but to Peter himself.

There were still issues to be clarified of course, specifically which elements of the Old Testament law Gentile Christians should be encouraged to observe in order to satisfy Jewish Christian consciences. This had huge practical significance since both groups must obviously be able in future to share in table fellowship, a point emphatically underlined by the fact that one of the primary legacies of Jesus was precisely a common meal. These questions would be addressed in the Jerusalem Consultation in 15:1-31. There was also the matter of how the mother church in Jerusalem would react to all this, for without their endorsement of the full acceptance of Gentiles the road ahead would be bound to be a rocky one. But this too was on God's agenda and the next section in 11:1-18 would bring a reassuring response.

Despite these two pieces of unfinished business, the significance of this section in 10:1-48 can hardly be overstated. The age-old promise to Abraham of the blessing of 'all the families of the earth' was at last fulfilled in the one who came to be a 'light to the Gentiles', as His gospel began to circle the earth. In principle, the great gulf had been crossed, or perhaps better, the door to the Gentile world had swung open, and would never close again. The life-bringing fruit of that day in Caesarea continues to be tasted all over the world. Christianity is a global faith, as history would demonstrate, not least in our own time. It is a faith for all nations, all peoples, all tribes, all tongues, and all ages. Jesus belongs to all of the world.

Peruvian missiologist Samuel Escobar expresses it memorably for today: 'The missionary facts of our time make me pause in wonder. Jesus Christ, incarnate Son of God, is the core of the gospel, which as a potent seed has flourished in a thousand different places. We can name a time on earth in which Jesus lived and taught. In other words we can place him in a particular culture at a particular moment in history. "The Word became flesh and lived for a while among us," in Palestine during the first century of our era. After that, the story of Jesus has moved from culture to culture, from nation to nation, from people to people. And something very wonderful has taken place. Although this Jesus was a peasant from Palestine, everywhere he has been received, loved, and adored, and people in hundreds of cultures and languages have come to see the glory of God in the face of Jesus Christ. Moreover they have come to feel that Jesus is "theirs", so that they say, "Jesus is one of ours." At the beginning of the twenty-first century the global church stands closer than ever to that vision of John in Revelation: "A great multitude that no one could count, from every nation, tribe, people, and language, standing before the throne and in front of the Lamb" (Rev. 7:9).'[32]

Study Questions:

1. We note Peter's Judean ministry, and in particular the transformed lives of Aeneas (9:32-34) and Dorcas (9:36-41). In both cases their transformation brought many others to faith in Christ (9:35; 9:42). Are we simply to dismiss this as only relevant to the apostolic period, or are there meaningful parallels, especially if we do not confine ourselves to medical transformations?

---

32. Samuel Escobar, *Global Missiology for the 21ˢᵗ Century* (Baker, 2000), 26.

2. This chapter covers one of the critical moments in the story of the spread of the gospel to the whole world, as Peter, the senior apostle, undergoes a 'second conversion' and crosses the 'great gulf fixed' between Jews and Gentiles. Trace the steps which Peter was led to take in the course of that journey (7:55; 8:15–17, 25; 9:43; 10:1-23). Can you identify similar moments in your own story?

3. What truths about his human neighbours did Peter learn through this experience? Where do you find it difficult to accept others? How can this chapter help you? How can this chapter help your church?

4. 'God does not show favouritism, but accepts men from every nation who fear him and do what is right...' (10:35). What do you understand Peter to be saying here?

5. The heart of Peter's message is the meaning of the life and mission of Jesus and its Easter climax in particular. List the truths about Jesus which he asserts here (10:36-43). Which of these truths about the Lord Jesus Christ has been most meaningful for you in your Christian pilgrimage to this date? Which is most meaningful at this particular moment, and why?

6. What did this 'Gentile Pentecost' proclaim? What truths about people different from ourselves do we learn in this chapter? What does this important section teach about how we are to relate to others? How good are we at implementing these things in our church? In our friendships? In life's casual contacts?

Scene 6: *Peter reports to the church in Jerusalem on the amazing events in Caesarea* (11:1-18)
News of the happenings in the home of Cornelius soon spread all the way back to Judea, and in particular to the 'mother church' in Jerusalem: **The apostles and the**

brothers...heard that the Gentiles had received the word of God. This clearly created considerable anxiety, even criticism, among them, not so much, apparently, that the gospel had been preached to Gentiles, but that Peter **went into the house of uncircumcised men and ate with them** (3). The primary issue was the threat to a rite of identity.

Religious rites and rituals, such as food laws or cultic actions and forms, can, if overemphasized, evoke the wrong kind of conservatism, as here, and even encourage a religion in which the performance and preservation of the rituals becomes an end in itself, a replacement for living faith. However, on the other hand, we can make an opposite mistake when we underestimate the importance of ritual in fostering and retaining religious adherence. No better example can be found than Islam. Among the pillars of Islam is the *Salat*, the daily prayer ritual. This requires that prayer be offered, either publicly or privately at five times: dawn, midday, mid-afternoon, sunset, and two hours after sunset, all facing Mecca. The sense of solidarity which is generated thereby with over a billion fellow devotees all over the world sharing together in an identical piece of religious ritual, goes a considerable way to explain why Islamic evangelism has proved, in general, so disappointingly unproductive over the centuries. Did our Lord Himself not make this point by instituting the Christian sacraments of baptism and the Lord's Supper, and teaching model prayers, most notably 'The Lord's Prayer'? Or again was the Spirit not pointing in the same direction in inspiring the 'Hymnal of the Jewish Church', the book of Psalms, along with the many ritual and festival features of Old Testament faith, as well as the whole series of creedal formulae and early Christian hymns dotted through the New Testament? While there is always going to be diversity in the forms of Christian worship under the leadership of the living Spirit of God, we cannot evade the question of how helpful for long-term depth of conviction and permanence of adherence, are Christian worship patterns which, as a matter of principle, are emptied of all elements of ritual and continuity of form.

The group raising questions were the more conservative wing, described here as **the circumcised believers**. Their tenacious retention of the Old Testament forms, of circumcision and the Gentile-discriminating food laws, makes it clear that for them the only road to the inclusion of Gentiles within the church was one that required the converts to become Jews on the way to becoming Christians.

Peter began and explained everything to them precisely as it had happened (4). Peter wisely confines himself to simply retelling the story of how he had himself been persuaded of the propriety of admitting Gentiles without requiring these Jewish 'boundary markers' – the vision at Joppa and its God-given interpretation, and Cornelius' parallel angelic encounter with the resultant meeting at his home. The account has inconsequential differences from that given earlier: the 'unclean animals now include 'beasts of prey', **wild beasts** (6). Peter's declaration of legal purity is more vehement, **nothing impure or unclean has ever entered my mouth** (8); and the Spirit's 'falling all over' is said to have happened **as I began to speak** (15). This last modification is essentially a matter of idiomatic translation and is no contradiction. There is the added detail of the number from Joppa who accompanied him, **six brothers went with me**. Bruce interestingly notes that according to the Old Testament law only two witnesses were required in order to confirm a matter, but that in Roman custom no fewer than seven seals (Peter and the six brothers?) were commonly attached to a will.[33]

In referring to the outpouring of the Spirit, Peter additionally reminds his hearers of the promise of the Risen Jesus, cited in Acts 1:5, **John baptized with water, but you will be baptized with the Holy Spirit**, which was fulfilled 'in a few days', as Jesus had readied them, at Pentecost. Hence **God gave them the same gift as he gave us who believed in the Lord Jesus Christ**, anticipated in promise and experienced in practice (17). The critical word here is **same** and once it is conceded Peter's conclusion is inevita-

---

33. Bruce 1990, 269; Rev. 5:1-8.

ble. To have refused these Gentiles immediate admission through baptism would have been to indulge in the unthinkable: to take upon his shoulders, consciously and deliberately, **to oppose God**.

Peter carries the day; **they had no further objections** (18). This seemingly grudging negative is more than balanced by a happy positive: **they praised God.**[34] That is always a blessed seal of the Spirit's operation: it leads to worship; God is glorified. Why so? Because clearly **God has granted to Gentiles repentance unto life**. We note that while the sovereign ministry of the Holy Spirit is underlined here this did not exclude the elements of human response: repentance (18) and faith (17). The reference to repentance is important. Gentiles had accrued religious guilt in addition to their personal moral shortcomings. They had not known, or worshipped, the true God according to the truths and principles revealed to Israel. In becoming Christians they needed to repent of their previous idolatries, as of course did Jews also, in their terms.

More generally, and here we anticipate the findings of the Jerusalem convocation in chapter 15, the church agreed that not every believer must follow an identical path on matters which did not touch the core of the gospel. This was clearly Paul's position, worked out not least in *Romans*. He insists in the early chapters of that letter that God's righteousness is available to Gentiles through faith in Jesus Christ, without their having to become practising Jews: 'We maintain that a man is justified by faith apart from observing the law' (3:28). That insistence is balanced by his plea in the later sections (14:1–15:7) that tolerance should prevail towards those whose convictions differ on secondary matters, such as 'unclean' foods and the observance of special days.

3. The Antioch Outreach (11:19-30)

In terms of personalities, attention now turns momentarily from Peter, back to Stephen and then forward

---

34. Bruce, 196, 'their criticism ceased; their worship began.'

to Saul. Geographically it moves from Jerusalem to Antioch, a critical change as Antioch becomes the hub for the expanding Gentile mission which will occupy the remainder of Acts.

We re-engage at this point with **those who had been scattered by the persecution in connection with Stephen,** as they **travelled as far as Phoenicia, Cyprus and Antioch, telling the message only to Jews**. They were earlier described at 8:4 as having 'preached the word wherever they went'. It would probably not be wrong to see these witnessing believers as Hellenistic Jewish disciples who had identified with Stephen's theology and its Gentile-laden missional perspectives. In a real sense Stephen and his vision lived on in these disciples. It is never too early in life to raise the question of our life-legacy. What will we leave behind us? Legacy can have few richer forms than that modelled by Jesus who invested so much of Himself and His time in the apostles, and by Stephen here, in similar terms, with respect to his spiritual fellow-pilgrims.

Three locations are noted for this 'Stephenite witness'. **Phoenicia** was a coastal territory to the north and west of Galilee. The reference at 9:31, to 'the church throughout Galilee', which we earlier noted with some degree of surprise due to there having been no reference in the text to that point of any explicit witness in the Galilee region, becomes immediately less surprising at this point. Here were at least some of the evangelists who may well have birthed these Galilean congregations, on their way to Phoenicia. The island of **Cyprus** was the place of origin of Barnabas (4:36), who will re-emerge shortly. It was home to a large Jewish population.

Antioch was by far the most significant of the three locations. Situated on the eastern Mediterranean seaboard, about 500 km north of Jerusalem, Antioch was the capital of the Roman province of Syria, a centre of trade, commerce and scholarship, and in size the third largest city of the Roman empire with a population estimated at around half a million. Like the Jerusalem of today it was divided into distinct ethnic sectors: Greek, Syrian, Jewish, Latin and African.

The combined Jewish populations of these 'mission points' was a significant one, and they were the initial evangelistic target-group in each of the three centres (19). A second wave of Stephen-inspired witnesses arrived at Antioch, however, hailing from Cyprus and Cyrene in North Africa (20). Cyrene was noted earlier as one of the places represented at Pentecost (2:10), and the hometown of Simon who carried Jesus' cross to Calvary (Matt. 27:32; Luke 23:26). It is tempting to believe that the emergence of the faith there can be directly traced back to that time-less scene on the *Via Dolorosa* (Luke 23:26), and hence that one of the major tributaries which flowed into and fed this Antioch mission led directly back to Jesus (John 12:24).

They joined in the Jewish mission in Antioch; how-ever, not content with proclaiming to the Jews the arrival of their long-awaited Messiah, they **began to speak to Greeks also, telling them the good news about the Lord Jesus**. The identity of these 'Greeks' has occasioned con-siderable debate. The actual Greek term used is found only here either in the New Testament or other ancient literature. Were they simply Hellenized Jews, so that the 'Greek' reference is essentially a cultural label rather than a reference to their nationality? Or were they addition-ally Greek nationals, i.e. full-blown Gentiles? The fact that Luke clearly distinguishes them from the Hellenized Jews in verses 19 and 20, as well as the fact that the message preached to them notably does not refer to Jesus as Mes-siah (Christ) but as **'Lord' 'Jesus'** = 'Lord' and 'Saviour', titles which would have resonated immediately in that eastern Mediterranean Gentile religious world, both sup-port the conclusion of their having been 'Greek-speaking Gentiles.'[35]

Some hesitate over this assignation as it would thereby assign the honour of initiating direct Gentile evangel-ism 'to anonymous evangelists in Antioch' [36] and hence diminish the innovation of Saul and Barnabas' evangelis-tic initiative to the Gentiles in chapter 13; but this caution

35. Barrett, 173.
36. Stott, 202.

appears unnecessary. In fact Paul and Barnabas were to be teamed in ministry to both Jews and Gentiles in chapter 12:25-26 prior to their Gentile evangelism in Pamphylia described in 13:46-48. What surely matters supremely, then as now, is the fruitfulness of their mission: **a great number of people believed and turned to the Lord** (21). If, as seems fairly clear, this was indeed a witness directly to Gentiles, it represented 'a quantum leap forward in Gentile evangelization'.[37]

It was a breakthrough moment, 'so exceptional that it became the fountainhead of an entirely new missionary enterprise'.[38] 'In Antioch some daring spirits...took a momentous step forward. If the gospel was so good news for Jews, might it not be good for Gentiles also? At any rate they make the experiment. So they began to make known to the Greek population of Antioch the claims of Jesus as Lord and Saviour...The enterprise met with instant success.'[39]

There were arguably two secrets of this astonishing blessing. First, and foremost, the preachers had *an omnipotent God* – **the Lord's hand was with them** (21). Every Christian conversion is, finally considered, a matter of divine initiative. We are, left to ourselves, 'dead in trespasses and sins' (Eph. 2:1). To become a Christian requires a miracle of the Holy Spirit: 'no one can say "Jesus Christ is Lord", except by the Holy Spirit' (1 Cor. 12:3). Accordingly no Christian ministry is more dependent on prayer than evangelism, since without God's regenerating intervention the gospel will ever be preached in vain.

Secondly, as noted, the preachers had *a relevant message*. The Gentiles of Antioch were, in common with their contemporaries across the empire, seriously religious. The Romans, like the Seleucids before them, had erected a number of magnificent temples there, and close by the city were the renowned groves of the goddess Daphne, as well as a sanctuary dedicated to Apollo where orgiastic rites were celebrated in the name of religion. There was a

---

37. Robert L. Reymond, *Paul: Missionary Theologian*, (Christian Focus, 2000), 99.

38. Merril C. Tenney, *New Testament Survey* (Eerdmans, 1961), 122.

39. Bruce, 239.

widespread longing in Antioch for a worthy Lord to worship, and for a power to save from the burdens of guilt and enslaving passions, and the hidden but menacing influences of astral forces and destructive fate. The evangelists in Antioch presented a message which was precisely tailored to these yearnings: the offer in Jesus of a **Lord** and **Saviour** ('Jesus') who could liberate and save them from their guilt and inner bondages, and from all threatening spiritual powers; one who could meet their deepest needs and fulfil their highest longings. He offers no less to our needy multitudes today.

News of this reached the ears of the church at Jerusalem (22), which leads once again to the sending of a representation from Jerusalem, this time in the person of **Barnabas** (cf. 8:14), to connect with and evaluate such a significant development. Although Jerusalem is about to be replaced by this 'new kid on the block' in Antioch as the central church in Luke's story, it still retains at this point, as the apostles' home congregation, a respected, 'mother church' role. It would be wrong to judge their initiative here too negatively. As Marshall justly observes, 'it is not necessary to assume that their action was prompted by suspicion, still less by hostility.'[40]

The choice of Barnabas as their envoy confirms that estimate. He was, of course, trusted in Jerusalem, but already renowned on all hands for his generosity of spirit. 'The man with the biggest heart in the church', is how Barclay appropriately describes him.[41] The choice of Barnabas proved critical: **When he arrived and saw the evidence of the grace of God, he was glad and encouraged them to remain true to the Lord with all their hearts** (23). Thus any potential for the emergence of distinct Jewish and Gentile branches of the faith was nipped in the bud. 'The fact that Barnabas had the spiritual insight to recognize that God's plan was being followed at Antioch was of decisive significance for the growth of the church.' [42]

---

40. Marshall, 202.

41. Barclay, 90; cf. 4:36-37; 9:26-27.

42. Marshall, 202.

There is a lesson here for congregational process: representatives need to be wisely and prayerfully chosen. The Old Testament carries a poignant warning of what can happen when that principle is not honoured. The negative report of the 'spies' who entered the promised land in Numbers 13 led to forty years of further wilderness wandering before the land could be possessed. The spies in Numbers who explored Canaan, in a sense, saw a glass half-empty: 'The land...does flow with milk and honey...But the people who live there are powerful, and the cities are fortified and very large...All the people are of great size...We seemed like grasshoppers...to them' (Num. 13:27-28, 32-33). Barnabas, exploring the Antioch 'revival', saw a glass half-full: **He saw the evidence of the grace of God**. No doubt there was much in Antioch that was less than perfect; the fact that he has to urge them all **to remain true to the Lord with all their hearts**, and that we read of the new converts requiring **a whole year** of teaching (26), makes that only too clear. But Barnabas focused on what he was seeing rather than what he was not yet seeing – he was seeing nothing less than God at work in His grace, saving many lost Gentiles in Antioch and liberating them in Christ, and so **he was glad.** His own name was Joseph, but they called him 'The Encourager' (in Aramaic 'son of encouragement' or 'refreshment', 4:36). In its Greek form, the root of the title is the word Jesus used in his Upper Room discourse for the Holy Spirit: 'I will ask the Father and he will give you another Encourager...the Spirit of truth' (John 14:16). We are not surprised to read in the following verse, concerning Barnabas, that **He was a good man** – the only instance of this particular epithet in the New Testament – **full of the Holy Spirit and of faith**.

How desperately all churches need such people. 'Good' people, authentically 'filled with the Holy Spirit and faith', are always encouragers and refreshers. Conversely, people who discourage others make it only too clear how little of the Spirit they possess, no matter how loud their claims. As Scott Peck famously observed in the opening sentence of his worldwide best-seller, *The Road Less Travelled*: 'Life is difficult. This is a great truth, one of the greatest truths.'[43] Unfortunately we are all so prone to self-absorption in our own issues and difficulties that we commonly have little or no time, energy, or even interest, in the difficulties and struggles of our brothers and sisters. Yet, is encouragement not what we ought to expect in a Christian family? Visually challenged songwriter Ken Medema offers this poignant plea in his song about the church, *If This is Not a Place*:

> *'If this is not a place where tears are understood,*
> *Then where shall I go to cry?*
> *And if this is not a place where my spirit can take wings,*
> *Then where shall I go to fly?...*
> *If this is not a place where my questions can be asked,*
> *Then where shall I go to seek?*
> *And if this is not a place where my heart cry can be heard,*
> *Where, tell me where shall I go to speak?'*

It would be hard to improve on a model for a Barnabas-like congregation than that expressed in the Congregational Covenant of Stoney Strattford English Baptist Church, in 1790, in which the members agree – 'To walk in love towards those with whom we stand connected in the bonds of Christian fellowship. We will pray much for one another...Those of us who are in more comfortable situations in life than some of our brethren...will administer as we have occasion, to their necessities. We will bear one another's burdens, sympathize with the afflicted in body and mind...under their trials, and as we see occasion, advise, caution and encourage one another. We will watch over one another for good. We will studiously avoid taking offences. Thus we will make it our duty to fulfil the law of Christ...looking to him who gives power to the faint, rejoicing that in the Lord we have not only righteousness but strength. Amen!' Amen indeed!

But Barnabas' visit did more than supply encouragement, it also added momentum to the ingathering to Christ in Antioch as a further **great number of people were brought to the Lord** (24). But even with this, Barna-

---

43. Scott Peck, *The Road Less Travelled* (Touchstone, 1978), 15.

bas' contribution at Antioch was not completed. The harvest from the Gentiles in Antioch had been spectacular, but there was now a huge challenge – to teach these new converts. Their Gentile nationality meant that they would have had only minimal, if any, connection with the Old Testament and its great foundational truths about God and humanity. Everything in their building of faith had to be constructed from the foundation up. Evangelism, however successful, which is not complemented by instruction receives no endorsement in the New Testament. It loses sight, as the biblical writers never do, of the great overall purpose of all ministry and witness, the glory of God. God is not glorified alone by impressive missional statistics, but no degree less by transformed, God-honouring lives. So the mass of new converts in Antioch must be taught, which was more than Barnabas could cope with on his own, and so he **went to Tarsus to look for Saul** (25).

Tarsus was Saul's home city, where he had been born and of which he was clearly proud (cf. 'I am a Jew of Tarsus in Cilicia, a citizen of no ordinary city', 21:39). It was some eight years since Saul had last been heard of, en route to his home city following a difficult time in Jerusalem (9:30). In the intervening period Saul had probably been engaged in the evangelistic endeavours he refers to very cryptically in Galatians 1:21: 'I went to Syria and Cilicia.'

The wording of **when he had found him** suggests Barnabas had some difficulty in locating Saul. Perhaps, as a number of the commentators suggest, in this period Saul had experienced some of the sufferings for Christ he refers to in 2 Corinthians 11:23ff, and also the pain, probably alluded to in Philippians 3:8, of being disinherited by his family.[44] We need to remember that Saul had been a devoted, and very probably, a star student of Gamaliel, the renowned Jewish teacher in Jerusalem (cf. 'advancing in Judaism beyond many Jews of my own age,' Gal. 1:14). That he should have renounced all that after his conversion would have sat very ill indeed with what was clearly a zealous Jewish family (Phil. 3:5). So it may

44. Stott, 204.

not be going beyond the evidence to see Saul at this point going through a period of considerable inner struggle as he contemplated his rather lonely and uncertain future, renounced by his family and with few Christian contacts. But Barnabas remembered him, and brought him back to Antioch. **So for a whole year Barnabas and Saul met with the church and taught great numbers of people** (26). Is there a Saul somewhere in our world, possibly connected at some level with our local congregation; gifted, called, but discouraged and somewhat sidelined from ministry? And is there a Barnabas in the house?

One other feature of the Antioch mission is noted, **the disciples were called Christians first in Antioch**. The citizens of Antioch were known for their instinct for nick-names, and that was probably the source of the title. It arguably reflects the degree to which the Christians 'were always talking about Christ.'[45]

Since 'Christ' means 'anointed one' = Messiah, the nickname may first have been applied during the earlier Jewish phase of the mission. However, as Bock notes: 'It also suggests that a separate identity is emerging for this group, which earlier was appealing to Jews only. It may well be that the mixed ethnicity is now forcing the issue of self-identity alongside the believers' messianic declarations about Jesus.'[46]

In other words, the Antiochenes were gradually real-izing that there was something here which had not been seen before. But what they had never seen before was not least the diversity-in-unity of this group, as we will have occasion to underline in chapter 13 when we encounter the astonishing ethnic diversity of the church's pastoral team. We noted earlier that ancient Antioch was divided into several sectors separated by dividing walls. Appar-ently in Antioch, people of different ethnic backgrounds began to cross the interior walls of the city to hear the gospel and join the church. What is clear is that Antioch had never before seen anything quite like this width of

45. M. Green, *Those Forty Years*, 57.
46. Bock, 416.

human diversity uniting in a deeply loving and committed unity. Nor could they find anything quite like it in Judaism, or in any Gentile religious tradition. Hence a distinct label was called for: 'the Christ-people.' Perhaps surprisingly, the name did not 'grab' people immediately, and there are only two other New Testament occasions of its use (Acts 26:28; 1 Pet. 4:16). Once it did catch on, it was never replaced, right down to this day. The challenge in the name is simple: the followers of Jesus were different and stood out, in particular because of their Christ-centred convictions, and their all-embracing width of relationships.

The shared contacts of Antioch and Jerusalem did not consist only of teacher/encouragers like Barnabas, but also in prophets like Agabus. These were often charismatic figures attached to a local church, as in 13:1, whether singly, or in groups as noted here: **some prophets** (27). We will meet Agabus again in 21:10 interfacing with Paul on his journey to Jerusalem and described there as having 'come down from Judea'.

In evaluating the ministry of such figures it is important to recognize that the New Testament was not yet written. Putting it more starkly, not a single member of the Antioch or Jerusalem churches had ever seen a Bible, nor would they during their entire lifetime! Yet clearly there was as urgent and extensive a need in these congregations, as in any of ours today, for instruction as to the nature of God, the will of God, and all the other areas of Christian truth. There were also innumerable issues around the shape and expression of a godly lifestyle, how to relate to one another in a Christian congregation, standards of sexually appropriate behaviour, direction in the many practical issues of living a Christian life, in family, the pursuit of a career, in handling money, in the workplace, and in general society. Furthermore the churches were new-born and had had no opportunity as yet to develop any extended history of failed or successful attempts at living the Christian life: there was as yet no 'Christian traditions' to afford guidance. True, there was certainly the LXX version of the Old Testament, and there were living apostles who might be consulted whenever they passed by, or later, should they write letters; and certainly there were traditions circulating about Jesus, some parts of His teaching and accounts of some events in His ministry. But all this fell very far short indeed of the full Scriptures we hold in our hands today. Consequently it was imperative in these first centuries that there be a special, Holy Spirit-provided source of knowledge in all these areas. Put otherwise, there was need for a significant prophetic ministry.

This fact does not imply the necessary secession of these Spirit-gifts with the completion of the New Testament canon. However it does certainly imply that whatever role these prophetic gifts continued to play in the churches thereafter it would never again be exactly that of the first centuries. We now possess, through the wise and loving providence of God the Holy Spirit, His living words in the New Testament Scriptures, and hence have a full and ever-available source for many, if not all, of the knowledge-needs mentioned above.

As far as the immediate prophetic ministry in Antioch was concerned, this could be declarative, but could also be predictive. In this case it was the latter: **Agabus stood up, and through the Spirit predicted that a severe famine would spread over the entire Roman world** (28). Much discussion has been generated by Luke's identifying the famine in question as **during the reign of Claudius**, who was Emperor from 41–54. Roman sources give evidence of a number of famines during this period; Josephus refers to a particularly severe one in Judea in A.D. 46.

Luke's concern, however, is not so much with the fulfilment, but with the response: **The disciples, each according to his ability, decided to provide help for the brothers living in Judea**. The wording nicely anticipates the Marxist slogan, 'From each according to his ability to each according to his need.'[47] The echo is not entirely accidental. Engels, in an essay entitled *On the History of*

---

47. K. Marx and F. Engels, *Basic Writings on Politics and Philosophy*, ed. Lewis S. Feuer (Anchor Books, 1959), K.Marx, '*Critique of the Gotha Programme*', 112-132; F. Engels 'On the History of Early Christianity', 168-194.

Early Christianity, published in 1894–5, draws the parallels between 'the early Christian communities' and the 'local section of the International Workingmen's Association'; though with history, of course, on the side of the latter. How wrong he was to prove; and, by an appropriate irony, one of the primary factors that undid Marxist regimes in eastern Europe in 1989 bringing about the collapse of the Soviet empire, was the faith and action of these despised, 'irrelevant' Christian communities.

The gift having been levied from the Antioch congregation is sent **to the elders** in Jerusalem **by Barnabas and Saul** (30). This visit by Saul and Barnabas appears to have been the one Saul (now renamed Paul) refers to in Galatians 2:1-10. There are striking points of parallel: the fact that Barnabas accompanied him, that he went there due to a 'revelation', and that there was a general concern about 'remembering the poor'. 'We regard it as most probable that the relief visit recorded here is the same as that in Galatians 2:1-10.'[48]

A further point of some importance is raised here. Clearly the Holy Spirit's identifying of the impending need in Jerusalem and Judea moved the hearts of the Antiochene congregation, and their resulting gifts are expressions of a deeply felt concern. But the gifts did more than that; they helped unify these congregations, representative as they were at that point of the Jewish and Gentile expressions of the church, and hence the gifts also contributed to a unified Christendom at a time when a division into separate Jew and Gentile streams must have seemed perilously possible.

The lesson of this was not lost on Paul. Years later, in the somewhat uneasy peace following the Consultation at Jerusalem in chapter 15 – a peace made no easier by Paul's subsequent confrontation with Peter in Antioch (Gal. 2:11-14) – Paul levied a significant collection from the Gentile churches he had founded under God in Achaia and Macedonia, for the 'the poor among the saints in Jerusalem' (Rom. 15:25-27; cf. 1 Cor. 16:1-4; 2 Cor. 8 and 9). Thus

---

48. Marshall, 205.

the collection became a highly meaningful expression of fellowship, and this explains the tremendous significance with which Paul invested it (Rom. 15:27; 1 Cor. 16:2; 2 Cor. 8:1–9:15). 'The collection was in its origin a symbolic gesture declaring the new fellowship between Jew and Gentile in Christ…it was the outward pledge of an inward unity which was as yet perilously fragile.' [49]

In 2 Corinthians 9:13 and Romans 15:26 Paul even goes as far as to refer to the collection as itself, *koinonia* = 'fellowship' (cf. Phil. 4:15 'koinonia…in giving and receiving'). Thus sacrificial financial support of brothers and sisters in Christ is viewed in the New Testament as a fundamental expression of love and fellowship, an expression in which fellowship is both demonstrated and deepened.

Perhaps at this point we need to take the language used around our weekly offerings in worship services out of the pious clouds with which we often surround them, 'the Lord's offering', 'our continuing worship', etc., and see them quite objectively, but not unbiblically, as what we are prepared to give to each other. The brother who requested that his wallet be baptized along with him surely had the Bible on his side. When the 'books are opened' on the great day of judgment (Rev. 20:12), will we be embarrassed if they include our bankbooks? As Helmut Thielicke put it: 'Our wallets have more to do with heaven and hell than our hymnbooks.'

But putting the issue positively, what a wonderful privilege this opens to us, that of being able to actually bless our fellow believers, and brothers and sisters in Christ in far-flung places of the globe, as we become the stewards of all our resources and see them at work, deepening relationships, and touching hearts for God.

Study Questions:

1. In the light of biblical models, reflect on the place of ritual in Christian worship. What are its dangers…and its benefits?

---

49. L.S. Thornton, *The Common Life in the Body of Christ* (Dacre, 1942), 9.

2. Do we, like Peter here (11:4-17), have a story to tell of how God has changed our minds during the course of our Christian lives?

3. What might be our equivalent to the 'Antioch break-out' to evangelizing the Gentiles there (11:20-21)? What are the things which make 'Christians' different in our society? What would be the nickname we have earned?

4. Identify the positive qualities shown by Barnabas in his visit to, and subsequent ministry in Antioch (11:22-26)? Which do you find the most challenging?

5. What sources to you draw upon to discern the will of God for your life (11:28)? What are our equivalents today to the collection in Antioch (11:29-30)?

4. Peter's Miraculous Escape (12:1-19a).

The focus now returns to Peter as his western Judean ministry recorded in 9:32-43, and his epochal experience in the house of Cornelius detailed in 10:1-48, is complemented by another frankly miraculous incident: his escape from prison in Jerusalem. Apart from his contribution to the debate at the Jerusalem Consultation, this is Peter's final spotlight moment as far as the Book of Acts is concerned; the remainder of Luke's story will feature the ministry of Paul.

Some discussion has been engaged as to the role this chapter plays in Luke's unfolding account. Its primary justification is simply that it happened. But since Luke is selective, as we have repeatedly noted, more needs to be said. Peter is of course the hero in this section, and his role as the chosen leader of the apostles obviously commends its inclusion. In its way it also underlines the costliness of the gospel mission. Thus even an apostle, James, will die for his faith, and Peter himself be brought to within an inch of a similar fate. But all the while God exercises His sovereign control as the church prays, Peter is liberated, and Herod, the leader of the anti-Christian movement at this point, dies under the judgment of God. Hence, in the spiritual warfare, which is what the church's mission ever continues to be, casualties are sustained, but the Lord keeps watch and faith, and the mission continues to move forward.

About this time (1) can be plotted with some confidence. Herod's death occurred in A.D. 44, so the events of the first part of this chapter would have fallen in the months prior to that. We are accordingly something over a decade into the church's life since Pentecost. **King Herod** is Herod Agrippa I, the grandson of 'Herod the Great' who had sought to slay Jesus in Bethlehem (Matt. 2:3-18). Raised and educated in Rome, he reigned in Judea from 41-44 at the behest of the Emperor Claudius. His son, Agrippa II, would meet with Paul in the vivid story told in chapter 25. Jewish historian Josephus speaks of Herod as mild in temper and popular with the Jewish leadership, not least on account of his public acts of piety while residing in Jerusalem. Herod was anxious to retain the goodwill of the Jews and saw a ready means to this by instigating a Christian persecution. Josephus' claim for Herod's 'mildness' accordingly needs some revision! Herod accordingly set his sights on the disciple community and **arrested some who belonged to the church** (1).

The apostles had been notably spared in the earlier persecution following Stephen's death, but that was not the case at this point. Clearly opposition to the faith had hardened in Jerusalem. Having arrested **James, the brother of John**, and son of Zebedee, one of the 'inner circle of three' among the apostles (Luke 8:51; 9:28), Herod had him **put to death with the sword** = beheaded (2). For this act Herod would have had to have Roman approval, and plainly he was motivated by the desire to have general Jewish approval in addition. Thus Jesus' prophecy concerning the sons of Zebedee, of their 'drinking the cup' of suffering (Mark 10:39), is fulfilled in James' case. Christian writer Clement of Alexandria (c.155–c.220), 'the first known Christian scholar', has left us a moving postscript on the death of James. The man whose denunciation had led to James' arrest was so impressed by James' testimony to Christ before Herod that he himself became a Christian, with the result that he was led away to execution along with James. Clement writes: 'On the way he asked James for forgiveness. James looked at him for a moment and said, "Peace be to you," and kissed him. So both were beheaded at the same time.'[50]

We ought not to forget the significant role which James, along with his brother and Peter, played in the ministry of Jesus. This 'inner circle' was not only afforded the special privilege of being present at the raising from the dead of Jarius' daughter (Luke 8:51-6), and the transfiguration (Luke 9:28-36); they were also those that Jesus turned to in a special degree for their human comfort and support in the hour of His agony in the Garden of Gethsemane (Mark 14:33). The death of James was a major loss: 'a great man has fallen in Israel this day' (2 Sam. 3:38). We need to be prepared for similar losses at times in the course of the mission 'to the ends of the earth'.

Seeing **that this pleased the Jews** Herod struck again, this time at the very centre of the church as **he proceeded to seize Peter also** (3). The timing of this action becomes critical for the unfolding events. Peter is seized **during the Feast of Unleavened Bread**, i.e. the Passover. This was precisely the time-frame of Jesus' arrest, and a similar dilemma arose for the authorities, that the 'holiness' of this period made executions impossible. In Jesus' case, the authorities had managed (barely) to squeeze Jesus' trial and execution into the last possible hours before sundown of 'Good Friday' signalled (with profoundest possible irony) the beginning of the 'holy days'. In Peter's case the Passover week is already under way, and so Herod had to **put him in prison** for the remaining days of the feast, intending to **bring him out for public trial after the Passover** (4). The strength of the guard around Peter, **four squads of four soldiers each**, probably reflects something of the known strength of the Christian presence, and perhaps is also a tribute to the legendary supernatural

50. Eusebius, *Historia Ecclesiastica*, 2:8.

powers associated with them: no misplaced fear, as events were to prove. The four-man squad was a Roman method, one soldier chained to each arm of the prisoner, and two others to maintain a constant guard at the cell door. They would have changed every three hours (a 'watch' was of three hours' duration) and hence covered twelve hours of night, and then daylight. Marshall (208) notes the 'careful balance' of verse 5: **So Peter was kept in prison, but the church was earnestly praying to God for him** (5).

Our having 'already read the last chapter' of the story somewhat erodes our ability to empathize with the seriousness of this situation; for serious it most certainly was. Peter being killed would have been a huge setback to the entire Christian movement, and would any of the apostles have been subsequently spared in such an event? Further, it is unimaginable that prayer had not been made with at least corresponding sincerity for James, and to no avail. This is veritably an 'hour of darkness' where faith is pushed to its very limits.

The praying, however, is notable. It is prolonged prayer, the tense of the verb **praying** is imperfect (*ginomene*), as is that referring to Peter's imprisonment, implying continuous activities: both lasted several days. Further evidence of the vehemence of the church's intercessions is supplied by the adverb **earnestly** (*ektenos*). Strikingly this is the precise word used of Jesus' praying in Gethsemane (Luke 22:44; 'being in anguish he prayed more earnestly, and his sweat was like drops of blood falling to the ground'). The disciples here represent the people of God in every generation, not least our own. When other options desert us, and all human recourse is gone, we fall on our knees and cry out, earnestly, to Him who alone is our final refuge and hope.

Donald Caskie was minister of the Scots Kirk in Paris when the Nazi forces invaded and conquered the city. He fled south to Marseilles where he played a significant role in helping Allied prisoners of war to escape. Caskie was eventually betrayed, taken into custody, tortured and thrown into prison, physically broken. His first thought as he looked around his cell was: 'This must be hell.' But he was a man of prayer, and he prayed as never before. And as he prayed from his cracked lips came lines from an old Scottish paraphrase learned as a boy:

> 'Art thou afraid His power shall fail
> When comes thy evil day?
> And can an all-creating arm
> Grow weary and decay?'

'As I sang these words,' he later wrote, 'I felt his arm go round me. I was with God and God was with me.' [51]

It is significant that there is no hint of the disciples organizing an escape attempt on Peter's behalf. Their hope was in God; they prayed for a miracle. The fact that there had been an earlier such miracle several years before (5:18-21) no doubt strengthened their faith, though the death of James would have been an understandable counterweight.

The story fast-forwards to the final night before Peter's arraignment (6). Despite the chains, and the added discomfort of his two guards beside him, the prisoner is asleep – when suddenly it happens – **an angel of the Lord appeared and a light shone in the cell. He struck Peter on the side and woke him up. 'Quick, get up!'** God has come! Immediately **the chains fell off Peter's wrists.** Centuries later, Charles Wesley was to borrow from these words in his timeless, thrilling song of salvation:

> Long my imprisoned spirit lay
> Fast bound in sin and nature's night;
> Thine eye diffused a quickening ray,
> I woke, the dungeon flamed with light;
> My chains fell off, my heart was free,
> I rose, went forth, and followed Thee.

Peter, still dazed and hardly comprehending what is happening, is instructed to **Put on your clothes and sandals. Wrap your cloak around you and follow me** (8). Peter obeys, still uncomprehending, thinking **he was seeing a vision**. The angel leads him past the layers of guards who are apparently blinded or in some other way rendered

---

51. Donald Caskie, *The Tartan Pimpernel* (Oldbourne, London, 1957), 196-7.

uncomprehending, and so they reach **the iron gate leading into the city**, which swings open allowing them to pass through it and down the adjoining street, where **suddenly the angel left him** (10).

The Western text adds the detail that they found themselves in the street 'after descending the seven steps'. Bruce believes that the circumstantial appearance of this detail stamps it as genuine, 'derived from an informant who knew Jerusalem before its fall in A.D. 70.' [52]

Peter, still somewhat befuddled, now comes wide awake, and the wonder of what he has just experienced dawns on him: **Now I know without a doubt that the Lord sent his angel and rescued me from Herod's clutches and from everything the Jewish people were anticipating** (11). He is on his own now; God's supernatural assistance is not offered prodigally when there are things we can do for ourselves. He makes his way through the darkness of the night to **the house of Mary, the mother of John, also called Mark, where many had gathered and were praying** (12). Some have conjectured that this was the 'house where they were sitting' when the Spirit fell at Pentecost (2:2). There certainly are indications of size, with an inner and outer section and household servants. We have no way of knowing if this identification is correct. More importantly for the Acts narrative, it brings Mark into the story for the first time.

Peter arrived and **knocked at the outer entrance** for admission. What follows is resonant with eye-witness authenticity. In answer to his knock, **a servant girl named Rhoda came to answer...When she recognized Peter's voice, she was so overjoyed she ran back without opening it and exclaimed, 'Peter is at the door!'** (14). No imaginative imitator would have created this detail. It is in the story because that is exactly what happened when Peter was miraculously delivered. The prayer meeting was sufficiently able to be disturbed to inform her that she was **out of her mind**. Since she refused to be dissuaded, the suggestion is then made that it was his angel. This reflects

---

52. Bruce, 249.

a Jewish belief in guardian angels, one which Jesus in some degree affirms (Matt. 18:10). Some extended it to include the thought that the 'angel' was a heavenly counterpart of the person being 'guarded'. The 'angel', however, proceeds to indulge in rather un-angelic behaviour by **keeping knocking**! (16). So they open up, and discover – Peter!

Why were they so surprised, we find ourselves asking? After all, God had displayed His ability to bring people out of prison on an earlier occasion in Jerusalem, as we noted above. No doubt the fate of James was a major explanation of their weakened faith. As we observed, it was unthinkable that similar prayer had not been offered in his case, as one of the 'inner circle' of Jesus' disciples. But additionally there is something endearingly human about this whole incident. We all know the experience of praying for something or someone and yet being totally unprepared for the prayer's being answered. 'Lord, we believe; help our unbelief!'

In the hubbub of emotion Peter wisely calls for **quiet**, and having **described how the Lord had brought him out of prison**, and asked that **James and the brothers** (presumably the rest of the Christian community in the city) be brought up to speed, he left (17). The hinted-at absence of other leaders from the prayer meeting, possibly most notably Peter's fellow apostles, was perhaps not surprising. Herod was in the full flush of his anti-Christian pogrom and probably they were, wisely, lying low; a church bereft of the entire apostolic community would indeed be in very serious trouble. This is the first mention in Acts of James, Jesus' natural brother (Mark 6:3). Initially a non-believer (John 7:3-5), James had been permitted a special meeting with the Risen Lord (1 Cor. 15:7) and come to faith. He would be a significant leader of the Christian witness in Jerusalem through the following years and already by the Consultation in Jerusalem had assumed a clearly leading role (15:13; cf. Gal. 1:19; 2:9; 2:12f).

In the morning there was no small commotion as Peter's escape is discovered. Herod, outwitted by God's miraculous intervention, vents his rage on the guards, ordering **that they be executed** (19). That fate was not out of keeping with general Roman practice in cases where important prisoners were allowed to escape.

5. The Death of Herod (19b-25)

Herod then withdrew to Caesarea. Unknown to him, the sand in the hour-glass of his life is fast running out. Herod had earlier become embroiled in an angry dispute with the coastal towns of Tyre and Sidon, who **depended on the king's country for their food supply** (20). They decide to make peace through the good offices of one **Blastus, a trusted personal servant of the king**. The day of their audience was apparently an occasion for the king to appear in **his royal robes and deliver a public address to the people** (21). They shouted, **This is the voice of a god, not of a man** (22).

The first-century Jewish historian Josephus gives an independent version of the occasion and the two accounts have many points of overlap. According to Josephus the event was a festival in honour of Caesar. Herod 'put on a robe made of silver throughout, of altogether wonderful weaving…The silver shone and glittered wonderfully when the sun's first rays fell on it, and its resplendence inspired a sort of fear and trembling in those who gazed on it. Immediately his flatterers called out…using language which boded him no good for they addressed him as a god…He did not rebuke them or repudiate their impious flattery…He was seized by a severe pain in his belly… He was carried quickly into the palace and when he had suffered continuously for five days…he died.' [53]

Luke uncovers the spiritual cause of the attack, **because he did not give praise to God, an angel of the Lord struck him down, and he was eaten by worms and died** (23).

The chapter concludes with another of Luke's 'state of the union' summaries: evangelism is flourishing in Jerusalem and elsewhere as **the word of the Lord continued to increase and spread** (24). Luke also reports on the movements of Barnabas and Saul who, having finished their mission to Jerusalem with the famine-relief gift

---

53. Josephus, *Jewish Antiquities*, XIX.8.2.

from Antioch, **return from Jerusalem, taking with them John, also called Mark** (25). There are numerous textual and syntactical problems in this final verse of the chapter, though the meaning is clear enough. Bock offers a helpful summary.[54]

Thus the chapter closes, rounding out the account of the mission of Christ in 'Jerusalem, all Judea and Samaria' (1:8). For the remainder of Acts the focus will move out and into the third, exciting, and certainly no less demanding dimension of the mission – witness 'to the ends of the earth.'

As we look back for a moment, we are struck by the vivid contrast this chapter reflects between the church's fortunes at the beginning and those at the end. When the chapter opens, Herod is in the ascendant, falling upon the church with murderous intent, killing James and imprisoning Peter as a prelude to his execution also. Nothing seems capable of restraining him, and the Christian community is cowering beneath his fearful shadow. When the chapter ends, the picture is vastly changed. Herod's plans have been thwarted by God's sovereign intervention, and Peter is free once more to continue his ministry. Further, Herod himself has been struck down for his unbounded personal idolatry, and dies a painful and demeaning death, while the church continues to prosper as the living word of God continues to run and be glorified. In its way the chapter is a parable; the evil one is ever abroad, and over the centuries regularly finds Herods, willing instruments for the expression of his hatred of the people of the Lord. At times evil seems to have unfettered sway and faith burns low. But 'the Lord is king' and again and again he thwarts the scheming of the enemy, overturns the tyrants, exalts his Son, and gives joyful increase to the followers of the Lamb.

Study Questions:

1. What is to be learned from the fact of James' execution (12:2)?

---

54. Bock, 434–5.

2. Herod is here clearly 'permitted power' over the church as expressed in James' execution and Peter's imprisonment (12:1-4). Can we identify other biblical examples? Are we able to accommodate this within our Christian world-view?

3. What are the lessons of Peter's escape (12:5-17)?

4. What do we learn from the church's prayer response (12:5, 12-16)?

5. Herod's death (12:19b-23) vividly expresses the fact of divine judgment, a reality clearly taught in both Testaments (cf. Ps. 2:9; 110:5; Isa. 51:5; Mal. 3:1-5; Matt. 25:32; Acts 10:42; 17:30-32; Rom. 2:3-16; 1 Cor. 4:5; Jude 14f). Have you come to terms with that? Are there truths in this story which help us grasp why judgment is inevitable?

7

Witnesses to the Ends of the Earth (I)
(Acts 13:1–14:28)

A. 'Paul's First Mission Journey' (13:1–14:28)

1. The Commissioning of Barnabas and Saul (13:1-3)

With our arrival at chapter 13 we reach one of the critical marker-points in the story-line of Acts. But more than that, we arrive at a major milestone in the history of the mission of God to the world. 'Reviewing the history of the Church it becomes clear that Christianity has never been more itself, more consistent with Jesus, and more evidently en route to its own future than in the launching of the world mission.'[1]

What we have traced over the last chapters is how the Holy Spirit, in a series of steps, brought the church closer and closer to the launching of a self-conscious, full-scale expression of its mission to 'go into all the world and preach the gospel to the whole creation' (Mark 16:15). Step one is of course the eternal heart of God for humanity and its expression in the covenant with 'Abraham and his seed' through the Old Testament period, culminating in the incarnation, death, resurrection and exaltation of Jesus. Step two was the great commission of the exalted

---

1. Meyer, 206.

Lord: 'you will be my witnesses in Jerusalem, all Judea and Samaria, and to the ends of the earth.' Step three was Pentecost and its global representation. Step four was the church in its power and spread in Jerusalem, culminating in the ministry and vision of Stephen. Step five was the 'scattering' from Jerusalem leading to Philip's ministry to Samaria and on the road to Gaza. Step six was the event outside Damascus, Saul's conversion and commissioning as the 'apostle to the Gentiles'. Step seven was the 'second conversion of Peter' in the home of Cornelius. Step eight was the witness of Stephen's followers in Antioch and the blessing of their direct witness to Greeks. And now comes step nine: the commissioning of Saul and Barnabas by the Antioch church to take the gospel into the wider world of Cyprus, and the Roman province of Galatia. In Bock's words: 'The move to the ends of the earth has started in earnest.'[2] In terms of the commission in 1:8 and the over-view it affords of Luke's whole book, this section at 13:1-3 extends to 21:36, and arguably all the way to 28:31.

We are first of all introduced to the Antioch congregation gathered for worship, and in particular to its leadership team. **In the church at Antioch there were prophets and teachers: Barnabas, Simeon called Niger, Lucius of Cyrene, Manaen (who had been brought up with Herod the tetrarch) and Saul** (1). We are immediately struck by the ethnic diversity of this group, consisting of Barnabas from Cyprus; Simeon the Black, an African; Lucius of Cyrene, a North African; Manaen, possibly a slave of Herod's father; and Saul, a native of Tarsus on the land-link to Europe. Ray Bakke comments: 'So the first large city-centre church we know anything about had a five-person pastoral team from three continents. This is the climax of Pentecost. In Jerusalem they spoke many languages, now in Antioch they were fleshing out multiculturalism in the structure of the pastoral team.'[3] This also meant that what would be realized through the mission, the planting of multicultural congregations in the provinces of the empire, was really

---

2. Bock, 436.

3. Bakke: 146.

an extension of the multicultural reality of the sending congregation in Antioch. While not wishing to limit the Holy Spirit's capacity to create the new and innovative, in this sense mission is commonly a form of church extension. Just as a child is to an important degree a print-out of the genetic map of its parents, so what we reproduce through our witness will be similarly shaped, to a significant degree, by who we, the missionaries, inherently are.

While they were worshipping the Lord and fasting, the Holy Spirit said, 'Set apart for me Barnabas and Saul for the work to which I have called them' (2). This worship context is critical, as we will note again at later points. The ultimate dimension of mission is worship: mission is a fundamental means to the honour and glory of God, as He draws the nations to Himself, and as His ever-blessed Son is thereby exalted as 'a Prince and Saviour' (5:31). Consequently the widely canvassed notion that somehow worship is about God, whereas mission is about humanity, could not be more mistaken. This is a profoundly unbiblical perception, separating 'those whom God has joined together.' It leads inevitably to the marginalizing of mission in the life of the church since how could the merely human possibly compete with the divine? Insofar as mission rates to any degree at all, it is viewed as the 'hobby-horse' of the 'mission people' (bless their hearts!), but not the overwhelming, fundamental responsibility of the church as a whole.

But mission is supremely about God, His glory, His power, His purpose, His amazing grace, His mercy, His love, His salvation, *Himself*! The keynote of mission is doxology. Murray McCheyne expressed it memorably: 'There are two things which it is impossible to desire with sufficient ardour, personal holiness of life, and *the honour of Christ in the salvation of souls.*'[4] If we truly care for God's honour – and if worship is not about that, what is it about? – then we will care deeply about how He is

---

4. R.M. McCheyne, in Andrew A. Bonar, *Memoir and Remains of the Rev. Robert Murray McCheyne* (Oliphant. Anderson and Ferrier, 1844), 281. Reprinted, London, Banner of Truth, 1966.

responded to in His world, whether or not the nations know of His Calvary love for them, and whether they honour Him by their embrace of His Son as their Saviour and Lord. Mission magnifies God; we go, for His glory!

Since mission is ultimately a 'God-thing' the initiative is with God, so **The Holy Spirit said...**(2). We are not informed as to how this 'word' was heard, though the reference to prophetic ministries in the church may well be a pointer. What really matters is less how God's voice was heard than what it expressed: the congregation's two prime leaders were wanted elsewhere!

Set apart for me; the essence of the call was less geographical than possessional, it was a call to be given up to God. Oswald Chambers expressed precisely this truth when he wrote: 'the bedrock of Christianity is personal, passionate devotion to Jesus Christ.' Missional service means at its heart our becoming entirely available to God (1 Cor. 6:19). The question of whose we are is always more critical than the question of where we are. Availability trumps itinerary in God's service. So Barnabas and Saul's being yielded to God was primary, and the geographical location of their service was in that sense secondary and would follow later.

...for the work. The missionaries are left in no doubt that they are not going off on vacation. They will be **workers** for God. In fact the cost will be extremely high as we will see. Work and witness are partners in mission. There is of course such a thing as overwork, and each must determine the balance here as best they may. Jesus is a supreme model as we discern in His ministry a regular rhythm of involvement and withdrawal (cf. Mark 1:29-38). But none should venture into a serious availability to God who are unprepared for hard work.

So after they had fasted and prayed (3); 'as always prayer and spiritual forces work together and play a role in guiding the church. These are realities which the modern world tends to shun but are the foundations of a Christian worldview.'[5]

---

5. Bock, 440.

They placed their hands upon them and sent them off. The laying on of hands was an affirmation and expression of God's hand laid upon His servants. Implicit in it is the assurance of the supply of all needed grace and enablement for the mission. But it does something further; this action identifies the entire congregation with the upcoming ministry of Barnabas and Saul. In a profound sense the entire church will go forth: the two missionaries by their hands-on proclamation, the congregation by their constant prayers, and gifts, in support. Hence a scene is enacted which has had its echo in a multitude of congregations of God's people over the passing centuries, and is being repeated all over the world at this very hour. This was the beginning. 'Everything about Acts shows us that its impetus is toward the church's call in mission. We build churches not just to go in for worship, but to go out with God's heart for people.'[6] It should also be noted that for the first time there is no direct Jerusalem involvement, nor any apostolic presence, other than Saul himself. The church is moving out beyond its first foundational forms to the apostolicity of its life as the people of God scattered through the world.

2. The Work Begins: Ministry in Cyprus (13:4-12)

So sent on their way by the Holy Spirit...(4) There is a wonderful reassurance reflected here. It is this conviction which not only launches mission and ministry but which alone enables it to be sustained through the harder stretches of the journey. They travel first to the coast at **Seleucia** and from there sail to **Cyprus**.

There is no reference to the Spirit's specific direction at this point, though it may be implicit in the opening phrase. Cyprus was, of course, Barnabas' home territory, just as the south of Galatia, where they would travel to afterwards, was broadly Paul's. It is therefore not impossible that they simply followed the obvious course of going to areas where they would have an immediate familiarity with the cultures and contexts; the Holy Spirit does not routinely

---

6. Bock, 440.

contradict common sense. Beyond these considerations of course, there was the additional reality – in both of these territories there were multitudes of men and women, boys and girls, entirely ignorant of the 'good news' about Jesus. **John** Mark accompanies them at this point (5). We are not told what his contribution was, possibly in the more practical aspects of the mission; besides which he too, having relatives on Cyprus, would have an initial familiarity with the setting. But there may also be here the first concrete expression of Paul's concern, perhaps best expressed in his 'son' Timothy, to train successors. Paul, not unlike his Master, was never blind to the reality of his own ministry's temporal limitations, and the need accordingly to think ahead to those who would carry the ministry forward after his day had passed.

Their landfall is at Salamis on the east coast of the island. Here they begin their mission, as **they proclaimed the word of God in the Jewish synagogues**. This was a potentially promising starting point as Cyprus was home to a significant Jewish population. However, it also reflected what was to become their practice; they go 'to the Jews first' (6:9; 9:2, 20; 13:5, 14, 43; 14:1; 15:21; 17:1, 10, 17; 18:4, 7, 19, 26; 22:19; 24:11; 28:17, 23-28). The inclusion of the Gentiles does not mean the exclusion of the Jews from the gospel and its proffered salvation. No report is supplied by Luke as to the effect of their preaching in Salamis, though clearly the gospel seed was faithfully sown there. It is to be noted that there already had been a 'Stephen-inspired', Antioch-led Christian witness on the island (11:19-20), which Luke does not refer to, but Barnabas and Saul's ministry would presumably have further encouraged believers already active there. This was all as might have been expected. Saul had not yet formulated his later 'ambition', 'always…to preach the gospel where Christ was not known' (Rom. 15:20).

From Salamis they make their way **through the whole island until they came to Paphos** on the far east coast (6). Here a fuller report is offered. There were many cults on the island (a feature which has its echo not infrequently today in island life), and the missionaries encounter this head-on in the person of **a Jewish sorcerer and false prophet named Bar-Jesus.** He was a type of the magicians who functioned within the popular, local folk religion. Barnabas and Saul appear to have come across him in the context of their witness to Sergius Paulus, the Roman proconsul of the island, and Bar-Jesus' employer (7). Sergius, whose **intelligence** is particularly noted, was also a religious seeker, and having come to hear of the missionaries, he **sent for** them **because he wanted to hear the word of God.**

Bar-Jesus, who was also known by a Semitic name, Elymas = 'sorcerer', **opposed them and tried to turn the proconsul from the faith** (8). Paul, described for the first time as acting independently of Barnabas, but under the inspiration of the Holy Spirit, confronted Elymas in a 'no-holds-barred' spiritual power-encounter: **You are a child of the devil and an enemy of everything that is right! You are full of all kinds of deceit and trickery. Will you never stop perverting the right ways of the Lord?** (10). Paul then added a judgment-curse: **Now the hand of the Lord is against you. You are going to be blind and for a time will be unable to see the light of the sun** (11). The judgment, though severe, is not without some lining of mercy in that the blindness will only be temporary. The effect is dramatic, however; and in this contest of light against darkness, Satan against God, the outcome is unsurprising, and registered **immediately** as **mist and darkness came over the magician and he groped about, seeking someone to lead him by the hand**. It was a striking re-enactment of Saul's condition in the immediate aftermath of his own encounter with the Lord outside Damascus. 'In a sense Saul here judges his old self.'[7]

The impact on Sergius, who was apparently present, was life-changing as **he believed, being amazed at the teaching about the Lord**. The reference to the proconsul's intelligence, and to the 'teaching' (when we might have expected a word like 'power'), points to the fact that the missionaries' message was clearly *both* demonstrated

---

7. Bock, 447.

power to the eye and heart *and* truth to the mind. Sergius both **heard** (v. 7) and **saw** (v. 12). We noted this same combination in Philip's ministry in Samaria (8:6); we meet it again here in Barnabas' and Saul's ministry in Cyprus. The world continues to both hear and see. That was true supremely of the incarnation: He who was the 'Word' of God, 'became flesh' with the result that 'we have seen his glory' (John 1:14). John makes the same connection in his first letter: 'That which was from the beginning, which we have *heard*, which we have *seen* with our eyes....this we *declare* to you' (1 John 1:1-2).

Christian witness is always both verbal and visible. This is true without exception. What we say is inseparable from what we do, and who we are. This is so blindingly obvious, yet frequently in danger of being overlooked in the multiple schemes and programmes of evangelism which are generated by local churches and larger Christian organizations. Nietzsche's challenge to the evangelical community of his day resonates for every generation, every church, and every last one of us: 'You will have to look more redeemed if you want me to believe in your redeemer.' All of which can be deeply discouraging – for 'who is sufficient for these things?' (2 Cor. 2:16). However Philip, Barnabas and Saul clearly *were* sufficient, not in themselves nor on the basis of their own resources, but by the power of God: the God who continues to be 'with us' in His mission (Matt. 28:20).

> *Make us to be what we profess to be;*
> *Let prayer be prayer, and praise be heart-felt praise;*
> *From unreality, O set us free,*
> *And let our words be echoed by our ways.*[8]

As the missionaries conclude their mission to Cyprus and **sail** northwards **to Perga** in the province of **Pamphylia,** today's southern Turkey, the abiding memory of this first, Cyprus, stage, is the remarkable conversion of Sergius Paulus. This is probably as Luke intends, because in a sense Sergius is a representative of the needy Gentile

---

8. Henry Twells.

communities that the missionaries have been sent to evangelize. As a man without any noted connection with the synagogue he represents the mass of the populations of the empire who must be reached without any intervening 'synagogue connection'; and in that sense, he represents the great mass of our world today who have had minimal contact, if any, with either the gospel or the historic people of God, but to whom the Lord continues to send his missionary disciples.

3. Ministry in Pisidian Antioch (13:13-52)

The journey to **Perga** was over a hundred miles, and when they arrived **John** Mark **left them to return to Jerusalem** (13). We are not told why, but it was to prove a divisive reality at a later stage (15:36-40). Clearly it is viewed by Saul as a failure on Mark's part ('he had deserted them in Pamphylia,' 15:38). Conjectures have been offered: did he resent the increasing leadership role that Saul was taking as against his uncle? Saul had seized the ministry initiative in Paphos, and the 'Barnabas and Saul' of earlier paragraphs (12:25; 13:2, 7), is now 'Saul and his companions' (13:13). If this *were* a factor, there is no sign that Barnabas resented it. He exhibits in a quite exemplary manner that rare quality of being able to celebrate success, irrespective of who is the subject of it. It is amazing what can be accomplished for God when it doesn't matter who gets the credit.

> It takes more grace than I can tell
> To play the second fiddle well.

Every church needs such musicians.

Alternatively, were the rigours of the travel and ministry too much for Mark? Was he missing the comfortable surroundings of his Jerusalem home with its household servants? Is there anything to be concluded from the fact that his name is added as a bit of an afterthought in 13:5, and there is no reference to his having been personally 'sent by the Spirit'? We simply do not know. What we *do* know is that Mark was later reinstated in his ministry, as his association with Peter (1 Pet. 5:13) expresses, to say nothing of the composition of his canonical Gospel which has blessed countless millions all over the world down the Christian centuries, and no less so today. His reaffirmation is also signally demonstrated by the fact that Paul, in almost his final recorded words, was to revise his judgment and reinstate Mark in his esteem and affections: 'Get Mark and bring him with you, because he is helpful to me in my ministry' (2 Tim. 4:11). There is a message of massive encouragement here: failure is never final with God – which is just as well, for all of us.

Perga (known today as Antalya) was a city of some size – 75,000 is estimated – as well as reflecting a considerable cultural life. Its Hellenistic culture inspired a School of Sculpture, and scores of perfectly preserved statues of figures from Greek mythology have been excavated. The early mathematician, Apollonius of Perga, had apparently already calculated that the moon went round the earth and that the earth went round the sun. All this makes it the more surprising that the missionaries decided not to evangelize there but to press on northwards, a further hundred miles, to the city of Pisidian Antioch. That called for climbing some 3,600 feet across the Taurus mountain range, along what has been described as 'one of the hardest roads in Asia Minor', and, due to brigands, dangerous as well. The additional fact that they stopped at Perga on the return journey, by which time they were probably eager to return to their home-base in Antioch, makes the omission of Perga at this point as requiring some explanation.

A perfectly plausible one is offered by Barclay,[9] among others: Paul's health. The coastal plain of Pamphylia was notorious as the home of a virulent malarial fever which involved 'prostrating paroxysms'. The Letter to the Galatians was very likely written to the churches in this area, and Paul there states that 'it was because of an illness that I first preached the gospel to you' (Gal. 4:13), and also that 'though my illness was a trial to you, you did not treat me with contempt or scorn' (4:14). Paul's illness may also have been a factor in Mark's decision to leave.

9. Barclay, 10.

Their destination was one of the sixteen 'Antiochs' of the time, all named by Seleucus Nikator, one of Alexander the Great's generals, in honour of his father, Antiochus. **Pisidian Antioch** had a large Jewish population, though we will note the wide range of types the missionaries were to encounter during their stay in the city. They begin, as customary, with the Jewish community. **On the Sabbath they entered the synagogue and sat down** (14). The typical synagogue order of worship began with the reciting of the *Shema* ('The Lord your God is one Lord, and you shall love the Lord your God...'); followed by prayers; two Scriptural lessons, one from the Torah, the other from the prophets; then an exposition of one of these passages, which might on occasion be a message of encouragement from any appropriate visitor present; and then a concluding blessing. In this case **after the reading from the Law and the Prophets, the synagogue rulers sent word to them, 'Brothers, if you have a message of encouragement for the people, please speak'** (15).

Paul, distinguished perhaps by his wearing rabbinic dress, rises in response. He **motioned with his hand** (16). Luke is clearly drawing upon an eye-witness source here, possibly Paul himself at some later point. The reference to gesture rather belies the later criticism offered by his Corinthian opponents that 'his speaking amounts to nothing' (2 Cor. 10:10). This criticism is probably to be explained by his later comment, 'I may not be a trained speaker' (11:6); Paul eschewed the finer points of the classical Greek rhetorical style highly esteemed in Corinth in order to speak directly to the heart.

The sermon is given in its full terms. Clearly Luke sees it as representative of Paul's witness in the synagogues, and to the Jews generally. In a similar manner, Luke will give a fairly full account of Paul's *Areopagus* address in chapter 17 as being representative of Paul's presentation to Gentile audiences.

Paul first identifies his congregation, never a bad starting point: **Men of Israel and you Gentiles who worship God**. The latter were the so-called 'God-fearers', a large class scattered throughout the Mediterranean world who were attracted to Jewish theology and worship. Judaism's unyielding monotheism along with its strong ethical stress were of considerable attraction to thinking minds, which were regularly repulsed by the multiple gods of the empire and their often questionable behaviour.

Paul then embarks, as was customary, on an overview of Israel's dealings with God (cf. 7:1-50). He mentions God's election, **God...chose our fathers**, and then their **stay in Egypt**, the **mighty power** of their Red Sea redemption, God's enduring their **forty years in the desert,** and his settlement of them **in Canaan** (19). Then followed the period of the **judges until the time of Samuel**, and the establishment of the monarchy, and **Saul**'s appointment and **removal**, which brought **David** to the throne, **a man after God's own heart** (22).

Paul now reaches his climax and the heart of his message: **from this man's descendants God has brought to Israel the Saviour Jesus, as he promised**. **John** (the Baptist) had prepared the way for Him, offering a **baptism** of cleansing, expressing **repentance** in readiness for the coming of the promised one, **whose sandals I am not worthy to untie** (25). This divinely sent Saviour meant that **salvation** was now offered to both you **brothers, children of Abraham, and you God-fearing Gentiles**. Tragically **the people of Jerusalem and their leaders did not recognize Jesus** and **condemned him** thus fulfilling the **prophets' words** that God's promised one would be rejected. Despite his innocence they **asked for,** and obtained, **a death-sentence** from the Roman procurator, **Pilate** (28). After **all that was written about him** was **carried out** (Isa. 52:13–53:12; Pss. 22; 69; 118) Jesus was **taken down from the tree** (Deut. 21:22) and **laid in a tomb. But God raised him from the dead and for many days he was seen by those who had travelled with him from Galilee to Jerusalem. They are now his witnesses to our people** (31).

Therefore – **the good news! What God promised our fathers he has fulfilled for us...by raising up Jesus** (33). Some scholars see the reference to the 'raising up' of Jesus as referring to a 'raising onto the stage of history' rather than more narrowly, his resurrection from the dead (so e.g., Barrett). [10] The Greek word he uses here (*anastesas*), is not the word usually applied to His resurrection (*egeiren*), so this is not impossible, though certainly not conclusive.

Paul then supports these claims by citing three Old Testament passages, first Psalm 2:7, **You are my Son; today I have become your Father** (33), legitimizing Jesus as truly the divine Son, 'in the same way as a father would accept his wife's child as being really his son and so promise him loving care and protection; the idea of begetting is purely metaphorical.' [11]

The second and third quotations stand together. The first of them, **I will give you the sure blessings promised to David** (Isa. 55:3) (34), probably refers to the fact that the promise given to David of the perpetuity of his kingdom is fulfilled in Jesus, which of course is only possible if He was raised from the dead, the thrust of the final quotation, from Psalm 16:10: **You will not let your Holy One see decay** (35), precisely the application of this passage made by Peter at Pentecost (2:27).

Having laid this clear biblical and historical basis concerning the person and mission of Jesus, Paul now moves to his application: **therefore, my brothers, I want you to know that through Jesus forgiveness of sins is proclaimed to you** (38). Here is 'good news' indeed: all our shortcomings and deliberate wrongdoings, from our earliest moral awareness through to our latest breath, can be forgiven, pardoned, and hence no longer stand against us in the moral register of heaven. Paul points to its theological basis and links this miracle to Jesus as he continues, **through him** (Jesus) **everyone who believes is justified from everything you could not be justified from by the law of Moses** (39). The key term is 'justified' which means 'declared or accounted righteous in God's sight'.[12] Thus one of the great fundamental categories of the New Testament theology of the atonement makes its appearance at the centre of one of the earliest forms of the Christian 'good news'.

---

10. Barrett, 645-6.

11. Marshall, 226.

12. cf. Bock, 459-60.

Positively this status of justification is made possible by 'believing in Jesus'. The NLT is helpful, 'Everyone who believes in him is freed from all guilt and declared right with God.' That implies the abandoning of every hope of attaining that righteous status by our own efforts, but of actually attaining it through a wholehearted trust in Jesus and what He has done for us. That 'done for us' is not spelled out here but is indicated in the earlier allusion, in verse 29, to His death interpreted in terms of Deuteronomy 21:22, 'cursed is every one who hangs on a tree.' Paul would refer to this Scripture directly in his letter to the churches of Galatia some months later, and apply it: 'Christ redeemed us from the curse of the law (= the condemnation which follows our failure to fulfil the law of God) by becoming a curse for us' (3:13); and again, 'the Son of God who loved me and gave himself for me' (2:20).

Negatively this forgiveness, the precondition of our justification before God, **cannot be** obtained **by the law of Moses** (39). The alternatives are therefore stark, faith in Christ and hence forgiveness, implying God's declaring us righteous; or the vain attempt at self-salvation through observing the Old Testament law, and hence condemnation.

Paul is alert to the possibility of a negative response to his presentation and so concludes with a solemn warning, that to reject God's offer would be to repeat the tragic error of those in the prophet Habakkuk's day who refused to consider that what was happening in the incursion of the Babylonian army was actually God's work. In a similar way God had been at work in their day in the coming, death and rising of Jesus. To fail to recognize this 'coming of God' would condemn them likewise to **perish** (41).

Luke then describes the reactions to the sermon. **The people invited them to speak further about these things the next Sabbath** (42). But the message has already borne fruit, as **many of the Jews and devout converts to Judaism followed Paul and Barnabas, who talked with them and urged them to continue in the grace of God** (43). Their being directed to God's grace is a clear indication of their having grasped the gospel and applied it to their lives; for

Paul's message in essence was a demonstration of how God's grace had appeared in Jesus Christ, in fulfilment of the promise to Israel, and was now available through faith in Him, with the resultant gift of a righteous status with God. They had already entered into this abandonment to divine grace; they were urged to **continue** to rest in it.

Word of this new message and its promise of salvation had clearly continued to resonate throughout the following week so that **on the next Sabbath almost the whole city gathered to hear the word of the Lord** (44). Clearly God's Spirit is at work as the entire community is stirred. The Christian centuries bear witness to such width of influence in times of revival. Jonathan Edwards, for example, writing of the awakening in Northampton, Mass., in 1735, writes: 'There was scarcely a single person in the town, either young or old, that was left unconcerned about the great things of the eternal world.' Similarly Charles Finney spoke of a revival in Rome, N.Y.: 'As the work proceeded, it gathered in nearly the whole population.' Or again, it was said of the awakening in the west side of Dundee in 1840, under the godly leadership of Robert Murray McCheyne, that at the height of the blessing you could walk from one end of that densely populated district to the other and never be out of the sound of the singing of the praises of God.

The very expansiveness of the influence, however, did not stir up any sense of thanksgiving in the hearts of the Jewish leaders. **When the Jews saw the crowds, they were filled with jealousy, and talked abusively against Paul and Barnabas** (45). Jealousy…it is sadly astonishing how quickly the skin of our piety can be penetrated by the 'success' of religious colleagues. Perhaps the best advice in such moments of temptation is that shared by the great Keswick Convention preacher F.B. Meyer, when asked how he coped with the enormous popularity which was attending the stirring, scholarly expositions of G. Campbell Morgan: 'I pray for him.'

There is obviously no repeat of the invitation to address the synagogue congregation, but Paul and Barnabas have a ready response, which they express with **boldness. We**

had to speak the word of God to you first (cf. Rom. 1:16; 2:9-10) (46). Is this 'had to' a reflection simply of a sense of responsibility to God's ancient people through whom Jesus had come for the world? Or is this something more personally felt, Paul's 'great sorrow and unceasing anguish of heart...for those of my own race, the people of Israel.' (Rom. 9:2-3)? Or again is this also a programmatic 'order' traceable back to Jesus (cf. 'Go rather to the lost sheep of the house of Israel', Matt. 10:6)? Marshall comments, 'the basis of this duty is never made absolutely clear in the New Testament but presumably rests on the nature of Israel as the covenant people of God to whom he continued to offer his promises of salvation.'[13]

Consequently, **since you reject (the word of God) and do not consider yourselves worthy of eternal life, we now turn to the Gentiles**. The Greek verb translated 'reject' (*apotheisthe*) means 'to thrust out or away', a forceful and energetic rejection. Paul's use of 'eternal life' here and in verse 48, immediately following, are the only occasions on which this synonym for salvation occurs in Acts.[14] It is particularly to the point here since Paul had drawn out, at the end of his sermon, the solemn future consequences of rejecting Christ's salvation (v. 41). Paul affirms the authenticity of the Gentile mission to which they will now turn, by citing Isaiah 49:6, a great text in which God addresses his Servant, **I have made you a light for the Gentiles, that you may bring salvation to the ends of the earth** (47). There is a whole Christology and a whole ecclesiology in that statement; here is why Jesus came, and what He continues to do through the church. Paul asserts that this represents a command from the Lord, **the Lord has commanded us** (cf. 10:42); world mission is no mere option as far as the church's responsibilities are concerned. 'It is sheer hypocrisy to pay lip-service to the Lordship of Christ if we do not heed his command to evangelize. A Church not engaged in mission is guilty of apostasy.'[15]

---

13. Marshall, 230.

14. Though 'life' occurs in 5:20 and 11:18.

15. John Stott, *Our Guilty Silence* (Hodder, 1967), passim.

The Gentiles greet this change of mission focus with delight: **they were glad and honoured the word of the Lord** (48). Here again we meet the doxological dimension of mission. God is 'honoured' when His gospel is proclaimed and responded to; a zeal for world evangelization is simply a fundamental means of worshipping God. Praising and adoring God with lifted hearts and hands is no doubt commendable, provided it is done sincerely, but we will have all eternity to express that particular form of worship (Rev. 5:13; 7:9-10). We only have our years on planet earth, this brief and ephemeral present life, to seek His glory through the global spread of the gospel. *'Sing to the Lord, praise his name…declare his glory among the nations!' (Ps. 96:2-3)*.

The Gentiles respond, as **all who were ordained to eternal life believed**, and the influence continued to grow as **the word of the Lord spread throughout the whole region** (49). The Jews, however, also expand their opposition to include the highest circles of influence in the city, **the God-fearing women of high standing and the leading men of the city**, with the result that the missionaries are **expelled from their region** (50). How tragically possible to be 'God-fearing' and yet opposed to God's heart for the world expressed for all time in the gift of His Son, and the obligation to share the good news of it; God-fearing, but not God-honouring. The apostles react by following the instructions of Jesus to His missionaries: 'The Lord appointed seventy-two others and sent them, two by two, ahead of him to every town where he was about to go… when you enter a town and are not welcomed, go into the streets and say "even the dust of your town that sticks to our feet we wipe off against you"' (Luke 10:1, 10-11). **So they shook the dust from their feet and went to Iconium** (51).

The terms in which the Gentiles' response is expressed, **all who were ordained for eternal life believed**, calls for comment. We need to recall that salvation involves two agents: God and the person or persons who believe the gospel. Their joint agency is clearly affirmed in Scripture (e.g. Eph. 1:4-5 with Eph. 1:13). There is no salvation without God's willing, and no salvation without humanity's believing. Spurgeon once put it in terms of the door into the kingdom of God which carries a text above it: 'Whosoever will may come'. We respond to the invitation, we believe in Christ and pass through the door into the kingdom. However, once inside, we look back and discover another text above the door on the inside which reads: 'Chosen from before the foundation of the world.' How these relate is a mystery for our present capacities. Both are true. This reference at verse 48 stresses the divine agency; properly understood, its fruit is boundless praise.

The disciples meanwhile continue to celebrate their salvation; they were **filled with joy and the Holy Spirit** (52). Could anything be better than that?

Study Questions:

1. We are struck by the astonishingly multicultural composition of the Antioch leadership team. In this increasingly multicultural age we need to open ourselves to this form of congregational life and leadership. How can Antioch (11:19-26; 13:1-3) help us? Consider the biblical bases of such churches; the attitudes they call for; and the encouraging potential they offer.

2. We note the context of worship here (13:2-3). Do we come to worship expecting God to meet with us and change things? What helps generate this kind of expectation? What can we do personally to promote it?

3. Consider the missionaries' Cyprus ministry (13:4-12). It centres on a 'power encounter' with demonic agencies and one of their human representatives. In what sense is all ministry and mission a species of these realities? What does this call for in our evangelistic efforts?

4. Paul's sermon in Pisidian Antioch is representative of his synagogue preaching (13:16-43). What are its most striking features? Its heart lies in its

offering 'good news' (13:32). What is this? Have we lost the joyous wonder of the gospel? What might we do to recover it?

5. The message provokes two contrary reactions (13:40-45); this is always so when the gospel is preached. Are we ready for that? Luke uncovers the deeper motives in those who oppose (cf. 'jealousy', 13:45). What other, similarly unworthy taproots to rejection of Christ's claims have we uncovered? This passage notes that 'those appointed to eternal life believed' (13:48), while also clearly reflecting human responsibility (13:45, 46, 50). What does the emphasis on *God's* action here teach us, and how does that serve as an encouragement in our witness?

4. Ministry at Iconium (14:1-7)

Paul and Barnabas would have travelled eastwards along the *Via Sebaste* to reach their next population centre, **Iconium**, known today as Konya. Situated in a plateau area, the central steppes in today's Turkey, the region was rather cold and bare of vegetation. Iconium was the ruling centre of the surrounding region.

After their rejection by the Jews in Pisidian Antioch, one might have forgiven the missionaries had they chosen a different place than the synagogue for their initial witness; however the principle of 'to the Jew first' is apparently more than a strategic one. **So they went as usual into the Jewish synagogue** (1). The Lord was clearly present, and empowering the missionaries, because **they spoke so effectively that a great number of Jews and Gentiles believed.** The by now familiar reaction soon set in, however, as the remaining Jews who had not responded to the gospel **stirred up the Gentiles and poisoned their minds against the brothers** (2). Nothing daunted, the missionaries **spent considerable time there, speaking boldly for the Lord**. The novel feature of the ministry here, at least in terms of what Luke reports, was to the effect that **the Lord confirmed the message of his grace by enabling them to**

do miraculous signs and wonders (3). So the message in words was confirmed by a message in deeds. We noted a similar combination in the conversion of Sergius Paulus in Cyprus. Ought we to expect, or even seek it, today?

Several comments may be ventured.

Firstly, the plain fact is that this area of the overtly miraculous, especially when promoted as a public accompaniment to the preaching of the gospel, has proved an extremely difficult area to handle at the pastoral level. Far too many have been caused to stumble, and even turned away from the faith altogether, by insensitivity, lack of balance, and the expression of personality and power complexes. That being said, the presence of such phenomena in Scripture, supremely in the ministry of Jesus, cannot be gainsaid, nor dare we set boundaries to God's power, nor become squeamish over what God may wish and choose to do among us.

Secondly, we dare not miss the clear unwillingness of Jesus to major His ministry around such phenomena, and perhaps even more significantly His strong rebukes to those who became 'sign-seekers' and lost sight of the importance of His proclamation of the kingdom of God. The emphasis on 'signs and wonders' carries an almost magnetic attraction towards the emotional and sensational to the neglect of the rational and gradual. It also often carries the implication that it is in such 'encounter' ministry that the real spiritual battles are fought and the real work of God is done. It is salutary in this connection to note that two of the primary autobiographical parables of Jesus, those of the sower and the tares, both present Him as essentially a teacher of God's Word (Matt. 13:1-9, 18-30). Further, in both these parables Jesus notes the presence of the evil one, in snatching away the seed in the first case, and in sowing the tares of falsehood in the second. In other words, Jesus makes it clear that His preaching ministry was every bit as much a spiritual warfare reality as his exorcisms. No one who has spent years expounding Scripture will need any persuasion on that point. They will have made the discovery that the front-line trenches in the battle between good and evil, God and Satan, run right through every Christian pulpit.

Thirdly, we can helpfully notice that the context of the signs and wonders at Iconium is **the message of his grace**. It is when this is lost sight of, when ministry in any of its expressions becomes 'ours', whether in preaching and teaching, or in any other manifestations or ministries of the Holy Spirit, we have moved beyond the safety of biblical truth. All that is done in the service of God is the work of God through us. The Risen Lord continues 'to do and teach' (1:1); it is all of grace; grace at the beginning, grace at the end, and grace all the way through; and hence it is only and all for *His* glory.

Fourthly, it is always helpful, more generally, to remind ourselves that *every* act of witness, whether congregationally or personally, is a combination of 'hearing' and 'seeing'; there is both the story we tell and the persons we are. In this sense Christian witness is always incarnational, and its greatest stumbling blocks lie here in many cases. 'People will not care what you know until they know that you care.' As with Jesus, people will only exclaim 'it is the Lord' when they see the print of the nails in our hands and feet.

Back in Iconium the work of the missionaries proves divisive, **some sided with the Jews, some with the apostles.** This, with verse 14, is the first and only passage where Luke uses the term 'apostles' to refer to Barnabas and Paul. Stott has helpful comment on the meaning of 'apostle' in the New Testament. 'The word is used in the New Testament in two senses. On the one hand, there were the "apostles of Christ", personally appointed by him to be witnesses of the resurrection, who included the Twelve, Paul and probably James (1:21; 10:41). There is no evidence that Barnabas belonged to this group. On the other hand, there were the 'apostles of the churches' (2 Cor. 8:23: rsv margin.), sent out by a church or churches on particular missions, as Epaphroditus was an apostle or messenger of the Philippian church (Phil. 2:25). So too Paul and Barnabas were both apostles of the church of Syrian Antioch, sent out by them, whereas only Paul was also an apostle of Christ.'[16]

---

16. Stott, 229.

The opposition grows and the missionaries hear of **a plot to mistreat and stone them**, and decide it is wise to leave, so **they fled to the Lycaonian cities of Lystra and Derbe and to the surrounding country, where they continued to preach the good news**. The closing of one door is the opening of another. We note also that the mission, while focused on larger centres of population, is not confined to them.

Whatever the memory they carry with them of their visit to Iconium, they certainly left an impression behind them. The second-century writing, *Acts of Paul*, preserves a description of the apostle by one, Onesiphorus, an Iconian resident. Bruce observes that this is 'so vigorous and unconventional that it must surely rest on good local tradition'.[17] 'And he saw Paul approaching, a man small in size, with meeting eyebrows, with a rather large nose, bald-headed, bow-legged, strongly built, full of grace, for at times he looked like a man, and at times he had the face of an angel.'

5. Ministry in Lystra (14:8-20)

The next stop in the road for the missionaries is at **Lystra**, some twenty miles to the south of Iconium, and a distinctly rural setting. Hemer refers to it as 'less developed'.[18] There is no reference to a synagogue which could well imply that none existed. Consequently Paul and Barnabas are here interfacing with a population which has had no previous contact with the God of Israel. Religiously this area could be described, not unfairly, as 'heathen'.[19]

We notice, however, that the reference in verse 7 to some preaching in the surrounding area may underlie the presence of some newly created 'disciples' in Lystra who appear in verse 20 (including Timothy? cf. 16:1-3). The ministry is initially focused on a healing miracle, which is introduced immediately: **in Lystra there sat a man crippled in his feet, who was lame from birth and had never**

---

17. Bruce, 288.

18. Hemer, 110.

19. Marshall, 234.

walked (8). The language here at several points contains echoes of the healing of the lame man at the Jerusalem temple in chapter 3: Paul has gifts akin to Peter's. Paul is preaching, perhaps in the town square which would be a natural site for a beggar, which this man presumably was. The apostle senses his interest, and his groping faith; **he saw that he had faith to be healed**, and calls out loudly (Gk. 'in a loud voice'), '**Stand up on your feet!**' (10). It is the one thing this man had been unable to do all of his life, yet he now does it; indeed **he jumped up and began to walk**.

This provokes reaction, though hardly one the missionaries are prepared for: the townspeople want **to offer sacrifices to them!** (13). The explanation for this lies in the region's history. A local legend, which is retold by Ovid the Latin poet, describes an incognito visit to the region of two of the traditional Greek gods, Zeus, the leader of the pantheon, and Hermes, the messenger. They sought hospitality but were repeatedly rebuffed, until finally a poor elderly couple gave them lodging in their meagre cottage. Later the gods returned to reward the couple, but also to destroy with a flood the homes which had rejected them. Marshall notes archaeological evidence of the cult of the two gods, side by side, dating from A.D. 250 near Lystra.[20]

So…here are visiting strangers with evidently divine powers (as seen in the healing miracle) – the gods have returned! Barnabas is seen as Zeus (did this mean he appeared older than Paul?). Paul is Hermes, the messenger. *This time* the townsfolk will attend them with due honour; and so the local priest of Zeus is dispatched to bring the appropriate offerings: **the priest of Zeus, whose temple was just outside the city, brought bulls and wreaths to the city gates!** (13).

Not having the local language, the meaning of all this activity is lost on Paul and Barnabas; their first awareness is when the sacrifices are about to be offered to them. Their reaction is both predictable and yet also striking:

---

20. Marshall, 237.

they tore their clothes and rushed out into the crowd, shouting: 'Men, why are you doing this? We too are only human like you' (15). One can only describe this as a violent reaction. But it is prompted by the deep-seated horror and revulsion, resident in the missionaries as sons of Judaism, of being seen to blasphemously claim divinity (Deut. 4:15-31; 5:6-10; 13:1-18; cf. Mark 14:63-64). A similar if less violent reaction is evidenced in Peter in response to Cornelius' adulation (10:25f); and we have observed the judgment that befell Herod apparently for precisely this idolatry (12:21-23). It is fair to ask the question whether we are as sensitive today at the adulation which can be heaped at times on Christian leaders. Appreciation and thankfulness are genuine virtues which should never be suppressed, but we also need to exercise a proper restraint, for the sake of the leaders themselves, as well as for the Lord's.

Having got their attention, Paul continues with his speech. **We bring you good news, telling you to turn from these worthless things to the living God, who made heaven and earth and sea and everything in them** (15). 'This is classic, prophetic Jewish natural theology like that seen in Isaiah 40–41.'[21] It is also the first speech to pagans recorded in Acts. Paul goes on to apply this theology of the one creator God to his hearers' immediate experience. **Yet he has not left himself without testimony. He has shown kindness by giving you rain from heaven and crops in their seasons; he provides you with plenty of food and fills your hearts with joy** (17). This ends his address as recorded, which has left many asking why there is no reference to Jesus. Marshall responds appropriately, 'this omission does not mean that Paul said nothing on this matter, but rather that Luke's purpose here is to supplement his earlier accounts of the apostolic preaching by showing what more was said when pagan Gentiles were being addressed.'[22] We remind ourselves additionally that verses 6-7 refer to preaching the 'good news' earlier in

21. Bock, 477.
22. Marshall, 239.

Lystra, and that Paul is already 'speaking' when he has his encounter with the lame man (9). Additionally, the address was a spontaneous response to the idolatry implicit in the crowd's preparations to offer sacrifices to the missionaries rather than a full-blown evangelistic address. It was an attempt to stop that, and it obviously succeeded.

This is not to imply, however, that this is not an important speech. It represents the necessary theological basis upon which the good news of salvation through Jesus requires to be based for effective witness to polytheistic pagans. 'One cannot discuss Jesus without first establishing that God is one'.[23] But this clarification of the nature of God carries an implicit call to repentance. **We are telling you to turn from these worthless things** (cf. 1 Thess. 1:9-10).

This call is appropriate because **God has not left himself without testimony** (17). This is an important assertion and is restated by Paul in Romans 1:18-20. Although, as Paul concedes there, 'men hold down the truth by their wickedness', they are nonetheless 'without excuse' for their idolatry and moral perversions (Rom. 1:18, 20 and 21-32). These Scriptures appear to justify the claim of the Princeton theologian Charles Hodge, that there is a universal human conviction 'that there is a Being on whom they are dependent and to whom they are responsible.' While this innate awareness should not be overvalued lest it render us insensitive to the difficulties many non-believers have in coming to faith, and since in any event it is not seen in Scripture as an adequate basis for a relationship with God, it nonetheless secures the important truth that God continues to address all people, and that He gives witness to Himself in His creation.

This last point is particularly pertinent at the present time through the accumulated scientific evidence of the astonishing degree to which the universe and its components are 'fine-tuned' to permit the emergence of human life on this planet. This may accordingly be seen as, in some sense, a modern equivalent to the divine **testimony** which Paul draws attention to here with respect to the

23. Bock, 478.

citizens of Lystra. There is of course a certain nuancing needed in drawing the parallel since the modern evidence is received at second hand from scientists; relatively few people are in any position to test these claims personally. However, with that qualifier added, we are faced today with highly significant evidence that points overwhelmingly, for those who are able to free themselves from the fallen tendency to 'suppress' the truth, to there being a Creator God, and that we need to repent, seek for Him, and worship Him.[24]

More generally, as far as Paul's speech is concerned, we cannot but admire its remarkable pertinence to its audience. We will have cause to comment similarly in chapter 17 when considering his message to the Areopagus in Athens. Paul has left us an abiding model of how to be faithful witnesses; in his own words, 'I try to please everybody in every way. For I am not seeking my own good but the good of the many, so that they may be saved' (1 Cor. 10:33f.). This implies absolutely no compromise on the fundamentals of the gospel, but endless flexibility in the ways we express it, a flexibility that expresses our unconcern for ourselves but our endlessly loving concern for those who need Christ, 'seeking *their* good, so that they may be saved.' He appropriately adds, 'Follow my example, as I follow the example of Christ' (1 Cor. 11:1).

Coming back to earth in Lystra, trouble begins to brew for the missionaries, when **some Jews came from Antioch and Iconium and won the crowd over**. This time the opposition is not confined to verbal abuse (13:45). The fickle crowd in Lystra are swept along into an act of mob violence. **They stoned Paul and dragged him outside the city, thinking he was dead** (19). This is a dark moment by any account. Paul, unsurprisingly, was never to forget it (2 Cor. 11:24f.; Gal. 6:17; 2 Tim. 3:11). The great nineteenth-century preacher Dr J.H. Jowett remarked: 'I once saw the track of a bleeding hare across

---

24. See for example: Antony Flew, *There is a God*, HarperOne, 2007, chap. 6, and passim; William Lane Craig, *Reasonable Faith*, Crossway, 2008, pp. 157-172.

the snow; that was Paul's track across Europe.' 'Mission sooner or later leads into passion...every form of mission leads to some form of cross.'[25]

> *From subtle love of softening things,*
> *From easy choices, weakenings,*
> *(Not thus are spirits fortified,*
> *Not this way went the Crucified)*
> *From all that dims Thy Calvary,*
> *O Lamb of God, deliver me.*[26]

For a moment in Lystra, the inconceivable hangs in the air...what if? The implications for the entire future shape and progress of Christianity were almost unthinkable; but God is there; He who holds the lives of all His servants in His hands; He whose plans must needs prevail. So...**after the disciples had gathered round him, he got up and went back into the city. And, the next day he and Barnabas left for Derbe** (20).

6. Ministry in Derbe, and Return to Antioch (14:21-28)

The eastern limit of the journey is now reached. The road to **Derbe** was sixty miles long, and one wonders how Paul's battered body could have coped with it, but clearly the extended journey, the undoubted 'tender loving care' of his companion, and the sustaining strength and love of the Lord brought renewal to Paul, so that on arrival **they preached the good news in the city and won a large number of disciples** (21). **Then they returned...**'We are hard pressed on every side, but not crushed; perplexed, but not in despair; persecuted but not abandoned; *struck down but not destroyed...So then, death is at work in us,* but *life is at work in you'* (2 Cor. 4:8, 12). 'Said Thomas, "except I shall see in his hands the print of the nails...I will not believe"....' What Thomas said of Christ the world is saying about the church. And the world is also saying to every preacher: Unless I see in your hands the print of the

---

25. Douglas Webster, *Yes to Mission* (SCM, 1966), 101.

26. Amy Carmichael, *Towards Jerusalem* (SPCK, 1936), 94.

nails, I will not believe...It is the one who has died with Christ that can preach the cross of Christ.'[27]

> It is the branch that bears the fruit,
> That feels the knife
> To prune it for a larger growth,
> A fuller life.
>
> Rejoice, tho' each desire, each dream,
> Each hope of thine
> Shall fall and fade; it is the hand
> Of Love Divine
>
> That holds the knife, that cuts and breaks
> With tenderest touch,
> That thou, whose life has borne some fruit
> May'st now bear much.[28]

It is significant to notice that the missionaries had another option at this point. They were already well down the *Via Sebaste* and only a few more days leisurely travel eastwards would have brought them to the connecting road southwards to Syria, and Antioch, and home! But despite its attraction they refuse this easier option. Instead they turn deliberately westwards and so, *retracing their steps,* **they returned to Lystra** (yes, Lystra!), **Iconium, and** (Pisidian) **Antioch.** What accounts for this inevitably risky choice? It was simply what Paul would refer to later in his list of sufferings for the gospel as 'the pressure of my concern for the churches' (2 Cor. 11:28).

Paul and Barnabas, as we have remarked before and will again, were not into winning converts but into making disciples; not into registering commitments but into building churches, congregations of God's people where there could be growth into God-honouring character, and mutual care. But congregations also which would be viable centres of witness from which the gospel could subsequently radiate outwards into the surrounding communities. Paul was never under the illusion that he was the

---

27. G. Cambell Morgan, *Evangelism*, 59-60.

28. Annie Johnston-Flint.

only evangelist to the Gentile world. Rather his ministry was like the match applied at critical places and times to the brushwood and kindling of strategic communities. He was there to set the fire alight and then move on to kindle another fire in another area or community. In that sense the spreading of the gospel was the work of the Spirit in and through the churches. The evangelists were as numerous as the converts. And so, with that as the overriding perspective, there was more to be done. So back it was, to do four things:

First, the 'apostles' (4) needed to **strengthen the disciples** (22). So many of those who had believed were still spiritually weak and vulnerable; they desperately needed teaching about the basics of their faith and on a whole range of issues which would deepen and strengthen their relationship with the Lord and one another, and bring a sense of ongoing commitment to their lives.

Second, they needed to **encourage them to remain true to the faith**, in face of its **many hardships**, and learn that these were not accidental or a sign that the Lord had forsaken them, but that such were in fact the divine seal of being citizens of the present and future **kingdom of God** (22).

Third, their community life needed structure and therefore there was need for the election of good leaders, wise and caring **elders** – to be **appointed**, after the model of Antioch, **with prayer and fasting** (23).

Fourth, they needed to direct them in everything to the Lord Himself, their supreme, ever-faithful, unfailing, everlasting resource, the ever-blessed Trinity. So, **they committed them to the Lord in whom they had put their trust**; to 'the grace of the Lord Jesus Christ, and the love of God, and the fellowship of the Holy Spirit.'

So on Paul and Barnabas went, until they were back at their point of disembarking, at **Perga** where they made up for their having had to pass it by on the outward journey as **they preached the word** there also (25). **Then from Attalia they sailed back to Antioch, where they had been committed to the grace of God for the work they had now completed**. Antioch, where the believers had been praying faithfully day after day for them and their mission. They were home again, and with such a story to tell! So **they gathered the church together and reported** (27). What one might give to have been a fly on the wall at that gathering!

Two things predominated, though they were really one thing: they reported, *not* what they had done, *but* **what God had done through them**. Thus the message of Luke is carried forward through this first mission journey: mission is the work of God, because it expresses the heart of God for all people everywhere, and His longing to embrace them in His arms and hold them in His heart for evermore. Which leads to the second theme, the celebration of the great truth which this mission journey has confirmed, that in His gracious, sovereign ordering the door of His everlasting salvation, received by **faith,** is now wide **open to the Gentiles**.

While this reality was to be joyfully celebrated it did not mean that all the questions were answered, or that every lingering concern about Gentile inclusion was laid to rest. So as the missionaries shared their well-earned rest and recovery, and **stayed there a long time with the disciples** (28), there were other teachers abroad, whose convictions were of a different order. Some of them were to arrive ere long at Antioch (15:1), creating inevitable disputes. Clearly matters could not be left in this condition. So we come to 'the Consultation at Jerusalem'.

Study Questions:

1. God 'confirmed the message of his grace' (14:3). What equivalents should we look for today? In what ways am I called personally to be a 'confirmation of the message of His grace'?

2. Chapter 14:6 notes the apostles' 'tactical retreat' from Iconium, and the not entirely dissimilar action of 'shaking the dust from their feet' in leaving Pisidian Antioch (13:51). Are there applications for us of these actions?

3. What is to be learned from the healing miracle, and its sequels, in Lystra (14:8-19)?

4. How does 14:19 challenge you personally?

5. Reflect on the apostles' 'return journey' to the newly planted churches of Asia (14:21b-25), when they might so easily have taken the open, much shorter, eastern road back to Antioch? What motivated them? Do these considerations motivate us? What were the particular goals of this 'follow-up' ministry (14:22-23)? How are they being expressed in our church? How are they reflected in our own lives? What might be our equivalents to the 'reunion' back in Antioch (14:26-27)?

8

The Consultation at Jerusalem
(Acts 15:1-35)

B. The Consultation at Jerusalem (15:1-35)

'Chapter 15 is the turning point, the "centre-piece" and "watershed" of the book, the episode which rounds off and justifies the past developments, and makes those to come intrinsically possible.' Such is the judgment of Haenchen,[1] and Stott concurs: 'this is not an exaggeration'.[2]

The events of this chapter have been a long time coming. In a sense they were implicit in the commission of Jesus; for if the good news was to be taken finally 'to the ends of the earth', and those far-flung Gentile lands should prove, in any degree, a responsive and fruitful field of witness, then the terms on which these Gentiles would be embraced would clearly, eventually, require to be determined. That moment had now arrived.

In a sense what we have surveyed in our exposition through the first 14 chapters of Acts is a church moving through a series of steps, inching ever closer, to this point of resolution. Step one was the inherited faith of Israel in the Old Testament with its revelation of a universal creator God who brought the earth with all its inhabit-

---

1. Haenchen, 461.
2. Stott, 241.

ants into existence and continually sustains them, and is accordingly the Lord and God of all its peoples. Step two is the global, redeeming purpose of God expressed in the covenant made with Abraham and his descendants that through his line 'all the families of the earth' were to be blessed. Step three is the promise of the fulfilment of this purpose through a Coming One who would be a 'light to the Gentiles' as well as 'for glory to your people Israel'. Step four is the coming of Jesus Christ, God incarnate, the long-promised Messiah and Saviour. Step five is His life and ministry culminating in His sacrificial death and resurrection. Step six is the commissioning of the apostles, and in them the entire community of Jesus Christ, to be His witnesses to the whole world, 'beginning in Jerusalem.' Step seven is the coming of the Holy Spirit at Pentecost to empower and enable the mission of the church. Step eight is the witness of the earliest church in Jerusalem culminating in the vision and sacrifice of Stephen. Step nine is the ministry of Philip in Samaria and to Ethiopia. Step ten is the conversion and commissioning of Saul. Step eleven is the 'second conversion' of Peter in the house of Cornelius. Step twelve is the witness to Gentiles in Antioch. Step thirteen is the newly completed mission outreach of Paul and Barnabas to Cyprus, Pamphylia and Galatia, whereby 'the trickle of Gentile conversions was becoming a torrent'.[3] Finally, step fourteen is the determination by the church of the terms on which believing Gentiles are to be admitted to, and find a full place within, the global people of God, thus freeing the church to fulfil step fifteen: the commission of its Lord, and in glad obedience take the gospel 'to the ends of the earth.'

In a sense the process just outlined was a journey to an understanding of Jesus Christ as the incarnation of the one Creator God of all people, and hence to seeing His ministry, mission, sacrificial death, resurrection, ascension and glorious return as *universal events* bringing a salvation intended for every human being, without any ethnic or other social distinction.

---

3. Stott, 240.

The Old Testament had given clear anticipation of eventual Gentile inclusion, in some sense, within God's purpose, but most Jews understood that as a process of absorption into Israel rather than as a fully authentic 'second people of God' alongside Israel. Thus the Gentiles would join Israel within its 'boundary markers', the receiving of the covenant sign of circumcision, and a submission to the basic requirements, social as well as ethical, of the law of Moses: to become a Christian would effectively mean also, in the process, becoming a proselyte Jew. The notion that the Gentiles' inclusion within the people of God would not include both, or even either, of these markers was very difficult for many and was to prove for some nearly impossible to accept; which brings us to chapter fifteen.

1. The Issue at Stake (15:1-4)

The issue of the terms of Gentile inclusion predictably comes to a head in Antioch, and around the question of circumcision in particular. **Some men came down from Judea to Antioch and were teaching the brothers: 'Unless you are circumcised according to the custom taught by Moses, you cannot be saved'** (1). We are not in the least surprised to read that **this brought Paul and Barnabas into sharp dispute and debate with them** (2). It is important to note the evident agreement of the two apostles on this issue since, assuming that Paul's letter to the Galatians was written during this period, Barnabas had been guilty of a 'wobble' on the matter of table fellowship with Gentiles during a visit to Antioch by Peter and some others from Jerusalem (Gal. 2:11-14). Paul's courageous challenge to the 'separating group' had clearly proved salutary both for Barnabas and, as events would soon prove, for Peter also.

The precise terms of the issue as stated here, **unless you are circumcised**...differs slightly from that put by the Pharisaic party at the Consultation, 'The Gentiles must be circumcised and required to obey the law of Moses.' However, the underlying principle, that faith in Christ was insufficient in itself for salvation but

required to be complemented, is the same in both for-
mulations.

Clearly matters could not remain in this confused and
contentious state, and so the Antioch congregation took
the initiative and **appointed** a delegation consisting of
**Paul and Barnabas...along with some other believers,
to go up to Jerusalem** and seek the mind of the wider
church, specifically **the apostles and elders** (2). They were
sent on their way by the church, language reminiscent
of the 'sending off' of Paul and Barnabas on the mission
journey (13:3), and in every sense the implications were no
less significant or far-reaching. For at its core the matter at
issue could not be more critical – what is the basis of salvation? who is an authentic Christian? how are people saved
and authentically related to God? At the more immediate,
relational level, it was the question: How can law-observing Jewish Christians and law-ignoring Gentile Christians
co-exist? How can authentic Christian fellowship occur if
Jewish Christians observe the law, in particular its dietary
regulations involving separation from those not observing
these practices, including non-observing Gentile Christians? This presenting issue was made all the more acute,
as Marshall notes,[4] by the fact that a sacred meal, 'the
breaking of bread,' was a fundamental element of Christian communication and worship.

As they travel through **Phoenicia and Samaria**, the
party take the opportunity to share the news of **how the
Gentiles had been converted** during the outreach to Pamphylia and Galatia, and the news was gladly received: **this
made all the brothers very glad** (3). The gladness would
have been particularly deeply felt in Samaria, one may
imagine, against the background of their centuries of religious exclusion. Arriving at Jerusalem, the delegation are
given a positive **welcome by the church and the apostles
and elders, to whom** also **they reported everything,** and
again we note the important emphasis – on *what God had
done* **through them** (4).

---

4. Marshall, 243.

2. Discussion and Resolution (15:5-35)

Before coming to the various contributions to the discussion, several matters need to be clarified. First, there is the question of how we should refer to this event. There has been a tendency traditionally to speak of the 'Council at, or of, Jerusalem', but that is to see the meeting through eyes attuned to later 'Councils', those widely representative ecumenical gatherings during the first five centuries of the church, called to resolve significant theological differences and attempt, authoritatively, to restate the faith of the whole church. Though the outcomes of this Jerusalem meeting were to prove no less significant than these later gatherings, it lacks their formality, self-conscious authority, and width of representation. It is accordingly, in our judgment, preferable to speak of the 'Consultation at Jerusalem'.

Second, to clarify again, the issue is *not* whether Gentiles should be offered salvation through Jesus-Messiah and hence included in the faith community – that was common to all parties; the issue is rather the terms in which this offer was to be presented, and how those responding to the offer should thereafter live. Must their faith *also* be expressed in being circumcised and adhering to the Mosaic law?

One other observation is that nowhere is there reference to discussion of the scope of the circumcision so advocated. Is this a male-only rite as in the Old Testament? Presumably so. But if it were so, how would this distinction relate to baptism which already was being performed on both 'men and women' (8:12; cf. 16:13, 33; Gal. 3:27-28). The relationship between circumcision and baptism is another issue, which we need not raise here (cf. Col. 2:11-12), but one of the 'better things' of the gospel (Heb. 11:40) is surely its clear and unambiguous declaration in its practice of baptism – at whatever age, and using whatever form – that it is administered identically to male and female recipients. Thus, apart from any other regrettable implications, had the Pharisaic party prevailed in the Consultation, a gender-discriminatory rite of entry would have been conferred on Christianity.

The meeting appears to have begun with the **Pharisaic party** being invited to state their position, which they do in its full terms: **The Gentiles must be circumcised and required to obey the law of Moses** (5). Then followed **much discussion**, as we would have expected. Luke does not give us any account of the debate but confines himself, surely wisely, to three defining contributions, those of Peter, Paul with Barnabas, and James, which lead to the consensual resolution.

Peter (7-11). This is Peter's final recorded contribution in Acts, but it is a critical one. His address is essentially a testimony to what they all already knew about, how God had **made a choice** that he should be the one to bring **the message of the gospel** to **the Gentiles** at the home of Cornelius **so that they might believe** (7). However it was not only the Gentiles *believing* that he appeals to but also their *receiving*; God **giving the Holy Spirit to them** (i.e. to these uncircumcised, non-Torah-keeping Gentiles) **just as he did to us** (8). The latter phrase means 'just as he did to us at Pentecost' (cf. 11:15). Thus the full divine attestation of the 'believing' was given in the 'receiving', as, at Caesarea, the Holy Spirit 'fell all over them'.

We can see now the critical importance of understanding, as we did in the earlier exposition, the three Pentecostal moments at Jerusalem, Samaria and Caesarea as distinguishable from other giftings and receivings of the Holy Spirit. In these unique, overtly and unmistakably supernatural, 'falling all over' experiences of the Spirit, God irrefutably authenticated the Samaritans and the Gentiles as, in His sight, equals in all respects with the original apostolic believers. **He showed that he accepted them; he made no distinction between us and them, as he,** through the ministry of the Holy Spirit, **purified their hearts by faith** (9). Consequently, since God has accepted them, to question their status is in effect to **test**, to pass judgment, on God.

Peter then adds a further supportive *ad hominem* argument by reminding the company what it is that is being asked for, the imposition of the law of Moses, **a yoke that neither we nor our fathers have been able to bear** (10).

This could refer to the general sense of burdensome obligation which always accrues to rules and regulations, and which Israel had experienced over the centuries with the multitude of laws calling for fulfilment. However in view of his final sentence (v. 11 below), which underscores the grace basis of salvation, Peter is probably thinking of the law-keeping which was being asked for in respect of the Gentiles as effectively eliminating grace and making human acceptance with God the grim matter of endlessly trying to save ourselves, a business which he and his fellow Jews have utterly failed to achieve, **a yoke** they could not carry. **No! We believe that it is through the grace of our Lord Jesus that we are saved, just as they are** (11).

Barnabas and Paul (12). As the two 'Antioch apostles' speak, there is a discernible hush, **the whole assembly became silent** (12). Paul had demonstrated in his exposition at Pisidian Antioch (13:47), and repeatedly in his synagogue preaching, as well as no doubt in the disputations in Antioch (15:2), and in the earlier 'discussion' at the Consultation (15:6), that the inclusion of the Gentiles is clearly foretold and affirmed in the Old Testament Scriptures. However in their more formal 'presentation' to the Consultation, as Luke records it, he and Barnabas choose to follow Peter's tack and bear witness to God's supernatural attestation of Gentile acceptance. So they tell of His **miraculous signs and wonders done among the Gentiles**, presumably such as the blinding of Elymas in Paphos leading to the faith of proconsul Sergius (13:9-11); the 'signs and wonders' in Iconium (14:3); and the 'jumping up' of the lifelong cripple in Lystra (14:9-10). The effect is predictable: the quieting of the clamour of debate and its replacement by a 'becoming silent' (12); a sense of the awesome presence of God and of His boundless power and majesty.

James (14-21). The advocates of circumcision and the law would presumably have anticipated something more affirming of their positions in James' case, as he was known to be a Jewish Christian with a strong commitment to the temple and other traditional practices. However, in this they are to be disappointed as he immediately aligned himself with the previous speakers, Peter specifically, whom James addresses as **Simon**, a brotherly touch. James, however, also supplies a further, utterly critical support to the testimonies which have preceded, by arguing that the full acceptance of Gentiles was **in agreement** with **the words of the prophets**. So he adds to the witness of the *works* of God in Caesarea and Galatia the *words* of God in Scripture, **as it is written** (15).

James appeals primarily to Amos 9:11–12: **After this I will return and rebuild David's fallen tent and I will restore it, that the remnant of men may seek the Lord, and all the Gentiles who bear my name…**(16-18). As Christopher Wright argues, 'James puts together several prophetic texts in an exegetical argument of considerable skill and subtlety.' Additionally to the Amos passage, Wright finds in James' quotation echoes of Hosea 3:5, Jeremiah 12:15 and Isaiah 45:21. 'Within this framework James quotes Amos 9:11-12 which looks forward on the one hand to the restoration of "David's fallen tent"' (which almost certainly was understood as the Messianic people of God) and on the other hand to the inclusion of Gentiles as those who 'now bear (the Lord's) name – that is, who are counted as belonging within Israel simply as Gentiles and not as proselyte Jews.'[5] In making this point from Amos 9, James uses the LXX Greek version rather than the Hebrew text which is not as clearly referenced to Gentiles, and the question has been asked whether James with his strong Hebrew-Jewish instincts would conceivably have departed from the Hebrew. However, the Gentiles are implicitly, if less clearly, included in the Hebrew version of Amos 9:11-12, and James, like all Galileans, would have been bilingual. Additionally, the proceedings of the Consultation were likely to have been carried out using Greek.

James concludes with a proposal, **it is my judgment** (= lit. 'I judge' v. 19, NIV). The verb here, *krino*, covers a range of meaning. JB has 'It is my verdict', ESV and NLT also have 'it is my judgment'. Stott offers, 'It is my conviction.' The critical issue however is, as they state in the letter to the

---

5. Wright, 518.

churches, that the decision was one that **seemed good to the Holy Spirit and to us** (28). It therefore was generally affirmed to be what God was saying, and also what they consensually agreed.

James states his view that **we should not make it difficult for the Gentiles who are turning to God** (19). This means no insistence on circumcision or the 'yoke' of the Mosaic law, the fundamental issue of salvation by grace alone should prevail; Gentiles do not need to become proselyte Jews in order to be Christians. However, in recognition of the need to be sensitive to Jewish scruples around foods in particular (and hence to make true table-fellowship possible), James proposes that certain minimal points of law-keeping be called for. He instances four, sometimes known as 'the Jerusalem Quadrilateral': abstaining **from food polluted by idols, from sexual immorality, from the meat of strangled animals, and from blood** (20). James justifies these by noting that **Moses has been preached in every city from the earliest times and is read in the synagogues on every Sabbath** (21). What James is implying in this final sentence is not entirely clear. Possibly he is making the point that since the law continues to be read in all the synagogues, Gentile Christians need to continue to show sensitivity of Jewish scruples even though they are not obligated to follow all of these themselves. Alternatively, he may be saying that since Moses and the requirements of the Torah will continue to be widely presented in local synagogues in every city, Gentile Christians who wish to know about Jewish concerns can easily find out about them. Or even, as a third possibility, is he perhaps saying, that since Judaism will continue to maintain its cultic life in its synagogue (and temple) worship which reaches back over the centuries, the Consultation should not be overly concerned with a decision not to propagate the law of Moses in Christian contexts, or require Gentile believers to obey it?

James' proposal clearly meets with general consent. The primary issue of retaining the grace of God in Christ as the one basis of salvation has been clearly established: 'the idea that circumcision is necessary is emphatically refuted'.[6] However, brotherly sensitivity to Jewish-Christian concerns is also observed by the affirming of the four prohibitions, which will enable warm communion to be established and maintained between Jewish and Gentile Christian believers.

The four requested abstentions have been variously viewed, some seeing them as all moral requirements, others as all ceremonial. The key consideration is the spirit of the recommendations. 'The abstinence here recommended must be understood...not as an essential Christian duty but as a concession to the consciences of others, i.e. of Jewish converts who still regarded such food as unlawful and abominable in the sight of God.'[7]. As Calvin puts it: 'He extracts nothing from them, which they do not owe to brotherly concord.'[8] All things considered, it was a judicious conclusion.[9]

It has been claimed that Paul could never have agreed to this resolution; however, that appears an unjustifiable objection. On the primary and all-important issue of the basis of salvation, he was utterly vindicated, and of the four abstentions, as Marshall notes, three of them are actually urged in places in his correspondence; immorality is strongly disavowed in 1 Corinthians 6:9;[10] eating meat offered to idols similarly so in 1 Corinthians 10:25-28; and he appeals for tolerance over issues arising from eating (or not eating) meat with blood in it in Romans 14.[11] Further, we cannot forget the Paul of 1 Corinthians 9:19f: 'to those under the law I became like one under the law (though I myself am not under the law) so as to win those under the law. To those not having the law I became like one not

---

6. Bock, 493.

7. Alexander, II, 84.

8. Calvin, II, 49.

9. See Neill, 174.

10. The insistence on sexual abstinence was hardly surprising in view of the prevailing sexual promiscuity which was a widely recognizable feature of the major population centres throughout the empire. cf. Wm. Neill, 'sacramental fornication was practiced as a religious act and many temples were little more than brothels', op. cit., 173.

11. Marshall, 246.

having the law (though I am not free of God's law but I am under Christ's law).'

Something of the larger and longer-term implications of the Jerusalem resolution are teased out impressively by missiologist David W. Smith. 'There is a clear distinction in the New Testament between proselytism and conversion. The former existed before the coming of Christ and was the means by which Gentile enquirers were incorporated within the people of Israel. They were circumcised, baptized in water and taught the Torah. In other words they became, to all appearances, Jewish.

'The early church, faced with a massive influx of Gentiles, might have been expected to follow precisely this pattern. But, astonishingly, they did not; instead they struck out in a completely new and revolutionary direction. They decided that Gentile believers in Jesus should be left to find a lifestyle of their own within Hellenistic society under the guidance of the Holy Spirit. In other words apostolic Christianity did not demand conformity to a single cultural pattern but accepted a valid cultural pluralism from the start. This was really revolutionary. As Andrew Walls points out, the proselyte model would have produced devout Gentile believers but "they would have had virtually no impact on their society." Conversion, by contrast, meant that they turned toward Christ as Gentiles, as Greeks, and now sought to open up their culture to him. The result was that a truly Greek, truly Hellenistic type of Christianity was able to emerge.' [12] There are lessons here for global mission in every age.

Agreement being reached, it was necessary to communicate the findings to the churches, particularly **Antioch**, so a letter is composed and messengers are chosen, **Judas (called Barsabbas) and Silas**, who are dispatched along with **Paul and Barnabas** (22). The letter, which has been described as 'a masterpiece of tact and delicacy',[13] begins with a clear distancing from the hard-line circumcision teachers, **who went out from us without our authoriza-**

---

12. David W. Smith, *Against the Stream* (IVP, 2003), 78.

13. Rackham, 255.

tion, and who had **troubled** them (24). The word translated 'troubled' (*tarasso*) was actually used by Paul in Galatians of these same people (Gal.1:7; 5:10). The letter then introduces the two messengers, along with **our dear friends Barnabas and Paul, men who have risked their lives for the name of our Lord Jesus Christ** (26). The messengers **will confirm by word of mouth what we are writing** (27).

In delicate or important communication, face-to-face contact is almost always the best medium. Letters on their own (or e-mails, or text messages) so often fail to carry the personal warmth of direct human contact and hence inevitably miss important, even critical aspects of the relating. This is especially true for Christian ministry and its pastoral aspects. It is beautifully anticipated in the traditional blessing in Numbers 6:24-26: 'The Lord bless you and keep you…the Lord *turn his face towards you…*'.

One of the enormous dangers of the current cultural dominance of electronic communication is that it can threaten the foundational insights of Christian anthropology deriving from its doctrine of universal human creation in the image of God, and its belief in the universal embrace of the death of Christ, His dying for all people everywhere. These twin truths, with their overwhelming affirmation of the intrinsic value of human persons, mandate a style of communicating in all congregations in which people and their concerns are the dominating reality. True shepherding after the model of Jesus (or Paul, cf. 20:18-31) cannot be done from a lap-top.

The Consultation then expresses its appeal: **it seemed good to the Holy Spirit and to us** (28). Bock sees the phrase **it seemed good** (*edoxe*) as 'the key term' in the letter.[14] The order of the two subjects is important: 'the Holy Spirit and us.' In the three expanded contributions to the debate which Luke records, in each case it is God's work and God's Word which predominates. The position which is arrived at therefore simply brings the church into line with God. The result is that there are no **burdens**, only **requirements** for **doing well**, which means the four abstentions (28, 29).

---

14. Bock, 512.

Thus the letter mandates a church which is not mono-chromatic in its practice but united in the centrality of Christ and in salvation by grace through faith in Him. Stott summarizes helpfully: 'Their vision was big enough to see the gospel of Christ not as a reform movement within Judaism, but as good news for the whole world, and the Church of Christ, not as a Jewish sect but as an interna-tional family of God.'[15]

One issue raised by this chapter's events but not cov-ered earlier is the much-debated issue of the relationship of the visit to Jerusalem described by Paul in Galatians 2:1-10, and the accounts of visits to Jerusalem given by Luke in Acts at 11:30 and 15:2-29 respectively. There are broadly three options: (1) Galatians 2 = Acts 11:30, the famine relief visit; (2) Galatians 2 = Acts 15, the Consultation visit; (3) Galatians 2 cannot be reconciled with either of these visits and has been created by Luke to try to paper over the highly regrettable reality ('the horrid truth' as one writer terms it) of the deep and unresolved divisions in the church on the matter of the inclusion of Gentiles.

In response, as far as this third option is concerned, we can note that, apart from the multiple evidences of Luke's faithfulness as a reporter (cf. appendix, 'Acts and History'), he makes honest admissions of the tensions in the church throughout his account, e.g. the immediately following paragraph (15:36-41). Further, the issue before the Con-sultation assembly was always likely to surface at some point, and in the process to raise deeply felt emotions, by the simple fact that what began as a predominantly Jewish movement became within a relatively short time a predominantly Gentile movement; and further that an instinct to resolve the issues raised by this development, and to do so with the help of apostolic insights was entirely to be anticipated. In other words, the essential historic-ity of the event appears fully credible. Of the other two options, there is much to be said for the first, Galatians 2 = Acts 11:30 (see earlier discussion at 9:20–30), and that the Jerusalem Consultation had not been held when Galatians

15. Stott, 241.

was written. Marshall argues the case for this identification in some detail with commendable clarity and fairness, and we concur.[16]

The messengers accompanied by Paul and Barnabas, and presumably the rest of the Antioch delegation, **went down to Antioch where they gathered the church together and delivered the letter** (30). Understandably, the letter was warmly received, **the people were glad for its encouraging message** (31). The principle of Gentile inclusion in the one people of God through faith in Christ alone was established without any additional requirements, beyond an appeal for a brotherly sensitivity to Jewish-Christian consciences in one or two particular areas. Judas and Silas remained for a period, using their prophetic gifts to further **encourage and strengthen** the congregation. After their return from Jerusalem, Paul and Barnabas continued **to teach and preach the word of the Lord** in Antioch (35).

Study Questions:

1. In what sense is this chapter a 'watershed' in the story of the Christian mission in Acts?

2. What was the issue at stake here? Is there any equivalent or similar challenge facing us today in the service of Christ?

3. Summarize the contributions of Peter (15:7-11), Paul and Barnabas (15:12), and James (15:13-21). In what sense was the resolution 'a judicious conclusion'?

4. What might correspond today to the concessions urged on the Gentile believers (15:28-29)? Are you ready to make these concessions in your church, and more generally, for the sake of the consciences of fellow Christians?

---

16. Marshall, 244-8.

9

Paul's Second Mission Journey
(Acts 15:36–18:22)

C. Paul's Second Mission Journey (15:36–18:22)

1. Silas replaces Barnabas (15:36-41)

Some time later Paul said to Barnabas, Let us go back and visit the brothers in all the towns where we preached the word of the Lord and see how they are doing (36). In calendar terms it is probable that the period of rest and refreshment in Antioch corresponded to the winter period (of A.D. 49–50); the coming of the spring would have reopened the travel routes on land and sea.[1] From what we already know of Paul, his proposal is entirely as we might have expected.

Perhaps it may be added that we notice no 'voice of the Spirit' in this case (cf. 13:2). While it is unthinkable that the missionaries agreed to this new journey without a deep persuasion that it was God's will, there is also a need to recognize that the initial responsibility having been conveyed, this 'follow-up' ministry in a real sense needed no further specific command. In the service of God, we recall the testimony of our Lord, 'I have brought you glory on earth by *completing the work* you gave me to do' (John 17:4). The honour of God is bound up not

---

1. Marshall, 257.

only with the enthusiastic commencement of a project, but with the faithful completion of it. 'He that endures to the end will be saved' has its application to service as well as to salvation.

Hence when we are wrestling with the possibility of engaging a new or different piece of ministry, for us in good conscience to accept the opportunity will normally require not only a 'call to' this new sphere of service, but also a 'call away' from that which is currently occupying us. Until that is given, silence implies our continuation, through, as always, the ever-renewed grace of God. Sir Walter Raleigh's prayer fittingly focuses this truth: 'O Lord, when you give your servants to endeavour any great matter, grant us also to know that it is not the beginning, but the continuing of the same to the end, until it be thoroughly finished, that yields the true glory; through him who for the finishing of your work, laid down his life, our redeemer, Jesus Christ. Amen.'

Just as we are happily affirming in our minds Paul's proposal for a 'follow-up' mission visit to the Galatian churches, and anticipating these further 'adventures in the Spirit' of our intrepid, closely bonded missionary pair, the light, as it were, momentarily goes out: **Barnabas wanted to take John, also called Mark, with them, but Paul did not think it wise to take him because he had deserted them in Pamphylia, and had not continued with them in the work**. Then it gets worse: **they had such a sharp disagreement that they parted company** (37-39).

We have had cause to underline the honesty of Luke in his account of these early years of the church. He is certainly honest here. Both Barnabas and Paul are by this point in the story both worthy Christian 'heroes' and we find our minds flicking back to the earliest connection between them – Barnabas' bringing Paul to the Jerusalem group in face of their suspicions (9:26-28), and then later finding him in 'the northern wastes' and bringing him to share in his own great ministry opportunity in Antioch (11:25-26); and then all their shared endeavours and rigours in the first journey (13:1–14:26), and standing side by side at the Consultation (15:12)...and now this!

Calvin does not exaggerate when he refers to 'this melancholy disagreement'.[2]

It is not difficult to sympathize with Barnabas. His gracious, supportive nature had given rise to his well-earned nickname ('Son of Encouragement', 4:36), and he himself had, more than once actually, given Paul renewed opportunities in ministry, as we noted. Mark's later biography, with his significant association with Peter (1 Pet. 5:13), his composition of the canonical Gospel of Mark, and, most significantly, Paul's own later recognition of his worth (2 Tim. 4:11), all underline the truth in his case that early errors need not eliminate later effectiveness. As with Jonah (Jonah 3:1)), 'the Word of the Lord' would come 'a second time' to Mark. In truth, if that were not regularly the case, could any of us be servants of Christ?

The presence of a family tie – Mark was Barnabas' cousin (Col. 4:10) – obviously complicates the picture. Such blood ties are notoriously difficult either to handle or evaluate in God's service, as Jesus in a sense conceded (Mark 3:31-35; Luke 14:26). A case recently in South Africa makes that point forcibly. A denomination had committed to a policy of monocultural church-planting in order to target specific ethnic groups in the community. The result was, sadly, the emergence of congregations with inbuilt family solidarities that were barriers to growth and credibility in their communities. In one case, family members all lined up behind a leader who was morally in the wrong purely on the basis of family loyalty rather than loyalty to God and *His* family.

On Paul's side there was the need to weigh the overriding seriousness of the issues involved, not just for the immediate parties, but in terms of the eternal implications for all the people that would be contacted in the course of their upcoming ministry journey. The presence of a colleague who did not fully share the commitment this demanded could place a significant limitation on what the ministry might accomplish. As Marshall concedes, 'this is a classic example of the perpetual problem of whether to

---

2. Calvin, II, 60.

place the interests of the individual or the work as a whole first, and there is no rule of thumb for dealing with it'.[3] Certainly the Antioch congregation sided in the end with Paul, and we have to concede that they were in touch with all the factors to a degree that we cannot be today.

So **Barnabas took Mark and sailed for Cyprus, but Paul chose Silas and left, commended by the brothers to the grace of the Lord** (39-40). In general, Calvin's application is salutary: 'We are warned by this example, that unless the servants of Christ are keeping a sharp look-out, many chinks are open to Satan, by which he may steal in to disturb the harmony among them.'[4] Bock's observation is similarly apposite: 'What resulted was a solution that allowed the advance of the gospel to continue, but in a way that recognized a need for distinct ministries. Sometimes this is the best solution.'[5]

So, at this point Barnabas leaves the stage, and the new pairing of Paul and Silas travel through the northern Palestinian regions of Syria and Cilicia, **strengthening the churches** (41).

2. Galatia Again: Timothy Joins the Team (16:1-5)

Continuing north and then west brings Paul and Silas to the stated goal of the journey, the revisiting of the churches birthed on Paul and Barnabas' journey; so, to **Derbe and Lystra.** Coming again to the latter must have called for courage; Paul certainly never forgot what happened there (2 Cor. 11:25; 2 Tim. 3:11). Strikingly, Lystra is identified here *not* as the place where Paul had been brutally attacked and left for dead, but as the place **where a disciple named Timothy lived** (1). God has a regular habit, if one may so put it, of bringing honey from the carcass of a lion (Judg. 14:5-18), in order to, among other things, demonstrate His easy sovereignty. 'Can any good thing come out of Nazareth?' (John 1:46) Quite!

3. Marshall, 258.

4. Calvin, II, 61.

5. Bock, 520.

Had Paul possibly come by this point to regret his rejection of Mark and now sought in Timothy another younger colleague to replace him? For whatever reason, **Paul wanted to take him along on the journey** (3). Timothy had strong credentials. **The brothers at Lystra and Iconium spoke well of him** (2), a major consideration. Writing years later to a maturer Timothy, tasked with appointing 'overseers' in Ephesus, Paul was to stress not only being 'spoken well of' by the church, but also having 'a good reputation with outsiders'. Additionally, Timothy had the rich blessing of a strong piety, 'sincere faith' as Paul calls it, in his home in the persons not only of his mother Eunice, **a Jewess and a believer** (1), but also his grandmother Lois (2 Tim. 1:5). The home, however, was also a problem, since Timothy's **father was a Greek** (3). In such mixed-marriage situations the children were regarded as Jewish and therefore liable to be circumcised. In Timothy's case this had apparently not happened; so **Paul circumcised him because of the Jews who lived in that area, for they all knew that his father was a Greek.** Paul's action here has been roundly criticized by some; he is seen as inconsistent, since he had trenchantly opposed circumcision in Antioch and in his letter to the Galatian churches, and was carrying at this point a letter from the Jerusalem Consultation to the effect that it was not required for salvation; yet here he actually performs it! The critics, however, have missed the way that Paul lived – by principled priorities rather than inflexible rules (Rom. 2:25–3:2; 1 Cor. 9:19-23; Gal. 6:15). For Paul the primary issue is the gospel and its spread. Circumcision is not necessary for gospel-believing Gentiles, though gospel-believing Jews have already received it. For Timothy, a Jew (through his mother), to be part of a mission team working among Jews, his not having been previously circumcised could easily have diverted the entire mission effort from the primary issue of the gospel to the secondary issue of circumcision. So Paul avoids that, **because of the Jews who lived in that area** (3), so that they might hear the gospel without distraction, and be saved. 'What is seen here is Paul's cultural sensitivity.'[6] One of the most important traits of leadership is knowing what is primary and what is secondary, what is worth dying for, and what can be let go.

So with the enlarged party the missionaries travel on, **delivering the decisions reached by the apostles and elders in Jerusalem for the people to obey** (4). This geographical reach was beyond what the Consultation itself had mandated (15:23). However if we assume, as we certainly may, that the *Letter to the Galatians* was addressed to these very churches – a letter written to Christians being deeply troubled by 'circumcision championing' teachers – their receiving details of the Jerusalem resolution was entirely to the point. **So the churches were strengthened in the faith and grew daily in numbers** (5).

This reference to the daily conversion growth actually echoes the aftermath of Pentecost, 2:47: 'The Lord added daily those who were being saved.' Though the circumcision debate had been a difficult, even costly one for Paul, as he had been thrust into the centre of it, the result of that nettle having been grasped was the opening of a new freedom to proclaim the gospel in a manner which was proving immensely fruitful.

There is a lesson here for all engaged in ministry. There are times when issues are best left alone and the sheer passage of time will deal with them. But when the issue is fundamental, and is clearly occupying everyone's attention and concern, the normally wise recourse is to face it, publicly if necessary, and have it resolved. One thinks of a church where a clear and courageous sermon setting spiritual gifts in their proper biblical perspective cleared the air in a congregation where charismatic expressions had become distracting and divisive. The result was renewed fellowship, and a period of discernible growth. Or in another setting, where gay activists had brought pressure on congregants, dampening the church's evangelistic ministries, a sensitive, yet uncompromising exposition of the biblical teaching on homosexuality brought renewed freedom and significant evangelistic fruitfulness in its wake.

---

6. Bock, 524.

3. A Vision calls to Macedonia (6-40)

The next paragraph, verses 6-7, is not easy to interpret. The main outline is clear enough: the missionaries have travelled **from town to town** retracing the earlier journey, and hence we can presume that, being already on the *Via Sebaste* and moving westwards, they would have delivered the Consultation findings also in Iconium and Pisidian Antioch. They apparently then continued on the Roman road, across into the province of Asia, possibly headed for Ephesus, the main city on this stretch, but they were **kept by the Holy Spirit from preaching the word in the province of Asia** (6). The missionaries then try turning north towards **Bithynia,** an extensive region bordering on the Black Sea; but again they are thwarted as **the Spirit of Jesus would not allow them to** enter it (7). Frustrated once again, they find themselves seemingly driven in a north-westerly direction, and **passing by** the loosely defined region of **Mysia** they finally reach **Troas**, the port city to ancient Greece (8). And so they find themselves gazing out into the blue waters of the Aegean Sea with its dotted islands, and beyond its distant shore-line, the Roman province of Macedonia, and beyond that again, etched on the horizon, the outlines of the distant Balkan mountains. There at Troas the negatives of their guidance, 'kept from preaching'…'would not allow them', turn dramatically to a positive: as **during the night Paul had a vision of a man of Macedonia standing and begging him, 'Come over to Macedonia and help us'** (9).

Before considering the vision, there are two issues of interpretation here. This occurrence of the phrase **Spirit of Jesus** is unique to the New Testament, though Philippians 1:19 has 'the Spirit of Jesus Christ.' However although 'the Spirit of God' is the commoner identity of the divine Director of the mission, the Spirit is ever 'the Spirit of Jesus' (John 14:26; 16:5-15). Luke's essential perspective in 1:1 is reflected in this phrase; the work of mission is finally presided over by the Son of God, the Risen Leader, 'continuing to do and teach', but in the indissoluble unity of the Godhead, working through the blessed, divine Holy

Spirit, He who is the 'extended arm of the exalted one' (Barth).

The other general issue here is to ask what we are to understand by the Holy Spirit's 'roadblocks'? Why no Asia, or Bithynia since these territories needed Christ no less than any other? And how was this 'refusal of the Spirit' expressed? The answer to the second question is that we can only conjecture. Both Paul and Silas are identified with a prophetic gift (13:1; 15:32), so we can perhaps conceive a Holy Spirit witness through that medium. Alternatively, circumstances may have intervened which the missionaries came to interpret as God's closing the door to an evangelistic initiative in these places.

Responding to the earlier question, that of the divine 'roadblocks', the need for the gospel was clearly, in this case, not enough in itself to justify the initiative. In point of historical fact, neither Asia nor Bithynia were long denied the message of salvation. At the end of this second journey, Paul would make a brief visit to Asia, to Ephesus, its pre-eminent city, on his way home to Antioch (18:19-20). After bearing witness in the synagogue, he would leave with a promise to return. This promise was generously kept as he would spend over two years there on his third journey, as a result of which 'all the Jews and Greeks who lived in the province of Asia heard the word of the Lord' (19:10).

As to Bithynia, there is an important historical allusion to the Christian community there in the correspondence, dated 111–113, between the Roman Emperor Trajan and Pliny, the governor of the province of Bithynia, concerning the empire's judicial proceedings against Christians. It contains fascinating details about Christian faith in the early second century; however most significantly for our present purpose, Pliny reports on 'the number of those who are accused (of being Christians). For many of every age, every class, and of both sexes are being accused and will be accused.' [7]

With hindsight we can today discern the larger pattern, viz. the immense importance of the gospel ministry being

---

7. cf. *Epistles of Pliny*, X, 96 and 97.

expanded to the province of Macedonia, which would bring a new breadth and width to the Christian movement, both culturally and geographically, and also give birth, in God's time, to some of the most important churches in Paul's ministry career. Looking still further ahead, to bear witness in Macedonia was to bury the living seed of the gospel in the future continent of Europe, the global region which would become the first Christian continent, and for many centuries thereafter the primary base of missionary outreach to the rest of the world.

So, we turn to the vision. As we address this 'word from God', it is worth drawing out the variety of means by which God has previously given His servants direction in Acts. The list begins with a direct conversation with the Risen Christ (1:1-9); the witness of Scripture (1:15-20); a sense of what was 'necessary' (to re-establish the twelve apostles, 1:21); prayers followed by the casting of a lot (1:24-26); the regular routines of worship (3:1ff); miraculous intervention, and angelic instruction (5:19-20; 12:7-10); communal discussion and decision, followed by prayer and laying on of hands (6:1-6); scattering through persecution (8:4; 11:19); an angel of the Lord (8:26); 'the Spirit of the Lord' (8:29, 39); encounter with the risen Jesus (9:3-6); a Christian leader (9:15-19); a clever escape strategy (9:23-25); a church's concern for a leader's safety (9:30); news of a medical emergency (9:38); visions (10:4-16); concern over new developments (11:22); the need for a teacher (11:25-26); a prophetic message (11:28-30); the Holy Spirit in worship (13:2-3); opportunities to tell the good news (13:13-39; 14:1-3; 14:9, 21); consultation with others (15:2, 22); concerns for discipling (15:36, 41). The obvious fact that this long and diverse list delivers is that God's guidance comes down many different roads to engage His servants. The biggest mistake we can make therefore, though it is often made, is to imagine that God's will for our lives is always going to be communicated to us in precisely the same way; but no, there is no 'one' method by which God guides His people.

We note that the vision is of **a *man* of Macedonia.** Obviously, an angel could have delivered specific instructions to go to Macedonia (cf. 8:26, 'Go south...'). The fact that the medium of the divine direction was a native inhabitant, and one moreover who was **begging** for them to come, would have greatly increased their sense of being needed. In other words, in this specific case the 'angel' was a man: it often is.

Macedonia was part of Greece, the country which had in its heyday embodied the finest cultural flowering of the human spirit. In the areas of philosophy, architecture, democracy, drama, poetry, history, science, and mathematics, Greece had contributed a national legacy which was to become one of the pillars of modern civilization. Yet in spite of all these sparkling cultural achievements, Greece was still needy; the 'man of Macedonia' is begging for help in the most important sphere of all – spiritual understanding and experience; he is begging for news of a Saviour.

There is an important signal in verse 10: **after Paul had seen the vision, we got ready at once to leave for Macedonia.** *We* got ready apparently implies that Luke is now part of the group. This is the first of the 'we' passages in Acts, running from here to 16:17, and then resuming at 20:5-15; 21:1-18; and finally 27:1–28:16. One view is that here Luke begins to use another member of the party's reminiscences, though without altering the grammatical style, which clearly remains Luke's. This, however, 'is most improbable in the case of a consciously careful writer like the author of Acts.'[8] The most obvious explanation is that 'Luke now joined the group.'[9] Michael Green offers the interesting suggestion that Luke might himself have been the man of Macedonia, and Paul had dreamed about him that night, though one has to say that there is no hint of that in the text.[10]

Macedonia was located in northern Greece. It was bordered by the Illyria and Nestos rivers, and had been a world power under Philip of Macedon and Alexander the

---

8. Marshall, 263; see also the researches of James Smith noted in 'The Sources of Acts' in the appendices.

9. Bock, 528.

10. Green, 26.

Great four centuries earlier. It was made a Roman province in 168 B.C. The Macedonians were viewed by the Greeks as barbarians. Its principal city at this time was Philippi and the party made straight for it. The sea approach route called for a stop on the way at the island of **Samothrace**, and then disembarking at Neapolis, Philippi's port, followed by a ten-mile walk along the most easterly section of the *Via Egnatia*, a major Roman highway which ended at Dyrrachium on the Adriatic coast, looking across to Italy.

Philippi is described as **the leading city of that district, and a Roman colony**. It had received that status in 42 B.C. when the army of Antony and Octavian had defeated the army of Julius Caesar's assassins, Brutus and Cassius. This 'colony' status meant that it was in effect 'a little fragment of Rome'.[11] A significant proportion of the citizens were retired Roman soldiers or other civil servants, the Latin language was widely spoken, Roman citizenship was granted to its citizens, Roman dress was worn in the city, the magistrates had Roman titles, and Roman customs and ceremonies were faithfully observed. The city additionally was absolved from tribute and taxation, had autonomous government, and Roman law obtained in its civic life. As a corollary, it meant that the citizenry were understandably anxious to maintain good relations with Rome and hence to preserve their privileges.

The account of the mission to Philippi has four parts: (1) Lydia (13-15); (2) the demon-possessed girl (16-24); (3) the Roman jailer (25-34); (4) the magistrates and civic leaders (35-40). The visit is full of notable incidents expressive of God's remarkable interventions, and is so vividly recorded that it has become registered ineffaceably on the Christian imagination.

(1) Lydia (13-15). The mission party **stayed several days**, settling into their new environment, and **then on the Sabbath went outside the city gate to the river where we expected to find a place of prayer**. The lack of mention of a synagogue must raise the possibility that there

---

11. W. Barclay, *The Letters to Philippians, Colossians and Thessalonians* (Saint Andrew Press, 1950), 4.

was not one in the city at this point. It required ten men to found a synagogue and the fact that the meeting which they discovered appears to have been comprised only of women probably confirms that no synagogue had as yet been established, but that the women met to go through the appointed Jewish service of prayer for the Sabbath. The location by a river may suggest some sort of purification rites. The missionaries sit down and converse freely with the women who have gathered. This points to a freedom in approaching women which Paul, contra his notorious reputation in this regard, clearly enjoyed. Paul shares a **message** (14), surely about Jesus, as the fulfiller of the Jewish hope.

One of those listening was **a woman named Lydia, a dealer in purple cloth from the city of Thyatira, who was a worshipper of God**. This indicates that she had come into contact with the Jewish faith in her home town of Thyatira in the district of Lydia (her name, despite the NIV translation, is actually not given; she was 'the Lydian woman') who had become a God-fearer. Thyatira was known for its production of fine cloths, and also for its purple dye, produced from a particular shellfish. ' She was presumably the Macedonian agent of a Thyatiran supplier.'[12] She hears 'the message' and believes. Luke expresses that with a not untypical note of the divine initiative: **the Lord opened her heart to respond to Paul's message.** There is no other way to salvation, and again the divine leadership of the mission is underlined. As a woman of some substance, she is accompanied by her household staff. They too, by implication, respond, and the proximity of the river offers the opportunity to immediately seal their faith: as **she and the members of her household were baptized**. As is ever the case, authentic faith leads to good works: Lydia's opened heart to the Lord leads to her opened home to His messengers – **'If you consider me a believer in the Lord, come and stay at my house.' She persuaded** them.

(2) The demon-possessed girl (16-24). As the mission party makes its way to the place of prayer on a subsequent

12. Stott, 263.

occasion, a second connection is made with a Philippian citizen – **we were met by a slave girl who had a spirit by which she predicted the future**. In vivid contrast to the first encounter which was within the broad sphere of Jewish faith and religious culture, this engages Paul and his companions with a vastly different world of sorcery and magic, and the demonic spiritual agencies underlying them, as well as with the all too human traffickers who lived on their potential earnings. In other words, Christianity is here confronting, and being confronted by, the very stuff of pre-Christian paganism.

The girl concerned is a **slave** and hence from the most dependent class, the chattel of her owners. She has a spirit of divination. The Greek is *pneuma pythona* which literally means, 'a spirit, namely a Python' or 'a Pythonian spirit', implying that she was inspired by the Pythian god, Apollo, the soothsaying divinity often portrayed as a snake. This spirit was said to direct women by overpowering them and allowing them to tell the future. These sorcerers generally were also linked in the popular mind with issuing curses, and were much feared on that account. Bock quotes in this connection Pliny the Elder, 'There is in fact no one who is not afraid of being cursed by terrible imprecations.'[13] Some interpreters note the common link with ventriloquism in such cases. The girl's fortune-telling was a source of rich pickings for her owners. She now proceeded to attach herself to the missionaries, **following** them, and **shouting, 'These men are the servants of the Most High God, who are telling us the way to be saved.'**

While the reference to the missionaries as **servants** (*douloi* = 'bondslaves') of the divine has Christian resonances (Rom. 1:1), **the Most High God** is not in fact the relatively orthodox confession that it might seem. This title was used in pagan religions, for example with reference to Zeus. The mission is here directly engaging polytheism. The girl's shouting becomes a daily event, and finally provokes **Paul** to action: he is **troubled** (*diaponetheis* = disturbed/burdened). He is probably influenced by the

---

13. Pliny, Nat. 28.19; Bock, 535.

negative publicity this is attaching to the party. He finally intervenes to free the girl from her demonic oppressor and to demonstrate the superiority of the power of the One True and Living God operating through Jesus; **he turned round and said to her, 'In the name of Jesus Christ I command you to come out of her!' At that moment the spirit left her.**

This is an act of exorcism, not the first Paul has carried out in Acts (13:9-11), nor will it be the last (19:12). For all the difficulties associated with this practice, and they are real, we dare not demythologize it out of the biblical record, or eliminate it in principle from the church's range of ministries. It does need to be noted, however, that this element is not all-pervasive in the accounts of New Testament mission: there is such a thing as demon obsession as well as demon possession. Ajith Fernando nonetheless makes salutary comment: 'How reluctant we are to see anything as demonic or as influenced by malevolent spiritual forces. We ignore such at our peril.'[14] This area is certainly not recommended territory for the spiritually immature, and mandates proper 'cover' from experienced leaders and discerning, praying, church communities. The girl's salvation is not explicitly noted nor her subsequent baptism; however, as Stott suggests, 'the fact that her deliverance took place between the conversions of Lydia and the jailer leads readers to infer that she too became a member of the Philippian church.' [15]

The outcome of the girl's deliverance quickly becomes a serious one for the mission team. Far from sharing in any celebration of her liberation, the owners, **realizing that their hope of making money was gone**, are angered; for them financial loss vastly outweighs spiritual liberation, 'not to mention her welfare or dignity.'[16] Their fury explodes into violence as **they seized Paul and Silas and dragged them into the market place to face the authorities. The market place** (*agora*) would have contained a raised judgment seat

---

14. Fernando, 453-4.

15. Stott, 265.

16. Bock: 537.

(bema) where the city magistrates sat to render judgment. This site has actually been excavated in Philippi.

The owners are clever in forming their accusations against Paul and Silas. They make no mention of the real reason for their anger towards the missionaries. Instead they lay two charges. First, they charge them with causing public disorder, **These men are Jews and are throwing the city into an uproar**. Second, they charge them with propagating anti-Roman teachings and practices: 'These men are...**advocating customs unlawful for us Romans to accept or practise**.' The first charge draws strength from the latent anti-Semitism of this Gentile community. In general, Jews were despised, even hated, throughout the empire. This may explain why it is the Jews, Paul and Silas, who are accused rather than the Gentiles, Timothy and Luke; the prominence of the former pair would probably also largely account for it.

As put, the two charges harbour a somewhat contradictory interface of racial prejudices: the former is anti-Jewish, the latter is pro-Roman. Both charges are serious ones, and particularly so in a Roman colony such as Philippi. Causing disorder was prejudicial to the Roman love of order and could, if serious enough, lead to the loss of their colony status and its privileges. While foreign religions might be practised within the empire it was critical that they did not threaten the official state religion centred in the veneration of Caesar, nor lead to significant proselytizing. The Jews had managed to obtain a certain official status for Judaism but Christianity was as yet untried in that area, and had as yet no distinct identity in the eyes of the empire.

The crowd joined in the attack, swayed no doubt by the charges, and hence siding with the slave owners. Proper process would have called next for the holding of the accused in custody until the case could be heard by the proconsul. This may have been somewhere in the magistrates' intentions; however for the present they **ordered them to be stripped and beaten** and to be imprisoned as 'high security' offenders. The question has been fairly asked why Paul and Silas at this point did not inform the magistrates of their Roman citizenship, a consideration Paul would not hesitate to bring to the authorities' attention on a later occasion (22:25). However, the proceedings have the marks of a 'rush to judgment', and Paul additionally may have taken the view that standing up for their rights might leave an unhelpful legacy for the church they were trying to bring to birth there.

The beating was no light matter: they were **severely flogged**. Even if this *admonitio*, or 'warning', was the lightest of the three levels of beating administered by the Romans, it certainly was no walk in the park. The recipients were stripped and the beating took place in public. Carried out by the 'lictors' (the 'rod-bearers), it was essentially a severe caning. It would have been one of those listed later by Paul in writing to the Corinthians, 'three times I was beaten with rods' (2 Cor. 11:25). **Afterwards they were thrown into prison and the jailer was ordered to guard them carefully**.

(3) The Roman jailer (25-34). His compliance with that order was ensured by the fact that under Roman custom if those responsible for the custody of important prisoners permitted their escape the lives of those guarding them would be forfeited. We have seen this enacted in the case of Peter's guards in 12:19, and will come across it again in respect of Paul's guards at the time of his shipwreck (27:42). So the jailer, understandably taking no chances, **put them in the inner cell and fastened their feet in the stocks**.

About midnight...it would be difficult to find a more pertinent phrase to express the state of the mission at this point. Despite the clear guidance of God to come to Macedonia, the promising beginning with the prayer group at the riverside, and the slave girl's liberation, things had clearly gone downhill fast since then. What now? Their two prime leaders had been shamefully treated and were beaten men, in a maximum-security prison cell with no immediate prospect of release in the foreseeable future... **midnight** indeed!

But what amazing words follow...**at midnight Paul and Silas were praying and singing hymns to God.** Here,

Calvin notes, 'we observe the general rule that we cannot pray properly as we ought, without praising God at the same time.'[17] That is certainly true, but there was something else at work in that Roman prison that midnight, what James Stewart once referred to as 'the indescribable gusto of the early Christian voice'. 'This wonderful sense of energy, exhilaration and vitality which meets you on every page of the New Testament; these men are almost uncannily efficient…supremely adequate to life's most difficult demands; not because "We are able", but because "He is able", and when they say that they are looking away from themselves to God. They are looking straight at Christ.'[18] So when everything appears to have gone wrong, and they seem helpless pawns in the hands of evil and merciless aggressors; in that seemingly final hour of darkness before the candle of faith finally flickers and dies, a beam of hope blazes across the sky, faith renews, and God's people rise up to victory.

And the other prisoners were listening to them, on that you can bet your life! Instead of the angry profanities and obscenities which invariably echoed in that inner cell after such treatment, they heard…**prayers** to God! and… the **singing of hymns**!! 'The legs feel nothing in the stocks when the heart is in heaven' (Tertullian). The **prayer** aspect is no surprise; every child of God knows the delight and privilege of moment-by-moment access to the throne of the heavenlies, and especially so whenever threats of any kind loom around us. 'Call upon me in the day of trouble and I will answer you' (Ps. 50:15). That Paul and Silas were fervently at prayer is only what multitudes of others before and since have done, and will continue to do, as we put ourselves and all our circumstances anew into the hands of our heavenly Father. But the **singing of hymns** takes us a step further. This implies joy in the midst of pain and suffering. Here is a Christianity of which the world knows nothing. 'Consider it pure joy, my brothers, whenever you face trials of many kinds' (James 1:2). The

17. Calvin, II, 82-3.

18. James S. Stewart, *The Wind of the Spirit* (Hodder and Stoughton, 1968), 158-9.

Jerusalem apostles had walked this extra mile after their beating at the hands of the Sanhedrin – 'the apostles left the Sanhedrin, rejoicing because they had been counted worthy to suffer disgrace for the Name' (5:41); here Paul and Silas fall into line behind them.

Then **suddenly there was a violent earthquake**...in a sense the surprise would have been if there had been no earthquake! Earthquakes were in fact a feature of life in that region, but this particular tremor was of such a precise force and location that **the foundations of the prison were shaken. At once all the doors flew open, and** everyone's **chains came loose**. 'Tremble, O earth, at the presence of the Lord' (Ps. 114:7). The jailer meanwhile, **awakened** by the earthquake, enters the prison where his worst fears are seemingly confirmed by the **doors** being **open** – the prisoners have escaped due to the structural damage and the resulting confusion! He needs no reminding of the implications...his life is forfeit and so, rather than face the public dishonour, and the inevitable executioner's sword, **he drew his sword and was about to kill himself.** Astonishingly his fears are in fact groundless, as **Paul shouted, 'Don't harm yourself! We are all here.' The jailer called for lights, rushed in and fell trembling before Paul and Silas.**

There are numerous questions which can be asked at this point concerning the details: if there was darkness such that lights were needed, how could Paul have been so sure that no one had escaped, etc.? While none of these questions are unanswerable, Marshall wisely observes: 'We are dealing as so often with a condensed story in which narrative is limited to the points significant for the author's purpose and he does not bother...to reconstruct the scene in every particular.'[19]

What is historically clear is that the jailer does *not* suffer execution, and that he with his family become members of the Philippian church. The jailer's **fear and trembling** would surely have included a significant ingredient of numinous awe. The missionaries' supernatural creden-

19. Marshall, 272.

tials would have been known, and possibly in addition the sorcerer's continual claim of their having a message of salvation (17); not only had they not escaped themselves but they had succeeded in restraining all the other prisoners – 'there was something uncanny about these two men!' [20]

So he brought them out and asked, 'Sirs, what must I do to be saved?' The jailer is forced by the supernatural confirmation of the missionaries' message to realize that he must come to terms with the God proclaimed by Paul and Silas.'[21] **They replied: 'Believe in the Lord Jesus, and you will be saved – you and your household.'** The Christian message has been expounded through these chapters of Acts in a variety of contexts, sometimes at considerable length. It was to receive significant restatement and further elaboration in the later New Testament writings. In the two millennia to follow, it would become the source of voluminous compositions and counter-compositions, both learned and popular, of sufficient number to stock and overflow the libraries of the nations. Yet in this dramatic moment, amid the ruins of the Roman jail in Philippi, it can be stated in a single sentence of five words (in both the Greek original and its English translation), 'Believe on the Lord Jesus.'[22] Such is the glory of the gospel, and the glory of the gospel's God; 'I thank you, Father, Lord of heaven and earth, that you have hidden these things from the wise and learned, and revealed them to little children' (Matt. 11:25).

Each word is important: **believe** or, 'have faith' = personal trust, a resignation of all self-trust, and a resting entirely on this Other, implied by the following preposition, 'believe **on**,' or 'on to'. **Lord Jesus** identifies the one to be thus trusted, the incarnate person who had lived, ministered, and died in Palestine and is now the risen and living Saviour (= '*Jesus*'), and *Lord* = God over all, and hence over Caesars and every other authority in time and eternity. 'This definition of salvation, that one is to believe

---

20. Bruce, 339.

21. Marshall, 273.

22. pisteusov epi ton kuriov Yesouv.

in Christ, is short and meagre in appearance, but yet it is ample. For Christ alone has all the elements of blessedness and eternal life included in himself.'[23] 'Faith is the empty hand that grasps Christ' (Barth).

In keeping with the Bible's uniform commitment to the family unit, the gospel's offer of salvation is extended to the jailer's household, which would have comprised his immediate family as well as various household servants. But they needed to hear and respond for themselves, so **they spoke the word of the Lord to him and to all the others in his house.** As with 'Lydia', so here with the jailer, faith spontaneously leads to works of mercy: **at that hour of the night he took them and washed their wounds.** Chrysostom aptly comments, 'he washed them and was washed; those he washed from their stripes, himself was washed from his sins.' Then **he and all his family were baptized**, and they share a celebrative **meal** together; the jailer was **filled with joy – because he had come to believe in God, he and all his household.**

It is an amazing account, and its power still resonates across the centuries. It has been repeated innumerable times over the intervening ages, as amid the pain, confinements, despair and darkness of impossible circumstances, God has stepped in with His gospel of grace, and brought astonishing deliverance, salvation and hope. 'He lifted me out of the slimy pit, out of the mud and mire; he set my feet on a rock, and gave me a firm place to stand. He put a new song in my mouth, a hymn of praise to our God.... Salvation belongs to our God who sits on the throne, and to the Lamb' (Ps. 40:2-3; Rev. 7:10).

(4) The magistrates and civic leaders (35-40). The following day the magistrates send the lictors to the prison with orders to the jailer, **release these men** (35). They probably sense that with the public beating and the night in prison they have gone as far as they dare to express the community's displeasure. To have prolonged the process involving a higher court would have exposed them to possible ridicule.

---

23. Calvin, II, 86.

Paul, however, is not prepared to slip away quietly; this man is no doormat! **They beat us publicly without a trial even though we are Roman citizens, and threw us into prison. And now do they want to get rid of us quietly? No! Let them come themselves and escort us out** (37). For one thing, a grave injustice has been done; and for another, Paul would have been alert to the fact that receiving appropriate official apology would bequeath to the remaining believers a status of respect, and potential protection. The report of Paul's response, and additionally no doubt the disturbing fact of his and Silas' status as Roman citizens, predictably creates no small **alarm** back at city hall, and so in a delightful reversal of fortune, **the magistrates came to appease them and escorted them from the prison, requesting them to leave the city** (39). The missionaries thus take their leave of Philippi with the representatives of the Roman power bowing and scraping around them.

Before leaving, **they went to Lydia's house, where they met with the brothers and encouraged them** (40). **Then they left,** though the disappearance of the 'we' subject in the next sections arguably implies that Luke, himself quite possibly a citizen of Philippi, remained behind to continue the work of instruction and encouragement in a church to which Paul was thereafter both deeply bonded and practically indebted (Phil.1:3-8; 4:14-18).

The final observation, as the main party travels westwards along the *Via Egnatia*, is to note the remarkable group of disciples they leave in their train. The three founding members of the Philippian church were, if the central paragraph implies commitment on her part, a recently exorcized, former slave-girl, a mature, sophisticated, high-class businesswoman, and the jailer of the local prison, a Roman civil servant. The families and household servants of the latter two would also have been part of the congregation. But the diversity of these three central figures is quite staggering. Yet it was out of similarly gaping human diversities that the early Christian churches in the Roman Empire were formed, and there is widespread support from the sources that it was precisely their ability to unite people across these massive gender, social, ethnic, age, cultural and linguistic divides, which attracted multitudes to the churches through the first and subsequent centuries.

Faced with the unprecedented social diversity of our modern communities, both urban, and increasingly also rural, that same quality of diversity-in-unity holds a similar promise if we can learn to open ourselves to the Holy Spirit whose chief fruit is agape-love, and learn to embrace those who are different from ourselves. In this dangerously polarized world there is only one who can offer that miracle of community: Jesus Christ. 'The future of Christianity in the twenty-first century depends on practical living examples of authentic reconciling faith. While multicultural congregations will never be perfect organizations, God's call to reconciliation through the life, death and resurrection and abiding presence of Jesus Christ compels us to embrace the challenge of moving towards this goal.'[24] 'There is neither Jew nor Greek, slave nor free, male nor female, for you are all one in Christ Jesus' (Gal. 3:28). Our unique privilege, and supreme opportunity, is to demonstrate that!

Study Questions:

1. How do you react to the 'melancholy division' between Paul and Barnabas (15:36-41)? Can you instance similar disagreements from your own experience of church life? How do you react to Bock's conclusion that 'sometimes a recognition of the need for distinct ministries is the best solution'?

2. What was the sense of priority which motivated Paul to circumcise Timothy (16:1-3) even though he must have known that it would be viewed by some as inconsistent? Apply this to our church life today, and to your own life.

---

24. 'All Churches should be Multiracial', *Christianity Today* (April 2005), 35. Also Curtiss Paul deYoung, Michael O. Emerson, George Yancey, Karen Chai Kim, *United by Faith: the Multicultural Congregation as an Answer to the Problem of Race* (Oxford University Press, 2003); Bruce Milne, *Dynamic Diversity* (IVP, 2007).

3. What are the lessons for us concerning God's guidance in this section (16:6–10)? How do you understand 'The Spirit of Jesus would not allow them'? What might this mean in your experience?

4. Consider in turn the three 'conversion stories' in this chapter; 'Lydia' (16:13-15); 'the slave girl' (16:16-18); and the jailer (16:25-34). What can each teach us about effective evangelism? Which of the three has the clearest resonances for you, and why?

5. What do we learn from Paul's refusal to be 'got rid of quietly' (16:36-40)?

4. Ministry in Thessalonica (17:1-9)

The next stop on the journey will be at **Thessalonica.** Thessalonica (today's Saloniki) was the capital city of Macedonia, referred to as 'the metropolis of Macedonia' and 'the mother of all Macedonia'. It was larger than Philippi, with a major harbour, and was an important trading centre. It was a 'free city' on the Greek model, and also known for its loyalty to Rome. It was obviously a strategic centre for Christian mission, as was to be confirmed: 'the Lord's message rang out from you, not only in Macedonia and Achaia – your faith in God has become known everywhere' (1 Thess. 1:8). Asserting the strategic basis of the choice of Thessalonica is made the more necessary by the fact that the hundred-mile journey to reach it along the *Via Egnatia,* took the missionaries through two not inconsiderable cites, **Amphipolis and Apollonia,** both full of people needing to hear the gospel. But these cities would hear the gospel as it radiated out from an effective 'planting' in Thessalonica.

We should be alert here to the constraining fact, as far as Paul was concerned, that being appointed 'apostle to the Gentiles' meant he was faced with the whole Gentile world as his parish. Patently there was no way he could reach it all in his lifetime. Consequently he needed to be highly strategic, planting the gospel in key centres of population and then trusting the churches formed therein to be responsible for witness to their surrounding communities. This 'key-centres plan' was not so clear in his first journey, though in a real sense that ministry in Galatia was part of the 'ringing out' of the gospel from Antioch. But thereafter his strategy was clear, and so the province of Macedonia will be reached through Thessalonica, the province of Achaia will be reached through Corinth (with some help from Thessalonica according to the reference above), and the province of Asia will be reached through Ephesus (19:10).

So...on to **Thessalonica**. His journey there was not without its internal struggles. Although we have just studied his ministry in Philippi and celebrated there the amazing triumphs of grace and the powerful interventions of God, Paul's own account is less enthusiastic. He tells the Thessalonians later 'we had previously been insulted in Philippi...but with the help of our God we dared to tell you his gospel' (1 Thess. 2:2). The length of the journey would have given Paul and Silas opportunity to heal physically from the wounds of their beating.

On arrival they follow their typical pattern and head for the **Jewish synagogue** (1). His ministry there covered **three Sabbaths** (though his overall stay probably covered a much longer period), as **he reasoned with them from the Scriptures, explaining and proving that the Christ (Messiah) had to suffer and to rise from the dead** (2-3). We have already studied this biblical-apologetic approach, both in the earliest sermons in Acts, and in Paul's address at Pisidian Antioch. Scriptures such as Psalms 2, 16, 110 and Isaiah 53 and Deuteronomy 21:22-23 were typically drawn upon. In the claims made for the Messiah, 'explaining and proving that he had to suffer', Paul would have faced instinctive scepticism. A **suffering** and crucified Messiah was certainly not the sort the Jews had been led to believe in. In general the Messiah was seen as a royal and powerful figure, the fulfiller of the promise to David of a continuation of his kingdom with its regal splendour. As we saw in expounding Acts 8:32-34, Old Testament passages teaching His suffering and death, such as Isaiah 52–53, were not viewed as Messianic since they were evidently, in principle, irreconcilable with these kingly dreams. The thought of **His resurrection** was also difficult in that the Jews had no anticipation of a single individual rising from death prior to the final resurrection at the end of history.

On Paul's general method, Calvin comments, 'Let us, for our part, realize that as faith can be founded nowhere else than on the Word of the Lord, so in all controversies we must take our stand only on its evidence...for Scripture is the true touchstone by which all doctrines must be tested.'[25]

Once having established the biblical base of a crucified and resurrected Messiah, Paul then in his second phase had the challenge of connecting the prophecies with Jesus: **This Jesus I am proclaiming to you is the Christ**. It says much for the effectiveness of Paul's preaching and the attendant work of the Spirit that **some of the Jews were persuaded**, and **joined Paul and Silas, as did a large number of God-fearing Greeks and not a few prominent women** (4). As was so often the case, Paul's evangelistic effectiveness is across the board. This very success however brought to a head the by-now anticipated Jewish opposition. This was apparently driven, as in case of the Jewish opponents in Pisidian Antioch, by **jealousy** (5; cf. 13:45). The tipping point in arousing this was probably the conversion of the God-fearing Greeks. That group were a fertile source of conversions to Judaism, which would have involved circumcision, and other law-observing requirements for becoming a Jewish proselyte. Now the Jews saw that potential mission field being reduced before their eyes, so they were jealous, and their jealousy turned to violence.

They rounded up some bad characters – how ironic this for a faith whose God was seen as the Righteous One who called for corresponding righteousness in His followers: 'Be holy as I am holy.' But once personal hurt and deeply felt envy are in the driving seat moral and religious restraints soon become dispensable. **They formed**

25. Calvin, II, 92, 101.

a mob and started a riot in the city. A character named **Jason**, who is Paul and Silas' host, now enters the picture. Haenchen suggests, plausibly, that he was initially only a landlord of convenience but through contact with the missionaries had been converted to Christ.[26]

The Jews **rush to Jason's house in order to bring them out to the crowd** (5), that is, before the popular assembly of the people where charges could be laid in this 'free city'. When the missionaries are not found there, the Jews resort to the other possibility as far as legal recourse was concerned, that of bringing a case before **the city officials** (6). The term Luke uses to refer to these leaders is a very unusual one, *politarchs*, but one which independent Macedonian sources have confirmed was applicable only in this province. 'From five inscriptions referring to Thessalonica, it appears that a body of five politarchs ruled the city during the first century A.D.'[27]

Here the Jews present their case. They describe the missionaries in their absence as **these men who have caused trouble all over the world** (6), which is their first charge, parallel to that laid in Philippi, that of being the instigators of public disorder. Their second charge follows: **they are all defying Caesar's decrees, saying that there is another king, one called Jesus** (7). This was a very serious matter if proven since it was effectively a charge of sedition, and it not surprisingly produced **turmoil** among **the crowd and the city officials** (8). It was the charge the Jewish authorities in Jerusalem had brought against Jesus before Pilate (Luke 23:2-3; John 19:12); though one Jesus denied under interrogation (John 18:33-36). There was, however, just enough truth here to leave suspicion in the minds of the uninformed. Jesus was, and is, King over all kings, as the title, *Lord* Jesus' indicates, and therefore king over Caesar. From study of 1 and 2 Thessalonians it is clear that Paul had majored on eschatological themes during his teaching ministry there, as well as in his subsequent contacts (cf.1 Thess. 1:3; 1:10; 2:19; 4:13–5:11; 5:23;

---

26. Haenchen, 512.

27. Longenecker, 469.

2 Thess. 1:6-10; 2:1-11; 2:14). Hence, while the Christian faith teaches responsible and law-abiding citizenship as a Christian duty, the situation becomes less clear where the state claims supreme homage and absolute obedience. In such circumstances, the Christian gospel has clear political consequences which have led to multitudes over the centuries dying for Christ's name due to their refusal to give to human kings and rulers, or to political totalitarianisms, the supreme and unqualified loyalty these authorities have demanded from them.

More generally, as Marshall pertinently observes, this formulation of the Christians' message, **another king, one called Jesus**, 'indicates how the focus in the gospel had shifted very naturally from the proclamation of the "kingdom" in the ministry of Jesus, to the proclamation of "the king" in the evangelism of the early church.'[28] It remains our focus today. Here is the supreme vindication, and endless attraction, of the Christian faith; not the church, which sadly is regularly disappointing, but the Christ Himself: 'another King: one called Jesus' fulfilling his own promise: 'When I am lifted up I will draw all people to myself'. It was true in the days of His earthly ministry, as Don Everts movingly records: 'There was just something so clear and beautiful and true and unique and powerful about Jesus that old rabbis would marvel at his teaching, young children would run and sit in his lap, ashamed prostitutes would find themselves weeping at his feet, and whole villages would gather to hear him speak, experts in the law would find themselves speechless, and people from the poor to the rugged working class to the unbelievably wealthy would leave everything...and follow him.'[29] They were doing it again in Thessalonica, and they do it still today, as King Jesus continues to draw the multitudes and expand His kingdom, from every corner of the globe.

Despite the concern about the missionaries' message, the officials manage to defuse the situation by **making Jason and the others post bond**, and then **let them go**. The

28. Marshall, 279.

29. Don Everts, *Jesus with Dirty Feet* (Downers Grove: InterVarsity, 1999), 26-7.

bond presumably called for the evangelists to leave the city forthwith and not return. So, **as soon as it was night, the brothers sent Paul and Silas away to Berea**. Though Timothy is not mentioned, it is clear that he accompanied the others to Berea (cf. v.14). The ban, however, clearly did not include Timothy as he would make a return visit to the city (1 Thess. 3:2–6). Stott suggests that this ban was what Paul had in mind in 1 Thessalonians 2:18 when he spoke of Satan 'preventing his return' to the city;[30] though in that case it would be important to specify the presenting 'enemy' here were those Thessalonian Jews whose opposition instigated the ban (1 Thess. 2:14–16).

Although Paul did not personally return to Thessalonica, as far as our knowledge goes, the gospel he had faithfully preached had been left there, and it continued to be 'at work' (1 Thess. 2:13) in many, many lives. The subsequent letters to the church reflect reports of persevering faith and courageous witness which was already spreading well beyond Thessalonica and being talked about 'everywhere' (1 Thess. 1:8), despite continuing Jewish-led persecution. The letters also bear testimony to Paul's deep and abiding affection for them all. This Thessalonian congregation was to supply two of Paul's later helpers, Aristarchus and Secundus (20:4).

5. Ministry at Berea (17:10-15)

To reach Berea required leaving the *Via Egnatia* and turning southwards, a journey of some fifty miles. Several commentators suggest that this move was occasioned by Paul's hope of returning to Thessalonica in the near future, the ban notwithstanding, and certainly there can be no questioning his longing to be back there (1 Thess. 2:17; 3:10-11). However, while we will never know for certain it would be surprising if the apostle, as a man of extensive education and wide cultural awareness, was not already feeling the pull of Athens, and Berea lay on the road to Athens. Although the Athens of the first century was in many senses a far cry from the glory of its prime in the

---

30. Stott, 273.

fifth century B.C., it remained in many senses, 'learned Athens' (Ovid), the intellectual and cultural capital of the world.

However, in the meantime, Berea also needed to hear about Jesus, and a start is again made at **the Jewish synagogue** (10). The reaction there was a notable improvement on the contentious spirit of their more recent synagogue encounters. **The Bereans were of more noble character than the Thessalonians, for they received the message with great eagerness and examined the Scriptures every day to see if what Paul said was true** (11). In a profound sense this was the ideal audience since (as good Greeks?), they applied the great Socratic principle of 'following the evidence wherever it may lead'. The locus of the relevant evidence with respect to the case the missionaries were presenting, was, as is implicit here, Scripture, God's written Word, and hence the supreme and final authority in all matters of faith and practice. What does the Scripture teach? That was their overriding principle. In this they anticipated by fifteen hundred years the slogan of the great Protestant reformers, *sola Scriptura*, expressed, for example, in *The Westminster Confession of Faith*, of 1647. Chapter I, X. reads: 'The supreme Judge, by which all controversies of religion are to be determined…and in whose sentence we are to rest, can be none other than the Holy Spirit speaking in the scripture.' But the Bereans were not only exemplary in their formal commitment to Scriptural authority, but a model also in the spirit with which they consulted them: they examined them **with great eagerness**. Come back to us, Bereans! Every church needs you! It is not surprising that this Jewish company were to lend their name centuries later to a number of Bible-study movements.

The result was predictable: **many of the Jews believed**, but not only they, **also a number of prominent Greek women and many Greek men** (12). The Greek wording implies that the 'prominent', possibly 'well-to-do', were of *both* men and women, but that the women were particularly noted for their responsiveness. What we see again is the breadth of the missionaries' appeal. Even among the Jews who were not as yet persuaded, there is no hint of any hostility towards Paul and his companions. This broad tolerance was not to last, however, once news that **Paul was preaching the word of God at Berea** reached back to Thessalonica, and prompted the arrival from there of his Jewish opponents who **agitated the crowds, stirring them up** (13). Paul is the personal focus of the anger and so the team decides to split up at this point, Paul with some of the new **'brothers'** in Berea going on **to the coast**, and then the further two hundred miles **to Athens**, possibly by sea. **Silas and Timothy stayed on in Berea** to continue to encourage the promising work there with its **crowds** of converts and enquirers, before, at Paul's request, **rejoining him** whenever possible at Athens (15). The work at Berea clearly was consolidated, as is indicated in the person of Sopater, son of Pyrrhus (20:4), who was to accompany Paul through Macedonia; Paul was once again drawing later support from one of his 'church-plants'.

6. Ministry at Athens (17:16-34)

From the perspective of human culture, Paul's arrival in the city was both dramatic and portentous. Here was the encounter of two worlds. The Athens of its earlier heyday represented an unprecedented flowering of human culture and creative genius which has remained, in many senses, one of the primary building blocks of subsequent Western and indeed global civilization. As a student and graduate of the not insignificant city of Tarsus, and the subsequent pupil of Gamaliel in Jerusalem, Paul would no doubt have been well aware of Athens' legacy and stature.

But however much Paul must have stirred with interest as he approached the city, he entered it not as a tourist but as an apostle of Jesus Christ. And so it happened, one spring day in A.D. 50, that the ancient order of classical paganism and the new order of nascent Christianity came face to face. Although nothing of this significance would have been discernible to the casual onlooker, Paul was bringing in his person ideas and convictions which within a few centuries would usurp the place of the pagan dynasties and usher in a new world of human experience, reflection and imagination. Here was a new order which would take its inspiration not from Athens but from Jerusalem, not from Mount Olympus but from a hill called Calvary, and, above all, from a crucified Judean carpenter rather than a Greek philosopher, poet or politician. In its meeting with Paul, however little it guessed the significance of that moment, ancient Athens was for the first time face to face with the 'world of tomorrow'.

As Paul is alone **in Athens, waiting** for his colleagues to rejoin him, he takes the opportunity to view the city – **as I walked about** (23). Whatever was his reaction to its cultural legacy is not indicated in the text at this point. What *is* made clear is his being **greatly distressed** at the ubiquitous, in-your-face, idolatry of the city (16). The verb here, *paroxyno*, has associations with deep feelings, including anger. So he was 'outraged' (REB), 'revolted' (NJB), 'provoked' (RSV/ESV). 'When Paul grew hot at the sight of the impious profanation of the name of God, and the corruption of his pure worship, he made it plain in that way that nothing was more precious to him than the glory of God.'[31]

But he did more than 'grow hot'; the sight of these multiple expressions of paganism with their patent ignorance of the true God, and the dishonour done by them to God's name, drove Paul to bear witness. He expressed this in turn in three places, in the **synagogue** to **the Jews and the God-fearing Greeks he met there** (17); in **the market-place day by day with those who happened to be there**, and where debate was the staple diet (17); and finally, at their invitation, at the elite intellectual club known as **the Areopagus** (18-31). Michael Green presents the challenge of Paul's reaction here: 'It broke Paul's heart to see the city captive to idolatry. At once we notice how different Paul is from us. We are surrounded by various forms of idolatry – worship of fame, sex, money, power, and it does not bother us. We have lost the ability to care.'[32] But Paul's 'care' was not simply at the folly of the Athenians' ignorance, nor even, we have probably to add, at their spiritual peril – though

31. Calvin, II, 104.

32. Green, 106.

he will warn them before he is done of the reality of future judgment (31), but finally *at the implications of all this for the honour of God*. As a Jew born and raised, no moral or religious duty was more deeply ingrained in Paul's heart and mind than the first commandment: 'You shall have no other gods before me' (Exod. 20:3). Here surely lay the source of the 'anger' that burned in his heart and opened his lips, the gross disrespect for God, the 'de-godding of God'[33] which this idolatry expressed. There can be no deeper or purer motivation for mission than this: a heart-yearning that the idols that burgeon in human hearts be dethroned by the gospel, and the one true and living God be thereafter exalted, honoured and worshipped in the shrines of the human hearts He has created for His praise. 'The mainspring of missions is not pity, but faith – not so much pity for perishing sinners as faith and zeal for the crown rights of Christ' (P.T. Forsyth). We recall in this connection the motto of the Moravians, the first great Protestant world-mission movement: 'To win for the Lamb the reward of his sufferings.'

The third witness opportunity arose from Paul's meeting with **a group of Epicurean and Stoic philosophers who began to dispute with him** (18). The **Epicureans**, followers of Epicurus who had died in 270 B.C., taught that the gods were remote from human affairs. The world and life within it were a matter of pure chance, there was no immortality and no judgment to come. The aim was, therefore, to enjoy life as far as possible without the shadows of pain, passion or fear. Paul may be reflecting a popular summary of the Epicurean philosophy in 1 Corinthians 15:32 (citing Isa. 22:13): 'Let us eat and drink (and enjoy ourselves as best we may), for tomorrow we die (and that will be the end of us)'. The **Stoics**, by contrast, disciples of Zeno who had died in 265 B.C., taught that there was a supreme god, the 'world's soul' who determined everything and acted in everything. Fate therefore reigned and life was best pursued by accepting it as it is,

---

33. D.A. Carson, *Becoming Conversant with the Emerging Church* (Zondervan, 2005), 184 and passim.

living according to nature, and developing indifference to pleasure and pain.

Some of the philosophers refer to Paul disparagingly, as **this babbler**; the word literally alludes to birds picking up seeds, so perhaps 'scavenger', or even, 'third-rate journalist.'[34] By whatever meaning it well expresses the arrogance of the Athenian intellectuals. Paul is given a slightly more positive rating by others of them: **He seems to be advocating foreign gods**. The surprising allegation of polytheism, in Paul of all people, is immediately explained: **They said this because Paul was preaching Jesus and the resurrection.** In Greek 'the resurrection' (*anastasis*) had been misunderstood by the hearers as the name of a goddess, a second deity alongside Jesus. Clearly Paul had been majoring on the central gospel realities. The auditors are however intrigued by Paul's **new teaching** and **strange ideas**, and wanting **to know what they mean, they took Paul and brought him to a meeting of the Areopagus** (19). This was a kind of intellectual discussion forum which additionally carried certain judicial functions within Athenian life, and so was a body of considerable significance and prestige. Some have suggested that Paul was arrested by them and that his address is his formal defence. The evidence, however, hardly supports that; he appears to speak as a Christian apologist and preacher. Luke interjects at this point a somewhat dismissive comment on the Athenian predilection for debate, their **doing nothing but talking about and listening to the latest ideas** (21); their breed is not dead.

We are then provided with the text of Paul's Areopagus address, or at least a condensation of its main themes. It is a remarkable utterance. Some have queried how well it meshes with the Paul of his letters, noting in particular the contrast between the apparently conciliatory tone towards pagan culture adopted here, and the more denunciatory stance, say, in Romans 1:18-32. 'This conclusion however fails to appreciate Paul's ability to contextualize.'[35] In

---

34. Barrett, 830.

35. Bock, 558.

Romans 1, Paul is addressing Christians concerning universal human fallenness as demonstrated in certain features of the cultural life of the Empire, rendering its citizens both ignorant of God and yet culpable in their ignorance. Here in Acts 17, he is attempting to build a bridge to the culture as he presents the gospel to some of its culturally alert but lost and needy representatives.[36] This criticism also misses the clear call for repentance in face of future divine judgment in Paul's conclusion here in Athens (30-31). In the address Paul further develops themes touched on in his message to the polytheistic audience in Lystra (14:15-17).

Paul is in no degree awed by the Athenians' philosophical traditions. Taking his point of contact from a local shrine, 'TO AN UNKNOWN GOD' ('a brilliant piece of contextualizing'),[37] he accuses them of a fundamental and pervasive ignorance of God. He then proceeds to educate them by expounding the character and deeds of 'the true and living God'. Paul asserts no fewer than seventeen truths about God:

1. God is the creator of all things: **God...made the world and everything in it** (24); **we are his offspring** (citing the pagan author Aratus) (28).

2. God is the sustainer of all things: **God...gives all men life and breath and everything else** (25).

3. God is ruler over all things: **God...is the Lord of heaven and earth** (24).

4. God is a transcendent spirit: **God...does not live in temples built by hands** (24); **we should not think that the divine being is like gold or silver or stone** (29).

5. God is perfectly complete in Himself: **God...is not served by human hands, as if he needed anything** (25).

6. God is a purposive and active God: **from one man he made every nation...that they should inhabit the whole earth; and he determined the times set for them and the exact places where they should live** (26).

7. God is a personal, relational being who seeks relationship with His creatures: **God did this so that men would seek him and perhaps reach out for him** (27).

36. Witherington, 533-5.

37. Green, 108.

8. God is immanent within the world: **God...is not far from each one of us; in him we live and move and have our being** (citing the pagan poet Epimenides) (27).

9. God is our Father, in the sense that our life comes to us ultimately from Him: **We are his offspring** (29).

10. God is a merciful being: **In the past God overlooked such [idolatrous] ignorance** (30).

11. God is a morally righteous being who calls all people to repent of wrong: **God...commands all people everywhere to repent** (30).

12. God is a God of justice: **God...will judge the world with justice** (31).

13. God's purpose in human history has reached its goal in the mission of Jesus Christ: **God...now...commands all people everywhere to repent... For he has set a day when he will judge the world with justice by the man he has appointed** (30-31).

14. God raised Jesus to life after His death: **God... [raised] him from the dead** (31).

15. God has already set a time when all people will be passed under judgment: **God...has set a day when he will judge the world** (31).

16. God will judge all people by Jesus Christ: **God... will judge the world by the man he has appointed** (31).

17. God has provided a universal sign of His future, universal judgment by raising Jesus from the dead: **God... has given proof of this to all men by raising him from the dead** (31).

One cannot read this list without astonishment. What Paul gave the Areopagus that day was nothing less than a crash course in basic theology. In particular he taught them a comprehensive doctrine of God. It is remarkably inclusive and expansive. It is, moreover, both effectively related to the philosophical positions of his hearers, and yet utterly faithful to the revelation of God in the Old Testament Scriptures. Virtually every primary attribute of God disclosed there is either asserted or implied. In a day when theology is routinely dismissed as an irrelevant preoccupation for Christian eggheads, it is time to learn again from Paul. Paul's gospel is rooted in Paul's God. And

Paul's God is not an innocuous, virtually absent being, who vaguely loves the world and is pleased about Jesus. Paul's God is the overwhelmingly real and ever-present embodiment of every one of the above list of attributes, and more besides.

More specifically Paul's God is the presupposition of every single act and attribute of Paul's Christ, and to ignore the former is in effect to empty the latter of true meaning. We need to be continually alert to the mistaken and mischievous notion, that to think long and hard about God in His triune majesty and mystery is somehow detrimental to a rounded and happy Christian experience.

The relevance of all this for Christian evangelism is powerfully spelled out by John Stott: 'all this truth about God is part of the gospel. Or at least it is the indispensable background to the gospel, without which the gospel cannot be effectively preached. Many people today are rejecting our gospel not because they perceive it to be false but because they perceive it to be trivial. People are looking for an integrated world-view which makes sense of all their experience. We learn from Paul that we cannot preach the gospel of Jesus without the doctrine of God, or the cross without the creation, or salvation without judgment. Today's world needs a bigger gospel, the full gospel of Scripture, what Paul later in Ephesus was to call "the whole purpose of God"'(20:27).[38]

We dare not miss Paul's unapologetic declaration of future judgment: **God commands all people everywhere to repent. For he has set a day when he will judge the world.** Paul does not hesitate to preach 'Jesus and the resurrection' to the philosophers of Athens, nor to call them to repentance, despite the fact that his sermon in most cases would probably have been the first time that they had heard of the name and saving work of Christ. This is because he clearly does not see the obligation of these pagans in Athens to repent as significantly mitigated by the fact that they have not previously heard about Jesus. **He commands all people everywhere to repent.** Specifi-

---

38. Stott, 290.

cally therefore this statement includes all the followers of other religious traditions. Why so? Because, as Paul taught in Lystra, 'God has not left himself without testimony' (14:17). God addresses all people everywhere in the moral conflicts of their lives. In that sense, no one can plead ignorance of him.

God's final judgment will be utterly just, of that we can be sure; indeed it will be the only perfectly just judgment in all of history. But that fact offers no ground for complacency in anticipation of it; particularly so when we recall that God has access 'to the thoughts and attitudes of the heart. Nothing in all creation is hidden from God's sight. Everything is uncovered and laid bare before the eyes of him to whom we have to give account' (Heb. 4:12b-13). We should also note that the proof of this universal, future arraignment is the resurrection of Jesus. Why so? Because His resurrection is His designation as the universal Lord, and consequently the one destined as the coming Judge of all, the heavenly Son of Man anticipated in Daniel's prophecy (Dan. 7:13).

But from all we know of the apostle's message, Paul's pointing to Jesus is not merely to confirm future judgment but to offer Him as the God-provided solution to the problems raised for us all by our moral accountability (cf. 17:18 'the *good news* about Jesus'). Calvin concurs: 'There is no doubt that Paul said a good deal more about Christ…but Luke considered it sufficient to give a brief summary of the discourse. However it is likely that Paul first spoke about the grace of Christ and proclaimed him the redeemer, before he made him the judge.'[39] Jesus' very name means Saviour, and it is as such that Paul exalts and proclaims Him. So 'a way of salvation' was offered at Athens, and some embraced it and 'believed' (34), and so may we, and so may all. 'For God so loved the world that he gave his one and only Son that whoever believes in him shall not perish but have eternal life. For God did not send his Son into the world to condemn the world, but to save the world through him. Whoever believes in him is not condemned'

---

39. Calvin: II, 125-6.

(John 3:16-18). 'Come unto me...and whoever comes to me I will never drive away' (Matt. 11:28; John 6:37).

It remains to consider the response to Paul's message. It is a threefold one, broadly representative of the responses made to all presentations of the gospel.

First, there were those who *dismissed*. **Some of them sneered** (32). The idea of the resurrection of the dead was a stumbling block, though as Paul was later to ask King Agrippa, 'Why should any of you consider it incredible that God raises the dead?' (26:8). So, some sneered; and some still do. God's amazing respect for the dignity of His creatures extends even to the point of permitting their rejection of Him. No greater mistake is imaginable, but it can be made, and then eternity will be spent with the regret.

Secondly, there were those who *deferred*; they said, **We want to hear you again on this subject** (32). This response is, of course, better than the first, and since most people who hear the gospel do not accept it on first hearing, this category is necessarily a large one. In a sense Jesus supported this form of response when He talked of the need to count the cost before committing ourselves to Him (Luke 14:25-33). Sooner or later, however, we need to move on from this, and enter the third category of response, since to remain indefinitely with the second will lead in the end to the same fate as the first.

Thirdly, there were those who *decided to believe*; they became **followers of Paul and believed** (34), at least one being **a member of the Areopagus**, a man named **Dionysius**, and another **a woman named Damaris**, as well as **a number of others**. And so a church was effectively begun in Athens also, after which **Paul left Athens and went on to Corinth** (18:1).

Bock offers a final comment. 'Despite being aggravated by all the idolatry he sees around him in Athens, Paul manages to share the gospel with a generous but honest spirit. The Paul of Romans 1 who speaks of the sad state of society is still able to love and connect with that society in Acts 17. This also is an important lesson: sometimes we Christians are so angry at the state of our society that all that comes through is the anger and not the love we are to have for our neighbour in need. Those who see this anger and want to represent the faith differently can overact the other way, almost pretending, as if there is no idolatry as long as the religious search is sincerely motivated. Paul avoids both of these extremes. He knows how to confront but does so honestly and graciously. Both message and tone are important in sharing the gospel. Here Paul is an example of both.'[40]

Study Questions:

1. Consider the mission to Thessalonica as described here (17:1-9), along with Paul's own report in 1 Thessalonians 1:1–2:19. What stand out as critical factors in its obvious effectiveness? Where do these points both encourage and also challenge us?

2. The Bereans 'examined the Scriptures every day to see if what Paul said was true' (17:11), and became thereby a model for the Christian ages. Reflect on your own experience in both corporate and personal Bible study, both its positives and its negatives. What steps might you take to experience the Bereans' 'great eagerness' in this area (17:11)?

3. Paul's reaction to the 'in-your-face' idolatry of Athens (17:16), and his response to it (17:17), deeply challenge us. What motivated these two rejoinders? What idolatries can you discern in your present culture and community?

4. What strikes you most forcibly about Paul's Areopagus address (17:22-31)? What can we learn from it?

5. Consider the threefold response to his witness (17:32-34). Can you identify similar reactions to the gospel being played out in your circle of con-

40. Bock, 573.

tacts? How might those in group A ('We want to hear…again') be helped towards joining group B ('a few…believed')?

7. Ministry in Corinth (18:1-17)

The ministry in Athens had brought Paul into the Roman province of Achaia, and he now heads for its capital and commercial centre, the city of **Corinth,** some forty miles to the west. 'Corinth and Ephesus were the two most important cities visited by Paul in the course of his missionary work, and he stayed in each for a considerable period in order to establish churches which would then evangelize the surrounding areas.'[41]

Corinth was a key administrative centre for the province and a major port to the southern Aegean Sea, with busy traffic sailing both to the eastern Mediterranean, and westwards to Rome. Corinth also housed the Isthmian games and the famous temple to Aphrodite, with its orgiastic rites which were partly responsible for generating the verb, *korinthiazomai,* meaning 'to practise immorality.' Prosperous and licentious, it was a city 'where only the tough survive', according to Horace. Farrer offers the epithet, 'The Vanity Fair of the Roman World', which Bock updates to 'the Las Vegas of its time'.[42] Above the city rose the impressive mountain, the Acrocorinth, from which, interestingly, one could view Athens in the distance, a not insignificant fact in view of some of the problems Paul had to later engage in the Corinthian congregation. This visit to Corinth was to initiate a deep bond which lasted through much of Paul's remaining years of ministry, and which would bring him considerable heartache, as well as periodic satisfactions. Due to his two lengthy letters *'To the Corinthians'*, we have a fuller knowledge of the church which eventually emerged there than of any other Paul founded.

Paul begins predictably by making a missional acquaintance with the Jewish community as **every Sabbath he**

41. Marshall, 291.

42. Bock, 577.

reasoned in the synagogue, trying to persuade Jews and Greeks (4), the latter presumably the customary God-fearers. Paul is still on his own as Silas and Timothy have yet to catch up with him, and he finds friendship and accommodation with a couple who were to be supporting colleagues over the next years, **Aquila, a native of Pontus, who with his wife Priscilla, had recently come from Italy because Claudius had ordered all the Jews to leave Rome** (2; Rom. 16:3-4; 1 Cor. 16:19; 2 Tim. 4:19). Paul's link is strengthened by their pursuing a common trade, **tent making,** which included leather-working. By Jewish practice, every rabbi was encouraged to learn a trade along with his more strictly religious duties and Paul apparently returned to it at this point. This was of course of significance for him with his itinerant lifestyle which was without a regular source of remuneration, as it allowed him, when so disposed, to be financially independent of the churches, a freedom which he greatly cherished (1 Thess. 2:9; 2 Thess. 3:8; 2 Cor. 11:9).

The reference in verse 2 to the forcible emigration of Jews from Rome, and the name of the proconsul in Corinth whom we meet shortly, allows us to date the period Paul spent in the city with some precision as A.D. 50–52.[43] The expulsion of Jews by Claudius, according to Roman historian Suetonius, was due to the Jews in Rome 'constantly rioting at the instigation of Chrestus'. Some have seen here a misinformed reference to 'Christus' = Christ, and hence to violence arising out of Jewish conflicts over Jesus. That the anger of an anti-Christian group could erupt into violence has been repeatedly evidenced in these last chapters of Acts, so this understanding of 'at the instigation of Chrestus' is certainly entirely possible, though the reference is of course not entirely clear.[44] The Jews trickled back over the next period, and we find Aquila and Priscilla relocated there when Paul writes his *Letter to the Romans* (16:3), along with other Jews included in his greetings (cf. 16:7, 11). One final comment here is with respect to Paul's

---

43. Fitzmeyer, 621-2.

44. cf. Bruce, 368, and for a more reserved judgment, R.T. France, *The Evidence for Jesus* (Hodder and Stoughton, 1986), 41f.

finding friendship in Corinth in the home of Aquila and Priscilla. The evidence of both Acts and the Pauline letters is of a man who covets, even is dependent upon, the ministry resource afforded by close associates. His mission work was always conducted in teams, and he clearly made deep relationships, often with a few people in particular, during his ministry in the churches. This rather tends to undermine one popular picture of Paul as a remote, doctrinaire personality.

The arrival **of Silas and Timothy from Macedonia**, bringing reassuring news of the churches in Thessalonica, Berea and Philippi – in the last case with a gift from the church (2 Cor. 11:8f; Phil. 4:15) – enables Paul to leave his manual work and **devote himself exclusively to preaching, testifying to the Jews that Jesus was the Christ** (5). Substantial, even **abusive opposition** develops which leads Paul to repeat the drastic step he took in Pisidian Antioch (13:51), **he shook out his clothes in protest. 'Your blood be on your own heads! I am clear of my responsibility. From now on I will go to the Gentiles'** (6).

The reference to 'responsibility' probably indicates a larger than merely strategic motivation for Paul's 'to the Jews first' evangelistic policy. This action, of shaking out one's clothes, which echoes that of Ezekiel (33:1ff), raises the question of whether we may be justified at times in turning away from an evangelistic initiative when it has been repeatedly rebuffed in order to expend our energies in a potentially more productive direction. These are not easy decisions to arrive at, and there are obviously contexts where the fruit we seek only comes after a long period of ploughing and sowing (Eccles. 11:1; Matt. 18:21; Neh. 9:30-31). However, Paul may be providing here some biblical support for such a decision. That may need to be qualified somewhat by reminding ourselves of the specificity of Paul's missional remit – the entire Gentile world, albeit his fellow Jews were never to be ignored (Acts 9:15; 22:21; 26:15-20; Rom. 1:16; 9:11; 15:17-20; Gal. 1:15-16; 2:8-9; Eph. 3:1-8; Col. 1:14-27; 1 Tim. 2:7).

Paul then moves to a strategic new location **next door** to the synagogue, **to the house of Titius Justus** (7), a God-fearer who was obviously sympathetic to the message, and whose home would obviously have allowed Paul continuing availability to those touched by his earlier synagogue witness. God 'gave the increase' as first the significant person of **the synagogue ruler, Crispus and his entire household believed in the Lord,** and then **many of the Corinthians who heard him believed and were baptized** (8). It is not clear who performed these baptisms as Paul in 1 Corinthians claims that he had only baptized Crispus, possibly the first person to turn to the Lord in Corinth, and one Gaius, and the 'household of Stephanas' (1:4-16).

The reason for his decision not to baptize is interesting, 'so that no one could say that you were baptized into my name' (1:15). Clearly issues of leadership rivalries and inappropriate personal adulation had arisen in Corinth from a very early point. Paul is as ever the soul of circumspection. This perhaps gives some hint of the difficulties which Corinth posed for the Christian church-planter. It accordingly makes sense of the vision which Paul was afforded: **one night the Lord** (= the Lord Jesus; 16:31-2; etc.) **spoke to Paul in a vision** (9). Such would hardly have been given had Paul not been in real need of it at this point. The words spoken have resonances of divine commissions in the Old Testament (cf. Exod. 3:12; Jer. 1:7-8, 17-19; Ezek. 2:3–3:11). In essence Paul is told four things: (1) not to back off in his preaching: **Do not be afraid…but keep on speaking, do not be silent** (9), 'It amounts to the same thing as if he said: "Do not let fear keep you from speaking."'[45] (2) to be assured that the Lord will be with him: **I am with you** (10); (3) that he will be protected: **do not be afraid…no one is going to attack and harm you** (10); (4) that his ministry is going to be evangelistically fruitful in the future: **I have many people in this city** (10). The message from the Risen Lord is comprehensive in its scope; every possible anxiety is assuaged, and so we are not surprised to read that following this divine encounter, **Paul stayed for a year and a half, teaching the word of the Lord** (11).

---

45. Calvin, II, 134.

These are promises that would lift and energize every witness for Christ anywhere in the globe, and some who serve today in dangerous places not least. The testimony of Dr Martin Luther King Jnr assures us that encounters such as Paul describes here are not confined to the biblical ages. 'After a particularly strenuous day, I settled in bed at a late hour. I was about to doze off when the telephone rang. An angry voice said, "Listen nigger, we've taken all we want from you. Before next week you'll be sorry you ever came to Montgomery." I hung up, but I could not sleep. It seemed that all of my fears had come down on me at once. I got out of bed and began to walk the floor. I was ready to give up. I tried to think of a way to move out of the picture without appearing to be a coward. In this state of exhaustion, when my courage had almost gone, I determined to take my problem to God. My head in my hands, I bowed over the kitchen table and prayed aloud. The words I spoke to God that night are still vivid in my memory. "I am here taking a stand for what I believe is right. But now I am afraid. The people are looking to me for leadership, and if I stand before them without strength or courage, they too will falter. I am at the end of my powers. I have nothing left. I've come to the point where I can't face it alone." At that moment I experienced the presence of the Divine as I had never before experienced him. It seemed as though I could hear the quiet assurance of an inner voice, saying, "Stand up for righteousness, stand up for truth. God will be at your side forever." Almost at once my fears began to pass from me. My uncertainty disappeared. I was ready to face anything. The outer situation remained the same, but God had given me inner calm.'

The final promise made to the apostle is particularly notable: **I have many people in this city**. This reflects two divine attributes. First, it affirms God's *foreknowledge* (2:23; Rom. 8:29; 11:2; 1 Pet. 1:2), which is a necessary corollary of his omniscience (Ps. 139:1-12; Heb. 4:13). God knows the future, including His people's future responses to Him. This is a great, reassuring truth. Because of it, Moses can be told at his call that 'When you have brought the people out of Egypt, you will worship God on this mountain' (Exod. 3:12); or Jeremiah, in a Jerusalem surrounded by the Babylonian army, is instructed the field in Anathoth, because 'fields will again be in this land' (Jer. 32:1-15). Or, most reassuringly of all, John can in vision see 'the holy city coming down out of heaven from God, prepared as a bride beautifully dressed for her husband' (Rev. 21:1-4).

Secondly, this great promise in the final words of verse 10 points to God's *eternal love*: **I have many people...** God's sovereign, saving purpose involves not just a prior awareness of our choice of Him but an anticipated personal embrace of us. Even those who have yet to hear and accept the gospel are even now, in a real sense, 'His people', gathered within 'His own'. There is the greatest possible encouragement here to persevere faithfully in God's service; we are not toiling alone, and He who is our divine fellow labourer will surely fulfil all that is on His heart, and complete and perfect His bride.

These glorious, reassuring truths are wonderfully expressed in a more personal sense in Revelation 7:9-10, a passage which affords us a fore-vision of the redeemed in glory drawn from 'every nation, tribe, people and language, standing before the throne and in front of the Lamb'. It is amazing to consider that as John for a moment, in his gaze, panned across that countless, white-robed throng, he might have seen you, or me! For if we are Christians in this day, then we will certainly be there, in that company on that day. We were actually seen there, somewhere in that blessed, countless, praising throng John glimpsed through that 'open door into heaven' (Rev. 4:1); we have already been seen in glory! God *has* His people!

At some point in the course of this period of missionary labour, **the Jews made a united attack on Paul and brought him into court. 'This man,' they charged, 'is persuading the people to worship God in ways contrary to the law'** (12-13). The commentators all find difficulty in deciding what exactly this charge comprised. A defensible view is that the Jews want Paul to stop evangelizing their community (presumably because Paul is being so effective) by trying to distinguish between Judaism, which as a *collegium licitum* had the protection of Roman law, and Christianity which does not and is therefore a *collegium illicitum*.[46] If this distinction was upheld, and the new faith was not one which Rome recognized, then Paul should be forbidden to propagate it in Corinth.

In the event Paul's defence was rendered unnecessary by the Roman proconsul, Gallio, who dismissed the case: **If you Jews were making a complaint about some misdemeanour or serious crime it would be reasonable for me to listen to you. But since it involves questions about words and names and your own law – settle the matter yourselves. I will not be a judge of such things** (14-15). The Jews, having been ejected from court, took their frustration out on **Sosthenes**, the current **synagogue ruler**, by **beating him in front of the court**; but Gallio remained totally unmoved. There is a Sosthenes who is mentioned as an associate of Paul in 1 Corinthians 1:1; however Sosthenes was a common name, so while the identification would seem likely since he would have needed to be a believer to have attracted the wrath of Paul's Jewish opponents, his continuing position in respect of the synagogue would seem to leave that uncertain. The larger reason for Luke's detailing these proceedings is to make the point, which will resurface again, 'that Christianity is not a threat to Rome'.[47]

The fruitfulness of the mission and the legal decision in his favour encourage Paul to **stay on in Corinth for some time** (18), before **leaving the brothers and sailing for Syria, accompanied by Aquila and Priscilla.** They travelled to **Ephesus**, the major city of the province of Asia, where, as we recall, Paul and his companions had received a sense of the Spirit closing the door to them at the beginning of the journey (16:6). **He reasoned with the Jews in the synagogue** (19) and received an invitation to remain; however he was anxious to be back in Syria and Judea, and so departed with the promise that **I will come back if it is God's will** (21). He would return and spend extended time there on his next (and final) journey.

---

46. Witherington, 552.

47. Bock, 583.

One remaining matter is **the vow** which Paul had taken before sailing back to Syria, involving **having his hair cut off at Cenchrea** (18), the outport of Corinth. There are several options as to what this vow was. One view is that it was a Nazirite vow (Num. 6:1-21). If that were so, then the cutting of his hair would be understandable. For the specified duration of the vow he would additionally have had to abstain from alcohol and 'uncleanness' such as that created by touching a corpse, and then be required, on completion of the vow, to offer a sacrifice in Jerusalem. This might explain his desire to return fairly immediately to Judea (the phrase in verse 22, **after he landed at Caesarea he went up and greeted the church**, could denote a visit to Jerusalem). Alternatively, the vow might have been a purely personal one, in token of his thanksgiving for the deliverances of the journey, and in particular for the fulfilment of the visionary promises of Jesus at Corinth (18:9-10). By the strict terms of the Nazirite vow, the hair cutting could not be done outside of Jerusalem, whereas if this were indeed a personal vow it might simply be a chosen, visible symbol of his renewed personal commitment to the Lord. Accordingly, 'a private vow seems more likely'.[48]

Back again to Antioch (18:18-22)
After landing at Caesarea he went up and greeted the church and then went down to Antioch (22). Paul's second mission journey was over.

It had been another epic adventure in the mission of Jesus Christ. Begun under the shadow of his unhappy separation from Barnabas, followed by the perplexity and frustration faced in trying to identify a new field of operation, it had finally taken Paul across into Macedonia and then through Achaia. In these significant provinces, amid exciting and memorable events, and while facing great hardships, he had seen living churches planted in Philippi, Thessalonica, Berea, probably Athens, and Corinth. Jewish opposition had dogged him consistently,

---

48. Bock, 586.

often evincing great bitterness and a willingness to resort to violence, though some among Israel continued to make the journey to faith in Messiah-Jesus, and all the while the Gentile wing of the church was becoming ever more securely established, and even giving promise of becoming the dominant form of Christianity for the longer-term future.

Study Questions:

1. 'Tent-making' (18:3), and 'exclusive devotion to preaching' (18:5), *both* feature in Paul's Corinthian ministry. What does the apostle's flexibility have to teach us? What, from this section (18:1-8), are the values and challenges of both these forms of missional endeavour?

2. Identify the elements of Paul's vision (18:9-11). In what ways would these realities have strengthened him for the months which lay ahead in Corinth (18:11)? In what ways do they strengthen us?

3. The ministry in Corinth was significantly advanced through the medium of preaching, by Paul (18:5), and by Apollos (24-28). The role of preaching has, in general, diminished in the Western church in the last period, a trend which goes against biblical models. What has contributed to this development? What convictions about preaching, and what practices in relation to preaching, would promote its recovery?

4. Taking vows has regularly been a significant feature of human society, as exemplified in marriage ceremonies all round the globe. Although we do not know what Paul's vow here exactly consisted in, it raises the place of vow-taking within Christian discipleship (cf. 18:18), e.g. in baptismal, confirmation and commissioning rituals. What are its possibilities and dangers? Has this been a feature of your own spiritual journey, and how helpful has it been?

10

Witnesses to the Ends of the Earth (II)
(Acts 18:23–21:16)

A. 'Paul's Third Mission Journey' (18:23–21:16)

Some writers have wondered whether speaking of this as a 'third journey' is in fact an appropriate way of referring to it since such a large part of it was spent in one centre, Ephesus. However Paul did travel from Antioch to get there, and he would return eventually to Syria from there, and there was ministry engaged in other places during that toing and froing. There is also the evidence that in his Acts account of these years Luke does not give us a complete picture of Paul's movements. At the very least, as we learn from his Corinthian correspondence, he broke his period in Ephesus at one point to make a visit to Corinth to deal with an emergency pastoral situation that had developed there. Taking the evidence overall, we accordingly feel justified in retaining the traditional title. So…to 'The Third Mission Journey.'

1. Ministry in Ephesus (18:23–19:41)

After spending some time in Antioch, Paul set out from there…(23). So begins this last of Paul's major itinerations for Christ. While he may well have had a further, fairly brief, period of freedom after his arraignment at Caesar's tribunal, before final rearrest and execution – a period during which the Pastoral Letters were composed – this 'third journey' would be his final extended piece of ministry.

Hence, rather poignantly, his leave-taking from his 'home church' in Antioch, rather cursorily noted here, was, unknown to himself, probably his last. That link had been immensely meaningful for the apostle. No one will know till the heavenly order breaks just how much was achieved for the kingdom of God as the Antioch believers prayed, and supported, and periodically refreshed him. We commented at the time of Paul's initial commissioning moment in Antioch (13:1-3) that the act of laying on of hands upon him and Barnabas, expressed, among other things, the sense of the congregation's ongoing involvement, even their real participation, in what the missionaries would attempt for Christ. Truly Antioch had been a 'sending congregation'. How greatly we continue to need such today, but how great is the privilege they open of literally 'reaching the world' through our local Christian community. As Paul sets out again, Silas may have stayed behind at Jerusalem (assuming that to be implied at verse 22), and Paul was most likely accompanied by Timothy, and maybe others, as he set out (19:22).

Ephesus, clearly Paul's goal, was a very important centre, the major city of the province of Asia. Just how critical, and hence how justified Paul was in investing so much time there, is proved by the comment at 19:10, that, even allowing for Luke's understandable exaggeration, because of Paul's Ephesian witness, 'all the Jews and Greeks who lived in the province of Asia heard the word of the Lord.' Estimates have the population of Ephesus in Paul's day at around a quarter of a million, making it one of the largest cities in the empire. Situated at the mouth of the river Cayster, it boasted a thriving economy. It was a free city with its own assembly (19:39), and was home to a large Jewish population who enjoyed special privileges. Its greatest claim to fame, however, was in the sphere of religion. Ephesus was home to the temple of Diana, or 'Artemis' in the terms of the Greek pantheon. The temple which housed Diana's image, 'fallen from heaven' (a meteorite? cf. 19:35), was one of the wonders of the ancient world. Made entirely of marble, and four times bigger than the Parthenon in Athens, it was the largest building in the Greek world. 'No religious building in the world ever knew a greater concentration of admiration, enthusiasm and superstition.'[1] This veneration, however, was also a major liability in that tradition had invested the temple with the right of asylum and hence anyone committing a crime would be beyond the reach of the law if he or she could reach the temple's precincts. This inevitably contributed significantly to Ephesus' reputation as a very wicked city. Heraclitus, 'the weeping philosopher', is alleged to have explained his tears: 'What else can I do when I look at Ephesus?'

Paul had left Ephesus, as we saw, with a promise to return (18:21), and it seems clear that, recognizing the immense strategic potential of the city, this was his focused goal for this third journey. However on the way there **he travelled from place to place throughout the region of Galatia and Phrygia** (23). So the churches at Derbe, Lystra, Iconium and Pisidian Antioch had one further opportunity to benefit from his teaching and general encouragement.

Before coming to Paul's Ephesus ministry, Luke helps set the scene by interjecting an introduction to **Apollos** (24-28). While Paul was on his way, **a Jew named Apollos, a native of Alexandria, came to Ephesus.** Luke underlines his special gifts. **Learned** could refer to eloquence as well as intellectual ability, though it would appear from the full description of Apollos' ministry that he was richly endowed in both areas. Alexandria in North Africa was another significant centre with a strong Jewish presence and culture. Apollos' **thorough knowledge of the Scripture** is in keeping with this.

There has been discussion engendered by Luke's account of Apollos' level of understanding. Was he even a Christian at this point? The answer appears to be that he was; his being described as **instructed in the way of the Lord**, and as one who **taught about Jesus accurately** seem fairly conclusive indications. There is also absent any mention of his being baptized following **Aquila and Priscilla's explaining the way of God more adequately**

---

1. Reymond, 180.

(26). The clinching consideration, however, may be one which is obscured in the NIV rendering of the phrase in verse 25 describing Apollos' teaching mode. The NIV opts for 'he spoke with great fervour'; however this = lit. 'burning in the Spirit he spoke…'. Admittedly 'spirit' could be a reference to Apollos' own 'spirit' but the presence of the definite article is more naturally a reference to the Holy Spirit, hence Bock's rendering: 'fervent in the Spirit',[2] along with his additional note of the parallel wording in Romans 12:11 'where it clearly describes Christians'. However Apollos, even if a true believer, had limitations in terms of his understanding. Despite the **boldness** of his **synagogue teaching, he knew only the baptism of John**.

The presence not only of a teacher of Apollos' stature who was deficient in certain theological basics, along with the immediately following account of Paul's meeting with the twelve disciples in Ephesus who had **not even heard that there is a Holy Spirit**, should not come as a great surprise. We today are so accustomed to assume the availability of the entire New Testament that we forget that it was not to be even completed till late in the first century, and not generally accessible in the churches for a considerable period thereafter. That being so, it was surely nothing less than the gracious overruling of the Holy Spirit that the church in the first few generations did not lapse into all manner of diverse parties, and that teachers with blank areas in their Christian understanding, or championing highly heterodox views, were not to be much more regularly encountered than in fact they were.

In Apollos' case 'his preaching is not inaccurate, merely incomplete'.[3] The deficiency was apparently in his understanding of baptism, and 'he may also have needed to hear about Jesus' commission, exaltation, and gift of the Spirit'.[4] Happily, present in the Ephesus synagogue congregation were Paul's friends, Aquila and Priscilla, **who invited him to their home and explained to him the way of God more**

---

2. Bock: 592.

3. Bock: 592.

4. Stott: 302.

adequately. Bruce's comment is certainly apt: 'How much better it is to give such private help to a preacher whose ministry is defective than to correct or denounce him publicly', or perhaps one may add, than to take him aside in the church foyer, in the emotionally vulnerable moments immediately following preaching, and attempt there and then to complete his theological education!

Apollos expressed a desire to minister also in Achaia, and the Ephesus **brothers encouraged him** in this prospect (27). They also, in brotherly fashion, **wrote to the disciples there to welcome him**. Apollos' ministry in Achaia, particularly in Corinth, was greatly appreciated and effective as **he was a great help to those who by grace had believed; for he vigorously refuted the Jews in public debate, proving from the Scriptures that Jesus was the Christ** (27-28). Apollos' preaching style with its rhetorical qualities would have been particularly appreciated in a Greek centre like Corinth where public speaking was a recognized and honoured vocation, and a staple of a rounded education. Paul would later refer to Apollos having watered the seed that he had sown in Corinth (1 Cor. 3:6). Apollos' qualities led later to his becoming a focus for party-spirit at Corinth, cf. 'I follow Paul, and I follow Apollos, etc.' (1 Cor. 3:4), however Paul refused to let that sour his relationship with Apollos, whom he refers to in the warmest terms as a fellow 'servant of Christ' (1 Cor. 4:1) and 'our brother' (1 Cor. 4:9; 16:12; Titus 3:13), perhaps even as a fellow apostle (1 Cor. 4:9). However the hero-worship in Corinth may have embarrassed Apollos, for he subsequently left Corinth and returned to Ephesus (1 Cor.16:12).

There is an encouraging picture here of the diversity and unity of ministries. At the public teaching and preaching level, Paul and Apollos, who have clearly different styles and quite different histories, can yet exercise complementary ministries, which benefit the witness and the growth of the churches in both Corinth and Ephesus. None of us are omni-competent as Christian leaders, preachers, or workers, however much we may be tempted at certain moments to imagine ourselves so. Congregations need a variety of input, both to reach the non-Christian community around them, and also to fully mature in Christ, and God will make opportunities for that to occur if we are open to it. There is often a similar complementariness called for in terms of historic succession as one minister of Christ follows another in a leadership role in a congregation. How critical that those completing their period should uphold the ministry of their successors, and that the successors in turn be quick to disavow criticism of their predecessors.

But there is also a complementariness at other levels illustrated here. Aquila and Priscilla illustrate the possibilities of a home dedicated in Christ's service, quite possibly one where there had not been the hoped-for gift of children, or where the children have matured and left home. God uses their supportive friendship of two public servants, one involved in hugely costly ministry (Paul), and in the second case, the quiet 'coming along side' of another gifted teacher with advice and faithful instruction (Apollos). The 'brothers' (18:27) representing the whole congregations at Ephesus and Corinth also contribute at that community level and this leads to enriched ministry in both churches. As Paul was to later instruct the Ephesians, 'When he ascended on high...he gave gifts...so that the body of Christ might be built up, until we all reach unity in the faith and in the knowledge of the Son of God and become mature, attaining to the whole measure of the fullness of Christ' (Eph. 4:8, 12-13).

Paul meanwhile had made his journey along **the road through the interior and arrived at Ephesus.** A helpful way of surveying Paul's Ephesus ministry is to see it as a series of conflicts.[5]

First, there was conflict with *inadequate knowledge of the gospel* (19:1-7). **There** in Ephesus Paul **found some disciples...about twelve men in all** (7) who gave him concern about their level of Christian understanding, and so he asked them: **Did you receive the Holy Spirit when you believed?** (2) to which he received the answer: **'No, we**

---

5. M. Franzmann, *The Word of the Lord Grows* (Concordia, 1961), 76.

have not even heard that there is a Holy Spirit.' 'Then, what baptism did you receive?' to which they reply: 'John's baptism (3). They are referred to as 'disciples', and there is reference to their having 'believed', though that may simply be Paul's polite assumption. It would appear that in fact, unlike Apollos' case, these men are disciples of John the Baptist, as in the case of Andrew and his unnamed friend many years previously (John 1:35-40), only in this Ephesian case the step of leaving John to 'follow Jesus' had yet to occur. As Stott observes, 'In a word, they were still living in the Old Testament which culminated with John the Baptist'.[6] Indeed how appropriately they can even claim the title of 'disciples of John' is somewhat doubtful since they apparently are not aware of what was by any account a central theme of John's entire ministry, including his administering of baptism, viz. the future appearing of the 'one coming after him', the Messiah (Matt. 3:11-12; John 1:19-36).

Paul clarifies their need immediately, and so the men, belatedly, do what John had urged his hearers to do by the Jordan; they recognize and follow the one 'the thongs of whose sandals I am not worthy to untie', 'the one who will baptize with the Holy Spirit', 'the Lamb of God' (John 1:27, 33, 36). They are, therefore, as the expression of their now believing in Jesus, baptized into the name of the Lord Jesus (5). Paul, possibly to make quite explicit to them the regenerating gift of the Spirit through Jesus, accompanies the baptism with the laying on of hands. The effect of the coming of the Spirit is not only their rebirth in Christ but additionally the Spirit's gifts of speaking in tongues and prophetic utterance (6).

We are left asking why these phenomena accompany conversion in this case. Lampe draws a possible parallel to earlier decisive comings of the Spirit by noting its location, viz. Ephesus, and suggests that this represents 'another decisive moment in the missionary history' since Ephesus is becoming the new centre of the Gentile mission in succession to Antioch. However the parallel to Antioch is not

---

6. Stott, 304.

particularly clear, and one would surely have expected the Spirit's outpouring to be upon the whole church rather than upon this marginal sub-group, if Lampe's view was in fact the case. We have earlier noted a distinction between the more regular Spirit's 'coming upon', or 'being received' at conversion, and the 'falling all over' of the Spirit at Pentecost, in Samaria, and in the house of Cornelius, corresponding, as we argued, to the three critical boundary points in the gospel's outward spread as specified by Jesus at 1:8. There is no 'falling all over' in the Greek text here, since the incorporation of these disciples of John does not represent a critical geographical boundary marker, as was the case in the three earlier Spirit outpourings. Nonetheless this coming of the Holy Spirit would certainly have been a very clear experiential confirmation of divine acceptance for these recipients, and therein probably lies its rationale. Here were a group whose passionate loyalty to 'the greatest of those born of women' in the entire Old Testament era (Matt. 11:11), required a decisive, divinely authenticated transfer to an even profounder loyalty to the one 'born of a woman, born under law, to redeem those under law, that we might receive the full right of sons (of God)' (Gal. 4:4-5).

Second, there was a conflict *with the synagogue* (8-10). Paul's previous visit had confined itself to the synagogue and resulted in a request that he spend more time with the Jews he met there (18:20). On this second visit they certainly could not complain of his failing to fulfil their request, as **he entered the synagogue and spoke boldly there for three months, arguing persuasively about the kingdom of God** (8). The terms in which the message is cast is notable, **the kingdom of God**. This meant that Paul was presenting Jesus as the Messiah who fulfilled the Old Testament hope of the future reign of God, his long-awaited kingdom (28:31). Thus Paul is proclaiming a large gospel with widest possible implications. Jesus has come to bring to fulfilment God's ancient promises of a salvation which will finally bring about the remaking of the whole world under His reign. The extra time spent in the Ephesus synagogue, however, did not mean a greater openness to the message on the part of **some of them, who refused to believe, became obstinate and publicly maligned the Way. So Paul left them** (9). The costliness of this initial Jewish ministry – **from the first day I came into the province of Asia** – comes to the surface in his later reflection with the Ephesian elders: **I served the Lord with great humility and tears, although I was severely tested by the plots of the Jews** (20:18-19).

There is a certain regression in the response to the gospel here; one that is sadly often observed. Those who express interest in the gospel, and a desire to **spend more time** learning more (18:20), can, if a positive response is too long deferred, come eventually to a critical moment when *not* to believe becomes itself a conscious choice, the choice *not* to surrender to the claims of Jesus Christ, **a refusal** (19:9) of His grace and atoning sacrifice. This only too often becomes an **obstinacy** (19:9); the middle voice of the verb here (*esklerynonto*) implies deliberate resistance, 'they hardened themselves', the same expression that is used regarding Pharaoh (Exod. 8:15f). It has thus become a conscious unwillingness to reconsider or revisit the issues, which may even be followed in turn by a **maligning** of the gospel (19:9), or the church, or Christians, or all three; and finally, at least in some cases, like tragic Esau, 'when he wanted to inherit the blessing, he could bring about no change of mind, though he sought the blessing with tears' (Heb. 12:17). The finding of the Barna Christian polling group, that, certainly for the USA, what you believe by the time you are thirteen is what in the great majority of cases you will die believing, is a sobering statistic, and not least an underwriting of Christian parenting and children and youth ministries. Happily, by the grace of God, there are glorious exceptions. But the lesson is nonetheless clear: 'Remember your Creator in the days of your youth, before the days of trouble come and the years approach when you will say "I find no pleasure in them"' (Eccles. 12:1, 6-7). 'There is a tide in the affairs of men...'

The synagogue witness had not been in vain however as Paul took **his disciples with him,** and then began a series of **discussions daily in the lecture hall of Tyrannus** (9).

It was an evangelistic master-stroke. Paul continued these daily 'seminars' and dialogues **for two years**, with a quite extraordinary influence – **so that all the Jews and Greeks in the province of Asia heard the word of the Lord** (10).

We would love to have been present at one of these sessions to see how it was conducted, who came along, what were the issues discussed, and not least how Paul presented the faith – obviously so winsomely, powerfully, and hence effectively, that all of the province of Asia was reached with the gospel. The Western text actually supplies the time-frame of these seminars, 11.00 a.m. to 4.00 p.m. If this is a solid piece of reminiscence, it would mean the sessions were covering the afternoon break and siesta period, when people would be free to listen to him. Paul is the strategist as ever – 'that I might by all means save some.' Larkin speaks of the example of the 'tireless Paul' who works in the morning and preaches in the afternoon.[7]

The remarkable spread of the faith during this period is attributable also to those, inspired by the seminars, who went out into the surrounding areas with the gospel. A likely example is Epaphras, who took the message northwards to the Lychus valley and planted the churches at Colosse, Laodicea and Hierapolis, and the now unknown witnesses who seeded the churches (other than Ephesus and Laodicea) that received messages from the exalted Christ in Revelation 2–3 (cf. Philem. 23; Col. 1:7; 2:1; 4:12-13; 1 Cor. 16:19).

The verbs used to describe this Ephesian missionary outreach are striking: Paul 'reasoned' (18:19); he 'argued persuasively' (19:8); he 'discussed' (19:9). In a word, he sought, not just an emotional response, but also an intellectual conquest. For Paul, Christianity was a religion of truth for the mind as well as all its other offerings. True, at the synagogue he also 'spoke', i.e. preached (19:8; cf. 19:13). But at the hall of Tyrannus it was much more dialectical. There is a place for both forms of presentation; but we need to note the second. We live in the midst of a communications revolution which has made information available on an unprecedented scale and opened up multiple channels

---

7. Larkin, 275.

of connection with others, and with it the possibility of dialogue-evangelism as never before. May God raise up in this day, and the next, a generation of effective gospel communicators who can courageously and effectively seize the opportunities in the many halls of Tyrannus which are available today through electronic communication.

Third, there was a conflict with *the prevailing practice of pagan magic* (11-20). The reference above to Paul's seeking 'an intellectual conquest' in his evangelism misleads if it seems to imply that he was only interested in winning verbal arguments, e.g. concerning how Old Testament prophecies were fulfilled in the life, death and resurrection of Jesus. Paul was deeply aware of the multiple facets of human experience and not least of all the dimensions of the spiritual order. He would later remind the Ephesians that 'we do not wrestle against flesh and blood.... but against the principalities and powers in the heavenly places' (Eph. 6:12; cf. 1:15-23; 3:10). Thus the ministry of reasoning and persuasive argument was complemented with a 'miracle ministry' in which **God did extraordinary miracles through Paul, so that handkerchiefs and aprons that had touched him were taken to the sick, and their illnesses were cured and the evil spirits left them** (12). Unfortunately our ability to appreciate what is described here is somewhat shaded by the practitioners of sensational media evangelism in which self-promotion, financial and lifestyle greed, and the exploitation of the vulnerable, are only too apparent, and tend to overshadow the cases where real spiritual and physical help is given, and where evil enslavements and demonic presences are effectively conquered. Nonetheless God was, and is, able to break savingly into human life at every level if He so chooses, whether in the first century or the twenty-first, and He clearly was so choosing here in Ephesus.

A particularly dramatic exorcism is described which significantly accredited Paul's ministry and the supreme authority and lordship of Jesus. Some Jewish exorcists tried to use **the name of the Lord Jesus** in their exorcisms: **In the name of Jesus whom Paul preaches I command you to come out!** (13).

This perfectly reflects the syncretistic spirit which was pervasive in the imperial world. It is also alive and very well in our cultures today. Our syncretism is to a significant degree the impact of what is arguably the most powerful single shaping factor in human culture today – the universal availability of information which has been fuelled by the electronic communications revolution. Its religious slogan and operational principle is no different than that of the first century: 'whatever works'; hence crystals, seances, gurus, mediums, nutritional supplements, herbal remedies, healing workshops, yoga meditation, channelling, sexual experimentation, and bits and pieces from Buddhism, Hinduism, Confucianism, Shinto and Islam, scientology, New Age, astrology, and Eastern Religion generally; you name it – we will try it. Welcome to the third millennium![8]

In one particular case in Ephesus a family of seven men were attempting an exorcism using the formula in verse 13 when the evil spirit responded, **Jesus I know, and I know about Paul, but who are you?** (15) There is a distinction in the meaning of the two verbs used in verse 15. Schneider helpfully suggests: 'Jesus I know, and Paul I respect.'[9] Whereupon the evil spirit suddenly so energized the possessed man that **he jumped on them, overpowered them, and gave them such a beating that they ran out of the house naked and bleeding** (16). This produced a general **fear** in both Jewish and Greek communities, **and the name of the Lord Jesus was**, as a result, **held in high honour.** The fear in turn provoked a spirit of genuine repentance among those who had already come to believe, or were now coming to faith. Those who had been involved in magic and sorcery came forward and made a public bonfire of **their**

---

8. The respected USA congregational polling publication, 'Pew Forum for Faith and Public Life,' in one of its 2009 editions, states its finding that one out of three Americans who attend religious services acknowledge that they go to multiple places of worship, across denominations and religions. Further the research found that two out of three American adults believe in experiences associated with New Age or Eastern religions, and that most of those who agree to these beliefs also identify themselves as Catholics, mainline Protestants, evangelicals or Jews.

9. G. Schneider, 1982, cited Bock, 604.

scrolls, the value of the same being estimated at **fifty thousand drachmas** (19). It was a remarkable movement of God's Spirit, and, Luke informs us without causing us any surprise, **in this way the word of the Lord spread widely and grew in power** (20).

The situation with these Ephesian believers in their initially retaining, despite their conversion, some of their magic practices, or at very least their trappings, has its resonances in every age. Clarity in terms of 'things permitted or profitable' does not come to the new convert overnight; maturity is a process. However, when believers do come under conviction and are led to repentance in a public manner, as here, the effect has often been powerfully renewing of the church. J.I. Packer refers to this as a recurring feature of revival: 'As God uses his Word to quicken consciences, the perverseness, ugliness, uncleanness, and guilt of sin are seen and felt with new clarity, and the depth of each person's sinfulness is realized as never before. Believers are deeply humbled; unbelievers are made to feel that living as they do with sin and without God is intolerable, and the forgiveness of sins becomes the most precious truth in the creed.'[10]

As an example, we can cite the revivals in Shansi, North-East China in the early 1900s, associated with the ministry of Jonathan Goforth. In the words of one present, 'God's Spirit was present in power. The text was from Revelation 3:15, "I know your deeds, that you are neither cold nor hot." An opportunity was given for prayer, and thereupon ensued such a scene as never before had I seen, nor again do I expect to see. One started to pray, but had not said more than half a dozen words, when another, and then another joined in, and in moment the whole company was crying aloud to God for mercy. All the sin of the past was staring them in the face, and they were crying in anguish to God for cleansing. Nothing in my mind can more fitly describe the scene than to compare it to the suddenness and violence of a thunderstorm.'[11]

---

10. J.I. Packer, *Keep in Step with the Spirit*, (Fleming H. Revell, 1984), 245.

11. Rosalind Goforth, *Goforth of China* (Dimension Books, 1937), 194-5.

Paul has one further conflict to engage at Ephesus. Luke, however, first supplies us with a sense of Paul's future plans. He is intent on a revisit to **Jerusalem**, which is implied, at 20:16, as a desire to be there for the anniversary of **Pentecost,** travelling by way of **Macedonia and Achaia.** Then **after I have been there I must visit Rome also** (21). This is the first surfacing of a desire to go to Rome, and the 'must' here (*dei*) expresses a sense of the divine necessity of that journey. In his letter to the church there, he would speak of having 'planned many times to come to you in order that I might have a harvest among you, just as I have had among the other Gentiles' (Rom. 1:13). It was a longing, perhaps a better word is a destiny, which Paul was indeed to fulfil, as Luke will go on to document, and in the process express the fuller terms of the commission of the Lord in Acts 1:8, 'to the ends of the earth'. Paul's realization of this goal will however be neither in the precise terms, nor in the precise time-frame, he anticipated.

Even Rome was not the limit of Paul's vision, however. As he shares in the *Letter to the Romans* which was written not long after, he was even dreaming of Spain (Rom. 15:24, 28). 'His vision had no limits', comments Stott, and adds Bengel's judgment '...no Alexander, no Caesar, no other hero, approaches to the large-mindedness of this *little* (a play on his name *Paulos*, little) Benjamite.'[12] As part of the preparation for this itinerary he sends **two of his helpers Timothy and Erastus** (cf. 2 Tim. 4:20) ahead into **Macedonia,** while he decides **to stay on in Asia a little longer** (22).

Fourth, there was a conflict with *the commercialized state religion of Ephesus* (23-41). We noted in our introductory comments on Ephesus the dominant place of the temple and worship of Artemis in the affections and self-identity of the city. It was also a source of financially rewarding business among the locals as well as the city's many visitors, a feature commonly replicated in celebrated world cities in our own time. The mention of **a silversmith named Demetrius, who made silver shrines of Artemis,**

---

12. Stott, 307-8.

brought in no little business for the craftsmen (24) could virtually be an excerpt from a current guidebook to Paris, London, Rome, Beijing, Cairo, Sydney, New York or Los Angeles, or...

But the gospel was affecting trade! **We receive a good income from this business. And you see and hear how this fellow Paul has convinced and led astray large numbers of people here in Ephesus and in practically the whole province of Asia. He says that man-made gods are no gods at all** (25-26). Thus while not going out of its way to confront the surrounding culture, due to different fundamental beliefs (the One invisible, transcendent creator God versus polytheism and the veneration of man-made idols), Christianity, by its very success, finds itself in confrontation with, and being opposed by, those who make a living from the alternative world-view.

However there is a deeper level of confrontation, which Demetrius clarifies in his further assertion: **There is danger not only that our trade will lose its good name, but also that the temple of our great goddess Artemis will be discredited, and the goddess herself, who is worshipped throughout the province of Asia and the whole world, will be robbed of her divine majesty** (27). Polytheistic, pagan gods and goddesses also inspire and elicit worship, and hence the engaging of spiritual loyalties. There is also a 'worship equivalent' here. So, to proclaim and encourage allegiance to the one true God is inevitably to discredit and seek the disaffection of all allegiances to the false gods and goddesses. In this sense Christianity is inevitably subversive in the pantheon of the gods and goddesses, and for this reason Christianity is endlessly at war in this present world. We Christians need to come to terms with that; it belongs to the 'given' of our faith. Put another way, to live with the dedicated intention of being endlessly at peace with all people of all persuasions in all respects, is not a Christian stance. It simply implies that we have abandoned the faith and are living in fundamental disloyalty to the One True and Living God revealed in Jesus Christ.

The reaction to Demetrius' speech is predictable, given the Ephesian admiration and enthusiasm for Artemis, and his linkage of the expansion of Christian witness to her being thereby discredited and demeaned. **When they heard this, they were furious and began shouting, 'Great is Artemis of the Ephesians!'** (28). The crowd identify two of Paul's companions, **Gaius and Aristarchus and rush into the theatre**.

The Ephesian theatre was a massive structure capable of seating 24,000. Still beautifully preserved, 'it is the most impressive of the wonderful collection of remains at Ephesus.'[13] Paul wants to address the crowd but is wisely restrained, both by **his disciples** but also, interestingly, by the entreaties of **friendly officials of the province**, known as 'Asiarchs' (31), of which more in a moment. The essentially emotional basis of the crowd's motivation not surprisingly meant that **confusion** reigned, with **some shouting one thing and some another**. In truth, as Luke observes, **most of the people did not even know why they were there** (32).

The Jews, disturbed no doubt that the antipathy towards the Christians would have serious implications for them and their privileged status in the city, try to address the crowd through a leader, one **Alexander**, who would possibly have tried to make clear the Jews' own hatred for Paul and all his works. Alternatively, he may have intended to try to defend Paul simply for fear that the anger would spill over into an anger towards all Jews in the city. Either way, whenever he was recognized as a Jew the crowd drowned him out by **shouting, 'Great is Artemis of the Ephesians!'**, and having got started kept it up for the next **two hours**! (34).

Finally, due in part no doubt to the crowd's eventual exhaustion, **the city clerk** was able to quieten them. He then gave a speech making four points (35-40): (1) everybody, everywhere knows about the city's loyalty to **Artemis,** so there is no need for this hullabaloo in her support; (2) the Christians have not committed any breach of

---

13. Bock, 610.

the law, by either **robbing the temple** or **blaspheming Artemis**; (3) if Demetrius and his colleagues have a complaint or charge to press against them, they should follow proper legal process and use **the courts and proconsuls**, or **a legal assembly** which would determine any further issues; (4) the present commotion carries the danger of bringing the city into disrepute because it has no rational basis. **After he had said this, he dismissed the assembly.** The speech has echoes of the similarly calming presentation by Gamaliel (5:34-39).

This scene is a solid confirmation of Luke's historical reliability. Sherwin-White, the leading classical historian, notes the local knowledge reflected in the references to the temple keeper (v. 35), the commerce surrounding silver shrines (v. 25), and the role of the scribe of the people, or town clerk (v. 35). Further, the way the people function, the appeal to the town clerk, and the march to the theatre all fit a first-century setting. 'Acts does not show such detailed knowledge of any other city as of Ephesus. Luke is very well-informed about the finer points of municipal institutions at Ephesus in the first and second centuries A.D.'[14]

There are important lessons for us in these chapters covering one of Paul's most fruitful periods of ministry. Stott summarizes them challengingly: 'When we compare much contemporary evangelism with Paul's its shallowness is immediately shown up. Our evangelism tends to be too ecclesiastical (inviting people to come to church), whereas Paul also took the gospel out into the secular world; too emotional (appeals for decision without an adequate basis of understanding), whereas Paul taught, reasoned and tried to persuade; and too superficial (making brief encounters and expecting quick results), whereas Paul stayed in Corinth and Ephesus for five years, faithfully sowing gospel seed and in due time reaping a harvest.'[15]

---

14. Sherwin-White, 87.

15. Stott, 314. cf. also Bock, 'In the end effective evangelism is rarely done in the context of a guerilla-like encounter but usually requires a sustained effort over time', 615.

We also hear the city clerk's testimony that the Christians had **not blasphemed our goddess** (37). Possibly in similar vein, we do not derive the impression of a programme to stamp out magic in the city. It is of course dangerous to generalize here from the admittedly limited reports contained in the text; however, there may well be a lesson in terms of the essentially positive tone of Paul's evangelism. There certainly was an inevitable conflict with Artemis worship in Ephesus, as we noted earlier, but it was one which arose from the commercial impact of the gospel's success rather than from a deliberate campaign to malign the cult's theoretical and moral inadequacies. In the case of magic, the impact on its 'empire' came from converts to Christ separating themselves from its practices. The line is a fine one here; one thinks for example of the Old Testament exposure of the limitations of idol worship (Ps. 115:4-8; Isa. 44:12-20; 46:5-7); false roads do need to be pointed out as part of the process in getting people to walk along the true ones. 'Prophetic' witness still needs to demonstrate the gospel's superiority to all the other 'ways of salvation' on offer in the religious and cultural market place. However Paul's essential goal consisted in being, in the terms of Jesus' commission, a 'witness to me' (1:8). The positive exaltation of Christ and the proclamation, and embrace, of His great salvation resulted in a glorious triumph for the gospel over the local idolatry and satanic entrenchments but without in the process deliberately alienating the local populace.[16]

Probably in the same vein we should be impressed by the fact that those who urged Paul not to attempt to go into the theatre (30) were the Asiarchs, described by Luke as **friends of Paul** who **begged him not to venture into the theatre** (31). These men, as part of their official duties, had the task of enforcing the imperial cult, which involved all the citizens sprinkling incense before the statue of the emperor. Yet they are 'friends of Paul'. Green draws out the lesson. 'Can you imagine Paul consenting to engage in something that smacked of idolatry? By no means, even if it cost him his life. No, Paul would be totally opposed to all the Asiarchs stood

16. See Bock's comments on p. 614.

for. Yet he had befriended these men. He was regarded so
warmly by them that they warned him (actually begged
him) not to go and risk his life in the theatre...Paul had
befriended these folk, he had tried to win them for Christ.
And although he had not succeeded, they respected and
liked him. It is a magnificent example to us.'[17]

Study Questions:

1. Consider the ministry of Aquila and Priscilla in
   this chapter (18:2-3 and 26). Have we any testimonies to share of the influence such people have
   had in our own lives? Are we alert to the continuing possibilities of such ministry in our own case?

2. Paul's strategic concentration on key centres (cf.
   1 Thess. 1:7-8) is again apparent in his focus on
   Corinth (18:11) with a view to reaching southern Achaia, and then here at Ephesus (19:10) for
   reaching Asia. Is this applicable to us? If so, in
   what ways can it be applied? Are there limits to
   such strategizing? (cf. John 1:46!).

3. Can people be true Christians even though they
   are fundamentally misinformed about the Holy
   Spirit (19:1-6)? What are the core beliefs required
   in order to be an authentic disciple of Jesus?

4. We note again Paul's remarkable flexibility
   (19:9-10). What might be the equivalent to the
   'Hall of Tyrannus' in your community? Are we
   in danger of seeing evangelism much too exclusively as only happening in 'Christian' settings?
   Is there a bold evangelistic initiative that God is
   calling you to take personally? Or is there one
   which you should encourage your church to venture upon?

5. Are we continually alert to the 'spiritual warfare'
   which is an invariable part of faithful mission

17. Green, 54.

activity (19:11-20)? What forms might it take? What are our resources?

6. Identify examples of syncretism you have encountered in your religious and cultural context. How do we best counter this highly pervasive spirit in our own time? In what ways might it affect our evangelistic message and methods?

7. Two passing features of Paul and his associates' evangelistic ministry in Ephesus (19:23-41) are not be missed: (1) that despite the overt idolatry practised at the Temple of Diana the missionaries are cleared of any charge of 'blaspheming our goddess' (19:37); (2) that Paul's safety is a deep concern of his 'friends' among the Asiarchs, who were responsible for the imperial cult of emperor worship (19:31). What do these things say about Paul's missional heart? What do they say to our hearts?

2. Ministry in Troas (20:1-12)

Following **the uproar** in Ephesus Paul decides the time has come to move on to other centres, notably Corinth. He had spent nearly three years in Ephesus, the longest single stay in one city of his entire travels, but an investment of time which its immediate fruitfulness, and its longer-term influence, would entirely justify (19:10, etc.). So he calls for **the disciples** (was he perhaps in seclusion at this point due to the threat of the mob?) and **after encouraging them, said good-bye and set out for Macedonia** (1), possibly intending to catch up there with Timothy and Gaius, whom he had earlier sent ahead (19:22).

His route would have taken him north through Asia to Troas once again where he engaged in some effective evangelism ('When I went to Troas I found that the Lord had opened a door for me', 2 Cor. 2:12). However he passes up the opportunity developing there to press on by boat, across the Aegean to Neapolis and probably Philippi. The reason, the situation in the Corinthian church, takes us into concerns which Luke, due to his familiar selectivity, does not mention.[18]

We did comment earlier on the fact that during his stay in Ephesus Paul made an emergency pastoral visit back to Corinth, and this concern about troubles at Corinth continues to be a significant factor. At his return visit to Corinth, Paul had been strongly opposed by an individual who was clearly a figure of impressive intellectual ability, and Paul left in some degree of humiliation, having failed to get the compliance with his teaching which he had hoped for, even expected (2 Cor. 2:1-10; 7:12). Back once more in Ephesus, and in the 'great distress and many tears' of the aftermath, Paul had written what is referred to as 'the 'severe letter' or 'epistle of tears' (2 Cor. 2:4). Unwilling to face a possible further humiliation, he had changed his proposed plan to revisit Corinth after Ephesus and instead sent Titus to Corinth, probably carrying the 'severe letter', having agreed to rendezvous with him in Troas following his visit to Corinth. Titus could then inform him at first hand how his letter had been received in Corinth, and whether the conditions now prevailing there would be conducive to another visit as part of his larger itineration through Achaia.

This background explains Paul's agitation as he awaits Titus in Troas, 'I had no peace of mind' (2 Cor. 2:13); so marked was this perturbation on his part that he had for once withdrawn from an evidently promising evangelistic opportunity in Troas and instead presses on into Macedonia to speed up his meeting with Titus. We will return to this when examining his 'ministry report' to the Ephesian elders later in the chapter (20:19). It vividly illustrates the 'sufferings' he mentions in his list of his trials in 2 Corinthians 11:23-29, which concludes with 'the daily pressure (*epistasis*) of my concern for all the churches. Who is weak and I do not feel weak? Who is led into sin and I do not

---

18. James Denney, *The Second Epistle to the Corinthians* (Hodder and Stoughton, 1916), 339, refers to this Corinthian preoccupation and its resulting determination of Paul's movements in this period (which Luke omits), as showing 'how fragmentary, or at all events how select, is the narrative in the book of Acts.' As we have repeatedly observed, Luke's theme is the outworking of the commission of Jesus at 1:8; everything is secondary to that chosen focus.

inwardly burn?' (11:28-29). The noun here is capable of a variety of shades of meaning; however 'pressure' = 'pressure of responsibility' seems best.[19] Calvin rightly observes, 'No one can have a heartfelt concern for the churches without being burdened by many difficulties; for the government of the Church is not a pleasant occupation which one undertakes with joy and delight; it is…a hard and bitter warfare, in which Satan again and again stirs up for us as much trouble as he can and leaves no stone unturned to annoy us.'[20] It is to be feared that at this point Paul leaves us far behind.

James Denney in a great passage expounds the meaning of 2 Corinthians 11:28-29. 'Paul's love individualized Christian people, and made him one with them. There was no trembling timorous soul, no scrupulous conscience, in all the communities he had founded, whose timidity and weakness did not put a limit on his strength: he condescended to their intelligence, feeding them with milk, and not with meat; he measured his liberty, not in principle but in practice, by their bondage; his heart thrilled with their fears; in the fullness of Christ-like strength he lived a hundred lives. And when spiritual harm came to one of them – when the very least was made to stumble, and was caught in the snare of falsehood or sin – the pain in his heart was like a burning fire. The sorrow that pierced the soul of Christ pierced his soul also; the indignation that glowed in the Master's breast, as He pronounced woe on the man by whom occasions of stumbling come, glowed again in him. This is the fire that Christ came to cast on the earth, and that he longed to see kindled – this prompt, intense sympathy with all that is of God in men's souls, this readiness to be weak with the weak, this pain and indignation when the selfishness or pride of men leads the weak astray, and imperils the work for which Christ died.'[21]

---

19. Arnt and Gingrich refer to this rendering as 'an outstanding possibility'; cf. P.E.Hughes, *Paul's Second Letter to the Corinthians* (Marshall, Morgan and Scott, 1962), 416-17.

20. *The Second Epistle of Paul to the Corinthians, and the Epistles to Timothy, Titus and Philemon*, tr. T.A. Smail (Saint Andrew Press, 1964), 152.

21. Denney, *The Second Epistle of Paul to the Corinthians* (Hodder & Stoughton, 1916) 340-1.

There is in all this a glimpse of what Denney eloquently shares above, and which every person with a pastor's heart will be able, even faintly, to understand and identify with. How profoundly we need such pastoral passion today; how vulnerable all of our Christian work becomes, no matter its statistical success, when such is lacking.

Once arrived there, **he travelled throughout Macedonia**. He presumably visited the churches in Philippi, Thessalonica and Berea, and possibly also at this point ventured into new territory north-westwards in the province of Illyricum where, in writing later to the Romans, he claims to have preached (Rom. 15:19); and 'this period is the most likely for this mission.'[22] During this journey he continues to build the collection 'for the poor among the saints in Jerusalem' (Rom. 15:25-26; cf. 2 Cor. 8:16-24). Luke makes no reference to this until 24:17 where it is only mentioned as an explanation for Paul's happening to be in Jerusalem at the time of his arrest there. This silence has perplexed the commentators. There appears to be no clear explanation for it, which is the more surprising in view of the importance which Paul himself placed on this offering (1 Cor. 16:1f; 2 Cor. 8–9).[23]

In every case, as he travelled again through Macedonia, he was **speaking many words of encouragement to the people** (2). Then it was on once again to **Greece** (the popular name for Achaia), greatly buoyed by Titus' most encouraging report on affairs in Corinth when they eventually met up, probably in Philippi (2 Cor. 7:5-16). The report probably caused Paul to write our canonical *2 Corinthians* in anticipation of his arrival in Corinth. He stayed **three months** in Asia, much of it we may presume in Corinth (3). He was not exactly idle there, as apart from all the pastoral, evangelistic and didactic work in and around that congregation, he wrote his great *Letter to the Romans* during this stay, committing it to the care of Phoebe (Rom. 16:1f.), who was headed for Rome. Paul's plan was now to sail straight back to Syria, and presum-

22. Marshall, 323.

23. cf. Bock, 617.

ably, among other things, make another report to his home base in Antioch; however **because the Jews made a plot against him just as he was about to sail, he decided to go back through Macedonia.**

Paul has by this stage developed a whole supporting cast of lieutenants, worthy souls who were attracted to him and whom he was training for future leadership. The list is impressive in its spread as well as its extent: **Sopater son of Pyrrhus from Berea, Aristarchus and Secundus from Thessalonica, Gaius from Derbe, Timothy also, and Tychicus and Trophimus from the province of Asia** (4). Somewhat surprisingly there is no mention either at this point, or elsewhere in Acts, of Titus. In a sense he represents the many 'unidentified others' who were very much part of the great enterprise and who contributed most surely to its success. This list is a reminder of Paul's missional foresight. Ministry in his mind never stopped with Paul; he himself was but a moment in a succession stretching back to God's plans and purposes through the Old Testament era, and stretching beckoningly on into the future, and for which he needed to plan and prepare beyond his own allotted span of service.

Paul sends his support group **ahead** from Philippi **to Troas** and rejoins them five days later, having in the interval shared in the **Feast of Unleavened Bread** (6), an indication that he continued to observe Jewish feasts, though with new Christian content. As Marshall suggests, 'He was probably celebrating the Christian Passover, i.e. Easter, with the church at Philippi.'[24] We notice the return at this point of the plural subject: **we** (6). Luke, as we earlier noted a likely native of Philippi, has rejoined the party.

This marks the beginning of Paul's final, and in terms of its implications, momentous journey to Jerusalem. It is described in considerable detail, which no doubt to some extent reflects Luke's presence in the company; however many have noted in addition the parallel which Luke appears to draw between this journey to the Holy City of the apostle Paul recorded in Acts, with the final jour-

---

24. Marshall, 325.

ney of Jesus to Jerusalem as recorded in his Gospel. Stott summarizes the points of parallel, which, though 'far from exact', he sees as 'too close to be a coincidence'.[25] He identifies six points of correspondence: (1) Both travelled to Jerusalem with a group of disciples. (2) Both are opposed by hostile Jews who plot against their lives. (3) Both make passion predictions on the journey, including their being handed over to the Gentiles. (4) Both declare a readiness to lay down their lives. (5) Both declare their determination to complete their ministry. (6) Both express abandonment to the will of God.

The entire Christian company comprising the local Christians and the visitors assemble at Troas **to break bread** (7), the earliest Christian name for the Lord's Supper (2:42, 1 Cor. 10:16). They do this **on the first day of the week** which is 'the earliest unambiguous evidence we have for the Christian practice of gathering together on that day.'[26] Paul preaches, and since in his mind this may well be his last opportunity to address them (cf. vv. 25, 38), he speaks at length, **until midnight**.

There follows an evidently eye-witness account of an interruption created by the hapless **Eutychus**. This **young man** (the word implies a youth between 8 and 14 years old) finds a vantage point in the obviously crowded third-storey meeting room, **seated** on the sill of an open **window** (9). One cannot but reflect on the countless multitude in every generation, right up to the present (including serried ranks of New Testament scholars!), who would have gladly emptied all their savings accounts, and even gone into debt for the rest of their lives, if they could have purchased Eutychus' seat in the house that Sunday evening! But…he falls asleep!! Luke perceptively describes his progressive loss of consciousness. Eutychus becomes drowsy, **sinking into a deep sleep**, and then falls into a **sound asleep**, and finally, by now effectively unconscious, **as Paul talked on and on**, falls out of the window all the

---

25. Stott, 315.
26. Bruce, 407.

way down to the ground below, where he **was picked up dead** (9).

The deep humanness of this incident has commended it to the Christian consciousness over the years. We need to be clear that Eutychus was killed by the fall, which is what Luke clearly asserts; **picked up dead** means exactly that. Paul's exclamation, **Don't be alarmed, he's alive!** does not mean he was never really dead, but rather – 'he's alive again!' 'A real raising of the dead is meant.'[27] Luke is present, quite possibly a medical man, but even if not, the ability to determine death was widespread enough in the first century, as it is today in the less developed parts of the world. In these cultures, corpses are commonplace. It is only in modern Western cultures that people are 'screened' from its stark reality. This simple social fact also clearly weighs, along with numerous other much more substantial considerations, against the claim in the Koran, and other critics of the resurrection, that Jesus was not truly dead when taken down from the cross.

Paul, alerted to the tragedy, hurries below, and proceeds to **throw himself on the young man**, i.e. to 'fall all over' him (8:16; 10:44, the same verb, *epipipto*; cf. 1 Kings 17:21; 2 Kings 4:34f.), **and put his arms around him** (10). Eutychus is miraculously resuscitated. So, a happy ending – **the people took the young man home alive and were greatly comforted** (12). This provides a natural break in Paul's message and so **they broke bread** at this point **and ate** a fellowship meal.

Paul, no whit discouraged, went on **talking until daylight** (11) (though one may presume that from this point on the window-sill seats would have remained vacant!). If the 'breaking of bread' here implies, as many suggest, an early celebration of the Lord's Supper – and we can recall Paul's claim in 1 Corinthians 11:23-26, written some time before these events, that he had 'received from the Lord' the theological basis and form of administration of the Supper – then this surely represents a fitting climax to Paul's ministry in Macedonia, Asia and Achaia. This

27. Conzleman: 169.

diverse family of believers in the Lord Jesus Christ, as they remember Him and His death in the bread and wine, and by faith commune anew with Him, the Risen One, are representatives of the fruit of Paul's missional endeavours over the last decade. It is profoundly appropriate that they should take their leave of one another thus – beneath the cross.

The magnitude of the achievement of these years is well summarized by Merrill Tenney: 'In little less than a decade Paul had won the freedom of the Gentile believers from the yoke of legalism. He had built a strong chain of churches from Antioch of Syria and Tarsus of Cilicia straight across southern Asia Minor to Ephesus and Troas, and thence through Macedonia and Achaia to Illyricum. He had chosen and trained companions like Luke, Timothy, Silas, Aristarchus, Titus and others, who were well qualified to maintain the work with him or without him. He had commenced an epistolary literature which already was regarded as a standard for faith and practice. In his preaching he had laid the groundwork for future Christian theology and apologetics, and by his plans he pursued a statesmanlike campaign of missionary evangelism. His plans for a trip to Rome and Spain showed that he wanted to match the imperial commonwealth with an imperial faith. Notwithstanding his bitter and active enemies, he had established the Gentile church upon a firm foundation and had already formulated the essence of Christian theology as the Spirit of God revealed it to him.'[28]

The sights are now clearly set on Jerusalem, for Paul **was in a hurry to reach Jerusalem, if possible, by the day of Pentecost** (16). The time between the Passover festival he had observed in Troas and the Pentecost celebration was, as it is today, fifty days. Reaching Jerusalem was do-able even by first-century shipping routes and timetables, but there was not a great margin for any diversions. The 'Jerusalem party' now engaged a series of short day-voyages, first **to Assos**, with Paul going across land **on foot**.

---

28. Merrill C. Tenney, *New Testament Survey* (Grand Rapids, 1961), 308.

We are not told why he chose this option, though Stott wonders if he was already sensing the crisis which awaited him back in Judea, and wanted the time alone to prepare his heart for what the journey would bring.[29] It is striking that in his address to the Ephesian elders he speaks of the Spirit already having begun to warn him 'in every city that prison and hardships are facing me' (23).

From Assos another 'leg' brought the entire party **to Mitylene**, then it was on again to **Kios**, then **to Samos**, and finally **they arrived at Miletus** (15). ' These short one-day trips from port to port are typical of ancient sea-trips.'[30] Miletus was only about thirty miles south of Ephesus and so the possibility of a final connection of some kind with the Ephesian church was naturally to be considered. **Paul had decided to sail past Ephesus to avoid spending time in the province of Asia** (16); a visit there might well detain him with congregational problems. However, there was the possibility of a meeting with the church's leaders, and so **he sent to Ephesus for the elders of the church** (17). It would have taken a messenger perhaps three days to get to Ephesus and bring the elders back to Miletus. **When they arrived** Paul addressed them.

3. Farewell to the Ephesian Elders (20:13-38)

What follows is a remarkable message of pastoral counsel and commission. Interestingly it is the only full account of an address to a Christian audience in Acts. It is Lukan in its written style, but the contents mesh very well with Paul's pastoral instruction in his New Testament letters. Those addressed are referred to variously as **elders** (= *presbtyeroi*, 17), **shepherds** (= pastors, 28), and **overseers** (= *episkopoi*, traditionally, bishops, 28). Whatever these titles imply they certainly rule out sole leadership responsibility, as well as hierarchical structures. Pauline leadership involves a team approach. The general temper is deeply serious and remarkably comprehensive. Overall the 'shepherding' function predominates; 'this is a pastoral

29. Stott, 322.

30. Bock, 621.

testament.'[31] Further, Paul could never be accused of 'decisionism'; 'Paul is concerned with more than evangelism. He seeks healthy churches.'[32] Leaders are key to realizing that goal.

The address can be variously subdivided. We will distinguish seven broad stages moving through it, but the pastoral spirit of the address binds all together and in some senses is more significant than any particular injunction.

1. *Paul's faithfulness* (18-21): Paul, both at the beginning, and again at the end (33-35) offers himself as a model. Critically however, it is a model of faithful service (Gk. *douleumon,* = the service of a bondslave): **you know how I lived the whole time I was with you, from the first day I came into the province of Asia. I served the Lord with great humility and with tears**. And just as critically it is service first of all of **the Lord** (19). Paul therefore establishes two primary qualities in Christian leadership: first, it is a leadership defined as *servant* leadership, hence leadership marked by **great humility**; second, it is a Christ-centred and Christ-exalting leadership, exercised in radical submission to Christ. That yieldedness to Christ is movingly and classically expressed by hymnwriter Frances Ridley Havergal: '...the being his very own; the serving him and pleasing him; the being utterly at his disposal; and with him, and in him, and all for him – on and on, through ages and ages of eternity...'[33] Further, these leadership fundamentals have been realized in face of **severe testing** (19) by Paul's Jewish opponents. So, a third quality is that of a leadership exercised not in a relaxed, secure setting, but resolutely pursued in the trenches of regular, ongoing conflict with opponents.

The other features in Paul's modelling belong to his actual practice of ministry. It has centred in a combination of **preaching** (20), the passionate, exhortatory form of communicating God's truth, and **teaching**, the more instructional, and perhaps interactive form. This

---

31. Schneider, 293.

32. Bock, 623.

33. Cited Gaius Davies, *Genius, Grief and Grace* (Christian Focus, 2001), 198.

'word-centred', 'truth-imparting' ministry has been comprehensive in its contents, covering **anything that would
be helpful**, and inclusive in its contexts, being carried out
both **in public**, and in the more intimate home setting,
from house to house. This last may imply some form of
systematic instruction of the entire congregation. 'Not sat-
isfied with general preaching he took pains to be of service
to individuals.' So notes Calvin, and applies this further:
'For Christ did not ordain pastors on the principle that
they only teach the Church in a general way on the public
platform, but that they also care for the individual sheep,
bring back the wandering and scattered to the fold, bind
up those who are broken and crippled, heal the sick, support the frail and weak.'[34]

Paul's ministry in Ephesus had also been comprehensive in its target audiences, addressing both Christians at
all stages as just indicated, and non-Christians among **both
Jews and Greeks** (21), calling both groups to an identical
response to God: **to turn to God in repentance and have
faith in our Lord Jesus**. This implies a comprehensiveness
also in conveying a message which, negatively, summoned
its hearers, without exception, to renounce their sin before
God, and positively, exhorting them to embrace by faith
the Lord Jesus Christ as their only hope of salvation, and
live henceforward to please Him as their Lord and Master.
We may appropriately hear from Richard Baxter: 'How
plainly, how closely and earnestly should we deliver a
message of such nature as ours is, when the everlasting
life or death of men and women is concerned in it...What!
Speak coldly for God and for people's salvation? Such a
work should be done with all our might – that people can
feel us preach when they hear us.'[35]

2. *Paul's plans* (22-24): Paul then shares his present
goals and constraints. He feels the **compulsion of the
Holy Spirit** to travel **to Jerusalem** (22), in the knowledge
that the **Spirit has** been **warning** him (23), presumably by
prophetic messages, perhaps in the general tenor of those

34. Calvin, II, 174-5.

35. Richard Baxter, *The Reformed Pastor*, 1655; (SCM, 1956), 97.

expressed at 21:4 and 21:10-11, **that prison and privations are facing him** (23). Indeed, if we may interject verse 25 at this point, Paul shares with them his conviction that his obedience to God's summons to Jerusalem will actually cost him his life, and hence **that none of you among whom I have gone about preaching the kingdom of God will ever see me again** (25).

Again Paul is a model of leadership: one in touch with God's direction of his life, and one who is ready to be obedient even when the results will be life-threatening and infinitely costly. However, and here Paul illustrates the 'servant leadership' of verse 19, he considers his life as **worth nothing** (24) to himself; that is, he is entirely expendable in God's service; his overriding goal being not to live long but to live well. That means living to the limit of God's will for him, by **finishing the race** marked out in advance for his life, that is, by **completing the task the Lord Jesus has given me – the task of testifying to the gospel of God's grace**. Once again leadership is linked to evangelism, a burning desire to direct lost people to the grace of God in Jesus Christ.

3. *Paul's resultant sense of innocence* (26-27): the reward of this faithfulness is a conscience which is free of guilt, one **innocent** (*katharos*= clean) **of the blood of all men** (26). Both 'innocent' and 'blood' are cultic terms and point to Paul's link between his service and his worship. cf. 'I am being poured out like a drink offering on the sacrifice and service coming from your faith' (Phil. 2:17). 'Paul likens his life-blood shed in death to the libation of wine or perfume poured out in the concluding rites of a sacrifice to a deity.'[36] (cf. also 2 Tim. 4:6.) 'Paul's ministry is an act of worship.'[37] Paul's sense of freedom from reproach is once more tied back to his teaching-preaching ministry. He refers again to its comprehensiveness; he has **not hesitated to proclaim to you the whole will of God** (27).

4. *The Leaders' Responsibilities* (28-31): Paul now addresses the Ephesian leaders directly concerning their responsibil-

---

36. R.P. Martin, *The Epistle of Paul to the Philippians* (Tyndale, 1959), 119.

37. Bock, 629.

ities and exhorts them in three regards. In general he calls for vigilance: this occurs both at the beginning and again at the end of this exhortatory section. **Keep watch** (28), and **Be on your guard!** (31). Paul is deeply concerned lest these leaders fail because they may lack continual watchfulness. The image of being on guard duty, which both imperative phrases reflect, is a powerful one in any time or culture. It obviously implies active enemies. Paul specifies who are to be the objects of their undistracted attention: two are identified.

First, they are to be on ever-watchful guard duty over **themselves** (28). Paul would later call Timothy to a similar vigilance: ' watch *your life* and doctrine closely' (1 Tim. 4:16). Murray McCheyne's often-quoted charge to a minister friend still resonates: 'Do not forget the culture of the heart. In great measure according to the purity and perfections of the instrument will be the success. It is not great talents God blesses so much as great likeness to Jesus. A holy minister is an awful weapon in the hand of God.'[38]

Second, they are to be on ever-watchful guard duty **over all the flock...the church of God**. Paul here employs an image which has strong Old Testament precedents, the leaders as **shepherds** caring for 'God's **flock, the church**' (Ps. 23:1-4; Ezek. 34:1-31). We note the comprehensiveness: *all* the congregation are to be the leaders' responsibility. Baxter speaks to us again: 'All the flock, even each individual member of our charge must be taken heed of and watched over...To which end it is necessary that we should know each person that belongs to our charge. For how can we take heed to them if we do not know them? We must labour to be acquainted with the state of all our people as fully as we can...what are the sins they are most in danger of, and what duties they neglect and what temptations they are most liable to. For if we know not their temperament and diseases we are likely to prove but unsuccessful physicians.'[39]

---

38. Andrew A. Bonar, *Memoir and Remains of Rev. Robert Murray McCheyne* (Oliphant, Anderson and Ferrier, 1892), 282. Reprinted, Banner of Truth, 1968.

39. Baxter, 50.

Paul indicates two weighty grounds for this vigilant watchfulness: (1) God the Holy Spirit has given them this responsibility, the congregation is the flock **of which the Holy Spirit has made you overseers**. Their appointment to their leadership responsibilities has been by the direct will of God the Spirit; hence they are directly accountable to him for fulfilling their calling. (2) The congregation are God's precious possession; so precious that He shed his blood for them: **the church of God which he bought with his own blood**.

Although this NIV rendering is a perfectly defensible translation of the Greek text here, the phrase 'blood of God' has no other New Testament occurrence. That the Father was personally present, to the very depth of His being, in the death of Jesus, by virtue of the hypostatic union of deity and humanity in Jesus' person is not in question; however this way of expressing that truth is unusual. One alternative is to understand the **his own** as a reference to Jesus, and hence **the church of God which he bought with the blood of his Own** = his own Son.[40]

Whichever translation is preferred the supreme consideration for the leaders to grasp here is the need to estimate the importance of their calling in the light of Calvary, which established for all time the value of God's church. Richard Baxter makes memorable application: 'Oh then, let us hear these arguments of Christ, when ever we feel ourselves grow dull and careless: "Did I die for them, and will you not look after them? Were they worth my blood, and are they not worth your labour? Did I come down from heaven to earth, to seek and to save that which was lost: and will you not go to the next door or street or village to seek them? Have I done and suffered so much for their salvation; and was I willing to make you my co-worker with me, and will you refuse that little that lies upon your hands?"'[41] This verse is 'one of two direct references to Jesus' sacrificial work in Luke-Acts'.[42]

---

40. This is supported by Bruce: 416; Marshall: 334; Stott: 327; cf. discussion, with alternatives, in M.J. Harris, *Jesus as God* (Baker, 1992), 132-41.

41. Baxter, 85.

42. Bock, 630.

Paul then underscores the importance of their unceasing watchfulness by developing the shepherding image a further stage, prophesying attacks from **savage wolves who will come in among you and will not spare the flock**. Indeed **even from your own number** (29-30) such men will arise. It is not clear whether Paul is here referring to some among the leaders themselves or, more probably, some from within the Ephesian congregation. These 'wolves' will be motivated by the self-promoting desire **to draw away disciples after them**. As Calvin adroitly observes, 'Ambition is the mother of all heresies.'[43] The means they will use to accomplish their destructive, preying ends will be **distorting the truth**. The verb here (*diestrammena*) means 'twist' the truth, so that it is no longer straight or true. These wolves still prowl. Paul closes this solemn charge by reminding them once again of his example, and by implication the quality of commitment he is pleading for; **remember that for three years I never stopped warning each of you night and day with tears** (31).

5. *The Leaders' Resources*: The demand just laid out is overwhelming, and so Paul immediately reminds them of the resources which are available to them: **I commit you to God and to the word of his grace** (32). The resource does not lie in the leaders themselves. In a profound sense fulfilling their responsibilities as Christian leaders is, quite simply, not a human possibility. So they are to cast themselves wholly on God; but that is all right – for He is sufficient. The resource in material terms lies in His **word**, that is, His self-revelation. For these leaders, there were the Old Testament Scriptures, and no doubt traditions of Jesus which would already have been circulating; early creedal formulae such as Ephesians 5:14, or even 1:3-14; or Philippians 2:5-11; or 1 Timothy 3:16; and additionally, of course, Paul's own apostolic teaching. That heaven-provided 'word of God' is the resource also when the wolves come sniffing around the flock, for 'All Scripture is God-

---

43. Calvin, II, 185.

breathed and is useful for teaching, rebuking, correcting and training in righteousness' (2 Tim. 3:16).[44]

That 'word' is a word of **grace**. It discloses a gracious God who would surely stoop to love and care for them, and for His people, and who will be their sufficiency in face of every challenge. As he would write to them later from his Roman prison, ' Unto him who is able to do immeasurably more than all we ask or imagine, according to his power which is at work within us. To him be glory...' (Eph. 3:20-21). The result of that dependence upon the gracious God is their being **built up** here, and their final **inheritance** hereafter, among those whom he has 'set apart to belong to him' (the force here of **sanctified**).

6. *The Leaders' Model*: As he concludes, Paul once again presents himself as a model – of a life of self-giving. This implies **not coveting** (33) material benefits such as **silver, gold or clothing**. It implies **hard work** so that they are not dependent on others unnecessarily, and also being thereby able to help the weak. This 'giving rather than receiving' lifestyle was expressed by **the Lord Jesus** who both lived, and taught: **It is more blessed to give than to receive** (35). This saying has been referred to, not unfairly, as 'the Ninth Beatitude'. 'It is one of the few places outside the gospels where Jesus is directly quoted.'[45]

7. *The Final Parting*: As Paul finally concludes, they, quite naturally, put themselves and all of the future into God's hands in prayer: **he knelt down with them all and prayed** (36). Their posture, kneeling, recalls Jesus' posture in Gethsemane. The Jewish tradition was to stand to pray (cf. Luke 18:11). Kneeling captures the solemnity and heart-yearning of the moment. Recognizing that this is a final farewell, as they recall his statement **that they would never see his face again, they all wept as they embraced and kissed him** (37-38). This last was culturally appropri-

---

44. 'It is simply a truism that there is nothing more important, more urgent, more helpful, more redemptive, and more salutary, there is nothing, from the viewpoint of heaven or earth, more relevant to the real situation than the speaking and hearing of the Word of God.' Karl Barth, *The Word of God and the Word of Man* (Hodder and Stoughton, 1928), 123.

45. Bock, 632.

ate. The Jewish Midrash taught that 'all kissing (in public) is indecent, with three exceptions: the kiss of high office, the kiss of reunion, and the kiss of parting.' We should note the emotion expressed. In some minds, Paul was not a very kissable man; but he was! **Then they accompanied him to the ship** (38).

It is perhaps appropriate to note the contrast between this parting and that recorded by Luke at the close of his Gospel with respect to Jesus and *His* disciples (Luke 24:50-53). There Jesus bids the disciples 'farewell' in similar circumstances: they too 'will never see his face again.' However, the mood is celebrative, even jubilant: 'they returned to Jerusalem with great joy and stayed continually at the temple praising God.' Why? Because…' I am with you always…I am ascending…I will come again.'

Study Questions:

1. 20:4-5 lists seven good men and true who accompanied Paul as he visited the churches of Macedonia. The spread of the churches they represented was the fruit of Paul's earlier years of ministry, and the promise of its future. Recall and give thanks for similar brothers and sisters in your own life, perhaps also in your case, from a variety of churches, who have accompanied and encouraged you as you have followed Christ.

2. Identify the elements of God's blessing shared during that memorable evening in Troas (20:7-11). Can you identify particularly with any of them in your own recent experience?

3. Paul's 'Farewell' to the elders at Ephesus is a deeply moving testament to pastoral ministry in every age (20:17-35). It covers many aspects of Christian leadership; notably, its essential character as service (20:18-19); its biblical base and content (20:20-21, 27); its submission to God, costliness and temporal limits (22-23); its pastoral charge, and grounds for diligence in fulfilling it

(28-31); its resources (32-35); and its unashamed loyalties (36-38). Review it carefully and prayerfully. Where do you find yourself most convicted of shortcoming? Where do you find yourself most encouraged? Where are our standards today most needing to be brought into line with Paul's here?

4. Journey to Jerusalem (21:1-16)

The leave-taking from Miletus was not easy; they needed to **tear themselves away** from the Ephesian brothers (1). One of Christianity's greatest glories is the bonding in Christ which happens, often in a comparatively short space of time, and often between those who were previously relative strangers, as we will note below at Caesarea. Here the ties had in many cases a solid history, and breaking them touched all the parties very deeply.

Paul's company now sail due south to **Cos**, then round the southern limit of Asia to **Rhodes,** and then on again, due east to **Patara** on the south coast of the province of Lycia (1). The account is cast again in the plural, '**we':** Luke is again in the party. At Patara they **found a ship crossing over to Phoenicia**, the sea-coast area between Syrian Antioch to the north and Judea to the south (2). Passing to the south of Cyprus the ship made land at **Tyre** (3).

This berthing for unloading cargo gave the party an opportunity to connect, and spend **seven days with, disciples they found there. Through the Spirit they urged Paul not to go on to Jerusalem** (4). We are not told how this message was discerned, though very probably one of the congregation there received what they understood as a prophetic message to that effect. Paul, however, retains his sense of God's direction to Jerusalem, and so **they continued on their way**. The passage here includes notes of a touching leave-taking, all the more impressive in view of the brevity of their contact, as **all the disciples including their wives and children accompanied us out of the city, and there on the beach we knelt to pray** (5). This surely is eye-witness writing.

With these touching farewells over, the company re-embarks, and after a stop further south at **Ptolemais**, and a time of fellowship with the church there, they finally disembark at **Caesarea** (8). Here they found hospitality with a leading disciple from a long way back, **Philip,** the companion of Stephen and one of the original **Group of Seven** appointed after Pentecost to take responsibility for an equitable food distribution in Jerusalem, and then so greatly used in Samaria, and later in Gaza (6:1-6; 8:4-40). It seems such a long time ago (actually some 25 years); so much has happened since; so much for which to thank God. Here we meet Philip's remarkable family, including **four unmarried daughters who prophesied** (9).

Some days later, another figure from the earlier history appears, **Agabus**, whose prophetic message some dozen years or so earlier, of the upcoming famine in Judea, had sourced the special offering at Antioch delivered to Jerusalem by Paul and Barnabas (11:27-30). Once again the Holy Spirit speaks through Agabus, this time in a piece of prophetic symbolism. 'In the Spirit' **he took Paul's belt, tied his own hands and feet with it and said, 'The Holy Spirit says, "In this way the Jews of Jerusalem will bind the owner of this belt and hand him over to the Gentiles"'** (11). Agabus' prophetic ministry clearly is deeply respected; on the last occasion mentioned in Acts, his oracle had been sufficient to spark a significant offering of money. Nor is he wrong on this occasion either, as events would fairly quickly prove. So, to no one's surprise, both those who had travelled with Paul, and the disciples there in Caesarea, **pleaded with Paul not to go up to Jerusalem** (12). Paul, however, is not to be deflected from his intention, **Why are you weeping and breaking my heart?** – clearly the apostle is deeply moved by the depth of this general concern for him, which even has people in tears of entreaty. However, he has already come to terms with the possibility of imprisonment, and worse: **I am ready not only to be bound, but also to die in Jerusalem for the name of the Lord Jesus** (13). Paul will simply not be held back from what he clearly and firmly believes is God's summons to the city. In the end the disciples come to accept it. **When he would not be dissuaded, we gave up and said, The Lord's will be done'** (14).

So, final preparations were made and **they went up to Jerusalem** accompanied by **some of the Caesareans** who **brought them to the home of Mnason where they were to stay** (16). **Mnason** hailed from Cyprus and **was one of the early disciples**, a believer of long standing, possibly even from Pentecost. Bruce sees him as a member of the Hellenistic wing of the Jerusalem church and hence an appropriate host for a party which included Gentiles.[46] His memories, which would have reached all the way back to the church's beginnings, might well have supplied Luke with further material on the 'early' days.

In reflecting on this section, we face the important and yet often perplexing issue of how to discern the will of God. The Holy Spirit through the sincere ministry of prophetic persons correctly puts before Paul what will befall him if he goes to Jerusalem; however Paul himself does not interpret this as a prohibition by the Spirit, but only as a warning. He therefore does not change what he has already discerned as God's will, viz. that he go to Jerusalem and face whatever awaits him there. 'The interaction between the believers and Paul about whether he should face suffering is significant because it shows that sometimes well-intentioned people can be wrong about what God desires. There is no doubt that those who warn Paul have his best interests at heart and are trying to protect him. It also is clear, however, that Paul has a real sense of what God is calling him to do, and that he has prepared himself to pay the human price to do it. What is so instructive about the scene is that once it becomes clear that Paul is being driven by the Spirit to face what is ahead, the believers who love him and God's will embrace the path and support him.'[47]

Study Questions:

1. In Tyre (21:5), as earlier at Miletus (20:37-38), there is a clear impression of deep emotion expressed

---

46. Bruce, 426.

47. Bock, 639.

around Paul and the prospect of his impending
death. Reflect on the way fellowship in Christ
evokes deep mutual commitment (cf. 1 John 3:14).
Have you shared such experiences? What might
be other equivalents to the embraces and kisses at
Troas? Are there brothers or sisters for whom you
are needing, in one of these ways, to show your
love for?

2. What do we learn about discerning God's will in
   21:10–14? In what ways is Paul a good model for
   us in these verses?

11

Paul the Prisoner: Rome at Last!
(Acts 21:17–28:31)

B. 'Paul the Prisoner: Rome at Last!' (21:17–28:31)

1. Riot and Arrest in Jerusalem (21:17-40)

The party now meets with the Jerusalem congregation. They are **received warmly** (17). The following day they meet with the Jerusalem leaders, **James and all the elders** (18). This may have been a semi-formal occasion. Bruce suggests that in view of the size of the Jerusalem Christian community there may have been seventy elders comprising a sort of 'Nazarene Sanhedrin'.[1]

Paul **reported in detail**, bringing them up to date on all that has happened in his own ministry, and the Gentile movement generally, since the Consultation (19). The response is again apparently very positive: **when they heard this, they praised God.** Luke makes no reference here (or earlier) to the offering levied by Paul from the Gentile churches, which he must have delivered on arrival, as he clearly states during his trial before Felix (24:17). This is frankly surprising, granted both its substantial nature and the significance attached by Paul to this offering, literally a 'peace offering' (Rom. 15:25f.; 1 Cor. 16:1f.; 2 Cor. 8–9) and, certainly in the terms he writes about it

---

1. Bruce, 429.

to the Romans, a primary reason for his travelling to Jerusalem in the first instance (cf. Rom. 15:25f.). Evidently its being received does not loom large as part of their 'welcome'. Witherington may well be right in suggesting that it met with a mixed response due to the deep underlying anxieties in Jerusalem about the Gentile mission.[2] These anxieties now come clearly to the surface as the Jerusalem leaders address Paul, **then they said**... (20-25).

It is a fairly long speech and leaves us in no doubt about the strains in the relationships between the two wings of the church at this point, a tension which may well be being influenced by events beyond the church's own experience. The date can be established with considerable confidence as A.D. 57, a point when Jerusalem was tense with a rising Jewish nationalism and political unrest, and the presence in Rome of a Palestinian Procurator, Felix, described by Tacitus as having 'the instincts of a slave'. This was accordingly no time for overtures towards Gentiles. The church was caught in the middle of this, and the presence of these political tensions probably goes a long way to explain both the irrationality and the depth of the violence shortly to be perpetrated on Paul. At this precise point the entire Gentile mission would probably have been viewed by the average Jerusalem citizen as highly suspicious. To describe Jerusalem at this moment as a powder keg waiting to explode would probably overstate, but the potential for violent emotion was certainly fermenting. Luke is probably very aware of all this and handles it perceptively in his account. It is in general a reminder that the church is always 'in the world', set there by and under the hand of God, and hence vulnerable to impacts from the rise and fall of wider forces in the surrounding culture.

The elders make two points, and offer a proposal. First, they tell Paul, whom they affectionately address as **brother**, of the continuing work of God among the Jewish and Jerusalem populace. It now has grown to **many thousands who believe** (20). 'Probably hyperbole for a significant response', but understandable in the circum-

---

stances[3] ('evangelistic counting' was no doubt known in the first century also). These disciples however have their continuing Jewish religious loyalty; specifically, they are in general **zealous for the law.**

Second, these Jewish, law-embracing believers have been given a very negative view of Paul personally, and of his work among the Gentiles. They have been informed that he teaches not just that Gentiles are not to keep the law – that was the issue resolved at the Consultation, and the elders are clearly not wishing to reopen that, as they will confirm in closing (v. 25). Rather, and here is the issue – Paul is believed to be teaching *all the Jews* who come to faith in the Gentile lands that *they too* should **turn away from Moses, not circumcise their children, or live according to our customs** (21). These Jerusalem believers **will certainly hear that you have come, so what shall we do?**

The elders have a proposal which they now lay before Paul. Before coming to the proposal, it needs to be kept in mind that there is another much larger reality in the background – the attitudes towards Paul and his mission held by the city's Jewish population at large, estimated at this time at between 30,000 and 50,000. If the believers have been misinformed about Paul's work, one can assume that the misrepresentations are much deeper in their case, a fact which will be emphatically proved in the following days.

The proposal in essence is an invitation to Paul to demonstrate to everyone that while an 'apostle to the Gentiles' he remains at heart a loyal Jew who upholds the observance of Jewish customs by Jewish believers in Messiah-Jesus. So, **there are four men with us** (i.e. believers) **who have made a vow** (actually not unlike Paul himself, 18:18). **Take these men, join in their purification rites and pay their expenses, so that they can have their heads shaved.** As a result **everybody will know that there is no truth in the reports about you, but that you yourself are living in obedience to the law** (23-24). The elders conclude by recognizing, as we noted, that the case of Gentile believ-

---

3. Bock, 646.

ers remains as agreed at **our decision** at the Consultation, their observing the 'Jerusalem Quadrilateral', which they rehearse (25).

Paul agrees to their proposal. **The next day Paul took the men and purified himself along with them. Then he went to the temple to give notice of the date when the days of purification would end and the offering would be made for each of them** (including himself) (26).

What exactly was this vow, and what are the implications of the fact that Paul agreed to their proposal? The first question can only be tentatively answered, so while we will lay out three proposed possibilities Bock's observation needs to be kept in mind: 'We simply lack enough detail and Luke's account is so compact that we cannot know which scenario is correct.'[4] The proposed answers are:

(1) The vow is to restore purity to Paul due to his having become 'unclean' as a result of his travels in Gentile territories. The men's vow is a Nazirite vow (thirty days) now nearing completion. Paul will join them for the final days and their shaving of hair.[5]

(2) The men are embarked on a Nazirite vow but have contracted some impurity during its course and require the wait of a further seven days before having their heads shaved and then making a final offering. Paul joins them for the final stages.[6]

(3) Paul's cleansing is not for his having been in Gentile territory but as a completion of the vow he himself had initiated at Cenchrea (18:18). The men are either themselves from overseas and needing cleansing, or are completing a Nazirite vow.[7]

The second question is more important: what are the implications of Paul's having agreed to participate in this act of purification? Bock comments: 'What we see here

---

4. Bock, 648.

5. So Larkin, 308-9; Fitzmeyer, 694: Schneider, 310, and with some modification, Haenchen, 610.

6. So Bruce, 407.

7. So Jervell, 526.

is Paul being asked to act with cultural sensitivity to the Jewish context he now finds himself in, without compromising the gospel. He is quite willing to do so for the sake of the unity it may create...Paul sensed that James' proposal made sense, so he willingly restricted his freedom. Liberty is a great thing but the expression of liberty can be counter-productive.'[8] Stott notes the 'generosity of spirit' shown by James and Paul here. He adds, 'they were already agreed doctrinally (that salvation was by grace in Christ through faith), and ethically (that Christians must obey the moral law). The issue between them concerned culture, ceremony and tradition. The solution they came to was not a compromise, in the sense of sacrificing a doctrinal or moral principle, but a concession in the area of practice.'[9] In ministry or social situations, we may at times be invited to share in morally neutral, cultural practices which can, as for Paul here, clear away barriers to our sharing the gospel, especially when, again like Paul here, we are visitors to an area. Several of the commentators cite a remark of Bruce: 'A truly emancipated spirit like Paul is not in bondage to its own emancipation.'[10]

However appropriate and meaningful to the 'believers' among the Jewish community Paul's response was, it all went terribly wrong. **When the seven days were nearly over** (better, 'when the seven days were going to be fulfilled', i.e. at the beginning of the week), **some Jews from the province of Asia saw Paul at the temple. They stirred up the crowd and seized him, shouting, 'Men of Israel, help us! This is the man who teaches all men everywhere against our people and our law and this place. And besides, he has brought Greeks into the temple area and defiled our holy place'** (27-28).

It is perhaps not altogether surprising to find Asian Jews as the instigators of the violence directed at Paul when we recall their reactions at Pisidian Antioch, Iconium and Lystra, and more recently, at Ephesus. The accusations

---

8. Bock, 648.

9. Stott, 342.

10. Bruce, 432, fn 39.

they hurl at Paul are a half-truth in the first case, and a plain lie in the second. **All men everywhere** is of course gross exaggeration, though this kind of context is not the forum for verbal precision. **Speaking against the people of Israel, the law and the temple** has echoes of what Stephen had been charged with years before (6:11-14). The half-truth is that with the coming of Jesus and His ministry the people, law and temple are necessarily taken to a new place, in that Jesus is the Promised One of Israel and the fulfiller of the law and the temple in His person. The law cannot offer salvation, and the temple sacrifices are fulfilled in Jesus' self-offering.

The second accusation is totally false. Paul had not violated the solemn prohibition of Gentiles being within the sacred inner area of the temple, the Court of Israel. This sacredness was indicated by an enclosing wall which bore the inscriptions (two of which have been excavated), 'No foreigner may enter within the barrier which surrounds the temple and this enclosure. Anyone who is caught doing so will have himself to blame for his ensuing death.' Paul had faithfully observed that stipulation. As Luke explains, **They had previously seen Trophimus the Ephesian in the city with Paul and assumed that Paul had brought him into the temple area** (29). The accusation, however, is immediately believed and Paul is mobbed in the temple, as **people came running from all directions** (30).

Ominously, they **drag** Paul **from the temple**, which may mean their taking Paul out of the sacred inner courts area into the outer courts since murder committed within the former would be a serious violation; the crowd by now clearly has murder in its mind; **they were trying to kill him** (31). Happily for the apostle, the Roman garrison in the city is quartered beside the temple in the Fortress of Antonia, where the commander is quickly informed **that the whole city of Jerusalem was in an uproar.** The commander is named Claudius Lysias, as we will learn later (23:26), and he **at once took some officers and soldiers and ran down to the crowd** (32). The reference to 'down' is due to the elevation of the fortress above the city level; we note the reference at verse 40 to the 'steps'. The effect is immediate, and saves Paul. **When the rioters saw the commander and his soldiers, they stopped beating Paul.**

Paul is **arrested and bound by two chains**, handcuffed in other words (33). The commander was perhaps hoping thereby to attain some sense of satisfaction for the crowd. He then tries to interrogate Paul, asking **who he was and what he had done.** This proves impossible **as some in the crowd shouted one thing and some another** (34). The truth is that there probably would have been no consensus in the crowd in any event as to who Paul was or why there was cause for his death. The commander then wisely decides to remove Paul and have him **taken into the barracks.** This proves no easy manoeuvre as the crowd are still massing and in violent mood. The soldiers eventually have to lift Paul bodily and **carry** him into the barracks. The crowd follow as far as they can, shouting all the while, *'aire auton!'* **Away with him!** (36). This was the identical cry that had echoed out across the city some thirty years before (Luke 23:18; John 19:15).

This section marks a major point of transition in Luke's account. Paul is now 'Paul the prisoner', and will continue to be so through the remainder of the narrative. In the process, he will carry his witness to Jesus Christ to Rome, the heart of the civilized world. In the course of that journey and its conclusion, his story will round out Luke's presentation of the church fulfilling its calling as Christ's witnesses 'to the ends of the earth'. In keeping with Luke's fundamental orientation (1:1), the church is therefore exhibited as the medium through which the Risen Lord continues 'to do and to teach' what He had commenced during the story Luke had previously told in his Gospel. Paul will also appear over the remaining chapters as a faithful witness, accepting his lot as a prisoner 'in chains for Christ' (Phil. 1:13), though whenever possible eloquently arguing his case within the Roman legal system. At the same time Paul will bear faithful witness to the gospel, refusing to take initiatives to escape, but waiting patiently for the Lord's sovereign direction of his affairs and circumstances. Paul courageously accepts the path of unjust suffering, in the footsteps of Jesus, and thus enhances the cause of Christ and commends the gospel to readers who may not yet be committed to his Lord.

As they are making their way into the barracks, Paul recovers sufficiently to ask the commander for a moment of his attention, **May I say something to you?** (37). The commander is immediately alerted, surprised by Paul's Greek fluency. Since Greek was widely spoken in Egypt, as well as being the lingua franca of the age, the commander now believes Paul to be a particular 'wanted' person he knows of: **Aren't you the Egyptian who started a revolt and led four thousand terrorists out into the desert some time ago?** (38). The commander is referring to an Egyptian false prophet who some three years previously had led an 'army' of 30,000 (according to Josephus, whose numbers are unreliable; cf. Luke's, and the commander's, **4,000**). He had brought them to the Mount of Olives with the promise that at his command the walls of the city would fall flat and allow them to take the city from the Romans. His men were killed or captured but the prophet himself had made his escape.

Paul corrects the commander's impression by identifying himself; he is no Egyptian revolutionary, rather **I am a Jew from Tarsus, a citizen of no ordinary city** (39). By this identification, and his place of origin not least, Paul is distancing himself from the kind of mindset and activities reflected by the commander's 'wanted' Egyptian. Tarsus was an illustrious home-town, 'the first city of Cilicia and one of the great university cities of the Roman world.'[11] Paul then requests an opportunity to make a public defence, **Please let me speak to the people**. The commander has by now radically revised his estimate of Paul and gives him **permission** (40).

Study Questions:

1. Consider Paul's flexibility on 'secondary matters' as exemplified in 21:23-26, and relate this to his statement of principle in 1 Corinthians 9:19–23. How is this 'principled flexibility' to be applied?

---

11. Sherwin-White, 180.

Can you offer examples of 'becoming all things... in order to save some'?

2. Paul is the victim of deep injustice and unwarranted hatred in this section (21:27-30). Are we prepared for this in our service for Christ?

3. God uses Roman military power to save Paul from being killed by the Jerusalem mob (21:32-34). What encouraging truth about God does this illustrate?

2. Paul's Defence before the Jerusalem Crowd (22:1-30)

So Paul stood on the steps and motioned to the crowd. When they were all silent he said to them in Aramaic: Brothers and fathers, listen now to my defence. (1)

This is the first of five Pauline 'apologies' which dot the final quarter of Acts. Though in most cases they are, necessarily, only summaries of his presentations, each one has its own emphases and each is suited to the particular setting and the specific audience being addressed. In general they contradict any lingering suspicion that Paul is anyone other than a sincere follower of Jesus Christ, or that the movement he represents is in any important sense a direct threat, either to the integrity of the Judaistic state, or to the Roman empire and its rule.

He begins with a polite address, **Brothers and fathers**; this to an audience which moments before had been energetically setting about killing him. **When they heard him speak to them in Aramaic they became very quiet** (2). Both these features underline Paul's great sensitivity. On the language choice, Bruce observes: 'If an audience of Welsh or Irish nationalists, about to be addressed by someone whom they regarded as a traitor to the national cause, suddenly realized that he was speaking to them, not in the despised Saxon tongue, but in the Celtic vernacular, the gesture would no doubt call forth at least a temporary measure of goodwill.' [12]

---

12. Bruce, 439.

We will follow Bock's helpful outline of the address which identifies three parts, each of which can be usefully focused in a phrase from their contents: ' I was where you are' (vv. 3-5); ' I was called by God' (vv. 6-14); ' I was called to be a witness to the nations' (vv. 15-21).

I was where you are (3-5)
Paul shares his personal upbringing within the strict standards of Judaism, leading to his active persecution of the Nazarenes. He mentions seven particulars: (1) **I am a Jew.** (2) I am from the cultured city **of Tarsus.** (3) **I was brought up** here **in** holy **Jerusalem.** (4) I was a student of the revered **Gamaliel** and **thoroughly trained in the law of our fathers.** (5) I was **as zealous** (*zelotes*) **for God as any of you are.** (6) **I persecuted the followers of the Way to the death, arresting both men and women and throwing them into prison (as the high priest and all the Sanhedrin can testify). (7) I even obtained letters from them to their brothers in Damascus, and went there to bring these people to Jerusalem as prisoners.**

I was called by God (6-14)
Then, **near Damascus,** God confronted me: **suddenly a bright light flashed around me. I fell to the ground, I heard a voice: 'Saul! Saul! Why do you persecute me?'** I asked, **'Who are you, Lord?' 'I am Jesus of Nazareth, whom you are persecuting.' My companions saw the light but did not understand the voice.** I asked, **'What shall I do Lord?'** I was told, **'Get up and go into Damascus. There you will be told all that has been assigned to you to do.' I was blinded and led by the hand into Damascus. There a man named Ananias, a devout and respected observer of the law, came to see me. He stood beside me and said, 'Brother Saul, receive your sight', and I was able to see him. Then he said, 'The God of our fathers has chosen you to see the Righteous One and to hear words from his mouth.'**

On Paul's falling to the ground, Calvin notes: 'As Paul was puffed up with pharisaic pride it was fitting for him to be thrown to the ground, and, as it were, deflated, so that he might hear Christ's voice.'[13] The title used for Jesus, the Righteous One, underlines His exalted position and His innocence; we recall, with respect to the latter, that Paul is here addressing some who could well have been in the Jerusalem crowd that had howled for Jesus' crucifixion. It was also a Messianic title (3:14; 7:52).

We note also the reference to God as **the God of our fathers**. Paul emphasizes that this Way is no innovation but precisely the longed-for fulfilment of the faith of their fathers. It therefore is not opposed to Judaism, or even intent on leaving it behind, but actually carries it forward to its glorious and promised climax.

I was called to be a witness to the nations (15-21)
Paul's calling is to **be his witness to all men of what you have seen and heard.** His calling meshes precisely with Christ's commission of the church in general (1:8). He was then asked: **what are you waiting for? Get, up, be baptized and wash away your sins, calling on his name**. This both seals his response to the divine revelation expressed in his meeting with the glorified Jesus, and also binds him to the community of faith, here in Damascus and increasingly, all over the world. Then, at a later point, **Paul returned to Jerusalem and was praying in the temple when he fell into a trance and saw the Lord speaking. 'Quick! Leave Jerusalem immediately, because they will not accept your testimony about me.'**

We note that Paul identifies with the temple here as a place where God is met, and he appears as a devout Jew, praying there. 'The Lord' here is apparently Jesus, and hence carries pointers to His deity. Paul resisted the need to leave Jerusalem on the grounds that his history of anti-Christian persecution was well-known to the authorities: **These men know that I went from one synagogue to another to imprison and beat those who believe in you. And when the blood of your martyr Stephen was shed, I stood there giving my approval and guarding the clothes of those who were killing him.**

---

13. Calvin, II, 214.

The Lord replied, **Go, I will send you to the Gentiles**. This command with its emphatic 'I', the personal *se* (you), and the verb *apostello* ('send'), could almost be rendered, 'I myself apostle you' or 'I myself make you an apostle'.

This has clear echoes of the moment of commissioning of the disciples in the Upper Room as recorded by John (20:21): 'As the Father has sent me, I am sending you.' The linkage back to the sending of the Son in the Johannine format underlines both the solemnity of the moment, and its ultimate character, as it links these apostolic 'commissionings' with the finality and mystery of the divine 'commissioning' within the Godhead. Paul is here claiming nothing less than that his ministry as the apostle to the Gentiles is an ultimate reality concerning which he had no choice, and the ongoing of which belongs within the eternal purpose of God in and for the world.

Paul in this address establishes his claim to be a loyal Jew. The new features of his faith, his knowledge of, and relationship to Jesus, and his entire ministry to the Gentile world, were not the product of his own eccentric notions, nor in any sense his personal initiative, but directly attributable to God's sovereign initiative and personal revelation (and confirmed by the fact of Christ's resurrection). Nothing less could have explained his transformation from fanatical persecutor to committed follower.

The reaction to these stated claims, however, is less than rapturous. Having thus far listened attentively, at the very mention of **Gentiles** the crowd erupts. **Then they raised their voices and shouted, 'Rid the earth of him! He's not fit to live!',** words which they embody in action by **throwing off their cloaks and throwing dust in the air**. Bruce fairly notes, 'it was as well for Paul and his captors that loose stones were not lying conveniently about the court.'[14] The trigger word, 'Gentiles', apparently confirmed all their worst fears, and also surfaced a visceral sense of violation, even blasphemy. In this moment there is memorably and fearfully framed the dark side of religiously-rooted, irrationally-intolerant nationalism.

---

14. Bruce, 439.

Paul is immediately withdrawn **into the barracks** (24). The commander, having no Aramaic, could only judge the address by its closing effect, and his more negative impression of Paul is restored. He needs to learn more about him and in particular **why the people were shouting at him like this**, so he **directed that Paul be flogged**, the normal Roman (and not only Roman!) means of eliciting information from suspects. The commander, having given the order, withdraws, leaving the preparation for the flogging to one of his attendant centurions (25).

This flagellation, the so-called *flagellatio*, represented a far worse physical beating than either a Jewish 'forty strokes less one' or the Roman caning at Philippi. The whip was cruelly studded with pieces of bone and metal, was even known to cause death, and its victim 'would certainly be crippled for life'.[15] Not surprisingly Paul senses that the moment has come to disclose his Roman credentials, and hence the entire illegality of this procedure in his case. He asks **the centurion, 'Is it legal for you to flog a Roman citizen who hasn't even been found guilty?'** The implied answer is of course 'certainly not!' Cicero wrote: 'To bind a Roman citizen is a crime, to flog him an abomination.' Immediately recognizing the significance of this information, the centurion **went to the commander and reported it**, bringing the commander in turn to Paul's side with his own question: **Tell me, are you a Roman citizen?** (27). Paul affirms it: **Yes I am**. This leads the commander to declare his own route to this privileged status, **I had to pay a big price for my citizenship** (28). Bruce suggests that since Paul does not cut a particularly noble figure at that point, with the marks of his near lynching still on him, the commander is provoked to comment, **It cost *me* a very large sum of money...**, the 'I' or 'me', should be accented: 'the implication being that the privilege must have become cheap of late if such a sorry-looking figure as Paul could claim it.'[16]

The commander had probably obtained his citizenship with a bribe, an apparently not uncommon practice during

---

15. Bruce, 445.

16. Bruce, 446.

Claudius' reign. Paul's citizenship, however, had been received from his father, probably for some conspicuous service to Rome. There is a clear indication here of some possibly illustrious heritage in Paul's case; tantalizingly, we have no other information to sustain or expand it. The surfacing of Paul's Roman citizenship, however, has an immediate effect; the commander must have been simultaneously both deeply **alarmed** and deeply relieved. To have submitted a Roman citizen to being heavily **chained** and then examined without trial by the *flagellatio* could have had serious repercussions for him (29).

Here we see, as we will regularly over the next chapters, Paul the Roman citizen using the shelter of imperial law, one of the supreme glories of the empire, and one of its most significant legacies to later civilization (despite, paradoxically, its having been party to the condemnation of the one perfectly innocent prisoner in all of history!). Paul uses it to support his innocence of the charges laid against him by the Jews, and also to obtain opportunities to continue to witness to the resurrection and lordship of Jesus, and the truth of the gospel. In the larger political picture, Paul will demonstrate that Christianity does not represent a threat to the Roman peace. This latter feature is sufficiently marked, in these final chapters in particular, that it has led some to see here the primary purpose of the book of Acts (cf. 'The Purpose of Acts' in the following appendices). This does not carry conviction; the primary purpose, as we have seen repeatedly, lies in Acts' affirmation of the glorifying of God through global mission. However there is certainly evidence that Luke saw this political reality as a significant secondary purpose, and one having particular significance in relating the story of the rise of Christianity to the un-churched reader.

Requiring to satisfy his need to understand **why Paul was being accused by the Jews**, the commander released him from formal arrest though he kept Paul in custody, and the following day convened a hearing to which **he summoned the chief priests and all the Sanhedrin. Then he brought Paul and had him stand before them** (30).

Study Questions:

1. What can we learn from Paul's using Aramaic in addressing the Jerusalem mob (22:2), and his addressing them as 'brothers and fathers' (22:1)?

2. In his account of his encounter with the Risen Jesus outside Damascus, Paul refers to the two questions he addressed to the Lord, viz. 'Who are you?' (22:8) and 'What do you want me to do?' (22:10) – if you like, the 'who' question, and the 'what' question. Notice the order in which the questions were asked. Is it true, as Dietrich Bonhoeffer suggests, that we cannot really put the 'what' question correctly until we have answered the 'who' question? Put another way, until we have seen something of the glory of Christ we cannot truly serve Him; worship must precede ministry and witness. How does this principle relate to your life today and tomorrow? How does it relate to the life of your church?

3. In 22:20 Paul refers to his having given approval, more than twenty years earlier, to the death of Stephen. This reminds us of the timeless quality of Stephen's faithful witness. Can you recall similar acts of faithfulness which may have brought you, or someone known to you, to faith years after they were expressed? How does this truth encourage us?

4. Consider Paul's appeal to his Roman citizenship at this point (22:25-29). What does his use of his political rights have to say to us today? What may have been Paul's motive for leaving this appeal to this point in the proceedings? Why, conceivably, did he not make use of this right when arrested and whipped at Philippi (16:22-23)?

3. Before the Sanhedrin (23:1-11)

Marshall informs us concerning 23:1–11 that 'there is scarcely a passage in Acts whose historicity has been so strongly questioned.'[17] Three particular objections have been raised. The first concerns the commander's ability to convene a session of the Sanhedrin. The second is Paul's use of the Greek form of his quotation from Exodus 22:28 in verse 5. Thirdly, it is claimed that the essential issue which had sparked this whole chain of events was the temple, and Paul's alleged desecration of it, not the resurrection, as reported here.

Barrett, among others, has defended Luke on all three points. First, this is not a regular session of the Council but an *ad hoc* meeting to enable the Romans to decide what to do with Paul; consequently the rationale for the meeting makes perfectly good sense. Second, the Greek version of Exodus 22:28 is verbally very close to the Hebrew version. Third, Paul's purpose in the proceedings was to get the commander to understand that the issue between himself and the Jews was essentially a religious one and hence not Rome's concern.[18]

The fact that the proceedings are begun with a statement by Paul and not, as we would have expected, with the Sanhedrin's laying of charges against him, plus the fact that they do not lay them at any later point in the scene as described, tends to vindicate Marshall's contention that Luke has significantly abbreviated the account, concentrating essentially on Paul's response. The reader already knows what concerned the Jews with respect to Paul (21:28), and these concerns will be repeated again in 24:5f.

So, Paul looked straight at the Sanhedrin and said, 'My brothers, I have fulfilled my duty to God in all good conscience to this day.' (1). This claim enrages the chairing **high priest, Ananias, who ordered those standing near Paul to strike him on the mouth** (2). Implicit in this claim was that Paul remained, as a disciple of Jesus-Messiah, a faithful, law-respecting Jew. Ananias presumably saw this as a blatant lie, even blasphemy.

This outburst, and his resort to violence, was not out of keeping with what is otherwise known of Ananias' char-

17. Marshall, 360.

18. Barrett, 1054-5; also Bock, 667-8.

acter. His avarice was proverbial and Josephus refers to his insolence and quick temper. Paul's response, **God will strike you, you whitewashed wall! You sit there to judge me according to the law, yet you yourself violate the law by commanding that I be struck!** (3), has, not surprisingly, evoked a considerable variety of interpretations. Paul's latter claim, concerning the injustice of his being struck as a person whose guilt has not yet been either demonstrated or ratified, is perfectly defensible. The earlier part of his statement has, however, proved more controversial. We may note first the reaction of at least some of those present: **You dare to insult God's high priest?**, eliciting Paul's further riposte, **Brothers, I did not realize that he was the high priest; for it is written: 'Do not speak evil about the ruler of your people'** (5).

Marshall, noting the contradiction this represents to Matthew 5:39 and 1 Corinthians 4:12, raises the possibility that Paul simply lost his temper. He reminds us that 'Paul was both human and sinful, and we do not need to credit him with a sinless perfection that he himself never claimed.'[19] It is certainly to be noted that Paul appears to step back from his accusation in verse 5, even citing Scripture in what seems to be a form of apology. Marshall moderates that view, however, by noting, alternatively, that verse 3 *may* represent a prophetic judgment (cf. 13:9-11), and that Paul may here be speaking in the name of God against Ananias' known corruption of the sacred office of high priest; the image of the 'whitewashed wall' has a clear parallel in Jesus' judgment of the Pharisaic corruption of his day (Luke 11:39-52; Matt. 23:1-36).[20]

Paul's further claim, that he **did not know he was the high priest**, has been variously explained. Stott, for example, attributes this to Paul's probably poor eyesight (Gal. 4:13–16; 6:11).[21] Another suggestion is that Paul's long absence from Jerusalem meant that he did not recognize Ananias as the current holder of the office, and notes

19. Marshall: 363.

20. Marshall: ibid.

21. Stott: 352.

that as this was not a regular session of the Sanhedrin Ananias may not have been wearing his usually distinguishing robes.[22] Calvin, following Augustine, claims Paul's comment here is ironic: meaning 'I, brethren, recognize nothing priestly about this man,'[23] which Marshall in the end thinks 'the most probable solution'.[24]

At this juncture the entire proceedings take a significant turn, which Paul initiates. Recognizing that he is highly unlikely to receive justice, or even a sympathetic hearing, at the hands of the Council, an assessment underlined only too clearly by Ananias' reaction to his initial plea of innocence, he opts to move the issue onto clearly theological ground, and in the process exploit the divisions which he well knows exist within the court itself.

Thus, **knowing that some of them were Sadducees and the others Pharisees, Paul called out in the Sanhedrin, 'My brothers, I am a Pharisee, the son of a Pharisee. I stand on trial because of my hope in the resurrection of the dead'** (6). Hanson sees this as 'an opportunist argument'.[25] In view of Luke's express reference to Paul **knowing that some of them were Sadducees and the others Pharisees**, this interpretation appears broadly justified. However it is worth recalling that the commander had convened this meeting for the express purpose of finding out what the issues were that the Jews had with Paul. In a real sense they were essentially theological issues, and so diverting the conversation into the theological arena was giving the commander a clearer picture of what lay at the root of the antipathy towards Paul.

The two groups, Pharisees and Sadducees, dominated the Sanhedrin. The Sadducees were the larger party and included the priestly aristocracy. The Pharisees were represented by the scribes. Politically the Sadducees supported appeasement with Rome, which of course allowed them to retain their hold on domestic power under Rome's

---

22. Bruce: 451.

23. Calvin, II, 229f.

24. Marshall, 364.

25. Hanson, 221.

ultimate authority. The Pharisees were silent protesters against Rome. Theologically the Sadducees were the disciples of Moses and held that only the books of Moses, the Pentateuch, were finally authoritative for doctrine. The Pharisees held to the divine inspiration of the entire Old Testament canon, the prophets as well as the law. Doctrinally the Sadducees were more conservative and in particular denied the notion of resurrection. 'The doctrine of the Sadducees is this, souls die with bodies.'[26] The Pharisees were more progressive and affirmed life after death. Paul's declared siding with the Pharisaic party therefore provoked immediate controversy: **a dispute broke out... and the assembly was divided** (7).

Luke reports the major doctrinal difference as above, but adds **angels and spirits** to the issue of resurrection. Since the Sadducees claimed the authority of the Pentateuch, as we noted, which appears to affirm both angels and spirits, discussion has ensued over what to make of Luke's explanatory comment: **the Sadducees say that there is no resurrection, and that there are neither angels nor spirits** (8). Of the numerous options, the more attractive appear to be that the Sadducees rejected *excessive speculation about* angels and spirits,[27] or that the Sadducees rejected the idea of *a hierarchy of angelic orders* who would be significantly involved in the finale of history.[28]

The critical issue, however, is the resurrection. It should be noted that in a profound sense the Christian claim for Jesus was a fundamental departure from all ideas of resurrection in all strands of Judaism, in two basic respects: it was the claim to a resurrection from the dead of a single individual, viz. the Messiah; and it was a resurrection which was claimed to have taken place within the historical continuum prior to the end of history. As we noted earlier, all Jewish understandings of resurrection were *corporate,* involving either all people, or all the righteous; and all Jewish understandings of resurrection were of an

---

26. Antiquities, 18.1.2-3.

27. Bruce, 466.

28. Polhill, 470.

event *at the end of history*. For Paul of course the real issue is the resurrection of Jesus in Jerusalem some thirty years earlier; however, since he saw a link between the resurrection of Jesus and the end-time general resurrection, cf. 'If the dead are not raised then Christ has not been raised.' (1 Cor. 15:16), his claim, **I stand on trial because of my hope in the resurrection of the dead** is not invalid.

Paul's further claim, **I am a Pharisee**, has proved more controversial; however it can perhaps be defended if we recall that Paul believed Jesus to be the promised Messiah of Israel, the fulfiller of the hope of Judaism for all within Israel who believed in Him; as well as the Saviour also of all believing Gentiles. Obviously Pharisaic practice was often at considerable distance from this, as Jesus had to repeatedly and trenchantly point out (Luke 11:39-52), and the Pharisaic and Christian views of the law were significantly different. However, a 'Christian Pharisee' was not an absolute contradiction, at least until A.D. 90 when synagogue worship introduced a prayer that 'the Nazarenes and the heretics might perish in a moment and be blotted out of the book of life.

The Sanhedrin was in uproar following Paul's claim, as **some of the teachers of the law who were Pharisees stood up and argued vigorously. 'We find nothing wrong with this man,' they said. 'What if a spirit or an angel has spoken to him?'** (9). The passion of the controversy effectively shuts down the proceedings, as Paul had perhaps anticipated. **The dispute became so violent that the commander was afraid that Paul would be torn to pieces by them. He ordered his troops to go down and take him away from them by force and bring him into the barracks** (10).

After the unedifying scenes at the Council, what follows is an event of an entirely different tone and temper. No doubt Paul would have returned to the barracks with a heavy heart. The deep hatred, wilful misunderstanding, and violent aggression of the Jews 'in the street' towards him, coupled with the intransigence, closed-mindedness and party-spirit of their leaders, must have left him wondering if he would ever get out of the city alive, never mind fulfil his dream of bearing witness to his Lord in Rome.

But, **the following night the Lord stood near Paul** (11). It is a beautiful picture, and one which would have ministered profoundly to his discouraged spirit. It is one of several special moments of vision given him in times of special need (16:9; 18:9f.; 27:23f.). **Take courage! As you have testified about me in Jerusalem, so you must also testify in Rome.**

Immediately Paul's fears were laid to rest; the future was secure; Rome was on God's agenda! How much this vision would no doubt come to mean to the apostle during the protracted legal process which lay ahead with its delays and frustrations – and, as a galling side-effect, his extended withdrawal from active ministry. In a profound sense the vision objectifies a truth which is endlessly enabling, no matter our circumstances: knowing that Jesus knows, and that He is there, the **Lord** of all; with us in His grace, in a love from which nothing can separate us in time or eternity.

Further, it is a presence and a love that will support us in the fulfilling of our calling, in Paul's case that of 'testifying about me' at the highest levels of influence in Jerusalem and Rome. For ourselves the details will no doubt be different in a whole range of ways, and yet we will be no less supported. In this sense Paul is not exceptional. Jesus stands near us also, even as we read these words. 'Fear not, I am with you...always. Take courage! Your future is in my hands.'

4. Transfer to Caesarea (23:12-35)

With the glory of the Lord's presence still suffusing his spirit, Paul discovers an immediate need for its reassurances, as he stumbles upon an exceedingly serious threat to his life. The Jews, frustrated in their open attack upon Paul at the temple, and no doubt also by the internal bickerings of the Sanhedrin, hatch a clever plot to finally exterminate the man they clearly perceive as their dangerous enemy. **More than forty** of them **formed a conspiracy and bound themselves with an oath not to eat or drink until they had killed Paul** (12). Their plan is simple enough. They take it to **the chief priests and elders** (so much for the moral and spiritual leadership of a people bound in covenant to the God who commanded: ' You shall not murder!'). The leaders will **petition the commander to bring Paul out to them on the pretext of wanting more accurate information about his case**. The assassins will then be **ready to kill him** at some vantage point on the route (15).

In one of those delightful reversals which illustrate the easy sovereignty of God, the plot just happens somehow to become known, not to a soldier or some other adult representative of the Jerusalem forces of law and order, but to a young man probably still in his teens, who just happens to be related to Paul, his nephew no less. Once again 'God chose the weak things of the world to confound the strong'; He regularly does.

Hearing of it, **he went into the barracks and told Paul** (16). Paul immediately put the lad into the care of **one of his** attending **centurions** (whose trust Paul has obviously won) with the instruction, **take this young man to the commander; he has something to tell him** (17). The centurion does so, and **the commander took him by the hand, drew him aside, and asked, 'What is it you want to tell me?'** And so the plot is revealed in detail: **The Jews have agreed...tomorrow on the pretext...Don't give in to them...waiting in ambush...they are ready now, waiting...**(21). The commander knows his Jerusalem Jews and so finds the information entirely credible. He thoughtfully tells Paul's nephew to keep entirely to himself the fact that he has shared this with the commander. **Don't tell anyone** (22).

The commander acts immediately on the intelligence received and issues the order: **Get ready a detachment of two hundred soldiers, seventy horsemen and two hundred spearmen to go to Caesarea at nine tonight. Provide mounts for Paul so that he may be taken safely to Governor Felix** (23-24). Caesarea was already a place of great significance in the storyline of Acts as the site of Peter's 'second conversion', and additionally the centre of Roman power for the entire area, the seat of the imperial governor, who at this point was one, Felix, the current successor to Pontius Pilate. We noted earlier his questionable character;

avarice and a disregard for justice were especially noted. In the next period, both in his dealings with Paul and with the accusations of the Jews, he will display both of these traits.

The commander writes an accompanying letter concerning Paul. **This man was seized by the Jews and they were about to kill him, but I came with my troops and rescued him, for I had learned that he is a Roman citizen** (27-30). This is, of course, a notable piece of air-brushing; no hint here of Paul's chaining, nor his being readied for the *flagellatio*. However it all serves Paul's, and the Lord's, purpose at this point. The letter concludes by referring to the commander's attempt to discover the Jews' essential issue with Paul, which turned out to be **questions about their law** but containing **no charge that deserved death or imprisonment** (29).

So Paul is transferred **to Caesarea**. The uncovering of the plot has led to this transfer to Felix's direct jurisdiction in anticipation of a proper trial process. Felix enquires as to Paul's place of origin and finds it to be Tarsus in Cicilia (34). Although this is a neighbouring province he agrees to hear the case since at this period 'it was normal for a prisoner to be tried in the province where the alleged offence was committed rather than in his home province.'[29] This regulation was altered by the end of the century, and further there was also a change in the status of Cilicia a few years after this conversation. Sherwin-White notes that a later author than Luke probably would not have got all this right, which is of course a further pointer to an early dating of Acts.[30] So Felix has Paul **kept under guard** pending trial (35).

Bock helpfully applies the lesson of these verses: 'This passage is rooted in God's providence, which moves to protect God's children though the means are not always known as they are here – though Stephen's martyrdom reminds us that providence does not always mean physical rescue. It is ironic that Roman justice

---

29. Marshall, 373.

30. Sherwin-White, 28-31, 55-7.

will bring Paul to Rome as a prisoner so that he will arrive safely and immediately be speaking to the highest levels of Roman society. It is unlikely that if Paul had journeyed as part of a missionary outreach to Rome such a high-level audience would have ever been possible. It is one of the mysteries of providence that many times we cannot see why things are happening as they are. Yet God is surely at work in ways that we could not have planned for ourselves.'[31]

> *If we could push ajar the gates of life,*
> *And stand within, and all God's working see,*
> *We might interpret all this doubt and strife,*
> *And for each mystery could find a key.*
>
> *But not today. Then be content poor heart;*
> *God's plans, like lilies pure and white, unfold.*
> *We must not tear the close-shut leaves, apart –*
> *Time will reveal the calyxes of gold.*
>
> *And when, through patient toil, we reach the land*
> *Where tired feet, with sandals loosed, may rest,*
> *There we shall truly know and understand,*
> *And there shall gladly say, 'Our God knew best'* (ANON).

Study Questions:

1. What do you make of Paul's outburst at 23:3, and his apparent retraction at 23:5, during his Sanhedrin trial?

2. Paul appears to have deliberately created a division in the Sanhedrin (23:6-7). Was he justified in this? It reminds us of Jesus', admittedly difficult, saying in Matthew 10:16. How may we faithfully apply this word of the Master?

3. In what senses was Paul correct in seeing the issue between himself and the Sanhedrin as centred in the question of whether or not the dead are raised? In what sense is this still the key ques-

---

31. Bock, 679.

tion in debates between Christians and those who oppose the faith?

4. Ponder the account of the vision of the Lord given to Paul in 23:11. What may we draw from the fact that Jesus is 'standing nearby'? How would the Lord's words be significant to Paul in the following years? What does this say about the Lord Himself? In what respects do Jesus' words to Paul have counterparts to your life with the Lord?

5. 'God chose the foolish things of the world to shame the wise; God chose the weak things of the world to shame the strong' (1 Corinthians 1:27). How does 23:12-22 illustrate this principle? Can you make application to the mission of the church in the world today? Can you make application to your own life?

5. Trial Before Felix (24:1-27)

This chapter falls naturally into four parts: (1) the trial – Tertullus' claims (1-9); (2) the trial: Paul's defence (10-21); (3) the trial: Felix' response (22-23); (4) Paul's witness to the Governor (24-27).

(1) The trial: Tertullus' Claims (1-9)
Five days later the high priest Ananias went down to Caesarea with some of the elders and a lawyer named Tertullus, and they brought their charges against Paul before the governor (1). As the proceedings get under way Tertullus, a hired legal gun, opens with the customary flattering eulogy in appreciation of Felix, **We have enjoyed a long period of peace under you...**(2) – in actual fact, his administration had been a time of unrest and deteriorating relations with Rome. There is also the regulation promise **not to weary you further** (4). He then presents four charges against Paul (5-8): (a) He is a **pestilence** or 'plague' (*loimon*); (b) he is an **agitator** (*kivounos*), a stirrer up of seditious behaviour **among Jews all over the world**; (c) he is a leader of a sectarian movement, a

ringleader of the Nazarenes; (5) he is a **desecrator of the temple**. In essence Paul is 'a seditious leader of a dangerous sect'.[32] All this explains why **we seized him**. The supporting group then **joined in asserting that these things were true** (9).

(2) The trial: Paul's Defence (10-21)
Paul responds by making five points.

(a) His behaviour in the temple had been above reproach, a fact that Felix can **easily verify**; he had only gone there simply and solely **to worship**. He was neither **stirring up a crowd** there, **or** elsewhere **in the synagogues, or** within **the city** limits (11-12).

(b) The accusers **cannot prove the charges** (13).

(c) It is true **he worships the God of our fathers as a follower of the Way**, a so-called sect. In fact it involves **believing everything that agrees with the Law and that is written in the Prophets**, including a belief in **a future resurrection of the righteous and the wicked** (14-16). 'The new movement is actually rooted in the old promises'.[33] Paul's **conscience** in all this is entirely **clear before both God and man**.

(d) The purpose of his visit to Jerusalem was **to hand over an offering** to alleviate the needs of **the poor** followers of the Way in Jerusalem, and **to present offerings** (in the temple). He was participating in a vow involving **ceremonial cleansing** when he was set upon in the temple. **No crowd** was involved **nor** was there **any disturbance** which he initiated. The instigators were **some Jews from Asia** who are the ones who **ought to be here** laying the charges (17-20). This last point implies the technical weakness of the case against him; Roman law did not view favourably people who made charges and then were unprepared to back them in court.[34]

(e) In the further event of his examination **before the Sanhedrin, no crime** had been found, except perhaps his

---

32. Bock, 691.

33. Bock, 693.

34. Sherwin-White, 52f.

claim to believe in the (Jewish) truth of **the resurrection of the dead** (21). 'The resurrection of the dead echoes like a refrain in these later chapters of Acts.'[35]

(3) The trial: Felix' Response (22-23)

Felix decides to **adjourn the proceedings** pending a personal report from Lysias, the commander in Jerusalem, (22). There is also Luke's note that Felix was **well acquainted with the Way.** Bruce thinks this understanding of the Christian movement was probably obtained from his wife Drusilla, who was Jewish. Meanwhile Paul is kept in custody, though one which allowed him some privileges, including the access of friends who could **take care of his needs** (23).

(4) Paul's witness to the Governor (24-27)

In the next period, Felix, with Drusilla, sought audience with Paul. It was a remarkable development and reminds us of the terms of Paul's call – 'This man is my chosen instrument to carry my name before the Gentiles and their kings...' (9:15). Paul faithfully shared the gospel, as **he spoke about faith in Christ Jesus.** The implication of the resurrection and hence the lordship of Christ would lead naturally, as it had in Athens, to a consideration of Christ's role in the final judgment (17:31). Thus Paul also spelled out the moral implications of faith, discoursing on **righteousness, self-control and judgment to come** (25). These were 'subjects which that couple specially need to learn about'.[36] Drusilla had been a child bride and been persuaded by Felix to leave her earlier spouse to marry him. Still only twenty, Drusilla was his third wife. It is fair to ask how regularly these themes are handled in our Christian witness and preaching today.

'Paul's major goal is to live in a manner that honours God, not just to talk about God.'[37] Paul's faithfulness at

---

35. Fitzmeyer, 737.

36. Bruce, 473.

37. Bock, 697.

this point is the more impressive recognizing that the man he was prepared to thus make **afraid**, or perhaps 'nervous',[38] was his earthly judge. Felix continued, however, to meet with Paul, though an ulterior motive also surfaces, his **hoping that Paul would offer him a bribe** (26). This is consistent with Felix's reputation for avarice. One suggestion is that Paul's mention of the 'offering for the saints' (24:17) had given Felix the impression that Paul had resources he could draw upon. Such veniality was unfortunately relatively common in the empire; however if Felix had hopes of an under-the-counter deal for Paul's liberation he had come to the wrong man. Felix, on the other hand, was anxious to keep in the good graces, relatively speaking, of the Jewish power-brokers in Jerusalem, and so declined to release Paul. This stalemate continued for **two years** (27).

This long hiatus in his case would represent a major challenge for anyone unfairly charged, in whatever place or time; but for Paul, whose heart was constantly recharged with his sense of commission as 'the apostle to the (entire) Gentile world', and who carried the 'daily pressure of my concern for all the churches' (2 Cor. 11:28), the delay must have been extraordinarily difficult to come to terms with, not least as it could have had no clear terminal point in Paul's mind.

Delays and deferments, however, appear regularly in Scripture as part of God's ways with His people. We recall the classic case of Abraham, 'the father of us all', as he waited through decades for his promised son and heir (Gen. 15:2–3; Rom. 4:16–22). We note too the more than four centuries of exile in Egypt, or the forty years of wilderness wanderings, or the long waiting period of another four centuries from the end of the Old Testament revelation until the ministry of John the Baptist; and in our own time, our longing, looking, and waiting, for the return of the Lord; 'Lord, how long?'

No doubt Paul would have regularly returned during this time to the promise of the Lord, imparted at his earlier vision, that he would indeed eventually 'testify about

---

38. Bock, 695.

me in Rome' (23:11). It would be no surprise also if these years did not seed the conviction Paul was to share from his later Roman prison, describing himself as 'the prisoner of Christ Jesus' (Eph. 3:1). The genitive here is critical = 'Christ's prisoner', implying that he viewed Christ as the one who, in His ever-gracious providence had brought about his imprisonment. It was the identical insight that Samuel Rutherford was to express in 1637 as he was imprisoned in Aberdeen: 'How sad a prisoner should I be if I knew not that my Lord Jesus had the keys of the prison himself.' But when all that is weighed, this was a hard trial by any reckoning. Every child of God needs to come to terms with this. Our Father knows; we are to trust Him, as much for His 'not yet', as for His 'yes' or 'no'.

With the hindsight of the centuries we can perhaps discern one specific shaft of light from these years of confinement in Caesarea, because, as Witherington and others have pointed out, they freed up Luke, who was among the friends attending to Paul in prison, to travel throughout Palestine, and carry out the necessary research for the earlier sections of Acts, and for his Gospel; cf. 'I myself have carefully investigated everything from the beginning...' (Luke 1:3).[39] Thus Felix's mendacity, in a beautiful expression of divine sovereignty, may have been largely responsible for the writing of the Gospel of Luke and this great book of Acts, and hence for all the unquantifiable blessings these Lukan texts have been to countless multitudes across the centuries and to this very day.

More generally, frustrations of this nature throw us back on the Lord Himself, and perhaps to a needed recovery of the recognition that what ultimately matters in our lives is our knowing Him.

> *Long is the way, and very steep the slope,*
> *Strengthen me once again, O God of Hope.*
>
> *Far, very far, the summit doth appear;*
> *But Thou art near my God, but thou art near.*

---

39. Witherington: 717.

And thou wilt give me with my daily food,
Powers of endurance, courage, fortitude.

Thy way is perfect; only let that way
Be clear before my feet from day to day.

Thou art my Portion, saith my soul to Thee,
O what a portion is my God to me.' [40]

The long wait was ended by Felix being replaced by a new governor, Porcius Festus, a man with a greater reputation for fairness than had attached to Felix (27). In general, the trial before Felix demonstrates once again that Paul personally, and the teachings of 'the Way', constitute no conscious disruption of social order, that they do not seek the deliberate undermining of the Jewish religion, and that they are no political threat to Rome.

Study Questions:

1. In the trial before Felix, consider Paul's defence in 24:10-21. What points does he make in rebuttal of the charges made against him?

2. How do you react to the terms of Paul's witness to Felix and Drusilla (24:24-25)? Where can we derive a similar courage and faithfulness?

3. Have we succumbed today to the temptation to downplay the moral dimension of the gospel and its summons? Insofar as we may have, why is that a serious declension?

4. Paul could have been immediately set free had he been willing to offer (or arrange for his friends and supporters to offer) a bribe to Felix. His freedom would have enabled him to further encourage his churches throughout the empire, possibly for many more years. Yet he refused this option. Why did he do so? What do we learn here from the apostle?

---

40. Amy Carmichael, *Towards Jerusalem* (SPCK, 1937), 52.

6. Appearance Before Festus and Appeal to Caesar (25:1-12)

As the newly installed Procurator, Festus is anxious to meet with the leaders of his new subjects, and so he **went up to Jerusalem from Caesarea** (1). Festus would in fact only last two years in the Procuratorship before dying prematurely, but during that time he would earn a reputation for being a good ruler. The two years of Paul's detention in Caesarea have clearly done little to appease the Jews' aggression towards Paul, and so they waste little time in **appearing before Festus and presenting the charges against Paul** (2). Their taste for intrigue and murder is in no degree lessened either, so **they urgently requested Festus, as a favour to them, to have Paul transferred to Jerusalem, for they were preparing an ambush to kill him along the way** (3). Festus however is unwilling to be thus at the beck and call of Jerusalem, and since **Paul is being held in Caesarea** to which Festus is shortly returning, he told them, **let some of your leaders come and press charges against the man there, if he has done anything wrong** (4-5).

So, once returned to his base in Caesarea, Festus **convened the court and ordered that Paul be brought before him** (6). On Paul's appearing, the Jews who had come down from Jerusalem **stood around him, bringing many serious charges** (7). Since the charges must have been broadly identical to those brought previously, and since the lapse of another two years would hardly have increased the likelihood of eye-witness credibility, the result was probably predictable from the start – their case could not be proved; however, as Marshall cautions, 'the history of litigation furnishes ample parallels of such folly'.[41] Paul responded and had no difficulty in maintaining his previous position: **I have done nothing wrong against the law of the Jews, or against the temple, or against Caesar** (8). Paul quite simply claims innocence of all the charges brought against him; he is a good Jew, and a good citizen of the empire.

---

41. Marshall, 384.

This plea of innocence is rooted finally in the statement he had made at the end of his defence before Felix: 'I strive always to keep my conscience clear before God and man.' Here Paul gives us an insight (literally) into his moral hinterland, and the demands he places upon himself as a servant of God, the God who 'knows and searches the heart', the God who is 'familiar with all of our ways' (Ps. 139:3; cf. 1-10), the God who 'desires truth in the inner parts' (Ps. 51:6). Living consciously, and daily, in the white light of the divine scrutiny can never guarantee sinless living, but it goes a long way to explaining the remarkable moral courage and tenacity which Paul displays through this succession of accusations, hearings, and trials. Here is a man who lives first of all *coram Deo*, before the eye of God, and accordingly is repeatedly able to survive the scrutiny of man. It is a lifestyle which appears entirely foreign to his accusers, as it is to the vast majority of our contemporaries, but it explains why he, and all his fellow pilgrims on the road to holiness, are able, as he most surely is here, to surmount the attacks of malicious accusers and continue in the face of them to faithfully uphold the gospel, and the gospel's God.

Festus, though unable to challenge Paul's claims, is nevertheless apparently unwilling to acquit him and set him free. It is still early in his tenure and he wants to keep the Jewish leaders 'on side'. So, **wishing to do the Jews a favour, (he) said to Paul, 'Are you willing to go up to Jerusalem and stand trial before me on these charges?'** (9). This question has caused discussion: what exactly is Festus proposing? It is difficult to see what advantage going over the same ground for a third time would have. Just possibly the setting in Jerusalem might help Festus himself arrive at a better understanding of the issues, but not surprisingly Paul is not prepared to commit himself to the proposal. He reaffirms his innocence, **I have not done anything wrong to the Jews, as you** (Festus, by now) **know very well. If I am guilty** (on the other hand) **of anything deserving of death I do not refuse to die** (10-11). Paul here is standing before God's tribunal. Since the Jews have again failed to make their case then **no**

one has the right to hand me over to them. Since Festus apparently lacks the courage to acquit him, Paul decides that the time has come to make his final move; it is time to be on his way to Rome! So **I am now standing before Caesar's court, where I ought to be tried** (10), and Paul invokes the *provocatio* by pronouncing the words –'*Ad Caesarem prouoco*' = **I appeal to Caesar**. Paul will exercise his right as a Roman citizen to appeal for Caesar's overriding judgment before a final judgment has been rendered by a lesser court.

The appeal to Caesar may be seen as serving two concerns of the apostle. It held promise of his receiving justice, and that clearly is not a small concern for him. Additionally, however, it would allow him the longed-for visit to Rome, and the possibility there of fulfilling the Lord's calling 'to carry my name before the Gentiles and their kings' (9:15) to an unprecedented level. With hindsight, it might seem that the then Emperor, Nero, was hardly the most likely to provide Paul with the justice he sought; however this was still the early period of his reign which was marked by relative tranquillity. Festus consults with his council of advisers and confirms Paul's appeal: **To Caesar you will go!** (12).

7. Festus Consults Agrippa (25:13-22)

A few days later King Agrippa and Bernice arrived at Caesarea (13). Agrippa II was a great-grandson of 'Herod the Great', the founder of the dynasty, i.e. the Herod who tried to destroy the infant Jesus, and in revenge slew the infants of Bethlehem (Matt. 2:1-18). His son had had John the Baptist beheaded for a whim (Matt. 14:1-12). His grandson, Agrippa I, had slain James, son of Zebedee, with the sword (12:1-2). Now Paul will be brought before Agrippa's son. It is not a promising scenario, albeit Agrippa has no judicial authority in his case.

Agrippa II had been too young when his father died to have inherited the throne of Judea, so Rome had given him rule of the northern territories (today's Lebanon) and Galilee. The Emperor Claudius had also given him responsibility for the temple in Jerusalem, and the right to appoint the high priest. His visit to Festus with his wife Bernice is **to pay their respects** to the new Governor (13). In the course of their visit the case of Paul comes into the conversation (14). Festus outlines the circumstances, and also his own dilemma of knowing exactly how to compose his brief to Caesar in preparation for Paul's arraignment at the emperor's tribunal (26).

Festus then details how on inheriting the prisoner, Paul, from Felix he was faced with the renewed **charges brought against him by the chief priests and elders in Jerusalem** (15). Festus had explained that **Roman** justice required that an accused be given **opportunity to defend himself,** and this had duly taken place shortly afterwards there in Caesarea (16-17). The charges when put had surprised Festus since they were essentially **about their own religion and a dead man named Jesus whom Paul claimed was alive** (18-19). At a loss to know how to proceed, Festus had offered a further **trial in Jerusalem** (20). Paul instead had made **his appeal to be held over for the Emperor's decision** (21). Festus was accordingly holding Paul pending his being sent to Rome. Agrippa's interest was stirred: **I would like to hear this man myself.** Festus promised him that opportunity the following day (22).

The critical point to note is Festus' summary of the charges against Paul: **about their own religion and a dead man named Jesus, whom Paul claimed was alive.** In other words there is no longer any mention of the alleged desecration of the temple, or of Paul being a threat to public order. The political charges have receded into the background and the issue has become essentially religious in the convictional sense, Paul's claim that Jesus has been raised from the dead. One can sympathize at this point with Festus' dilemma. As Marshall shrewdly observes, 'The Jews had managed to convert their religious charge against Jesus into a political charge when they brought him before Pilate. They had not succeeded in proving it (Luke 23:4, 14, 22), but they were even less successful in the case of Paul.' [42]

---

42. Marshall, 389.

8. Paul's Appearance and Defence Before Agrippa, Bernice and Festus (25:23–26:32)

Luke vividly sets the scene for what is Paul's final public defence of his ministry as Luke has recorded it. The following day **Agrippa and Bernice came with great pomp and entered the audience room with the high ranking officers and the leading men of the city** (23). Festus commands that **Paul be brought in**. This will be, in a sense, a 'show trial'.[43] He then clarifies the nature of the occasion and what lies behind it, and in the process introduces Paul to the assembled dignitaries.

Bruce has a wry and highly perceptive comment: 'There is probably quiet humour in Luke's description of the "great pomp" with which they all assembled: Luke had a very true sense of values, and knew that in his friend and teacher Paul there was a native greatness which did not need to be decked with the trappings of grandeur that surrounded his distinguished hearers. History has vindicated Luke's perspective. Most people nowadays who know anything about Agrippa and Bernice and Festus know of them as people who for a brief space of their lives crossed the path of Paul and heard him speak words which might have brought much blessing to them had they been disposed to pay serious heed to them. All these Very Important People would have been greatly surprised, and not a little scandalized, had they been able to foresee the relative estimates that later generations would form of them and of the handcuffed Jew who stood before them to plead his case.'[44]

Festus then addresses Agrippa and his other guests, and rehearses the case: the virulent accusations of **the whole Jewish community** calling for Paul's death, and Festus' own investigation and conclusion that Paul **had done nothing deserving of death** (24-25). However, since he had **appealed to the Emperor** he had **decided to send Paul to Rome**. Festus then confesses his difficulty in

---

43. Johnston, 428.

44. Bruce, 484.

having nothing definite **to write to His Majesty** in Rome **about Paul**. However, this occasion before Agrippa will hopefully give Festus **something to write** to Caesar, particularly in **specifying the charges against Paul** (26-27). This clarifies the nature of this encounter; it is not a formal trial in any sense, but rather a public hearing before this invited audience, to provide opportunity for Agrippa, as a prominent Jew and one well-versed in Judaism, both to hear Paul, and thereafter to help Festus in framing the charges on account of which he will be sending Paul to the Emperor.

Agrippa then 'assumes the chair' and invites Paul to address the company: **'You have permission to speak for yourself.'**

This is Paul's final defence in Acts. It is also 'the longest and most stylized.'[45] It is a classic *apologia pro vita sua*. In content it does not vary greatly from that presented to the Jerusalem mob in chapter 22, but it is longer overall, and carefully nuanced for this audience, being couched in terms that would appeal to Herod in particular with his being **well acquainted with all the Jewish customs and controversies** (3). On the matter of style Witherington notes nine elements of Greek rhetoric which is not without interest, possibly confirming the view of some that Paul's education in Tarsus university had included study of classical rhetoric.[46] This however is proclamation as well as apologetic, or even mere oratory; Paul as ever is the evangelist, concerned not only to defend himself and clear his own name and those of his fellow Christian believers, but seeking also his audience's allegiance to his Master

So Paul motioned with his hand and began his defence (1). This vivid touch recalls the similar reference to gesture at 13:16. Clearly it was a significant movement, perhaps a characteristic Pauline mannerism, indicating the immediate grasping of initiative on Paul's part, as well as the animation and intensity of his presentation. It is also an eye-witness element; and while it is hardly likely

45. Bock, 705.
46. Witherington, 737.

that Luke would have been among Festus' invited guests, he may well have had a source among those who were present and, besides, considerable opportunity in the following period to have Paul's own account. It is even possible that he also had access to one of Paul's personal parchments giving the contents of the address.[47] Paul's address can be divided into eight sections.

(1) Appreciation of Agrippa as one eminently fitted to understand Paul's case (2-3).
This opening, in rhetorical terminology the *captatio benevolentiae*, was a standard introductory gambit in classical rhetoric (24:2-4, 10). **King Agrippa, I consider myself fortunate to stand before you today as I make my defence against all the accusations of the Jews, and especially so because you are well acquainted with all the Jewish customs and controversies** (2-3). This was no doubt sincerely expressed, and is simply an acknowledgement on Paul's part of what was in fact the case. That it was also rhetorically correct does not imply Paul's engaging in mere flattery. Paul then asks to be heard **patiently.**

(2) Paul's early life and upbringing as a Pharisee (4-8)
Paul then sets off on an encapsulated account of his life and religious experience, beginning with his earliest years growing up in Tarsus and his continuing education in Jerusalem. All this was something **the Jews all know. They have known me for a long time and can testify...that according to the strictest sect of our religion, I lived as a Pharisee** (4-5). The 'our' here is significant, Agrippa is being addressed as a fellow Jew; he and Paul have had the same nurturing influences. It was one of the keys to Paul's entire effectiveness as an evangelist to the Jews that their religious world and its convictions were not something Paul had learned only at second-hand from others. It was the world-view by which he himself had lived during the larger part of his life.

---

47. See 2 Tim. 4:13, which T.C. Skeat argues should be rendered, 'the books – I mean the parchment notebooks.' *'Especially the Parchments'*: A Note on 2 Timothy IV.13. *JTS* 30 (1979), 173-7.

Herein lies at least part of the reason why those who experience a dramatic conversion and a radical moral 'about-turn' are subsequently often such effective evangelists to the pagan society around them. It is also a reason why they regularly ought to be such. To have a testimony like the psalmist, 'He lifted me out of the slimy pit, out of the mud and the mire, and set my feet on a rock', carries a real potential that, by God's grace, the testimony can continue, 'many shall see and fear and put their trust in the Lord' (Ps. 40:2-3). This fact underlines a truth experienced in extended pastoral ministry, that there is literally nothing in our lives that God is unwilling to use if we will dedicate it to Him.

Paul reiterates here his Pharisaic upbringing and its attendant religious practices, **I lived as a Pharisee** (23:6). Pharisaism was a way of life ('Pharisee' lit. = 'separated one') as well as a number of specific doctrinal convictions, and Paul had lived it to the full extent of his powers (Phil. 3:6: 'I obeyed the law so carefully I was never accused of any fault', NLT). This biographical foundation is theologically critical to Paul's whole case, and in particular his defence of his apostolic career, as he will clarify in the next verses. This is because it enables Paul to continue, with entire integrity, **now it is because of my hope in what God has promised our fathers that I am on trial today. This is the promise that our twelve tribes are hoping to see fulfilled as they earnestly serve God day and night** (6-7).

In other words, the so-called 'Nazarene heresy' which he unashamedly embraces and gives leadership to, is not a heresy in any meaningful sense whatever, nor is it a bastardized form of Judaism. *It is Judaism in fulfilment!* This is why the Bible consists of two inseparably unified corpuses of divinely inspired writings. It is why Christians revere the Old Testament as fully as the New Testament. It is why Christians bear witness to the same God addressing them in both. It is why the tragedy of Israel is not merely that it has refused to accept the New Testament, but that it has refused to accept the New Testament because it has fundamentally *failed to understand and submit to the Old Testament*. For the religion of the Old Testament is essentially a religion of **promise (what God has promised our fathers**, v. 6), whose essence lies in its hope of a future divine revelation and intervention, call it the 'Messianic Age', 'the Kingdom of God', 'the Day of the Lord', it matters little. The issue for Israel is simply this: *the promised fulfilment has been realized in the ministry, life, death, rising, exaltation and glorious return of Jesus Christ and the present renewing ministries of the Holy Spirit* – do you not realize that, can you not see that, and will you not humbly and joyfully acknowledge it, and enter into its blessings, for the glory of the one eternal God?

Thus Christianity is no blasphemous denial of the faith of Israel; it is in fact its true inheritance, its long-promised fulfilment, and its greatest day. Thus, for the Jew to become 'a follower of the Way', or in our commoner parlance, 'become a Christian', means affirming the Old Testament, not denying it; it is to become 'a completed Jew'. As Conzlemann strikingly expresses it: 'The true Jew must become a Christian in order to remain a Jew.'[48]

This, as Paul testifies, is the essential issue between himself and his opponents, **O King, it is because of this hope that the Jews are accusing me** (7). But that hope is not merely theoretical; it is specific – the Old Testament and its promise have been fulfilled in a specific person, in Jesus of Nazareth, the incarnate, eternal Son of Yahweh. Accordingly Paul focuses this challenge in a question: **Why should any of you consider it incredible that God raises the dead?** (8). Put directly in this manner, the question at first blush seems somewhat disconnected from what Paul has said up to this point, and here the summary nature of Luke's account becomes quite clear. No doubt Paul would have included a series of steps leading up to the question, such as Jesus' coming and His fulfilment of the Old Testament promise, His death, and then resurrection. However the goal of Paul's argument in this section (vv. 5-7) correctly lies in the question he puts here. For once the fact of Christ's rising from the dead is conceded, His credentials as the Promised One, the Christ, the Mes-

---

48. Conzlemann, 210.

siah, and the embodiment of the fulfilment of the entire
Old Testament revelation are established. Additionally, as
Paul will immediately affirm, once Christ's resurrection is
conceded, Paul's own experience outside Damascus and
his subsequent personal mission career are likewise vindicated. And further again, the charge against Paul of being
an agent of sedition is also effectively eliminated. 'Here is
the irony. The coming and preaching of the very resurrection hope that Jews should respond to as the goal of their
worship is why they charge Paul with sedition.'[49]

Paul's question, however, has universal apologetic force,
as well as immediate relevance to Agrippa and the listening
audience in Caesarea. Granted the existence of God, and
in particular the God of the Old Testament whom Agrippa
and many of the other attendees would have recognized,
then resurrection in principle cannot be excluded. He who
is the author of all life is endlessly capable of restoring and
renewing life. He who is in Himself eternally the Living
One can grant, and express, death-vanquishing resurrection life, whenever, and in whomever, He pleases. This is
exactly the point Jesus made in response to the scepticism
of the Sadducees with respect to the resurrection of the
dead – 'You are in error because you do not know...*the
power of God'* (Mark 12:24). To leap from Paul's defence into
the world of today, we consequently affirm the words of a
lifelong, highly articulate, champion of atheism, who has
now turned theist: 'You cannot limit the possibilities of
omnipotence except to produce the logically impossible.
Everything else is open to omnipotence.'[50] 'Why should
any of you consider it impossible that God raises the dead',
or that He will raise them yet again when Christ returns?

(3) Paul's fanatical Persecution of Christ (9-11)
**I too was convinced that I ought to do all that was pos-
sible to oppose the name of Jesus of Nazareth"** (9). As
we observed above, there is no better or more persuasive
witness than a 'turned enemy'. **And that is just what I did**

49. Bock, 715.
50. Anthony Flew, *There is a God*, Harper One, 2007, 213.

in Jerusalem – this **was not done in a corner** (26). **On the authority of the chief priests I put many of the saints in prison, and when they were put to death I gave my vote against them. Many a time I went from one synagogue to another to have them punished, and I tried to force them to blaspheme.**

This account of Paul's anti-Christian crusade is fuller than we have at any other point, and some have queried Luke's reliability here, specifically since he refers to '*they* were put to death', clearly indicating that Stephen's was not an isolated case. Since the Romans retained the right to apply the death penalty, could this have occurred without their legal participation? Marshall suggests that we may need to allow for Paul being 'somewhat rhetorical' here.[51] Alternatively since this period in Paul's career covered, at least in part, an interim between two Roman governors, it may be that the Romans were more willing to look in the other direction at this point; their close links with the ruling Sadducean party are certainly documented. Paul's reference to having **cast my vote against them** (10) is interesting, literally this = 'I set down a stone' which was how votes were recorded in the ancient world. It carries the suggestion that Paul may have been for at least part of this period a member of the supreme Sanhedrin. The reference to his touring the synagogues to root out the Nazarene heresy is a new detail, though entirely credible. The attempt to force them to blaspheme 'probably means demanding that they deny who Jesus really is, or even curse him.'[52] Paul failed; the 'saints' were not for turning!

The depth of Paul's fanaticism is further reflected: **I even went to foreign cities to persecute them.** Well may he speak of his **obsession** (11). 'He does not spare his own character, but freely makes known his own disgrace, so long as the mercy of God may be revealed more clearly out of it.'[53]

---

51. Marshall, 393.

52. Bock, 715.

53. Calvin, II, 394.

Saint did I say? With your remembered faces,
Dear men and women, whom I sought and slew!
Ah when we mingle in the heavenly places,
How will I weep to Stephen and to you![54]

It is important here to notice that Paul obviously brought to his once anti-Christian career something of the energy and wholeheartedness which was later to so evidently mark his life as a Christian. In this, he was not the first or last to serve the devil with a zeal comparable to what would later be offered, yet more completely, to Christ. This has an important pastoral lesson. It is a clear reminder of the fact, which psychological studies have repeatedly documented, that the fundamentals of human personality do not change with a religious conversion. Character of course changes, lifestyle and behaviour change, attitudes, goals, world-view and motives all change, but 'Grace does not change us as personalities. Traits, easily measured by psychologists, are aptitudes which we inherit and develop because of our genetic potential. Our faith in Christ and his grace working in us enable us to use them in new ways. But to try to change our basic personalities, rather than accepting them as part of what we are given, leads to endless problems. It is to look for magic, not the miraculous changes that grace brings. It is like looking for spiritual cosmetic surgery, or a brain transplant.'[55]

Thus Paul was always, in certain respects, the Saul of his earlier life; and it is so for all of us. While drawing the line of distinction here is not always easy, there is much peace to be experienced in making the attempt. Some Christians spend much energy, and needless, often painful, guilt-ridden effort, trying to become someone God never intended them to become. All the characteristics of grace listed in the New Testament are certainly to be sought earnestly by us all, as God's Spirit works within us – the call to holiness is unequivocal and universal – but personality traits

---

54. Fredrick W.H. Myers.

55. Gaius Davies, *Genius, Grief, and Grace* (Christian Focus, 2003), 20-1.

and aptitudes are part of the given-ness of our creature-hood, that which God has 'made us like' in our basic cast of personality. The good news is that it is in, and through, our 'given' personalities that God is willing to use us, and to fulfil His eternal purpose for our lives; and eventually, without eradicating the unique ' I' whom we each are, to conform us to the likeness of Christ.

(4) Paul's Conversion and Commissioning (12-18)
Paul now comes to the great turning-point of his life. He had introduced it obliquely by mentioning his persecuting zeal driving him to 'foreign cities' to try to eradicate the 'Nazarene heresy'; now he addresses it directly. **On one of these journeys I was going to Damascus with the authority and commission of the chief priests**...Then it happened –...**About noon, O King, I was on the road –** the intimacy of this moment evokes a desire to connect more intimately with Agrippa, 'O King!' – **I saw a light from heaven, brighter than the sun blazing around me and my companions. We all fell to the ground, and I heard a voice saying to me in Aramaic...**

Several significant features of the experience are high-lighted, which counter dismissive interpretations of the event. First, it was not purely subjective. Paul was travelling in company. His **companions** would have been temple police from Jerusalem sent along to bring the 'Nazarene prisoners' back to Jerusalem from Damascus for the Sanhedrin's retributive process. They are also impacted by the **light from heaven...blazing around** Paul; **we all fell to the ground**. In his account before the Jerusalem mob in 22:9, Paul affirms that his companions also saw the light. In Luke's conversion account in 9:7 as well as in Paul's Jerusalem version in 22:9, we are told that they also heard the sound of Jesus' voice though they did not understand what was being said to Paul. These 'companions' were presumably available, both immediately and subsequently, to confirm or deny this claim. In other words, this was not a purely private experience, a visionary projection out of Paul's own mind, what one recent critic, Richard Carrier, refers to as 'a convincing ecstatic event – his unconscious mind producing what he really wanted to hear'.[56]

Second, the experience was radically and unalterably life-changing. There is not the slightest hint at any point over the next thirty years of Paul's life of supremely demanding, costly, sacrificial and regularly life-threatening ministry, that the veracity of the experience as an authentic, objective meeting with the risen Jesus was in question for him. It literally remade Paul's entire worldview. From this point on, everything he either experienced in his travels or reflected in his mind was evaluated in terms of the authenticity of this event and the things which he claimed to have heard spoken to him during it.

This also speaks powerfully against a merely circumstantial projection of some alleged inner conflict, such as Carrier opines. The claim that it represented some kind of wish fulfilment is really remarkable when one considers the incredible price Paul was to pay for having experienced it; the loss of 'whatever was to my profit', no small loss this (cf. Phil. 3.7, cf. 4-7); and its replacement by the almost unbearable catalogue of sufferings he would endure as a Christian apostle (2 Cor. 11:23-28). 'What he *really wanted* to hear'? – Are you serious? At this point the critic becomes much less credible than the biblical text.

Saul, Saul, why do you persecute me? It is hard for you to kick against the goads (14). This is the only occasion in the three accounts that these words are recorded, though they are in no way reduced thereby in their appropriateness to the circumstances. Marshall, commenting on the different nuances in the three Acts accounts, remarks, 'Something of Luke's literary ability may be seen in the way in which he varies the details of the story so that it comes over freshly to the reader each time.'[57] Jesus' address uses the Semitic form of his name, *Saoul, Saoul* (14), though elsewhere in Acts Luke uses the Greek form, *Saulos*. The repetition of the name echoes other 'encounter moments' in Scripture (cf. Gen. 22:11; 46:2; Exod. 3:4; 1 Sam. 3:6).

---

56. Richard C. Carrier, *Empty Tomb* (Price and Lowder), 184.

57. Marshall, 394.

The point made thereby is the profoundly personal character of the greeting. In such moments we are opened to the heart of a God for whom every individual in His creation, or who breathes on this planet, is not a statistic or a human life form, but a person, unique, special, endlessly and limitlessly loved. In a profound sense God is not aware of 'people', 'citizens', 'consumers', 'congregations', even 'families', or whatever other collective noun we may employ. These do not exist for Him. He is only and always aware of 'Saul', 'Moses', 'Samuel', 'Mary' 'Priscilla', 'Peter', 'John', 'Luke', 'Rhoda', 'Agrippa' 'Bernice' 'Festus'......The list is as endless as the human race; each of us appears in it, *by name*.

The next words, which occur in all three accounts, must have blown to pieces all Paul's years of carefully assembled self-sufficiency: **why do you persecute me? It is hard for you to kick against the goads.** The comment about the goads reached right into Paul's mind and cast a beam of light across his inner consciousness. 'These words reflect a proverbial way of speaking, attested in several classical Greek writers.'[58] The goad was a stick which served as a whip, used to prod and hence direct an animal. 'Jesus is asking why Paul is kicking against God's discipline and direction.'[59] Longenecker sees it as a metaphor for 'useless opposition to deity'.[60] Bruce understands this allusion as reflecting Paul's struggling against his conscience.[61] Hanson prefers a reference to a struggle against his destiny.[62] Whatever way we view it, there appears here a clear indication that God had been at work in Paul's heart, probably through the testimony of Stephen (22:20), and the other Christians whom he was encountering. Consequently, despite the frenzy of what he, at least initially, perceived as his righteous struggle to maintain God's truth, even to honour God's name, Paul was also facing an ever-deepening inner uncertainty.

---

58. Marshall, 395.

59. Bock, 716.

60. Longenecker, 552; cited Stott, 370.

61. Bruce, 491.

62. Hanson, 238.

More generally, from the vision and these first words, Paul is immediately aware that he is in the presence of a divine figure, hence his own question: **Who are you Lord?** (15). The answer is devastating in its import: **I am Jesus, whom you are persecuting** (15). While it is of course impossible to recover the cataract of thoughts which must have cascaded through Paul's consciousness at that moment, two things at very least must have registered with overwhelming force. First, that he was indeed in the presence of Jesus of Nazareth, risen and alive, and therefore the promised Messiah of God; second, that the Nazarenes were right, and were truly Yahweh's people, indeed Jesus' own people, to whom Jesus (and Yahweh by implication) was personally committed and with whom He was to be identified. It is certainly arguable that we need look no further than these ever-remembered words for the origin of Paul's later doctrine of the church as the body of Christ, and hence, not unlike Paul here, our need to review our attitudes towards fellow Christians. They are those in whom Christ now lives! 'Inasmuch as you did it to one of the least of these...you did it to me'; or 'Inasmuch as you did not....'

But there is more. **Now get up and stand on your feet** (16). This, as Stott suggests, implies standing up 'as a necessary preliminary to the command to go.'[63] We are already therefore at this point moved into Paul's account of his commission. This also explains why Paul does not make any reference to the command to go into Damascus, or the gracious ministry there of Ananias. Though personally significant, these details are unnecessary to sustain Paul's primary thrust, which is to justify his lifestyle and mission, and to exercise that evangelistic mission towards those in his present audience in Caesarea.

I have appeared to you to appoint you as a servant and as a witness of what you have seen of me and what I will show you (16). This was the general *content* of the task. Paul has been met and claimed for the **service** of Christ; he is destined to be henceforth Christ's love-bound slave

---

63. Stott, 373.

(Rom. 1:1). From this hour for Paul, 'to live means Christ' (Phil. 1:21). Myers again catches this memorably:

> *Christ! I am Christ's! and let that name suffice you,*
> *Ay, for me too He greatly hath sufficed;*
> *Lo with no winning words I would entice you,*
> *Paul has no honour and no friend but Christ.*
>
> *Yea thro- life, death, thro' sorrow and thro' sinning*
> *He shall suffice me, for he hath sufficed;*
> *Christ is the end, for Christ was the beginning,*
> *Christ the beginning, for the end is Christ.*[64]

Specifically Paul's work will involve being a **witness,** particularly to Jesus, both to what he has seen of His risen reality and glorified person, and to what will be further revealed to him. Witness and service are key Lukan themes (cf. Luke 1:2; Acts 1:8; Luke 24:48; Acts 1:22; 2:32; 3:15; 5:32; 10:39, 41). We can also note Paul's account of this commission in Galatians 1:1 and 1:15-16.

The *sphere* of his future work is next declared: **I will rescue you from your own people and from the Gentiles. I am sending you to them** (17). The 'them' is inclusive of both Jews and Gentiles. Paul will be the apostle to the Gentiles in a primary sense, but will ever also be Christ's witness to the Jews, as Luke's account of his ministry through the previous chapters has made abundantly clear – however unwilling to heed his message many of the Jews would prove. There is a clear imperative intent in the verb here: 'I am sending you.' Stott suggests the force is effectively: 'I myself apostle you', or 'I myself make you an apostle.'[65] This is Paul's moment of apostolic commissioning, his equivalent to the setting apart of the original apostles (1:8; Matt. 28:18-20; Mark 14:15; Luke 24:46-49; John 20:21-22). So, 'Paul, an apostle – sent not by men nor by man, but by Jesus Christ and God the Father, who raised him from the dead' (Gal. 1:1).

---

64. Frederick W.H. Myers.

65. Stott, 373.

Paul is further assured of *protection*: **I will rescue you** (17) would be repeatedly important for Paul, and echoes prophetic calls in the Old Testament (Ezek. 2:1-9; Jer. 1:8).

The *goal* of Paul's witness is then conveyed in a richly layered series of phrases and images: **to open their eyes, to turn them from darkness to light, from the power of Satan to God, so that they may receive forgiveness of sins and a place among those who are sanctified by faith in me** (18). The passage has significant echoes of the account of the Servant's ministry in Isa. 42. It is focused round three infinitives: to open blinded eyes (*avoixai;* cf. Isa. 42:6-7, 16; John 9:1-41); to turn people from darkness to light, and from Satan to God (*epistrepsai;* cf. Acts 8:11, 20-23; 13:10; 19:13-19; 2 Cor. 4:4-6; Col. 1:12f; Eph. 5:8-14; 1 Thess. 1:9); and to enable them to receive forgiveness of sins and sanctification by faith in Christ (*labein;* Luke 1:77; 3:3; 4:18; 5:20-21; 7:47-49; 11:4; 17:3-4; 24:47; Acts 2:38; 5:31; 10:34; 13:38). 'Sanctified' here has the force of 'set apart for the possession of' (cf. Acts 20:32; 1 Cor. 1:2; Titus 2:11-14; 1 Pet. 1:2).

In reviewing the terms of Paul's commission as detailed here, it is pertinent to note with Bock the implication of its rich expression of basic New Testament theological convictions. 'If Paul came to faith in the mid-30s, then the core theology about which he wrote was clearly in place by then. In other words, the only way Paul could process this vision and understand it as he did was by having heard and now believed the apostolic message from figures like Peter or Stephen. Even though Paul argues in Gal. 1 that he received the gospel by revelation, his ability to understand that appearance of Jesus assumes a pre-understanding that the apostolic preaching would have supplied. Thus the event shows how old the core theology of Christianity is; it goes back to the earliest days of the apostles' preaching.'[66] That being so, it also shows how inadequate to the facts are the claims made repeatedly, and still widely encountered in scholarly circles, that the explanation of the exalted status attributed to Jesus in the New Testament

---

66. Bock, 717.

is the product of the early Christian religious imagination whereby a very human figure was, through the following decades, progressively exalted in their minds.

(5) Paul's Response and Subsequent Ministry (19-20)
So then, King Agrippa, I was not disobedient to the vision from heaven (19). The opening 'so then' (*othen*) is the foundation for Paul's subsequent career detailed in verses 19-20. Paul has been personally met with by the living God and commissioned for a specific task. Consequently he is obedient to the terms of his commission (Rom. 1:16). Paul thus defends his life and ministry by appeal to the highest possible authority: God has commanded it, and hence God continues to authorize it.

So...I preached...(*appangellon* = lit. 'I evangelized', 'I preached the good news'). Here is both the primary implication of the commission Paul has received, and also the content of the message which he has been set apart to proclaim. This message has the potential to open sin-blinded eyes to spiritual reality, to enable its recipients to know the living God; it can liberate from the dominion of dark and evil forces into the glorious freedom of God's children; it can bring those who believe it and commit themselves to the Christ who is offered therein, the forgiveness of all their sins and a place among the people of God who are His own possession. Accordingly the responsibility is clear and comprehensive – the message must be shared and declared, to all people everywhere, both Jews and Gentiles. The challenge lies no less surely upon all who have met Christ throughout the rolling centuries. It challenges us anew today. 'I was met by the living Jesus Christ...so...I evangelized'.

Paul had accordingly begun immediately to preach **to those in Damascus**, then **to those in Jerusalem and in all Judea**, and finally **to the Gentiles also, that they should repent and turn to God and prove their repentance by their deeds** (20). The grammatical construction of the link between Paul's ministry in Damascus and that to all Judea is odd. There is the further difficulty noted by some that Paul explicitly denies having preached in Judea in the early period (Gal. 1:22; cf. Acts 9). Some suggest an early 'gloss' (a later scribal addition) in the text here. However, Bock notes helpfully that 'the remarks here may well be a compression of events over a long period (Rom. 15:19).'[67] Fitzmyer simply refers to a Lukan hyperbole, meaning that Paul preached everywhere to anyone; he suggests – 'I preached repentance and turning to God to those in Damascus and Jerusalem – I evangelized Judea – and to the nations.'[68] In essence Paul asserts that the message he preaches is one and the same for both Jew and Gentile alike: to Jews in Jerusalem, Judea and wherever else in the *diaspora*, and to Gentiles everywhere. It contains three consistent elements: repentance from sin, turning to God in Christ with reliant faith, and resultant godly living.

We should not miss the intrinsic link between 'turning to God' and its proof in 'good deeds'. 'None more than Paul rejected works, before or after conversion, as a ground of salvation, and none more firmly demanded good works as a consequence of salvation.'[69] We can add, no theologian of the church has ever more clearly insisted on that very connection than Calvin. In his monumental *Institutes of the Christian Religion*, perhaps the most influential theological writing ever penned, Calvin audaciously devotes a major section of his exposition of Christian doctrine to 'The Life of the Christian Man' (and Woman). In other words how the justified live out their faith is itself part of the faith. We are saved by faith alone, but true saving faith is never alone. Justification and sanctification are inseparable.

(6) Paul's Consequent Arrest (21)

This message, with its explicit equation of Jews and Gentiles in their spiritual and moral need, and in their being equally offered God's gracious salvation through Christ, is, Paul asserts in his concluding moments, **the reason why the Jews seized me in the temple courts and tried to kill me** (21).

---

67. Bock, 720.

68. Fitzmyer, 760.

69. G.H. Lang, *The Gospel of the Kingdom* (London 1933), 23.

Hence the issue underlying Paul's incarceration is finally Christological, Jesus Christ, and who He is; and soteriological, how salvation from sin and its consequences, is attained. This is the line in the sand which runs throughout the book of Acts, between the apostles and the Jewish leadership in chapters 4 to 12, and between Paul and the Jewish leadership, and Jews more generally, in chapters 13 to the end.

That same line marks the sands of our own age of religious pluralism. On the one side of the line is biblical Christology, its revelation of the person of our Lord: not just a special holy man, a great religious teacher and genius, a spiritual master or miracle-worker, or even all of these combined. He is nothing less than Immanuel, God Himself with us in person, fully human, fully divine. Hence to bracket Jesus with Muhammad, or the Buddha, or Krishna or any other religious luminary of the ages, is to fail to understand Him, indeed it is to detract from His proper glory. He is the unique, the one and only: He is the Lord Jesus Christ!

On the same side of the line is biblical soteriology, its doctrine of salvation. Jesus comes not only to reveal God to us but to bring us effectually to God. We cannot save ourselves from sin and its entail. As sinners we are separated from our Creator and the objects of His just wrath. No amount of religious practice or devotion at whatever shrine and from within whatever religious faith or tradition (including Christianity) can, in itself, atone for our sins and restore us to a right relationship with God. We are helpless; we cannot save ourselves.

In infinite mercy and indescribable love, Jesus as God incarnate makes our need His own. At the cross in sheer grace He accepted in our place the entire responsibility of all our sins and their implications, bearing the divine judgments on our behalf. He died for us. By that act of atonement, He has made it possible for sinners, through reliant personal faith in Him, to be forgiven and restored in relationship with God as His own children. Of necessity, since He alone as the God-*man*, *can*, as man, *take our place*; and since He alone as *God*-man *can achieve reconciliation with God*, His death and rising are *the only way to salvation*. Peter expressed it at 4:12, 'There is salvation in no one else for there is no other name under heaven given to men by which we must be saved.'

So the line of division remains in the sands of our own day. No matter how lovingly and winsomely the message is presented, by the apostle or his contemporary third millennium witnesses; no matter how effectively Paul, or his contemporary third millennium witnesses, may claim that all this is no innovation, but what God Himself actually teaches in Scripture; in the end there are those who repent and believe and receive salvation, and there are those who reject and will not receive it, and may even raise up against those who proclaim it. So they try to kill Paul, and the terms may not be different for us today and tomorrow. In the final analysis, like Martin Luther, we are constrained from beyond ourselves: 'Here we stand – we can do no other, so help us God.'

Despite the physical assault and further plots on his life, **'I have had God's help to this very day and so I stand here to testify to small and great alike'** (22). The reason Paul has escaped up to this present moment has been finally due to his having had 'God's help'. The Romans had, of course, intervened on his behalf at the temple, and we may be confident that Paul was not unthankful for their intervention; however behind these 'intermediaries of aid' he discerns, as all Christians in similar circumstances would do, the hand of God.

(7) The Message Paul Preaches (22-23)

These two verses are a final statement of the apostle's message. Although the following verse mentions that **Festus interrupted** at this point, Marshall seems justified in noting that 'in fact the speech has reached its conclusion.'[70]

We can ask four questions of this final summary (22): *How* has Paul fulfilled this preaching ministry? **with God's help**. *When* has he fulfilled it? **to this very day**. *To*

---

70. Marshall, 398.

whom has he directed it? **to small and great alike**. *What* is its content; what has he preached?

(a) The message is no more and no less than **what the prophets and Moses said would happen**. Yet once again Paul reiterates that the gospel is the fulfilment of the Old Testament revelation, in both law (Moses) and the prophets.

(b) The message asserts, in its fulfilment of Old Testament Scripture, that **the Christ would suffer** (23). Paul thinks here surely of the 'suffering servant', 'led like a lamb to the slaughter…cut off from the land of the living… who poured out his life unto death' (Isa. 53:7, 8, 12; also Pss. 22:1-18; 118:22; Zech. 12:10).

(c) The message asserts that the Christ **would be the first to rise from the dead** (Pss. 16:8-11; 2; 110:1; Isa. 53:10; 42:6; 49:6; 60:3; Hosea 6:2).

(d) The message asserts that the Christ, risen and alive, **would proclaim light to his own people and to the Gentiles** (Isa. 61:1f.; 42:1-7; 49:6; Deut 18:18). This last represents a significant underwriting of Luke's foundational insight in 1:1, of the apostolic ministry as the continuing ministry of Christ Himself (cf. Romans 15:18: 'What Christ has accomplished through me…').

(8) The Judges Respond (24-32)
At this point Festus interrupted Paul's defence, 'You are out of your mind, Paul!' (24). '(Festus) is portrayed as a man who is still unable to comprehend the subtleties of Jewish theology.'[71] To this Roman, while the idea of the immortality of the soul would have had some familiarity, the notion of the resurrection of the dead, in the sense Paul was applying it to Jesus, would have seemed utterly incredible, pure fantasy. Yet he cannot question Paul's obviously massive intellect and learning. But perhaps that is just the point…**Your great learning is driving you insane**. Pohill suggests 'all your learning…has lifted you out of the real world.'[72] Not all Roman officials were so dismissive (13:7, 12).

---

71. Marshall: 398.
72. Pohill: 507.

Paul replies courteously to **most excellent Festus**; he is emphatically **not insane** (25); on the contrary, his case, as argued in his presentation, is **both true and reasonable**. Here is the bedrock as far as the gospel is concerned, and one of the supreme reasons for preaching it – it happens to be true! Paul is consequently not unprepared to claim that it is consistent and rational.

This is our final sight of Festus; we can only hope that he was helped by all this in formulating the charges against Paul for Caesar's benefit. For confirmation of his claim as to the truth and reasonableness of his case, Paul turns from the Roman governor to the Jewish king, Agrippa; **The king is familiar with these things** (unlike Gentile Festus) **and I can speak freely to him. I am convinced that none of this has escaped his notice, because it was not done in a corner** (26).

This assertion of the openness and accessibility of Christian claims continues to be significant. God's acts of redemption, whether in the call of Abraham and his seed, the Exodus from Egypt, the restoration of Israel after the captivity, the life and ministry of Jesus Christ, His death and resurrection, the coming of the Holy Spirit, and the global publication of the gospel, are all public events, written into the soil of history. Christian truth is public truth, open to enquiry, defensible as a faithful account of what actually occurred, and thus helping people 'to know the certainty' of the things which are taught in its name (Luke 1:4).

But Paul is not finished; the evangelist in him stirs: **King Agrippa, do you believe the prophets? I know you do** (27). Paul is in essence challenging Agrippa to take the next step towards personal faith, by examining the prophetic writings, which he already reveres, in their anticipations of the ministry of the Messiah, and to compare these prophecies with the terms and Easter climax of Jesus' ministry. Paul is pointing Agrippa to Jesus. This of course puts Agrippa on the spot. To deny Paul's assertion about his belief in the prophets would be a serious public gaffe, with leading Jews no doubt among the, by now, riveted audience. Yet it would hardly be appropriate to his status to meekly accept Paul's evangelistic directive. He resorts to a reply which has left the interpreters debating: **Do you think that in such a short time you can persuade me to be a Christian?** (28). Some see this as a sarcastic, even caustic response. However, it is probably as Marshall suggests: 'light-hearted, but not ironic'.[73]

This is only the second occasion of the term 'Christian' in Acts (cf. 11:26); however, it was later to catch on universally. Luke's reserve here is in keeping with his faithfulness to the historical setting. Paul has the final word; he can go no further in such a public setting, but he is at least able to witness to his deep spiritual concern, the supreme importance, even urgency, of the issues he has represented in his defence, and his longing accordingly for the salvation of Agrippa and all those present through their joining him in his commitment to Christ: **Short time or long – I pray God that not only you but all who are listening to me today may become what I am, except for these chains** (29).

There is no extant evidence that Agrippa ever followed up on Paul's urging to study the prophetic writings and thus open himself to the Christian claims for Jesus. Oftentimes evangelism is unsuccessful as far as the immediate impression goes. But success lies also in the faithfulness of the witness which is offered. People saying 'no' to Christ's claims, though always disappointing, does not imply the failure of the sharing. Furthermore, we need to keep constantly in mind that the supreme evangelist is God the Holy Spirit, who takes and uses the truth which we share. What that finally means in any individual's life will only become clear on the judgment day. As Jesus reminds us graphically, witness to God's Word is like sowing seed in the ground; the greater part is always unseen. So we sow in faith, and water with prayer, and wait in hope, 'until the harvest' (Matt. 13:30).

The hearing is over, and the dignitaries rise, **talking with one another**, and expressing their general conclusion, **This man is not doing anything that deserves death or imprisonment** (31). Agrippa's judgment concurs, **This man could have been set free if he had not appealed to**

---

73. Marshall, 400.

Caesar (32). The question which arises is why then Paul was not set at liberty. Sherwin-White draws upon his extensive knowledge of classical society in responding: according to strict Roman law acquittal at this stage would have been possible; however, 'to have acquitted him despite the appeal would have been to offend both the emperor and the province.'[74] But behind all this we trace, with Paul, the hand of God, who had set in the apostle's heart a longing to bear witness to the gospel of his Lord also in Rome, at the perceived centre of the world (Rom. 1:13-15); and while the means by which he would travel there may not have been those Paul anticipated, to Rome he would go as the Lord had promised him (23:11).

So ends the first part of Paul's prolonged period as a prisoner. More will follow though that will carry the story beyond Luke's time-limit. In these last chapters, Paul had been subjected to a series of trials and hearings in which he acquitted himself, and by implication 'the Nazarenes', most effectively. 'Paul's three defences were successful. Neither Felix, nor Festus nor Agrippa found him guilty. Instead each indicated that he was innocent of the charges made against him...He proclaimed in court his threefold loyalty – to Moses and the prophets, to Caesar, and above all to Jesus Christ who had met him on the Damascus road. Paul was a faithful Jew, a faithful Roman, and a faithful Christian.' [75]

Study Questions:

1. Consider Paul's plea of innocence (25:8). Behind it lies his testimony in the earlier trial before Felix: 'I strive always to keep my conscience void of offence before God and man' (24:16). What light does this throw on Paul's inner life, and on his public ministry? What does it say to us?

2. What motivated Paul's appeal to Caesar? How was God's purpose to be fulfilled through all this legal process and the political manoeuvrings

---

74. Sherwin-White, 65.
75. Stott, 378.

which underlay it? What encouragement is there for us here?

3. Review F.F. Bruce's perceptive comment, cited above, on the scene at Paul's 'show trial' before Agrippa. Can you think of similar applications from today's world, and from your own experience? We can recall at this point Jesus' often repeated prophecy of the final judgment: 'The first shall be last and the last shall be first' (Matt. 19:30; 20:16; Mark 10:31; Luke 13:30). Why should this lift our hearts?

4. Paul's claim is that his faith in Jesus Christ is fully in accord with Old Testament promises, i.e. that the New Testament is to be understood as the divinely intended fulfilment of the Old (26:6-7, 22-23). Does the Old Testament figure significantly in your understanding of the Christian faith? Does it so figure in the teaching of your church? If the answers are negative, what steps might we take to recover Paul's perspective here? 'It takes a whole Bible to make a whole Christian' (William Still). Do you agree?

5. Which attributes of God make the resurrection of Jesus, and the general resurrection at the parousia, both inherently possible and inherently likely?

6. 'Grace does not change us as personalities' (Gaius Davies). Do you agree? If this is a valid insight, what are its implications for teaching about Christian holiness? What are its implications for our lives personally?

7. Consider Paul's commission (26:16-18) and identify its salient features. Which of these are relevant to Christian mission today? How well are we fulfilling them?

8. In what ways is Paul a model evangelist in this discourse generally, and in 26:25-29 in particular?

9. The Journey to Rome (27:1–28:16)

And so we came to Rome... These words from 28:14 serve as a 'text' for these final two chapters. But in a real sense Rome has been the goal ever since Paul had appealed to Caesar (25:11); and in an even deeper sense it has been the goal ever since 1:8 and Jesus' words of commission, 'you shall be my witnesses...to the ends of the earth.' As we argued in our exposition of chapter one, Isaiah 49:6 underlies the commission in both its unifying vision and ultimate global scope: 'God says, "It is too small a thing for you to be my servant to restore the tribes of Jacob and bring back those of Israel I have kept. I will also make you a light for the Gentiles, that you may bring my salvation to the ends of the earth."' Indeed a good case could be made for this Scripture being the 'text' of Luke's unified literary project in his 'Gospel plus Acts'...and so to Rome!

We earlier noted Paul's long-standing yearning to preach the gospel in Rome (Rom. 1:10-15). His desire to visit it would surely reach back to his early education in Tarsus; being himself a Roman citizen it could hardly have been otherwise. Described with justice as 'the grandest political achievement ever accomplished',[76] the very longevity of the Empire, already in its eighth century, and in the full flush of its growth when we encounter it in the New Testament, dwarfs in many respects every other imperial project of history. 'To a Roman the city of Rome was the centre of the world; from the golden milestone of the Forum at Rome roads went in all directions as to all parts of the Empire.'[77] But Paul was also the eternal strategist and no doubt salivated at the missional possibilities of Rome as the centre from which 'the gospel can go out to all people since everything comes to and from there.'[78] But first Paul has to get there, and that brings us back to chapter 27.

Writers have long commented on the length of the account of Paul's journey to Rome in proportion to the

---

76. S. Angus, art. 'Roman Empire', ISBE, first edition, 1915, ed. J. Orr.

77. F.V. Fison, Gasque and Martin, 76.

78. Bock, 726.

book as a whole, 'especially since at first sight the narrative appears to contribute little to the theological aim of Acts.'[79] There was certainly a strong interest in sea voyages in classical literature: one survey counts eleven such, many involving shipwreck. One possible further motif is Paul as the heroic survivor, from the threats of storm, shipwreck and deadly snakebite. Broadening that, Paul, having been vindicated by man in terms of his judicial process, is now similarly vindicated by God. In terms of the length of the narrative issue, there may be, as we noted earlier, a deliberate parallel to Jesus. In Luke's Gospel the journey of Jesus to Jerusalem occupies the final third; here Paul's journey to Rome covers arguably the final quarter (21–28). A clear underlying theme throughout is God's sovereignty, and His entire faithfulness to His servants.

Coming directly to chapter 27, surprisingly, Luke's historical integrity has been called into question once again at this point, some claiming to discern a non-Lukan source which he has taken over and adapted. In response we note that quite apart from the return of the 'we' material (v. 1f.), it is nearly incredible that so vivid an account, with its battery of eye-witness details, should be questioned at this level. 'It is completely improbable that it should be either invented or taken over from another source.'[80] Further, 'there is no such detailed record of the working of an ancient ship in the whole of classical literature.'[81] In other words, if we question the integrity of Luke's account here then nothing of a similar nature in all of classical literature has a credible claim to authenticity; which might not disturb a deconstructionist, but leaves the rest of us shaking our heads.

One of the most persuasive vindications of the historical authenticity of Luke's account dates back to a nineteenth-century book written by a Scottish yachtsman, geographer, and Fellow of the Royal Society, James Smith, of Glasgow. He spent the winter of 1844–45 in

---

79. Marshall, 401.

80. Marshall, 402.

81. Walker, 543.

Malta investigating Paul's voyage, familiarizing himself with the weather patterns of the Mediterranean, and studying the navigation and seamanship of both first and nineteenth-century worlds. 'His general conclusion was that Acts 27 was the work of an eyewitness who neverthe-less was a landlubber, and not a professional seaman: "no sailor would have written in a style so little like that of a sailor; no man not a sailor could have written a narrative of a sea voyage so consistent in all its parts, unless from actual observation."'[82]

The account of Paul's 'march on Rome' in these final two chapters can be readily divided into four stages.

Stage 1: Caesarea to Phoenix (27:1-12)

Paul is joined by **some other prisoners** for the voyage to **Italy**, conceivably part of the human freight daily carried to Rome from all parts of the Empire to die in the Colosseum and other arenas of the city. They are of course under arrest, and in the hands of a Roman security force headed by **a centurion named Julius.** Paul, however, also has a Christian support team accompanying him in the persons of Luke and **Aristarchus, a Macedonian from Thessalonica**, who had been in the party accompanying Paul to Jerusalem over two years earlier (20:4) (2). The Western text also mentions Secundus, a fellow Thessalonian and travel-companion of Aristarchus (20:4). Clearly Paul is respected by the authorities, as well he might be, and so this personal accompaniment is permitted him. It is also encouraging to note the continuing contribution of Paul's earlier work in Thessalonica, with all its hardships, in this significant fellowship support of one, or perhaps two of its converts. 'Cast your bread upon the waters, for after many days you will find it again' (Eccles. 11:1), a text which all involved in ministry over the years find graciously, and repeatedly, fulfilled; it was fulfilled now in rich measure for Paul.

The voyage gets under way as the ship's company, comprising its crew and owner, Julius and his soldiers,

---

82. James Smith, *The Voyage and Shipwreck of St Paul*, (1880, Longmans, 4th ed.) cited here as in Stott, 386.

an array of prisoners, and a few other travellers like Luke and Aristarchus (and Secundus?), numbering some 276 persons in total (37), board **a ship** whose home port was **Adramyttium** in the Province of Mysia, north of Ephesus (2). The vessel was calling at Palestinian ports en route **to ports along the** (south) **coast of the province of Asia.** The voyage to Rome would have taken some five weeks, even if sailing directly; however long-distance 'direct flights' were not the order of the day in the first century, and so typically Julius would be looking to transfer to another ship once the Asian ports were reached.

Their first 'leg' is a short day-trip to Sidon, north of Caesarea, where Paul is afforded a further favour: **Julius, in kindness to Paul, allowed him to go to his friends so they might provide for his needs** (3). No doubt the replenishing at this stop by the believers at Sidon would have helped equip the travellers for the long voyage ahead. All this must have deepened Paul's sense of travelling in what he would later refer to as 'the good, pleasing and perfect will of God' (Rom. 12:2). From Sidon the ship moved out into the open Mediterranean waters, and passing **to the lee of Cyprus** they reached the Asian coast and continued westwards along its shores, finally berthing at their destination, the port of **Myra** in the province of **Lycia** (5).

Here Julius was successful in finding a North African ship out of **Alexandria** which was **sailing for Italy**, and so they went **on board** (6). They **made slow headway**, however, presumably sailing into a contrary wind, and arrived, **with difficulty** off the port of **Cnidus** in the province of Caria in South-West Asia (7). Here the captain had to decide between fighting the wind through the Greek islands or making for the open sea around **Crete**. He chose the latter and eventually reached the island, and, passing **Salmone** at the east end of Crete they reached **Fair Havens** on its south coast (8).

The slow pace of the voyage now caught up with the ship and it was clear that to proceed further would be dangerous, due to winter storms which virtually shut down all sailing from early November onwards. Luke notes the date as **by now after the Fast**, a reference to the Day of Atonement, which Ramsey computed fell that year on October 5 (9). Clearly they would need to winter in a Cretan harbour. Fair Havens, however was **unsuitable to winter in. The pilot and the owner of the ship** were of a mind to sail on to the harbour at **Phoenix**, some forty miles along the south coast with a harbour which faced **both south-west and north-west, and winter there** (12).

At this point, **Paul** spoke up; we are not told in what context, though some general discussion of the options seems possible. Marshall reminds us that 'within the comparatively cramped conditions of a ship it would be difficult to keep the various groups entirely segregated from one another.'[83] **Men, I can see that our voyage is going to be disastrous and bring great loss to ship and cargo, and to our own lives also** (10). They ought therefore to stay put in Fair Havens, even with its limitations.

It is difficult to know whether Paul is speaking here from a sense of divine revelation or simply offering a common-sense judgment. The former is certainly not impossible, and would assuredly be the case as the voyage proceeded (cf. vv. 22-23). The latter, however, is also an option since, as Barclay claims, Paul was arguably 'the most experienced traveller on board that ship'.[84] Haenchen actually catalogues eleven voyages of Paul prior to this one and calculates that he had already travelled at least 3,500 miles by sea.[85] Hence his sheer experience as a sailor may have provided an adequate basis for his judgment.

Whatever its source, Paul's counsel is overridden as Julius favours the combined judgment of the ship's owner and its pilot, and so, buoyed up by the favourable sign of **a gentle south wind, they weighed anchor and sailed along the shore of Crete** bound for the safe winter harbour at Phoenix (12).

Stage 2 (27:13-44)
The dreams of an easy, uneventful voyage to Phoenix and the prospect of pleasant winter months relaxing there were

---

83. Marshall, 407.

84. Barclay, 182.

85. Haenchen, 716.

soon banished by **a wind of hurricane force, called 'the north-easter'** ('Euraquilo' literally) **which swept down** on them **from the island** directly to the north, and soon succeeded in forcing the ship out into the open sea away from the island and its protection (14-15). Hemer cites a reference to this formidable wind in an early Latin inscription.[86] Early ships had no capacity to tack in face of a wind and so the ship is soon being helplessly **driven along.**

As they are thus swept on at the mercy of the wind and sea, the sailors attempt a series of manoeuvres. First, as they passed near **a small island called Cauda** they managed with some difficulty to hoist on board the small dinghy which was trailing behind them (16). **We** did this, reports Luke, perhaps indicating his being involved, and **with difficulty**, 'probably remembering his blisters!'[87] Second, they 'frapped' the ship, undergirding it with cables. The Greek word for this[88] is a nautical term attested in both Aristotle and Philo. There are a number of possible ways of carrying out this procedure and several of the commentators list them. In essence it was a way of securing the integrity of the vessel, and thus to **hold it together**, against the danger of its breaking apart under the pounding of the waves (17). Third, fearing the dreaded **sandbars of Syrtis**, a first-century 'Bermuda triangle' [89] which ran right out into the sea from the north African coast, they **lowered the sea anchor and let the ship be driven along,** implying that the aim was to slow the ship down and hence reduce the danger of the sandbanks which lay to the south (17). The reference here is somewhat vague and some think it refers rather to lowering the mainsail. This procedure, whatever it was, apparently had no positive effect as they continued to take **a violent battering from the storm.** So **the next day** a fourth remedial action was taken; **they began to throw the cargo overboard**, possibly indicating that they were taking on water (18). This process of lightening the ship

86. C. Hemer, 'Euraqhilo and Melita', JTS 26, 1975, pp. 101-111.

87. Bruce, 509.

88. *hypozonnyntes.*

89. Marshall, 409.

was taken a stage further **on the third day** of the storm as they **threw the ship's tackle overboard** (19). 'The tackle would be all the spare gear and might even include the mainsail and main yard. They were that desperate.'[90] This was done **with their own hands**, implying probably that this had to be done without any of the lifting gear such as would normally have been available for this work in a harbour setting.

The lowest point of their despair was reached soon after as heavy clouds effectively blotted out all sighting of **sun or stars for many days**, and as **the storm continued raging, we finally gave up all hope of being saved** (20). The combined effects of seasickness from the endless tossing of the boat, and the sheer anxiety and apparent hopelessness of their position, combined not surprisingly to produce a serious loss of appetite: **the men had gone a long time without food** (21).

At this point of darkest (literally) despair, God's servant **stood up before them.** No longer is he Paul the great apostle to the Gentiles, the powerful preacher and debater, the man of learning, the veteran survivor of countless threats to life and limb, not excluding three previous shipwrecks (2 Cor. 11:25). He is Paul the prisoner, on his way to trial in Rome; but also Paul the Pastor bringing a word of gracious and desperately needed encouragement to that congregation of nearly 300 men who were staring death in the face.

Though they would, in almost every case, know nothing of Paul and his life and ministry they were ready to listen to any words of hope. He begins by noting that had he been listened to at Fair Havens, **you would have spared yourselves this damage and loss** (21). Bruce sees this as Paul's sheer humanity poking through, unable to entirely miss the opportunity to tell them 'I told you so.'[91] We should not feel it necessary to exclude that possibility; however, even if something of that underlies his first sentence – and we really cannot be sure as we have no real access to the specific human context into which Paul is

---

90. Bock, 736.

91. Bruce, 512.

speaking – his further words are replete with encouragement and hope. **But I urge you to keep up your courage (22)** – one can sense the spirits rising – **because not one of you will be lost**, – 'now if only we could really be assured of that!' – **only the ship will be destroyed** – 'well we can cope with that if only we escape alive ourselves!' Perhaps we ought to add, however, that the owner of the ship might have lost his brighter spirit at that point!

But this is no mere whistling in the dark; Paul has a basis for this confidence, which he immediately shares: **Last night an angel of the God whose I am and whom I serve stood beside me and said, 'Do not be afraid, Paul. You must stand before Caesar; and God has graciously given you the lives of all who sail with you (23-24)**. Once again a heavenly vision is given to Paul at a moment of crisis (9:3-6; 16:9; 18:9-10; 22:17-21; 23:11). The crisis of the storm has clearly not disturbed the foundation of his relationship to God; Paul remains God's possession and servant, in His hands as always, given up to whatever his Master should choose for him, whether in life or death (Phil. 1:20-23).

The mention of God 'giving' the entire ship's company to Paul surely reflects his having been interceding for them. Marshall recalls Abraham's intercession for Sodom and all of its people for the sake of a righteous remnant there.[92] Three (or perhaps four) would prove sufficient in this case! The 'must' of Paul's appearance before Caesar would offer deep reassurance, and echoed the earlier visionary word (23:11). So Paul draws the implication: **keep up your courage, men**, and the reason for it: **I have faith in God that it will happen just as he told me (25)**. Here is the heart of faith; belief in God's promise, like Abraham, 'who did not waver through unbelief regarding the promise of God, but was strengthened in his faith and gave glory to God, fully persuaded that God had power to do what he had promised'(Rom. 4:20-21). 'Faith means holding to the word and promise of God, in spite of all that stands against it'[93]. Faith is trust in truth. 'Lord, I believe, help my unbelief.'

92. Marshall: 410.

93. K. Barth, Dogmatics in Outline (SCM, 1949), p. 15

The prophetic message goes even beyond the generalities of their universal preservation to the specifics of the circumstances of it: **we must run aground on some island** (26). This message is a symbolic representation of the gospel Paul has been commissioned to preach to the world. Here is our human condition vividly illustrated – we are overwhelmed by forces which cannot be controlled, driven helplessly before them, out of touch with our bearings, lost and losing all hope as darkness falls. Into the darkness steps the Christian preacher and witness, who points us to another entire dimension, to a living God who is Lord of all things, and is fully aware of all the details of our condition and need; a God who makes promises that He is pledged to fulfil; a God who is able to master these fearful forces and bring deliverance against all the odds; a God who can save everyone who calls upon Him and can organize the very circumstances of their deliverance.

On the fourteenth night, presumably since the ship left Fair Havens; 'calculations show that this period fits in with the time it would take a ship to cover the actual distance involved if it was drifting in the manner described';[94] **about midnight the sailors sensed they were approaching land** (27). The prophecy concerning their deliverance and its precise circumstances is about to be fulfilled. This reference to divine intervention, or direction, is entirely appropriate since, as Bock notes, 'the only island for them to hit, given where they are and where they are headed, is Malta.' Granted the vastness of the ocean and the size of the island 'it would be like finding a needle in a haystack.'[95] God is rather good at haystacks, however, since He made them all, and needles too when necessary!

The sailors take soundings and find them to indicate a depth of **a hundred and twenty feet**, and then a little later, **ninety feet deep**, clearly indicating the approach of land (28). The depth measurements recorded actually agree

---

94. Marshall: 411.

95. Bock: 738.

with those established by modern soundings at the probable site of the landing. **Fearing that we would be dashed against the rocks, they dropped four anchors from the stern and prayed for daylight** (29). The final phrase should probably not be taken to imply Paul's leading a night-long prayer meeting attended by the entire company; however it is probably an indication of a desperate piety on the part of some, and maybe even the first stirrings of genuine faith in others, and of course three (or four) of those present would have been fervently at prayer in the name of Jesus.

The ship is now resting at anchor some distance from the shore awaiting daylight to determine the best way of safely reaching land. Believing that the best hope lay in abandoning the ship and getting ashore using the lifeboat-buoy **the sailors, on the pretence of lowering some** (more) **anchors, let the lifeboat down into the sea** (30). Paul, sensing what was in mind, called upon Julius and the other soldiers to intervene, **Unless these men stay with the ship you cannot be saved** (31). Without the crew, the remaining passengers would be at the mercy of the waves, and Paul may additionally have sensed that their staying all together was in some sense necessary to their all being brought together to land by God's merciful hand.

This recorded judgment of the apostle (31) has evoked not a few sermons over the centuries on the need to remain within the church to find salvation, a need encapsulated in Cyprian's famous aphorism that 'outside the Church there is no salvation'. Whatever the truth or otherwise of that claim, it needs to be asserted that it cannot receive biblical justification from the shallows off Malta! At best this passage may offer a certain 'picture' of salvation, but to learn its theological truth and meaning we need to go elsewhere in Scripture.

The soldiers at Julius' command **cut the ropes that held the lifeboat and let it fall away** (32). Marshall interestingly recalls the shipwreck in *Robinson Crusoe* where the ship ran aground in the early morning, and the crew took to the boat and all perished except for Crusoe, who later came back to the boat and observed, 'I saw evidently, that if we had kept on board, we had all got safe on shore.'[96]

Just before dawn Paul spoke up once more, urging them to eat, reminding them that they had been **in constant suspense and gone without food for the last fourteen days. Now I urge you to take some food; you will need it to survive** (33-34). He then reaffirms God's promise: **Not one of you will lose a single hair from his head**. Paul then gave the lead by taking food himself: **he took some bread and gave thanks to God in front of them all. Then he broke it and began to eat** (35). Some have claimed this was a Christian 'breaking of bread'; however, while not impossible, that appears more than the language will justify. The result was salutary: **they were all encouraged**, and afterwards completed the lightening of the ship by jettisoning what remained of the grain cargo (38). At this point Luke gives us the total number of the company, 276. Had they been counted for the sake of the food distribution? Stott asks thoughtfully.[97]

As morning dawned the shore became clearer, unrecognized by anyone, but containing an inviting **bay with a sandy beach, where they decided to run the ship aground if they could** (39). Preparations were made: the loosing of the anchors, freeing the rudder, and the hoisting of the foresail (40). However, the attempt foundered on **a sandbar** where the ship **stuck fast and would not move**, and began to break up due to the **pounding of the surf** (41).

We have already noted the Roman custom of holding guards' lives forfeit if their prisoners escaped, and since escape seemed likely once the party made their way piecemeal to shore, we are not surprised to learn that at this point **the soldiers planned to kill the prisoners to prevent them swimming away and escaping** (42). Julius however, concerned to ensure Paul's safety, intervened, and then gave the command **that those who could swim should jump overboard first and get to land. The rest were to get there on planks or on pieces of the ship.** Thus, incred-

---

96. Marshall, 412.

97. Stott, 414.

ibly it must have seemed, but entirely credible from the perspective of a present, all-powerful, gracious God, who keeps His promises, **in this way everyone reached land in safety** (43-44).

Study Questions:

1. The journey to Rome is essentially another story of God's sovereign providence. Identify the evidences of that through the account in 27:2-44.

2. If Paul's advice in 27:10 was in fact based on a divine revelation, we have here the classical alternatives of revelation *or* reason, the 'common sense' of human knowhow and experience. Discuss ways in which these alternatives are posed still in our culture, and in our lives. Is 'common sense' never to be trusted?

3. Consider 27:13-20 as a vivid picture of humanity without God and His salvation. Are there ways in which this stirring account speaks to your own condition, or to others known to you?

4. Can we echo Paul's testimony in 27:23 of God as the one 'whose I am and whom I serve'? What would help to make that an authentic personal testimony?

5. What lessons can we learn from Paul's speeches in 27:21-26 and 27:33-36? How did Paul 'encourage' the entire company by his words? Can we see ourselves as 'encouragers' of others around us who are in regular need of encouragement, including, as here, those who are not fellow believers?

Stage 3: Malta (28:1-10)

As the party gradually reassembles on the shore they discovered, presumably from their subsequent contact with the local people, that **the island was called Malta** (1). Its people were of Phoenician extraction and spoke a Phoenician dialect. Although such people were generally despised by the Greeks and Romans as 'barbarians' (cf. our often derogatory 'natives'), and traditionally were hostile to visitors, this particular island people **showed an unusual kindness**. They **built a fire and welcomed us all because it was raining and cold** (2). The fire leads to another moment of Paul's prominence. In the process of helping collect sticks to add to the fire, he also gathers up a snake, **a viper**, which **fastened itself on his hand** (3). **The islanders,** knowing at first hand the implications of a venomous snake-bite, and aware of Paul's status as one of the prisoners in the party, interpret it as a judgment: **This man must be a murderer; for though he escaped from the sea, Justice has not allowed him to escape** (4). The capitalizing of 'Justice' reflects the reference here to the goddess '*Dike*' (= Justice) who was believed to be the personification of justice and revenge. Nemesis, as we might say today, clearly had Paul's number. They watch Paul, expecting him to succumb to the poison injected by the viper, **but Paul shook the snake off into the fire and suffered no ill effects** (5). The islanders accordingly revise their view of him; **they changed their minds and said that he was a god**. As Stott notes, in Lystra they hailed Paul as a god, and then stoned him (14:11-19); in Malta they see him as a murderer, and then hail him as god.[98] The truth is of course that Paul was at neither extreme. He was, in his own just estimate, 'once a blasphemer, a persecutor and a violent man...the chief of sinners', but one on whom 'the grace of our Lord was poured out abundantly...(and, hence) an apostle of Christ Jesus by the command of God' (1 Tim. 1:13-15). So 'instead of being drowned or poisoned by *Dike*, Paul had actually been protected from both fates by Jesus.'[99]

The survivors have come ashore near the island **estate** of Malta's **chief official**, one **Publius** (7). The welcome already shown is now extended as Publius **welcomed us to his home and for three days entertained us hospitably**. Publius has an invalided father residing with him. Luke,

98. Stott: 394.
99. Stott: ibid.

possibly reflecting previous medical training, defines his condition as **suffering from fever and dysentery**, a condition, tentatively identified as 'Malta fever', which was classified over a century ago and said to be endemic to the island and other Mediterranean locales.[100] Paul visited him and **after prayer, placed his hands on him and healed him** (8). Not surprisingly this brought others similarly unwell and they too **were cured** (9). Luke does not indicate how this happened in the other cases, though there is the implication that a miraculous element was also involved for them. Paul has exercised this gift on earlier occasions (14:8-10; 19:11-12; 2 Cor. 12:12), though as ever the ultimate healer is Jesus (1:1). This ministry deeply touched the Maltese community who **honoured us in many ways**, reports Luke, **and when we were ready to sail furnished us with supplies** for their onward journey (10).

Marshall notes the absence of any reference to a Christian witness or a legacy of new converts from this island ministry.[101] It is of course dangerous to argue from silence. That many, both in the travelling party and among the island inhabitants, would have been deeply impressed by the Christian bearing and healing impact of Paul and his companions is not to be doubted. However, the absence of explicit reference to any 'converting' effect may be a reminder that there are times and places where verbal proclamation is not a necessary part of authentic Christian witness. Perhaps we meet here an implication of the combination of hearing and seeing which we have referred to several times when commenting on evangelistic models in Acts. The point from this 'Malta ministry' is that in bringing particular people to Christ the Holy Spirit can blend the 'hearing' and the 'seeing' even if offered by different Christians at widely separated periods in the convert's life. We should take heart; David Wells' title of the Holy Spirit as *God the Evangelist* is an entirely appropriate one.[102] He is the best of all evangelists…He has been part of every

---

100. Longenecker: 565.

101. Marshall: 418.

102. David F. Wells, *God the Evangelist* (Paternoster, 1987).

single Christian's coming to Christ since the day of Pentecost. We can trust Him.

The plain fact is that there are countless multitudes of people, both across the ages and around the world, who, like this present author, were brought to a commitment to Jesus Christ as personal Lord and Saviour largely through one or two Christians whose lives were so attractive that it drew them towards Christ, and softened their hearts towards the gospel message; a message which they would only hear, understand, and respond to some years later, when it was presented verbally by others.

Stage 4: Rome at last (28:11-16)
The months of winter now concluded, the resupplied party **put out to sea** once more (11). They travelled on another north African vessel, this one with a characteristic figurehead which Luke notes. The first stop is at **Syracuse** on the island province of Sicilia (today's Sicily) where they have a three-day stopover, and the next is at **Rhegium** at the southernmost tip of Italy (13). A favourable south wind blew them northwards up the Italian coast to **Puteoli**, where the travellers, presumably with their fellow prisoners and Roman custodians, finally disembarked (13). It must have been some relief to get back on land for the remaining portion of the journey. There at Puteoli they **found some brothers who invited us to spend a week with them** (14). Paul's being able to do this while still a prisoner of Rome is somewhat puzzling, though clearly he is not seen as a significant threat, and his own desire to get to Rome would be well known to Julius and others. Not for the first time in Acts, Luke tantalizingly omits details which we would be glad to have had.

Luke's next comment is the hugely significant one: **and so we came to Rome** (14). However this too appears, at least on the surface, rather misleading since in fact they have not yet reached the city. Marshall suggests, 'And in this way we made our journey to Rome', and footnotes another suggested rendering, 'and so we came to Rome as follows…'[103]

---

103. Marshall: 419.

The next verse describes, not surprisingly, how word of their approach had gone ahead of them and how a number of the Christians in Rome **travelled as far as the Forum of Appius and the Three Taverns** to meet them (15). The journey was no short step in either case: Three Taverns was over twenty miles from Rome and the Forum of Appius forty-three miles. These distances simply underline how heartfelt was the welcome extended to Paul, and in this light we can well appreciate Luke's comment that **at the sight of these men Paul thanked God and was encouraged** (15). It is perhaps worth bearing in mind, however, that these Christians had been basking in the glories of Paul's *Letter to the Romans* for the previous three years, so perhaps the enthusiasm of their welcome is not entirely surprising! The extensive list in Romans 16 of people in the Roman Christian community with whom Paul had close links also underlines the credibility of this exuberant welcome.

It is the more surprising, therefore, as the commentators note, that Luke has no further reference to the church in Rome in his remaining paragraphs. Two factors may go some way to explaining that. First, Luke clearly wishes to leave us with a picture which complements and restates his primary theme, the publishing of the gospel 'to the ends of the earth' (so vv. 28-31). Secondly, and more conjecturally, Luke may have been nearing the end of his papyrus scroll. The overall length of both his Gospel and the Acts are not dissimilar and may have been designed to fit within a single scroll. It is perhaps a supportive consideration in this connection that the final chapter of the Gospel of Luke has a similar (editorial?) 'conflation' in the accounts of the resurrection appearances.

On arrival in the city, **Paul was allowed to live by himself, with a soldier to guard him** (16). This arrangement 'seems to fit with Roman practice, attested at least for later times.'[104] Luke sees this arrangement having continued throughout his two years in Rome (30). If we follow the traditional dates for the New Testament letters of Paul, four of them were written during this Roman imprisonment as

---

104. Marshall: 420.

he awaited his arraignment before Caesar, and in three of them he refers to being 'in chains' (cf. Eph. 6:20, Col. 4:18, and Phil. 1:13-14). Thus while the conditions were relatively relaxed and did not prevent Paul being ministered to by visitors, or his exercising ministry towards others as the next passage makes clear, he continued to be under the surveillance of a Roman soldier to whom he was continually chained by his wrist (20). This also concludes the 'we' passages. However, Luke remained with Paul for at least part of these next two years, as Philemon 24 and Colossians 4:14 demonstrate.

'The most important theme of this section is that God can be taken at his word.'[105] Sometime during his long ministry in Ephesus, God had put into Paul's heart a conviction that he should visit Rome in Christ's service (19:21). Later, following his appearance before the Sanhedrin, God had confirmed that goal: 'you must also testify about me in Rome' (23:11). That destiny had been threatened in a whole series of life-threatening circumstances: the murderous assault of the mob in Jerusalem (21:30-31; 22:22); the plots of the Jews to ambush and kill him when he was en route to, and then from, Caesarea (23:12-14; 25:3); the terrible storm in the Mediterranean Sea (27:14-20); the serious threat of being killed by his Roman guards (27:42); and the deadly bite of a poisonous snake (28:3-6). Yet in spite of all these multiplied dangers, here he was, in Rome at last. God keeps His word. It is a lesson taught repeatedly in Scripture. Stott reminds us of the preservation of the baby Moses from the murderous pogrom of Pharaoh by his bulrush basket on the Nile, and of the saving of the Jews from Haman's evil plan in Esther's day, and the baby Jesus preserved from the callous slaughter of the Bethlehem infants.[106] David Livingstone's claim was certainly borne out in the case of Paul, 'A man (or woman) is immortal until his work is done.' 'God told Paul that he would reach Rome and he did; God told Paul that no lives would be lost, and they weren't; God told Paul that the

105. Bock: 747.
106. Stott: 402.

ship would run aground, and it did. God's word can be trusted because God can be trusted.'[107]

10. Ministry in Rome (28:17-31)

Having arrived in his new setting, Paul launches into ministry: **three days later Paul called together the leaders of the Jews** (17). Romans 1:16, 'first for the Jew, then for the Gentile' is honoured once again. He begins by addressing them as **brothers** – Paul is as ever the loyal Jew addressing his fellow Jews. He then explains the reasons for his imprisonment, clarifying that **I have done nothing against our people or against the customs of our ancestors**. He further asserts the Roman verdict: **they examined me and wanted to release me because I was not guilty of any crime deserving death** (18). The problem was with the Palestinian Jews whose objections meant that Paul was **compelled to appeal to Caesar** (19).

Paul then restates the real issue at stake in his rejection by the Jewish leaders and his subsequent arrival in Rome as a chained prisoner: it is **because of the hope of Israel** = because our religion is a religion of hope, with its central focus on the promise of the coming Messiah and the Messianic salvation, involving resurrection from the dead (20). The Roman Jewish leaders tell Paul that this is news to them. No report to this effect, **or anything bad about you**, has reached them from Jerusalem (21). At first sight, this seems somewhat surprising; however, apart altogether from the long delays in the legal process, as Bruce notes, 'The leaders of the Sanhedrin may have realized that if they could not proceed successfully against Paul before provincial magistrates there was still less chance of a successful prosecution in Rome...They may (at this point) have wished to have as little to do as possible with Paul and his Christianity.'[108] Further, while the Jewish community had plenty of awareness of the Christian presence – the church in Rome may have been one of the earliest churches outside of Palestine – and **we know that people**

---

107. Bock: 747.
108. Bruce: 530-1.

everywhere are talking against this sect, they would not have easily forgotten the riots ten years earlier which were probably due to tensions in the Jewish community sparked by Christian witness. Accordingly they confine themselves to a request to hear Paul's **views** (22).

This meeting involving even larger numbers took place **where Paul was staying. From morning till evening he explained and declared to them the Kingdom of God and tried to convince them about Jesus from the Law of Moses and from the Prophets**. We are struck again by the degree to which Paul seeks a rational assent to the case he presents. The verbs 'explained' (*exetitheto*), 'declared' (*diamarturomenai*), 'tried to convince' (*peitho*), all imply, as a goal, what we have earlier referred to as 'an intellectual conquest'. We may recall Paul's defence to Festus, 'what I am saying is true and reasonable' (26:25). Paul recognizes the critical importance of having the mind, as well as the emotions and will, brought into captivity to Christ (2 Cor. 10:4-5). But it is reason based upon divine revelation; it is conviction grounded in the ancient promise of God now fulfilled in the person and mission of Jesus as the Christ (Messiah).

As ever, the message divided the audience: **some were convinced by what he said but others would not believe**. Luke's phrase is insightful: not 'others were not convinced' but 'others would not believe.' Unbelief always, at a certain point, becomes a choice, and hence a culpable rejection of the Word and truth of God. Paul's message also led to their **disagreeing among themselves**, provoking Paul's **final statement: 'The Holy Spirit spoke the truth to your forefathers...'** (we note, not '*our* fathers'); then follows the citing of Isaiah 6:9-10 where the prophet complains of the people of Judah's response to God's word: specifically their dullness of heart, **this people's hearts have become calloused**, their enfeebled hearing, **they hardly hear with their ears**, and their deliberately blinded eyes, **they have closed their eyes**. This means that they cannot **turn** to God (cf. 3:19) and receive His **healing**. The identical passage was cited by Jesus (Matt. 13:14-15) when faced with similar intransigence. It is ironical, and tragic, that when they refuse to receive the Prophet's words **about Jesus** (v. 23), they actually in the event confirm the Prophet's words about them!

Before we follow Paul as, faced once again with the intransigence of the Jews, he turns to the Gentiles, it is important to note that **some *were* convinced**. And thankfully that remains the case to this day…some Jews are still being convinced, and thereby becoming 'completed Jews'.

But there is a further implication as far as Paul's evangelistic witness is concerned: **Therefore I want you to know that God's salvation has been sent to the Gentiles, and they will listen**. So, for the next two years awaiting his final appearance before the Emperor, Paul continues witnessing to all who came to him, not least the Gentiles. It was a God-honoured witness, as he reports later from his Roman prison to the Philippians: 'I want you to know that what has happened to me has really served to advance the gospel. As a result, it has become clear throughout the whole palace guard and to everyone else that I am in chains for Christ. Because of my chains, most of the brothers in the Lord have been encouraged to speak the word of the Lord courageously and fearlessly.' And he signs off with a probable further indication of his evangelistic fruitfulness: 'All the saints send you greetings, especially those who belong to Caesar's household' (Phil. 1:12-14; 4:22). We observe that the fact that 'God's salvation has been sent to the Gentiles' is a reassertion of the gospel's universal scope, and hence the global scope of the church's missional responsibility. This does not carry as a corollary, however, that the gospel should not continue to be also sent to the Jews. As he had argued to the Romans, 'Has God rejected his people? By no means!…there is a remnant chosen by grace' (Rom. 11:1, 5; 11:25-32).

Luke completes his story at this point, as we are afforded our final glimpse of the apostle: **boldly and without hindrance he preached the kingdom of God and taught about the Lord Jesus Christ** (31). Thus the book ends with this picture of 'the apostle to the Gentiles', although a prisoner, established in Rome, 'the centre of the world', freely preaching the Christian faith and bearing faithful witness to the Lord Jesus Christ. Here is a clear fulfilment of the programme mapped out by the Risen Lord Himself at the beginning of Luke's account: 'you shall be witnesses to me in Jerusalem, all Judea and Samaria, and to the ends of the earth.' This accordingly is a fitting conclusion to Luke's story.

'In sum, the book of Acts, a book of witnesses to the risen Jesus, ends with one of the key witnesses living out his calling despite having suffered unjustly. We see the continued tragic nature of Jewish unbelief, yet Paul continues to (literally) keep an open door to anyone who will listen to him and consider his message. Paul loves his enemies, whom he views as brothers who have lost their way. Nothing, including prison, persecution, or possibly death, has hindered Paul's ability to minister and to preach the message. We are led to marvel at how God has protected Paul and accomplished His word. We can also see that Paul has suffered well. He has kept the faith and continued to serve, living out his call.'[109]

The intriguing question remains, as we conclude the text: what happened to Paul after this? And why does Luke not answer that question, even briefly? That Luke does not tell us is in one sense entirely proper since the story of Acts is not the story of Paul but of the spread of the gospel through the world, of which more will be said below. The hero of these chapters is the gospel or, more precisely, the God of the gospel, not its messengers, even one as illustrious as Paul. However we can at least ponder why Luke leaves us at this point, and what in fact eventually happened to Paul.

One possibility is that Luke leaves us here because, when he completed Acts, Paul was still a prisoner in Rome awaiting his appearance before Caesar. That would require a very early date for the writing of Acts, sometime in the early sixties, and an even earlier one for the Gospel of Luke. This is not entirely impossible, but that in turn requires dating Mark's Gospel even earlier still, again not impossible, though not a widely supported view.

---

109. Bock: 759.

Another is that at the conclusion of his Roman imprisonment Paul appeared before Caesar, was found guilty,
and duly executed. That he did eventually end his life as a
martyr at the hands of the Romans is uniformly supported
in all the sources. But if it was at *this* point it leaves us
with two difficulties; one, that the attitude of the imperial
authorities is uniformly favourable throughout Acts, and
two, how to fit the Pastoral Letters into this time-frame.

A third possibility is that Paul was eventually acquitted, *either* because the Jews failed to carry through their
case against Paul – having failed to get their own provincial imperial authorities to condemn him, they possibly
recognized that there was even less likelihood of a successful prosecution in faraway Rome; *or* because the case
was heard but thrown out. This option, on either of these
two grounds, appears the most likely eventuality, and one
which would allow for a final, relatively brief, period of
ministry during which the letters to Timothy and Titus
were composed. This period was brought abruptly to an
end when a hardening of Roman attitudes towards Christians developed, as is certainly documented in Nero's
later reign. During this period of severe persecution, Paul
was rearrested and, after a further Roman arraignment,
was sentenced to be beheaded at the execution place on
the Appian Way outside Rome. If this is a fair account
of the last mile of Paul's remarkable life and ministry,
his anticipation as expressed in 2 Timothy 4:6 was truly
realized: '...the time has come for my departure. I have
fought the good fight, I have finished the race, I have kept
the faith. Henceforth there is laid up for me the crown of
righteousness...'

The final note is wholly positive. The mission in these
chapters of Acts experiences regular obstacles and setbacks, and the seemingly endless attacks of powerful,
fanatical enemies. Persecution is experienced, sacrifices
are demanded, lives are lost. Yet, despite the paucity of
their resources, the ordinariness and the modesty of the
witnesses themselves, and their almost total lack of backing from influential individuals or organizations, by grace
they prevail. The gospel continues to go forth, multitudes

respond to it, and the commission is fulfilled. The ultimate theme is the triumphant progress of the gospel.

Postscript: So...

As we conclude our journey with Luke through this great sequel to his Gospel, we face the question: what is the overall message of the Book of Acts for us today? It is not difficult to express this. As we have argued repeatedly, 1:8 is the essential perspective of Luke himself: Acts tells of the sending of the apostles, and the apostolic community they generated, to be 'witnesses to me in Jerusalem, and in all Judea and Samaria, and to the ends of the earth.' Acts is the story of the launching of that programme of witness during the first thirty years of the church's existence, from the initial, glorious outburst at Pentecost in chapter two to Paul's unhindered witness in Rome in chapter twenty-eight. Acts is the story of the first thirty years of the Christian world-mission.

But while that way of expressing the message of Acts is not wrong, it misses the greater reality. Because, as we have seen again and again through these chapters, the primary actor in the drama of Acts is neither the apostles as a body, nor Peter, nor Stephen, nor Philip, nor Paul. It is *God Himself*: the Father, whose age-long plan this fulfils; the Son, whose death, rising and ongoing presence commissions, inspires and energizes the work; and the Holy Spirit who supernaturally empowers and directs it. In other words, it is the story of the mission of the triune God, or put another way still, it is the story of the God of mission. Acts tells us not just who we are, nor what the church is, nor even what the gospel is; supremely, Acts tell us *who God is*. He is the missionary God.

And that has hugely significant implications.

It has implications for the church. How are we to think of the relationship between the church and mission? One way is to say 'Mission is something the church is meant to do' (like worship, discipleship, fellowship, etc.); thus mission is a function of the church. Here 'church' is the primary term and 'mission' is the secondary one. The second way to relate them is to say 'Mission is why we need the church.' Here 'mission' is primary and the church 'secondary'. The second option is the perspective of Acts. It is a perspective which I honestly acknowledge has come home to me with fresh power and persuasiveness as I have worked on this commentary. Looking back now over a lifetime in Christian ministry, I cannot but sense how far we in the modern Western church have moved away from this perspective of the Book of Acts. And that is serious because it means we have, to the same extent, moved away from God. It is difficult not to see parallels here to the church in Jerusalem in the opening chapters of Acts, where for all the undoubtedly good, even remarkable, things which were happening, and all the effort being expended in worthy ministries, there is no obvious sign of a community whose very reason for existence was to glorify God by evangelizing the globe. When that church lost sight of its global purpose, God, through the ministry of Stephen, blew it away from its base in Jerusalem out into the wider world of Judea and Samaria, and then by further Holy Spirit initiatives into the Gentile world. Here key city churches were established from which the gospel radiated outwards into the major imperial provinces, and was finally proclaimed boldly in Rome itself. While worship, discipleship, fellowship and ministries of compassion are certainly, and rightly, not neglected in this process, there is no question that for Acts, 'the primary task of the church is mission',[110] and furthermore, that 'for Luke mission means evangelism: the proclamation of the good news of Jesus Christ and the call to repentance and faith.'[111] Hence the challenge of Acts is clear: the church's priority is the proclamation of the good news of Jesus Christ in all the world.

But the challenge is also personal. Acts is in a real sense an unfinished book. All of us who claim to belong to God are called to add our names and stories, as the contemporary witnesses of Jesus, to those we have examined in these chapters. In other words, we are called to be part of what Jesus 'continues to do and teach'; to be available, day

---

110. Marshall: 50.

111. Marshall: 50.

by day, year by year, decade by decade, for the mission of God, personally, locally and globally; until that day when the risen and reigning One will be revealed in His glory, and the triune God will be all in all for evermore.

The implications are accordingly uncomplicated. At the communal level, where does mission come in the activities and vision of our church? At the personal level, am I available to be a 'witness' to the Risen Lord Jesus Christ, not as one feature of my life among a number of others, but as a fundamental constituent? How we express our response to this challenge is no doubt personal. For some who because of circumstances or age are no longer in their 'active years', it will mean a call to become in a new way 'prayer warriors' in the battle for the spread of the gospel among the nations. For others it will be commitment in the sphere of stewardship or other forms of supportive ministries. For some it will be engagement in ministries of compassionate service for Christ. For others again it will call for direct engagement in witness and proclamation of the gospel. The possibilities for a missional lifestyle are multiple, and will vary at different times in our lives, but that mission is to be a fundamental element of our identity is true for all. Hence, if God were to call me, am I willing to undertake service for Him in another world-area? Or, similarly, am I available to be His 'witness' within my 'native' culture, within a career vocation, a domestic vocation, or in whatever way my life is directed?

As we noted in the frontispiece, 'The Study of the Book of Acts can be very bad for your health.' As we conclude, it is time to revisit those paragraphs. But, in the final resort, we do so in a spirit of gladness, not gloom. Why so? Because, for starters Acts, whether in its biblical chapter, or its continuing story across the ages, is about 'what Jesus began to do and teach...' So to launch our lives into the seas of His global mission is, like Peter, to walk on the water *with Him*. Jesus is the great 'frontiersman' who travels the no-man's land between God and the fallen world. As we commit ourselves to be available to Him in His mission we are guaranteed new experiences of His blessed presence. Not only that, as we saw in Acts 2, the Holy Spirit is our promised empowerer. New experiences of His enabling are also assured us as we step out in God's missional service. Further still, as we noted in several places in our exposition, Acts assumes a significant link between the church's witness and God's glory. Here lies the ultimate motivation and the supreme inducement for us all. Mission glorifies God, because the gospel we are commissioned to proclaim reveals Him, as nothing else does, in the glory of His unending, life-giving righteousness; His regal sovereignty; His boundless, self-giving love; and His infinite and endless mercy; here we meet, as nowhere else, the glorious, endlessly adorable, 'three-in-one', God of the Bible. But mission glorifies Him also because as men and women, boys and girls, respond, all around the world, to the invitation of the Saviour, their hearts are cleansed from the idolatries of sin, and become instead the shrines where the living, ever-blessed, triune God begins to be loved, adored and served. Enlisting in the age-long mission of the church, of which Acts is only the first chapter, therefore means living a life of worship. It is finally a matter not so much of obedience but of privilege, the privilege of honouring Him 'who loved me and gave himself for me.' It is to become a doxological disciple. It is to discover and live out our destiny. It is to be supremely fulfilled, for God's eternal praise.

Jesus still speaks the words with which the story began, and He speaks again as the story ends. 'You shall be my witnesses in Jerusalem, all Judea and Samaria, and to the ends of the earth.' 'Do not say, "Four months more and then the harvest." I tell you, open your eyes and look at the fields! They are ripe for harvest.' And he breathed on them and said: 'Receive the Holy Spirit.' 'All authority in heaven and on earth has been given to me. Therefore go and make disciples of all the nations, baptizing them in the name of the Father, and of the Son and of the Holy Spirit, and teaching them to obey everything I have commanded you. And surely I am with you always, to the very end of the age.'

> 'Whom shall I send, and who will go for us?'
> 'Lord, here I am, send me!'

Appendices
Issues which call for comment

1. The Authorship of Acts

Traditionally the author of Acts has been viewed as the same individual who wrote the third Gospel, viz. Luke, the 'beloved physician', the friend and companion of Paul (Col. 4:14; Philem. 24; 2 Tim. 4:11). This view of the authorship of Acts held universal sway in the church until recent times, and it remains the majority view of scholars to the present.

Why has Luke's authorship been so confidently affirmed? We can distinguish internal and external evidences.

A. Internal Evidence

(1) Acts begins with a dedication to Theophilus (1:1), exactly paralleling the dedication of Luke's Gospel (Luke 1:3). The two 'works' are to be seen as 'former' and 'later' accounts of the ministry of Jesus Christ. Thus the strong case for Luke's authorship of the third Gospel carries identical weight in the case of Acts.[1]

(2) The writer is a companion of Paul. This is particularly clear in the so-called 'we' sections (16:10-17; 20:5-15; 21:1-18; 27:1-28:16). These sections lack any hint of studied literary device and, additionally, they occur fairly haphazardly through the account, thereby pointing to the

---

1. On Luke as the author of 'The Gospel According to Luke' see, for example, D.L. Bock, *Luke*, Vol. I (Baker, 1994), 4-7.

authenticity of their implied association with Paul. There is also lacking any literary precedent for this 'we' format in other secular 'histories'; again a pointer to authenticity. The 'we' implies authorship by one of Paul's companions, and the candidates for this 'we' identification are numerous: Aristarchus, Timothy, Silas, Luke, Titus, Epaphras, Barnabas. However the external evidence (below) invariably gives us only one of these as the author of Acts.

This is the more significant in that Luke was not a prominent figure in the New Testament in terms of missionary or church leadership. Furthermore, the author is not a witness personally to the events and material he records in the Gospel, and in the non-'we' sections of Acts. This raises the issue of Luke's sources, which we will comment on below. These facts, however, are confirmatory of a writer who joined the Christian story in the 'second generation' as it were, not meeting Jesus directly, becoming acquainted subsequently with His life and mission; but someone who had access in the closest way to the expanding mission of the nascent church. Luke meets all these criteria.

(3) The Greek of Acts is 'notably good',[2] and appears to reflect a writer who is utterly at home in the language, befitting one whose cultural inheritance was the Graeco-Roman world. This points up the interesting question of this author's cultural background. Acts, like the Gospel, at many points reflects the larger, global perspectives of an imperial citizen, albeit one deeply committed to the person of the Jewish Messiah, Jesus. Most writers accordingly see him as a Gentile, though there is debate on exactly which Gentile background he reflects.[3]

(4) Was he also a doctor? Colossians 4:14 refers to him as 'our dear friend, Luke, the doctor.' W.K. Hobart's nineteenth-century attempt to find classical medical vocabulary in Luke and Acts is largely discounted today,[4] though prin-

---

2. Barclay: xiv.

3. cf. Bock, *Luke*:5–6

4. W.K. Hobart, *The Medical Language of St Luke* (Dublin University Press, 1882, rep. Baker, 1954).

cipally because there was not, in point of fact, an extensive medical vocabulary at that time, rather than that Luke and Acts do not in fact reflect what there was. Perhaps just as relevant to the 'medical man' identity is the way the author comes across as a person with 'an intense and sympathetic interest in, and treatment of people…His outstanding quality is his feeling for people.'[5]

(5) The opening dedications. Martin Dibelius notes the importance of the opening dedications to Theophilus of both the Gospel and Acts, as indicating the intention to circulate these writings among the educated. For such readers the name of the author would necessarily have been included. If the prologue 'gave the name of the person to whom the dedication was addressed, the name of the author could hardly be omitted from the title.'[6]

B. External Evidence

Tradition unanimously affirms Luke to have been the author of both the third Gospel and the Acts. The attestation goes back to Marcion (d. 160; Luke, because of his association with Paul, was the only Gospel in his canon). Luke, as the author of Luke-Acts, is so listed in the important Muratorian Fragment towards the end of the second century. The Anti-Marcionite Prologue to Luke (which also includes the information that Luke was a native of Antioch, that he was a physician, that he wrote his Gospel in Achaia, and that he died at the age of eighty-four, unmarried and childless) is a further early witness. Luke's authorship of Luke-Acts is also asserted by Justin Martyr (d. 165), who refers to Luke as writing a 'memoir of Jesus' and being a companion of Paul; Irenaeus (c.180), who adds the detail that Luke was 'inseparable' from Paul; and the Lukan identification is affirmed also by Tertullian and Clement of Alexandria in the early third century, and others.

Doubts concerning Luke's authorship are confined essentially to the last few decades. They can be represented

---

5. D.J.W. Milne, *Let's Study Luke* (Banner of Truth, 2004), xiii.

6. M. Dibelius, *Studies in the Acts of the Apostles* (SCM, 1956), 148.

by Vielhauer.[7] Vielhauer claims to find important inconsistencies between the Paul of the New Testament letters and the portrait of Paul in the book of Acts; of such significance that they call in question the latter's historical value. Four such are alleged, relating to natural law, Jewish law, Christology, and eschatology. Vielhauer alleges (a) that the teaching of Romans 1 and Acts 17 are inconsistent on the possibility of a 'Natural Theology'; (b) that the atonement and work of Christ on the cross are not central in Acts in the way they are in Paul's letters; (c) that Acts has no real place for the return of Christ; (d) that the actions of Paul in Acts, e.g. in taking a vow in Jerusalem in Acts 21:26, are not compatible with the Paul of Galatians and Romans.[8]

In reply to Vielhauer it is urged:

(1) In essence the place of 'natural law' in terms of creation's bearing witness to the pagan world, is common to both Romans 1 and Acts 17; the apparent differences are due to the different contexts; evangelistic proclamation to educated pagans in the Acts 17 case, and didactic teaching for committed believers in Romans 1.

(2) Acts does not lack a stress on Christ, and salvation through His work. Indeed salvation is in fact one of the book's primary themes, and it is always salvation through Christ who died and rose again, as with Paul's letters. Explicit references to the cross occur in Acts, e.g. 1:3; 2:23, 36; 3;15, 18; 4:10 with 12; 5:30; 20:28; etc.

(3) A futurist eschatology is not absent from Acts; cf. 1:11; 3:18-22; 10:40-42; 17:30-31.

(4) That Paul's attitude throughout his ministry is governed by the principle which he states in 1 Corinthians 9:19-23: 'To those under the law I become like one under the law, so as to win those under the law; to those not having the law I become like one not having the law...' His teaching in Galatians for example, and his actions in

7. 'On the Paulinism of Acts' in *Studies in Luke-Acts: Essays Presented in Honour of Paul Schubert*, ed. L.E. Keck, and J.L. Martyn (Nashville, 1966).

8. All four of these contentions have been answered by, e.g. E. Ellis, *The Gospel of Luke* (NCB, 1974); F.F. Bruce, 'Is the Paul of Acts the Real Paul?', *Bulletin of the John Rylands Library*, 58, 282-305, 1976; and J.A. Fitzmeyer, *The Acts of the Apostles, A New Translation with Introduction and Commentary* (Anchor Bible, Doubleday, 1998).

Acts, are not incompatible in this light. We have looked at this issue at closer quarters during our exposition of the text.[9]

We may conclude with Bock: 'In sum, the external evidence strongly favours Luke as the writer of Acts. That no other Pauline companion was ever put forward as the author of this work when many such candidates existed is key evidence. It is true that the internal considerations and theological emphases raise questions…but not to the degree that cancels out the likelihood that he was the author, and that the tradition has the identification correct.'[10] We note, in similar vein, the judgment of Howard Marshall: 'The tradition in favour of Luke's authorship of the Gospel and Acts is as good as that for any other of the Gospel writers.'[11] The case for Lukan authorship is a very strong one, and hence we make no apology for having adopted it in our exposition of the text.

Finally on authorship: it is surely not out of order to consider the place and function of the book of Acts from the *divine* perspective. Salvation has come to the world through Jesus Christ…but it needs to be shared globally, because God is finally the God of *all* the earth, and *all* of its peoples. Anything less reduces God to a tribal deity, even if the tribe be the people He chose as the historic vehicle of His purpose, Israel. An account of that earliest period when the apostles are still alive and many of the primary principles of the Christian global mission are being hammered out under the Holy Spirit's direction, would clearly be of enormous assistance to the church in succeeding generations. The apostles in general are still (understandably) struggling with the ethno-centrism of their upbringing (cf. 1:6; 10:9-16). The early leaders who are most profoundly grasped by this global vision are Stephen and Paul; but Stephen is martyred, and Paul needs someone else to do the research and the writing-up of a story in which he himself is a central actor, ideally someone who is utterly

---

9. On this more generally, see D.L. Bock, *Acts.*, 16-19.

10. Bock: 19.

11. Marshall: 45.

sympathetic to the faith, and who has obtained an intimate knowledge of Jesus, but also one whose world is the global world of the Graeco-Roman empire. It would also be very helpful if the one so chosen is a person of evident education and intelligence, has the freedom to travel freely, a wide cultural awareness, an intense perceptivity with an eye for detail, a companion of Paul, and withal, a gifted writing style. Who meets all these criteria? – Luke, the author of Acts!

2. The Date of Acts

The linked authorship of Luke and Acts means that the dating of Acts is necessarily bound up with the dating of the Gospel. This issue is well surveyed by D. Guthrie in his *New Testament Introduction*,[12] and D.L. Bock, *Acts*,[13] and *Luke*.[14] The student is referred to these sources, but additional discussions are to be found in all the standard commentaries on *Luke* and *Acts*. There are broadly three options: a date before 64, a date in the 64–70 period, and a date post–70, extending for some as late as the second century. I will simply list the arguments for an early, pre–64 date and then note other considerations which lead some scholars to propose a later point of writing. All the issues here touch the Gospel as well as Acts.

For a date before 64

(1) *The absence of reference to key events in the 60s*: specifically the martyrdom of James, the leader of the Jerusalem church, in c.62, and the great fire of Rome in 64 leading to the Neronian persecution of the church. The first of these is the more significant. Lack of reference to James' death is an argument from silence and hence needs to be used with reserve, and Nero's fire, as Bruce points out, was an embarrassment to the Romans, and hence seen as aberration, which might explain its omission. However, the general attitude of tolerance of Christianity by the Empire

12. Donald Guthrie, *New Testament Introduction* (Tyndale, 1970), 340-8.

13. D.L. Bock: *Acts* (Baker academic, 2007), 25-7.

14. D.L. Bock: *Luke*, 2 vols (Baker, 1994), vol. 1, 16-18.

all the way through to the conclusion of Acts does need to be weighed. Further, the absence of allusion to the outbreak of the Jewish War in 66 and the fall of Jerusalem in 70, or any sign of its impact, is probably more important than either of the above, though this of course would imply only a date earlier than 70.

(2) *The absence of reference to the death of Paul.* This is probably the strongest supporting circumstance favouring a pre–64 date. The date of Paul's martyrdom is commonly set at 64, however some support a later time, up to 67. It is pointed out, however, that there is possibly a veiled reference to Paul's upcoming martyrdom at 20:25. It should also be noted that the goal of Acts, as we will argue later, is the global spread of the gospel not the career of Paul with its heroic climax. That goal is arguably achieved by the arrival of the gospel in Rome (28:14).

(3) *The primitive nature of the subject matter.* It is striking how appropriate the opening speeches are to the setting of the earliest witness in Jerusalem. Further the Jewish-Gentile relationship is a central issue, as it certainly was in these first years, but declined in importance after the fall of Jerusalem and the scattering of the Jerusalem-based Jewish church to Jamnia and other Palestinian centres after 70. In other words, Acts reflects authentically the issues and ideas of the earliest stages of the church's life. In this connection the prominence and authority of the Sadducees in the opening chapters belongs to the pre-70 situation.

(4) Closely associated is *the primitive character of the theology of Acts.* Thus titles such as 'the Christ', 'the servant of God' and 'the Son of man' are common, and there is little sign of a fully developed doctrine of the atonement. Also notable are references to the Christians as 'disciples' and the people of Israel as *laos.*

(5) *The attitude of the state towards the church.* The impartiality towards the church in Acts is in notable contrast to that which obtained in many provinces after 64.

(6) *The relation to the Pauline letters.* The writer of Acts shows no acquaintance with Paul's letters, and certainly not with the early attempts to collect these in a *Corpus Paulinum.*

(7) *The 'Immediacy' of Acts, particularly of its closing chapters.* These are marked, Hemer notes, 'by the apparently unreflective reproduction of insignificant details, a feature which reaches its apogee in the narrative of Acts 27–28… The locations of insignificant places in Crete, the frustrated plans of the ship's company, the nautical manoeuvres, and the topography of the Maltese shore, are not only theologically irrelevant, but hard to explain except as vivid experience recalled before the details could blur or be merged in a longer perspective of reflection.'[15]

For a date later than 64
The biggest obstacle to dating Luke-Acts prior to 64 is the Gospel's proven use of Mark. Clearly the evidence of the text of Luke means that Mark must be dated even earlier than both Luke's writings, which is not impossible but, among other things, has to take the view that Mark 13:14's reference to the 'abomination of desolation…in the Holy Place' is purely inspired prophecy and not influenced in any way by events during the sack of Jerusalem in 70. However, on the other hand of course, one dare not set limits to the prophetic possibilities inherent to the mind of Jesus, or to the inspiration of the Holy Spirit (2 Pet. 1:21).

For a date after 70
Some interpreters have even favoured a date well into the second century, but their case is a weak one at best, and would call for quite remarkable literary powers on the part of the author in his evident ability to capture so fully realities obtaining a century and more previous to his own time of writing. Additionally such a late date would require mastery of the many points of detailed local knowledge of first-century affairs, such as the names and official titles of Roman officials, on which Luke, writing in Acts, has been thoroughly exonerated. Such dating also runs into clear

---

15. C. Hemer, *The Book of Acts in the Setting of Hellenistic History.* Ed. C.H. Gempf (Tubingen, Mohr, 1989), 380; Hemer presents fifteen arguments for an early date of composition, opting personally for A.D. 62; cf. 376-82.

difficulty with the unanimity of the external support for Luke as the author of both volumes.

Marshall cites Bruce as suggesting that the composition of Luke-Acts may have taken place over an extended period of time and been finally issued 'towards A.D. 70';[16] Bock concurs.[17]

3. Acts and History

It is customary to understand Acts as a fairly straightforward 'history of the early church'. Its very title 'Acts' (which is the entire title of the earliest manuscripts, and hence arguably Luke's title also), prepares us for a description of historical events and their impact. The text does not disappoint in this regard. The storyline begins with what purports to be scenes in Jerusalem during the final period of Jesus' ministry and the beginning of the Christian movement which emerged out of it. In geographical terms the account then moves us on beyond Jerusalem to critical moments in Christianity's spread to surrounding territories, notably Samaria and Judea, and then we are carried on, with the spreading message of Jesus, as the church begins to root itself in the wider Graeco-Roman world, successively in the Roman provinces of Syria, Cilicia, Pamphylia, Galatia, Asia, Macedonia and Achaia, before we find ourselves, finally, accompanying Paul, as a prisoner, on an exciting journey, by way of Crete and Cilicia, to Rome, the imperial capital, where he continues to preach the gospel as he awaits his impending arraignment before Caesar.

This relatively straightforward, historical view of Acts appears to be in accord with Luke's own view of his work and its method, as expressed in his Prologue to the Gospel of Luke (1:1-4). In antiquity, the preface to a two-volume work carried over to the whole, and hence this passage is to be viewed as the 'real preface to Acts as well as the Gospel'.[18]

---

16. Marshall: 48.

17. Bock: 27.

18. FJ. Foakes-Jackson and K. Lake, *The Beginnings of Christianity* (Macmillan, 1920–23), Vol. II, 492.

Luke's method, he informs us, consisted of a series of steps or stages. He delineates five. First there are the events themselves, which he refers to as 'the things fulfilled' (Luke 1:1). In the case of the Gospel they are primarily the events of the life and ministry of Jesus. Luke was not himself directly present for any of this, though he notes that others have 'drawn up accounts'. The verb 'fulfilled' (*plerophorew*) probably points to Luke's conviction that Jesus' life and ministry had been prophesied in the Old Testament.

Second is the evidence of those who were actually present, and have 'handed down' their recollections of the ministry of Jesus. Luke appears to have in mind particularly the original apostles since he refers to them as 'eye-witnesses, from the first (beginning)' and 'servants of the Word'.

Third, there is Luke's own work of research, his having 'carefully investigated everything from the beginning', implying as part of this, his personal interrogation, of some at least, of these 'first-generation' eye-witnesses. This is important in indicating his unwillingness to uncritically transmit the information conveyed to him. It has all been subjected to a process of careful scrutiny on Luke's own part.

Fourth, Luke had composed his book(s), Luke and Acts. He refers to this in the opening verse as 'drawing up an orderly account'. Thus the material at his disposal from others, and the fruits of his own direct research, has all been subjected to a certain organizational 'ordering'.

Finally, in the last stage, Luke-Acts was offered for reading and study, and Luke's hope is that it will effectively undergird the convictions of his sponsor, and now reader, Theophilus, and others like him. They, through reading Luke's account, will come to 'know the certainty' of what they had been taught concerning Jesus and the Christian religion. Luke's account accordingly 'conveys in a permanent and assured form what Theophilus had previously learned in a less systematic manner.'[19] That is, it

---

19. Creed, *The Gospel According to St. Luke* (Macmillan, 1942); cf. also Marshall: 21.

will tell what actually took place and enable his beliefs to be rooted in historical actuality.

It is difficult to read the terms of Luke's statement of method without sensing a kindred spirit. Here resonates something of the critical, investigative spirit of Luke's inherited classical civilization which was, and has continued to be, a primary constituent of the post-medieval mind and its pursuit of truth.

This 'assured history' approach to Luke's work has, particularly in the modern period, been assailed by interpreters. F.C. Bauer, leader of the Tubingen school in the later nineteenth century, which approached the history of the early church on the basis of the assumption of a major division between the Petrine and Pauline factions, saw Acts as an attempt by Luke to pour oil on the troubled waters by writing a fairly imaginative account of Christian origins which would paper over the cracks of the controversy. Acts' reliability as actual history was, therefore, dubious at best.

This view never held unchallenged sway. Harnack, the influential German theologian, through his visits to the Holy Land, was deeply impressed by Luke's reliability in the Palestinian portions of his writings with respect to topographical and chronological details, as revealing 'the care, the consistency, and the trustworthiness of the writer.'[20]

Famously Sir William Ramsey, writing at the end of the nineteenth century, having previously absorbed Bauer's critical views, was led by his own 'on the ground' research of Paul's journeys as recorded by Luke in Acts to an entirely different judgment. He discovered at point after point that Luke was entirely faithful to the Roman sources, and was led to place 'the author of Acts as among the historians of the first rank'.[21]

This respect for Luke's historical trustworthiness finds echo in the recent period in the work of Graeco-Roman

20. A. Harnack, *The Acts of the Apostles* (Williams & Norgate, 1909), 112.

21. W.M. Ramsey, *St Paul the Traveller and the Roman Citizen* (Hodder & Stoughton, 1895), 4.

historian A.N. Sherwin-White, not himself a professing Christian, who writes: 'For Acts the confirmation of historicity is overwhelming...Any attempt to reject its basic historicity even in matters of detail must now appear absurd. Roman historians have long taken it for granted.'[22]

Of similar force is the recent work of the late, and sadly missed, evangelical scholar, Colin Hemer, whose volume, *The Book of Acts in the Setting of Hellenistic History* (1989) is already a landmark in Acts study. After Hemer's thorough investigation of every major point of historical overlap, the conclusion reads: 'Contrary to modern opinion on the subject, ancient historians were capable of very rigorous and critical methods and principles... (In the case of *Acts*) we discovered a wealth of material suggesting an author or sources familiar with the particular locations and the times in question. Many of these connections have only recently come to light with the publication of new collections of papyri and inscriptions. We considered these details from various perspectives... in the way they supported and confirmed different ways of reading the text. By and large these perspectives all converged to support the general reliability of the narrative.'[23]

The appearance of post-modernism in the last forty years or so has further impacted the entire historical project by arguing, in keeping with its premise that all attempts at knowledge are subject to the obfuscating biases and tendentiousness of the knower, that 'history' is essentially a fictive art, a matter of construction on the part of the historian, rather than a description of objective events. To ask questions concerning special interests and subjective biases in accounting for the past, as post-modernism does here, is of course entirely legitimate, as it always has been. Indeed the Christian doctrine of universal fallenness would offer clear biblical support for this very insight. But

---

22. A.N. Sherwin-White, *Roman Society and Roman Law in the New Testament* (OUP, 1963; Baker, 1978), 189.

23. C. Hemer: 412.

to move from that to an elimination in principle of every effort to determine what happened in the past, is a step which defies even common sense, and one which in fact the proponents of post-modernism, like everyone else on planet earth, do not in practice consistently live by in their everyday lives.[24] As has been pointed out, it is surely striking that professional historians in many fields continue to do their research, and publish their findings along with the customary presentation of supportive evidences, with a confidence apparently unaffected by the post-modern critique.

To defend Luke in terms of his method and general reliability, however, does not imply that he is only interested in presenting objective facts and events. Luke is a theologian as well as an historian; that is, he comes to his work with certain convictions about God and Jesus Christ, and the human condition and God's salvation. In other words, how he tells the story of the spread of the gospel is necessarily impacted by his own view of what the gospel is. In this Luke is no different from any other New Testament or Old Testament writer.

In the recent period, however, the recognition of Luke's theological convictions has been carried to extreme limits so that, in words of William Neill, 'The trend of recent scholarship has been to move away from the traditional picture of "Luke the historian" to "Luke the theologian" or even "Luke the mythographer".'[25]

The issues here obviously relate to the Gospel as well as Acts. It is sufficient to note that:

(1) the assumption that holding personal convictions inevitably imports significant distortion into a writer's

---

24. Those wishing to explore these issues at greater depth may like to refer to chapter five of William Craig's *Reasonable Faith* (Crossway, 1994) and his extensive bibliography of works relating to this area on pp. 313-16. cf. also D.A. Carson, *The Gagging of God* (Zondervan, 1996), esp. chapters 2 and 3.

25. Wm. Neill, *The Acts of the Apostles*, NCB (Marshall, Morgan & Scott, 1973), 17. Influential in this development has been the work, among others, of C.F. Evans, 'The Central Section of Luke's Gospel' in *Studies in the Gospels*, ed. D.E. Nineham, 1955; Hans Conzlemann's *The Theology of St Luke*, ET 1960; and J.C. O'Neill, *The Theology of Acts*, 1961.

composition is debatable. Quite apart from the reality of the Holy Spirit's sovereign supervision (cf. 2 Pet. 1:21: 'men spoke from God as they were carried along by the Holy Spirit'; John 14:26-27; 15:26; 16:13-16; 2 Tim. 3:16; 1 Cor. 2:2-16; Heb. 3:7; 10:15; etc.), it is far from self-evident that personal conviction necessarily eliminates the ability to faithfully report events and spoken testimony.

(2) In the case of Acts the proven reliability of Luke in multiple matters of detail; his making good, in other words, on his claim to have 'carefully investigated everything' (Luke 1:3) retains its currency value. So whatever may be said about Luke as a theologian can never be allowed to eliminate the fact that he is also, in Ramsey's words above, 'a historian of the first rank.'

(3) The real question with respect to Luke's theological outlook is not whether he has one. In a real sense every living, breathing person on planet earth has a theology, i.e. they have certain views, however inchoate and unsystematized, of God – whether or not He exists, who He is and what He may be expected to do, about the world and human beings in general, and about themselves in particular.

The real challenge concerning Luke's theology is to identify what his theological convictions actually are, whether they are congruent with those expressed by other New Testament writers, and with the theology of Scripture as a whole, and hence to what extent they seriously undermine his claim to record an orderly and reliable account of the early years of the Christian mission. Important issues in this regard are the relationship of the teaching of Acts to that of Paul's letters; the view of Jewish law in Acts; the decrees of the Jerusalem Consultation in relation to other New Testament witness; Luke's portrait of Paul; and the Speeches in Acts. These questions have all been addressed in the text of this commentary as they arose. At no point did we find Luke's stated views inimical to our conviction of his entire faithfulness as a witness to the events he records, and to his being a truthful and reliable scribe in the hands of the Holy Spirit, contributing in the Book of Acts a work worthy to set alongside his Gospel of Luke and together holding a place of eminent worthiness in the Holy Scriptures.[26]

4. The Sources of Acts

In his apology for his method in Luke 1:1-4 the evangelist refers to the testimony of 'eye-witnesses' (v. 2), and to his bringing everything together in an 'orderly account' (v. 3). Thus affirming, as we did above, the presidency of the Holy Spirit does not eliminate the value of identifying how the Spirit worked in Luke's case, where clearly his ministry involved a work of inspiration effected through, rather than apart from, Luke's sources. This raises the fascinating and important question of what were the sources which Luke employed.

There are of course the 'we' sections already referred to (16:10-17; 20:5-15; 21:1-18; 27:1–28:16) where Luke's personal memory of the events would have provided most, if not all, that he needed. In that connection it is interesting to note the work of James Smith, a lifelong mariner and sailor, first published in 1848, *The Voyage and Shipwreck of St Paul,* in which the author, after making an extensive study of ancient ships and their methods of navigation, argued persuasively that Acts 27 must have been written by an eye-witness, but one who was not himself a sailor.

But what about the other sections? Despite energetic efforts over a long period, very little of generally acknowledged conclusion has been arrived at. The Catholic scholar, Jacques Dupont, after a searching examination in *The Sources of Acts* (1964), concluded 'it is impossible to define any of the sources used by the author of Acts in a way that will meet with widespread agreement among the critics.'[27] The basic reason for this rather bleak conclusion is that Luke 'has successfully managed to conceal what-

---

26. On this general issue of Luke as a historian and theologian, see D. Guthrie, *New Testament Introduction*, 354-63; I.H. Marshall, *Luke: Historian and Theologian* (Paternoster, 1970); Colin J. Hemer, *The Book of Acts in the Setting of Hellenistic History*, ed. C.H. Gempf (J.C.B. Mohr, Tubingen, 1989), chaps. 3–5; Craig L. Blomberg, *The Historical Reliability of the Gospels* (IVP Downers Grove, 1987); and P. Rhodes and G.A. Boyd, *The Jesus Legend* (Baker Academic, 2008).

27. J. Dupont, *The Sources of the Acts: The Present Position* (London, 1964), 166.

ever sources he used beneath a uniform editorial style'.[28] In other words Acts is from beginning to end Luke's own literary work; he clearly uses a variety of sources but has written the final text himself in a manner which makes the sources exactly that, his servants rather than his masters.

Bock offers some general perspectives. Chapters 1–12 are obviously informed by a source or sources in the Jerusalem community. Chapter 6:8–8:40 may indicate insights from more Hellenistic-leaning disciples. Acts 9, with its account of Paul's conversion and some of his early ministry, most probably may have come from Paul himself. The latter part of 9 and 10–11 may have come directly from Peter or from disciples who were present at Lydda or Caesarea. From 13 onwards Paul would be an obvious source, with perhaps some supplementary material provided from the various centres such as Philippi, Antioch, Corinth and Ephesus, a possibility suggested perhaps by the vividness of some of the descriptions; though Paul's memory of these events must have remained strong. That brings us to the 'we' sections, and the final journey to Rome, interspersed by the judicial process and the speeches delivered in the course of it in 22–26. As with the speeches throughout Acts, these fit tightly and authentically into their settings. We considered the Speeches in detail in the course of our exposition.[29]

For numerous scholars the inability to detect with assurance what Luke's sources were, due to his working them so thoroughly into his own writing style, has generated a lack of confidence in his historical reliability. Marshall offers two reasons to question this scepticism. First, 'the activities of the apostles and the establishment of congregations were events that formed part of the missionary proclamation of the church, and thus conditions were favourable to the preservation of traditions about the history of the church.'[30] Second, Luke's Gospel gives us a

---

28. Marshall: 37.

29. Bock: 19-20.

30. Marshall: 38; following J. Jerwell, *Luke and the People of God* (Minneapolis, 1972), 19-39.

significant opportunity to check Luke's standards for the use of sources from his use there of both Mark and 'Q' (the presumed lost source which he shared with Matthew). What emerges upon careful examination is Luke's significant faithfulness to these sources even though casting them at points in his own language. To quote F.C. Burkitt, 'What concerns us is not that Luke has changed so much, but that he has invented so little.'[31]

5. The Speeches of Acts

Acts to a significant degree is composed of speeches. These include legal defences both ad hoc and carefully rehearsed, sermons in synagogues, impromptu sermons, and more specific words of encouragement or witness. There are nineteen of these scattered through the book.

Specifically they comprise: Peter's speech on the need to replace Judas (1:15-22); Peter's Pentecost sermon (2:14-39); Peter's sermon after the healing of the lame man (3:12-26); Peter's defence before the Sanhedrin (4:8-12); Peter and the apostles' defence before the Sanhedrin (5:29-32); Stephen's defence before the Sanhedrin (7:2-53); Peter's sermon in the home of Cornelius (10:34-43); Peter's subsequent defence before the Jerusalem church (11:4-17): Paul's sermon in the synagogue at Pisidian Antioch (13:16-41); Paul and Barnabas' message in Lystra (14:15-17); Peter's speech at the Council in Jerusalem (15:7-11); James' speech at the Council in Jerusalem (15:13-21); Paul's sermon before the Areopagus in Athens (17:22-31); Paul's message to the Ephesian elders (20:18-35); Paul's defence before the mob in Jerusalem (22:3-21); Paul's defence before the Sanhedrin in Jerusalem (23:1-6); Paul's defence before Felix (24:10-21); Paul's defence before Festus, Agrippa and Bernice (26:2-23); Paul's sermon to the believers in Rome (28:25-28); nineteen in all. This amounts to 'twenty-five percent' of the book (Stott);[32] 'fully one third' (Bock).[33]

---

31. In F.J. Foakes-Jackson and K. Lake, *The Beginnings of Christianity* (London, 1920–33), II, 115.

32. Stott: 69.

33. Bock: 20.

Are all of these verbatim reports of what was said? Or are they at least highly reliable accounts of what was said? Those who dismiss these possibilities draw attention to the obvious fact that in many cases they are too short to be full statements. Clearly some degree of summary is being adopted. Further there appear to be some evidences of common stylistic features, indicating some level of editorial reworking. It is also noted that there was no such thing in ancient literature as quotation marks.[34] Hence we must not bind Luke to contemporary levels of accuracy in such matters. Further, standards of reporting verbal testimony in ancient times were notoriously fluid. Josephus, for example, admits to making little attempt to provide an accurate account of such, and Thucydides allows for some creativity by the author. In view of these considerations, we are urged to set aside any thoughts of precise verbal correspondence to the spoken words.

There are however significant points to be made on the other side. For example, dealing in a fast-and-loose manner with spoken testimony was 'not a universally accepted practice' in classical times.[35] Thucydides speaks of his attempt to 'as nearly as I could to gain the general purport of what was said.' Further as many commentators have noted, Luke's accounts are remarkably fitted to their historical settings. In particular we can note that the speeches in the early chapters of Acts are notably 'old-fashioned' in respect of their phraseology and theology.[36] Thus the Christology of these early sermons focuses on the Messiahship of Jesus rather than His deity; cf. 'Jesus the Nazarene,' 'your holy servant Jesus.' Similarly 'a primitive concept of redemption is used: Jesus is seen in terms of his redemption of Israel as a nation...When one compares 1 Peter, Mark (which tradition says came from Peter), and Peter's speeches in Acts, the language, style and emphases are almost identical. This

---

34. cf. C. Blomberg, in Wm. Craig, *Reasonable Faith*, second edition, 207.

35. W.W. Gasque, *A History of the Criticism of the Acts of the Apostles* (Grand Rapids, 1975), 226-8.

36. H.N. Ridderbos, *The Speeches of Peter in the Acts of the Apostles* (Tyndale, 1962), 10.

makes sense if one assumes that all three actually refer to statements which came from Peter himself.'[37] C.H. Dodd notes that the 'kerygma is primitive'.[38] Other writers have drawn attention to further primitive elements, particularly in the use of Old Testament citations. The uniqueness of some of the speeches stands out clearly showing a 'tight fit' with their settings, e.g. Stephen's defence before the Sanhedrin, or Paul's sermon to the Areopagus. Marshall further notes that 'Luke's accounts are not as polished as would be the case in literary creations. They show the kind of redundancies and minor incoherences which mark the incorporation of traditions into a redactional framework.' So, for example we can ask, 'What sort of things would Peter have said to the Jews if he did not say the things Luke ascribes to him?' 'It is very difficult to imagine him taking a line very different from that which he is alleged to have taken.'[39]

There is some evidence that Luke is not claiming exact reproduction in every case, as the two accounts of Peter's sermon in the home of Cornelius may indicate (chs. 10 and 11), though there would appear no requirement that Peter should have used exactly the same words in his subsequent report in any case. The three forms of Paul's conversion may appear to have similar import, but again there is an antecedent likelihood that Paul would have adapted his accounts to the settings, as is notoriously the case when people today share an important biographical moment. We can note that, on a few occasions, conversations which Luke could have had no direct access to, are reported, e.g. that between Festus and Agrippa, or the closed sessions of the Sanhedrin. However in the latter case sympathetic persons were present (Joseph and Nicodemus), and in the former they may have been civil servant eavesdroppers or subsequent public reports of policy decisions. F.F. Bruce comments, 'Taken all in all, each speech suits the speaker,

---

37. J.P. Moreland, *Scaling the Secular City* (Baker, 1987), 155-6.

38. C.H. Dodd, *The Apostolic Preaching and its Development* (Hodder and Stoughton, 1936), 35.

39. Marshall: 40-1.

the audience, and the circumstances of delivery...and this gives good ground for believing these speeches to be, not inventions of the historian, but condensed accounts of speeches actually made, and therefore valuable and independent sources for the history and theology of the primitive church.'[40]

Other points in Luke's defence are his clear concern for accuracy in his reporting, as reflected through the twenty-four chapters of his Gospel. Guthrie refers for example to his use of Mark 13 in Luke's Gospel, and claims 'there is no evidence that Luke invented material not found in his sources.' Further, Moreland observes the way in which the speeches of Acts 1–2 translate very well into Aramaic, and the otherwise unlikely presence of a seven-week delay between the event of the resurrection and its public proclamation; not at all the kind of detail which would be created by a freely inventing apologist. Renowned classical historian Sherwin-White notes that it takes more than two generations to wipe out a historical core.[41]

In general, we can echo the judgment of Hengel: 'Luke is quite simply not concerned with pious edification at the expense of truth. He is not just an "edifying writer", but a historian and theologian who needs to be taken seriously.'[42] Additionally, we need to note Luke's regular opportunities to access primitive tradition in the churches during his journeys and to actually hear apostolic speeches.

Further, it is certainly not unlikely that some written transcripts may have existed in first-century culture, and we dare not minimize the capacity for people in the largely non-literary world of the first century to have possessed highly developed memorization skills which have been proven, as the Dead Sea Scrolls have demonstrated, to enable considerably detailed, highly accurate, reproduction over a long period of major amounts of traditional material.

---

40. F.F. Bruce: 'Speeches in the Acts of the Apostles' (Tyndale, 1942), 27.

41. Sherwin-White: 186-193.

42. M. Hengel, *Acts and the History of Earliest Christianity* (SCM, 1979), 61.

Finally, we need to set no limits to the inspirational power of the Holy Spirit. Our Lord on one occasion bore testimony to the possibilities inherent in the divine supervision of human language: 'I did not speak of my own accord, but the Father who sent me commanded me what to say, and how to say it' (John 12:49). If it be replied that this refers to a perfect mind, we can recall the not dissimilar claim of the apostle Paul: 'we speak not in words taught us by human wisdom but in words taught by the Spirit, expressing spiritual truths in spiritual words' (1 Cor. 2:13).

Bibliography

Alexander, J.A. *A Commentary on the Acts of the Apostles* (1875, Banner of Truth, 1963, 2 vols.).

Barclay, William. *The Acts of the Apostles* (Saint Andrew Press, 1953, 1955).

Barclay, William. *The Letters to the Galatians and Ephesians* (Saint Andrew Press, 1954, 1958).

Barrett, C.K. *A Critical and Exegetical Commentary on the Acts of the Apostles*: Vol. 1: Acts I–XIV (T&T Clark, 1994); Vol. 2: Acts XV–XXVIII (T&T Clark, 1998).

Bavinck, J.H. *An Introduction to the Science of Missions* (Presbyterian and Reformed, 1961).

Bock, D.L. *Acts* (Baker, 2007)

Bosch, D. *Transforming Mission* (Orbis, 1991).

Bosch, D. *Witness to the World* (Marshall, Morgan and Scott, 1980).

Bruce, F.F. *Commentary on the Book of Acts* (Marshall, Morgan and Scott, 1954).

Calvin, J. *The Acts of the Apostles*: Vol. I: 1–13. 1552. Tr. J.W. Fraser and W.J.G. McDonald (Oliver and Boyd, 1965); Vol. II: 14–28. 1554. Tr. J.W. Fraser (Oliver and Boyd).

Conzlemann, H. *The Acts of the Apostles*, tr. J. Limburg. A.T. Kraabel, D.H. Juel (Fortress, 1987).

Dunn, J.D.G. *Jesus and the Spirit* (SCM, 1975).

Eddy, P.R. and G.A. Boyd. *The Jesus Legend* (Baker Academic, 2007).

Fernando, A. *Acts* (Zondervan, 1998).

Fitzmyer, J.A. *The Acts of the Apostles* (Doubleday, 1998).

Gasque, W.W. and R.S. Martin. *Apostolic History and the Gospel: Biblical and Historical Essays* (Paternoster, 1970).

Gasque, W.W. *History of the Criticism of the Acts of the Apostles* (Morh, Tubingen, 1975).

Green, M. *Thirty Years That Changed the World* (InterVarsity, 2002).

Haenchen, E. *The Acts of the Apostles* tr. B. Noble and G. Shinn (Blackwell, 1987).

Hanson, R.P.C. *The Acts* (Clarendon, 1982).

Hemer, C.J. *The Book of Acts in the Setting of Hellenistic History* (Mohr, 1989).

Jenkins, P. *The Next Christendom* (OUP, 2002).

Johnson, L.T. *The Acts of the Apostles.* Sacra pagina 5. (Collegeville, MN: Liturgical Press, 1992).

Larkin, W.J., Jr. *Acts* (InterVarsity, 1995).

Longenecker, R.N. *The Acts of the Apostles* (Zondervan, 1981).

Marshall, I.H. *The Acts of the Apostles* (Tyndale, 1980).

Marshall, I.H. 'Palestinian and Hellenistic Christianity', *NTS 19*; 1972–3; 271-87.

Neill, Wm. *The Acts of the Apostles,* NCB (Marshall, Morgan and Scott, 1973).

Pohill, J.B. *Acts* (Broadman, 1992).

Reymond, R.L. *Paul: Missionary Theologian* (Christian Focus, 2000).

Sherwin-White, A.N. *Roman Society and Roman Law in the New Testament* (Clarendon, 1963)

Smith, D.W. *Against the Stream* (IVP, 2003).

Stott, J.R.W. *The Message of Acts* (InterVarsity, 1990).

Witherington, B., III. *The Acts of the Apostles* (Paternoster, 1998).

Wright, C.J.H. *The Mission of God* (IVP Academic, 2006).

Wright, N.T. *The Resurrection of the Son of God* (Fortress, 2003).

Scripture Index

Subject Index

Aaron 106
Abraham 102, 116, 156-8, 440
Aeneas 227, 228
Agabus 265, 266, 410
agnosticism 64
Agrippa II 445-6, 447-68
alms, giving of 94
Ananias (Damascus)
    instructed by Jesus 212-14
    restores Paul's sight 210, 216, 422
Ananias (high priest) 428-9, 430, 437-42
Ananias and Sapphira 87, 120, 123-5
Annas 108, 129
Antioch
    'Christians' in 264-5
    diversity in 264-5, 280
    Gentile mission in 257-60, 263
    as Paul's 'home church' 374
    receives letter to Gentiles 324
    sends relief to Jerusalem 267
Apollos 375-7
apostles
    appoint administrators 141
    bear witness to Christ 37-8, 76
    deal with Judas Iscariot 'issue' 47-52
    definition of 299
    'dim-wittedness' of 32, 33
    disavow their own worth 97
    fear of 178
    filled with the Holy Spirit 56-8, 60, 119
    freed by an angel 130
    hastiness to appoint Matthias 50-2
    imprisonment of 107, 130
    instructions from Holy Spirit 19, 20, 24-5, 30-1, 246

    meet in Jerusalem 45
    mistrust of Paul 221
    mockery of 63-4
    prayer of 46-7
    receive lashes 134-5
    status of 25
    taught by Christ 66-7
    as teachers 85-6, 130
    see also individuals (i.e. Peter)
Aquila and Priscilla 365, 370, 375-6
Aquinas, Thomas 94
Areopagus (Athenian forum) 357-62
Aretus, King 217, 218
Aristarchus 388, 472
Artemis (Temple of Diana) 374-5, 386-7, 388
Asiarchs 388, 390-1
atheism 64, 216, 247, 381
Athens 354-63, 354-6
atonement 291

Babel 62
Bakke (cited) 280
baptism 31, 38, 59, 82-5, 204, 315
Bar-Jesus (Elymas) 285
Barclay, William (cited) 233n, 260, 288, 474
Barnabas
    brings Paul to the apostles 221-2
    called on by Holy Spirit 281, 282
    character of 120, 122, 261, 287
    disagreement with Paul 326-7
    flees to Lystra 300
    and letter to Gentiles 321-2
    ministry in Cyprus 283-7
    ministry in Iconium 297-300
    ministry in Lystra 300-5
    ministry in Pisidian Antioch 289-96

527

FOCUS • ON • THE • BIBLE

1 SAMUEL

LOOKING ON THE HEART

'The best expository commentary I have read in years.'
Eric Alexander

DALE RALPH DAVIS

1 Samuel

Looking on the Heart

Dale Ralph Davis

Dale Ralph Davis has developed a reputation as someone who is able to communicate the meaning of biblical texts with a freshness that does not compromise the content. That he has managed to do this is an achievement in itself, that he has managed it in a popular commentary is exciting!

Comments about Ralph Davis' commentaries in this series

'an excellent... crisp, lively... exposition'

Bibliotheca Sacra

'the most practical expository work that this reviewer has ever encountered'

Southwestern Journal of Theology

'Dr. Davis has a great sense of fun. He must often have his class or his congregation in stitches!'

Christian Arena

'...presents historical and theological material in a way that can only excite the expositor.'

Warren Wiersbe

'a great feast of biblical truth made so digestible, garnished with so many apt illustrations.'

Alec Motyer

ISBN 978 1 85792 516 6

2 KINGS

THE POWER AND THE FURY

'Excellent, crisp, lively exposition.'
Bibliotheca Sacra'

DALE RALPH DAVIS

2nd Kings

The Power and the Fury

Dale Ralph Davis

2nd Kings provides a fast-paced narrative of insight into the history of Israel under its monarchy. This book is a continuation of the narrative begun in 1st Samuel, and continued through 2nd Samuel and 1st Kings. Ralph finishes it off with a captivating and rewarding journey through 2nd Kings.

Written between 561 BC and 538 BC, 2nd Kings gives us a warning about the consequences of sin, especially the catastrophic repercussions of Israel's love affair with idolatry. Despite struggling with other problems, we see that the Jewish people learned from their experience, They never made a mistake of this enormity again.

Through prophets such as Elisha and Elijah we see God's compassion for his people and the opportunity for repentance. An opportunity spoilt by Judah, climaxing with the subjugation of the kingdom by the Babylonians.

Illuminating, accessible and laced with his unique sense of humour, Davis' practical devotional expository applies events to the contemporary reader providing parallels to alert us in the 21st century.

ISBN 978 1 84550 096 2

FOCUS · ON · THE · BIBLE

JOSHUA

NO FALLING WORDS

*'New insights abound. No one who reads this book
will ever find Joshua dull and tedious again.'*
Richard A. Bodey

DALE RALPH DAVIS

Joshua

No Falling Words

Dale Ralph Davis

'A happy blend of exegetical and historical study on the one hand, and homiletical treatment and application on the other. Ideas pop out everywhere, even in the most unlikely places. New insights abound. No one who reads this book will ever find Joshua dull and tedious again.'

Richard A. Bodey,
formerly Trinity Evangelical Divinity School

'One of the reasons I enjoy Davis's exposition so much is that I feel confident that he has done his exegetical homework, and so is not just delivering blessed, unhistorical thoughts on the text.'

Themelios

'Davis' expositions in the Former Prophets put us in his debt. Davis plots a straightforward course through this potential minefield…'

Ed Moll, The English Churchman

This exposition is rooted first in a thorough analysis of the Hebrew text, employing helpful insights from archaeology and linguistics, and second in the major theological and literary themes discovered in each section. Finally the author brings the fragments together in an expository treatment *'that is not ashamed to stoop to the level of application.'*

ISBN 978 1 84550 137 2

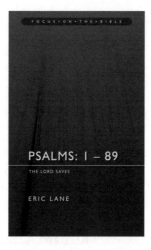

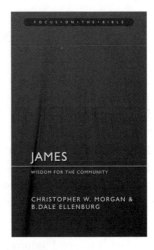

Christian Focus Publications
publishes books for all ages

Our mission statement –

STAYING FAITHFUL
In dependence upon God we seek to help make His infallible Word, the Bible, relevant. Our aim is to ensure that the Lord Jesus Christ is presented as the only hope to obtain forgiveness of sin, live a useful life and look forward to heaven with Him.

REACHING OUT
Christ's last command requires us to reach out to our world with His gospel. We seek to help fulfil that by publishing books that point people towards Jesus and help them develop a Christ-like maturity. We aim to equip all levels of readers for life, work, ministry and mission.

Books in our adult range are published in three imprints.

Christian Focus contains popular works including biographies, commentaries, basic doctrine and Christian living. Our children's books are also published in this imprint.

Mentor focuses on books written at a level suitable for Bible College and seminary students, pastors, and other serious readers. The imprint includes commentaries, doctrinal studies, examination of current issues and church history.

Christian Heritage contains classic writings from the past.

Christian Focus Publications, Ltd
Geanies House, Fearn,
Ross-shire, IV20 1TW, Scotland, United Kingdom
info@christianfocus.com

www.christianfocus.com